# REASONS AND CONTEXT IN COMPARATIVE LAW

In honour of the work and writings of Professor John Bell, leading scholars present essays on factors affecting the course of 'legal development' in common law and civilian systems. The reasons and context for legal development in a comparative perspective embrace the law both in action and in the books, legal institutions, legal cultures and extra-legal environment. Offering an accessible pathway into understanding comparative law, the collection introduces the core features of understanding foreign legal systems. With a range of illustrative case studies, the essays explore topical problems and debates in tort, contract, legal history and judicial studies. In a tribute to one of the defining legal scholars of our time, this volume draws a rich, nuanced picture of the object of comparative legal research, and indicates new and exciting avenues for further research.

SOPHIE TURENNE is a fellow and senior lecturer in law at Murray Edwards College, University of Cambridge. She is President of the British Association of Comparative Law and an associate member of the International Academy of Comparative Law.

# REASONS AND CONTEXT IN COMPARATIVE LAW

## Essays in Honour of John Bell

Edited by

SOPHIE TURENNE

*University of Cambridge*

CAMBRIDGE
UNIVERSITY PRESS

CAMBRIDGE
UNIVERSITY PRESS

Shaftesbury Road, Cambridge CB2 8EA, United Kingdom

One Liberty Plaza, 20th Floor, New York, NY 10006, USA

477 Williamstown Road, Port Melbourne, VIC 3207, Australia

314–321, 3rd Floor, Plot 3, Splendor Forum, Jasola District Centre, New Delhi – 110025, India

103 Penang Road, #05-06/07, Visioncrest Commercial, Singapore 238467

Cambridge University Press is part of Cambridge University Press & Assessment, a department of the University of Cambridge.

We share the University's mission to contribute to society through the pursuit of education, learning and research at the highest international levels of excellence.

www.cambridge.org
Information on this title: www.cambridge.org/9781009246378

DOI: 10.1017/9781009246361



First published 2023

*A catalogue record for this publication is available from the British Library.*

*A Cataloging-in-Publication data record for this book is available from the Library of Congress*

ISBN 978-1-009-24637-8 Hardback

CONTENTS

# CONTRIBUTORS

CRISTIÁN A. BANFI LLB (Pontifical Catholic University of Chile), LLM (University of Chile), LLM (Darwin College) and PhD (Pembroke College, University of Cambridge) is Associate Professor of Civil Law at the University of Chile. He has written extensively on the law of tort in Spanish and English.

MATTHEW DYSON is Professor of Civil and Criminal Law at the Faculty of Law, University of Oxford, and a Tutorial Fellow of Corpus Christi College, Oxford. He is also an associate member of 6KBW College Hill, and a visiting professor and senior fellow at the Notre Dame London Law Program.

PAULA GILIKER FACSS is Professor of Comparative Law at the University of Bristol, former President of the British Association of Comparative Law and President of the Society of Legal Scholars (SLS), 2023–4. She has published extensively on private and comparative law, with a particular interest in vicarious liability in tort from a comparative perspective.

DAVID IBBETSON has been Regius Professor of Civil Law at the University of Cambridge since 2000 and was President of Clare Hall between 2013 and 2020.

MITCHEL DE S. O.-L'E. LASSER is the Jack G. Clarke Professor of Law at Cornell Law School. He teaches and writes in the areas of comparative law, law of the European Union, comparative constitutional law, and judicial process.

ELAINE MAK is Professor of Jurisprudence at Utrecht University. Her research focuses on judges and judicial decision-making in evolving legal and societal contexts. She studied law in Rotterdam and Paris and obtained her PhD at the Erasmus University Rotterdam.

JOANNA MCCUNN is Lecturer in Law at the University of Bristol. After studying at the University of Oxford and working at the Law Commission for England and Wales, she completed her PhD at the University of Cambridge. Her research focuses on the history of English private law.

COLM PETER MCGRATH is Senior Lecturer in Tort Law at the Dickson Poon School of Law, King's College London. His research focuses on comparative private law and professional liability, with an emphasis on the liability and regulation in healthcare in both the common law and civilian legal traditions.

SOLÈNE ROWAN is Professor of Contract Law at the Dickson Poon School of Law, King's College London and Honorary Professor at the Australian National University.

GEOFFREY SAMUEL is Professor Emeritus at the Kent Law School and formerly a professor *affilié* at the École de droit, Sciences Po, Paris. He received his legal education at the University of Cambridge and holds doctoral degrees from the Universities of Cambridge, Maastricht and Nancy 2 (*honoris causa*).

SOPHIE TURENNE (PHD, PARIS II PANTHÉON-ASSAS) is Fellow and Senior Lecturer in Law at Murray Edwards College, University of Cambridge. She is President of the British Association of Comparative Law and an associate member of the International Academy of Comparative Law. She has published extensively in the field of judicial studies.

# FOREWORD

The purpose of this collection of essays is to pay tribute to the career and work of John Bell. It does so admirably. Within its pages we find many of John's abiding interests explored and analysed by colleagues, friends and former students. The focus of most of the essays reflects John's particular passion for comparative law, especially French law, by which I mean to include not only substantive and procedural comparative law but also his fascination for European judiciaries. There are in addition essays on other topics that have featured in his work, such as the interpretation of legal texts, especially statutes, and legal education. Throughout the Festschrift, the warmth towards, and respect for, John shines through.

I first came to know John in 1978. He had the desk behind mine in the postgraduate seats of the Bodleian Law Library in Oxford. I was studying for the Bachelor of Civil Law. He was working on his DPhil, supervised by Ronald Dworkin, on policy arguments in the reasoning of the courts. Subsequently, I followed his career with great interest and admiration from his early fellowship years at Wadham College through to his Chairs and administrative positions at Leeds and Cambridge. It was also a pleasure for me to follow in his footsteps, although I was seventeen years behind him, as President of the Society of Legal Scholars (SLS). Among many other administrative roles, he has been a formidable editor of *Legal Studies* and the *Cambridge Law Journal*.

In the second of my judgments after being appointed to the Supreme Court of the United Kingdom, I was delighted to cite an aspect of John's writings on the European teleological approaches to legislative interpretation: see *R (on the application of Highbury Poultry Farm Produce Ltd)* v. *Telford Magistrates' Court* [2020] UKSC 39, [2020] 1 WLR 4309, at para 27.

John epitomises all that is good about legal academia. Committed selflessly to teaching and administration, as well as research, he has been an inspiration to students and colleagues alike. As a comparative lawyer, especially in respect of French law, both public and private, he has had few equals; and, in the words of one of the contributors at the conclusion of his chapter, John has been 'the finest of all scholars of French and European judicial cultures'. His work is characterised by rigorous clarity, by the depth and quality of his research, and by the range and originality of the questions he has explored. If I have ever had a question on French law, and how it relates to English law, I have almost always been able to count on John's writings to point me in the right direction. A few years ago, I had the privilege of attending a presentation on an aspect of comparative law given by John at the annual SLS conference. As I listened to him, my abiding impression was that I was listening to one of the great academics of our times, a master of his subject.

Readers of this collection will find themselves inspired by the analysis of topics as diverse as vicarious liability in England, Australia and France; the historical and comparative development of the law of unjust(fied) enrichment; the reforms to the French civil code on contractual interpretation; the standard of care in medical negligence in English and German law; and the Chilean law on economic torts. The reader will see the incorporation of John Bell's belief that comparative law, to be done properly, must go beyond the mere comparison of rules and principles, to the societal values lying behind the law. You will see the lessons to be learned from John's ground-breaking research on judicial cultures in the European Union. The reader will be led into analogies between comparative legal reasoning and the rules of the road for junctions and roundabouts. You will learn, perhaps with shock, about the prohibition in France on research concerned to evaluate and predict the professional practices of named judges. You will find out why legal professors may not be welcome guests at a dinner party of social scientists. You will be introduced to the student primer on legal interpretation written by the Elizabethan lawyer William Fulbecke. And the reader will discover that, on a long train journey, John is as happy settling down to read *Wisden* (the cricketers' bible) as he is to read a doctoral thesis on French public law.

Each of the essays provides a stimulating and thought-provoking read. The editor and contributors are to be warmly congratulated on providing a fitting tribute to their esteemed honorand.

***Lord Burrows***
***Justice of the Supreme Court of the United Kingdom***

# PREFACE: JOHN BELL

John Bell was educated at voluntary-aided Catholic schools. Given its place in the church of the period, Latin was well taught at both Salesian College in Cowley and Marist College in Hull. Encouraged by his father, who had been an interpreter during military service, he learnt French and German to A-level. After his BA studies in Law at Trinity College, Cambridge, he had planned to study for the LLM but was dissuaded by Gareth Jones and Tony Weir, and was offered the chance to be a research assistant at Paris II, the patronage of which was exercised by Jack Hamson.

His year as an assistant in Paris (1974–5) provided an introduction to French law. He attended lectures by Denis Tallon and Philippe Malinvaud, and talked with André and Suzanne Tunc, whom he had known in Cambridge. He also researched the history of French product liability and land registration (at Tony Weir's suggestion). Under Denis Tallon he taught English legal terminology in French, and developed his love of teaching.

After two years at the English College in Rome studying philosophy and theology at the Gregorian University and acquiring a knowledge of Italian, he returned to the law. At Oxford, he studied for a DPhil under Ronald Dworkin on 'Policy Arguments in Judicial Decisions'. Although the work was in jurisprudence, attending lectures in Oxford persuaded him that he was not a philosopher. When he started at Wadham he had to fit in with college needs, and so taught contract, tort, administrative law, constitutional law, jurisprudence and comparative law. He taught jurisprudence at university level, but also took on the role in comparative law vacated by Barry Nicholas on his election as Principal of Brasenose. He started teaching French constitutional and administrative law, which he had previously never studied.

The reorientation of his research towards comparative law was assisted by the invitation from Barry Nicholas and Don Harris to take part in an Anglo-French working group on French contract law, along with Bernard Rudden,

Anthony Ogus and Patrick Atiyah (to be joined later by Hugh Beale). That project led to the book by Harris and Tallon, *Contract Law Today*, which involved joint chapters between English and French authors. It was also published in French. The book led to an invitation to succeed Bernard Rudden as professeur associé at the Universities of Paris 1 and 2 in 1985–6.

That period in Paris proved a turning point. Although the teaching was mainly on English contract law (in French), he had two research projects. The first was to write the second edition of *Cross on Statutory Interpretation* with Sir George Engle QC, then still First Parliamentary Counsel. The second was to find out more about French constitutional and administrative law, which he had been teaching for a few years. Roger Errera facilitated an opportunity for him to be a *stagiaire* at the Conseil d'Etat from January to June 1986. That enabled him to see judicial and administrative sections of the Conseil at work, to read files and to sit in deliberations. This helped him to gain a much better understanding of how the French administrative court system worked than could be found in books.

Subsequent books and research followed from this period. The research on statutory interpretation was the kind of applied jurisprudence that he preferred and had already undertaken in his thesis and its subsequent book. It led to an invitation from one of his thesis examiners, Neil MacCormick, to work on artificial intelligence and legal reasoning and to give lectures on statutory interpretation in Rotterdam. The research on French administrative law resulted in an invitation to work with Neville Brown on a new edition of Brown and Garner's *French Administrative Law*, which Brown was undertaking after his retirement. Neville Brown's presidency of the Society of Public Teachers of Law (now Society of Legal Scholars) had already resulted in a workshop on comparative liability of public authorities organised by the United Kingdom National Committee of Comparative Law (now the British Association of Comparative Law) and an edited collection with Tony Bradley. The absence of a textbook on French Constitutional Law then led to a major project that culminated in *French Constitutional Law*. It involved significant amounts of translation, but provided an explanation of French constitutional ideas from a legal point of view. Work of political scientist Alec Stone Sweet on the French Constitutional Council was also published by Oxford University Press in the same year, but the authors did not meet at the time. This book and the book with Neville Brown were published in 1992, because the work at Leeds provided more time for research.

The period at the University of Leeds consolidated these developments in his research interests. Statutory interpretation became a regular teaching subject and led to further work on legal reasoning and a third edition of *Cross*. But the main work was comparative and much of that was disconnected from teaching, which focused on the French private law of obligations and some jurisprudence. (There was also regular teaching on the theory of comparative law in Brussels at the invitation of Mark Van Hoecke and François Ost.) In the 1990s, regular workshops took place on the judiciary with the Institut des Hauts Etudes de la Justice, headed by Antoine Garapon. This resulted in work on judicial appointments with Carlo Guarnieri and Giuseppe di Federico among others. Given the constraints of major university administrative duties, much comparative work was briefer, involving regular reports on English law for French law journals and, later, articles on French law for *European Public Law*.

The work with Antoine Garapon on judiciaries led to an interest in legal culture, which began with book reviews and was consolidated by a British Academy Fellowship from 1999 to 2001. The Fellowship allowed some relief from administration and teaching and the chance to travel. The first book, *French Legal Cultures*, was completed during the Fellowship and tried to explain how French law was composed of several distinct legal cultures that went beyond the classic *droit public–droit privé* division. In particular, the role of institutions and social relations within professions offered significant explanatory power for differences. The second part of the research involved looking at judiciaries not only in England and France, but also in Germany, Spain and Sweden. This necessitated learning Spanish and Swedish, and reading key materials in those languages. A particular interest of the research arose from discussions with colleagues in Leeds and the work with Antoine Garapon – the role of lay judges, whether as jurors or assessors. The methodology of court observation was helped by discussion with colleagues in Leeds. Although the book *Judiciaries in Europe* was not finally completed until 2005, much of the work was undertaken during the British Academy Fellowship.

The move to Cambridge in 2001 led to more focused teaching and research in comparative law, including supervision of research students. It also renewed discussions with David Ibbetson. The two of them made an application for a major research project in 2003 to the Arts and Humanities Research Council (AHRC) as part of its Centres competition for the study of European Legal Development. Though unsuccessful, the bid led to an AHRC research grant and a project which ran from 2005 to

2008. It brought together over seventy researchers from across the United Kingdom and western Europe. It involved regular meetings between scholars from a variety of countries on themes defined at the beginning of the project. The model of preliminary meetings in person in Cambridge and then subsequent meetings to present drafts and discuss them produced an alignment of attention among the relatively small group of researchers on each topic – technology, medicine, products, road traffic, relations between neighbours, as well as doctrinal writing, legal professions and links to wider ideas. The subjects were chosen to reflect the common social problems which tort law in different countries had to deal with in the late nineteenth and twentieth centuries. The output from the project included eight edited volumes, with a joint overview book by Bell and Ibbetson, *European Legal Development: The Case of Tort*. The project also funded two PhDs – by Matt Dyson on the borderline between criminal and tort liability and by Colm McGrath on German medical liability.

The final part of Bell's career involved three projects. The first, with Sophie Turenne, returned to the legal professions, particularly the judiciary. It involved interviews with barristers and solicitors about why they did or did not want to apply to become judges. The conclusions were then presented to the Senior Salaries Review Body. The work drew on Turenne's previous work on judicial appointments in England and Bell's experience of judicial appointments in other countries.

The second project followed on from teaching comparative law in Cambridge and involved the major revision of *Markesinis German Law of Torts* with André Janssen. The new edition benefited from use of the work for students over many years and the understanding of tort law issues gained from the European Legal Development project.

The final project was a completely new book on French administrative law with François Lichère. By then the Brown and Garner approach had reached its limit and a new book was required. Many of the good features of Brown and Garner were copied, especially the use of illustrative cases and explanations of French legal issues in ways that English lawyers would understand. But the major theme was to show how French administrative law had developed, absorbing European influences as a natural part of its current environment at a time when English law perceived them as irritants.

Throughout his career, Bell has also undertaken significant university administration. He was Dean and then Senior Tutor at Wadham. He was the first Pro-Vice Chancellor for Education at the University of Leeds, then Head of the Department of Law, followed by first Chair of the School of Social Sciences and Law. In Cambridge, he was Chair of the School of Humanities and Social Sciences from 2005 to 2009 and briefly Head of the Faculty of Law in 2018. He was also a member of the Higher Education Funding Council for England (HEFCE) research assessment panels for law in 1996 and 2008, and an assessor in 2000. He was editor of *Legal Studies* from 1992 to 1998, and of the *Cambridge Law Journal* from 2010 to 2019, as well as acting as a member of the editorial board of the *International and Comparative Law Quarterly* from 1995 to 2009. And he was a Quality Assurance Agency for Higher Education (QAA) auditor from 1998 to 2005. The experience of administration provided insights into writing and assessing research grant proposals and research outputs, which proved useful for personal research and for advising others.

**

Many leading scholars of today might feel unable to emulate the remarkable range of John Bell's achievements and contributions. In all his various endeavours John has enjoyed the support of his wife Sheila and his two sons, Damian and Martin, and we will say more of the personal qualities of John in our Introduction.

# ACKNOWLEDGEMENTS

I would like to express my gratitude to the authors who have contributed to this volume, and to all the participants of the workshop that marked John Bell's retirement in September 2019. This volume is the fruit of the lively discussions we had then, in the presence of John Bell and in the beautiful surroundings of Murray Edwards College. Not even the Covid-19 pandemic could halt the publication of this collection of essays, but it did lead to delays and adjustments throughout, and I would like to thank those who bore the brunt of these adjustments for their patience with me. I am especially grateful to David Ibbetson and Paula Giliker for their invaluable suggestions during the editing process, to Stelios Tofaris and Simon Whittaker for kindly assisting with the reviewing process, and to Marianne Nield from Cambridge University Press for her stewardship. I received precious editing assistance from Tony Zhou and Khomotso Moshikaro and appreciated the constructive feedback from two anonymous peer reviewers. Finally, I am grateful to Murray Edwards College and the Centre of European Legal Studies at the University of Cambridge for their financial support.

1

# Introduction

SOPHIE TURENNE

In September 2019, John Bell KC (Hon.), FBA, FRSA retired from his (1973) chair at the University of Cambridge. His scholarship has had a profound and lasting influence on comparative research on the study of foreign law, and on French law in particular. Not only that, his immense intellectual curiosity has been matched only by an equal measure of generosity to others. All those who have worked with John, attended his classes or undertaken research under his supervision can testify to his tireless enthusiasm for sharing his knowledge and experience of the law. Moreover, much of John's scholarship causes us to reflect on what is distinctive about comparative law, and why its methods should interest those in other legal disciplines. John's pioneering way of understanding comparative law is echoed in many contributions to this volume, and we offer this volume in the deepest appreciation of John as a scholar and colleague.

## 1.1 The 'Bigger Picture' of Legal Development

Thirty years ago,[1] John praised the virtues of a comparative study of law for its capacity to convey the complex relationship between the legal rules and their environment more satisfactorily than other disciplines. Law is (at least) as much about norms that are discovered by experience and then developed by reason as it is about norms first discovered by reason and then tested by experience:[2] it is, by nature, an integrated phenomenon. This is easily overlooked, however, by those who study the law in one jurisdiction. They might stop at the appearance of unity and singularity of 'law' in its abstract formality. Instead, a comparative study of law requires us to do the extra work that all lawyers should be doing, because

[1] J. Bell, 'Studying Statute Law' (1991) 11 *Oxford Journal of Legal Studies* 130.

[2] R. Pound, 'Philosophy of Law and Comparative Law' (1951) 100 *University of Pennsylvania Law Review* 1.

to make sense of the paths taken in other jurisdictions, lawyers need to discover the plurality of legal principles, knowledges, and events which have shaped legal change over a period of time. As Watson noted, comparative law is concerned with 'the study of the relationship of one legal system and its rules with another', so that we 'understand the particular factors which shape legal growth and change'.[3]

John Bell and David Ibbetson, in their research project on *European Legal Development*,[4] have suggested that the key to understanding legal development in jurisdictions is to identify the way in which a rule is formulated and interpreted, the relevance and context of the rule so formulated, and its operation. Importantly, the strength of any given justification for what the law is depends on the strength of and the complex relationship between the surrounding factors and various dimensions of context: the institutional structures, the constitutional and political systems and values, philosophical and historical questions of meaning and legal practices. Without such support, we might expect many changes to be short lived. Significant interactions exist between these factors too. For this reason, John Bell and David Ibbetson consider four factors together: the 'law in the books' – that is, the legal rules and principles found in legislative enactments, court decisions or doctrinal writings; the legal outcomes, namely the results reached in actual cases; legal institutions, or the framework within which the law operates; legal culture, understood as the set of beliefs and attitudes which give meaning to, and condition, activity; and the broader legal and extra-legal environment. The correlative values of these different factors are not always easy to identify, hence a comparative enquiry is a reflective exercise on insights drawn from social sciences. This encourages a commitment to interdisciplinarity as, on our understanding, socio-cultural norms feed and inform legal developments, and the autonomy of law from social power or social morality is relative.[5]

[3] A. Watson, *Legal Transplants: An Approach to Comparative Law*, 2nd ed. (London: University of Georgia Press, 1993), p. 6; A. Watson, *The Evolution of Western Private Law* (Baltimore, MD: Johns Hopkins University Press, 2001).

[4] See J. Bell and D. Ibbetson (eds.), *European Legal Development: The Case of Tort* (Cambridge: Cambridge University Press, 2012), pp. 4–10, with references to the other (eight) volumes of their breathtaking research on the development of fault liability in tort in Western Europe between 1850 and 2000, see *Comparative Studies in the Development of the Law of Torts in Europe* (Cambridge: Cambridge University Press, 2010–12).

[5] J. Bell, 'Sources of Law' (2018) 77 *Cambridge Law Journal* 40, 46.

As Geoffrey Samuel emphasises, this calls for a demanding approach to the study of the basic sources of doctrinal legal knowledge.[6] In this respect, comparative studies have much to offer to traditional legal teaching: on our understanding, a comparative enquiry expands the boundaries of the law's domain beyond 'black-letter' legal knowledge of the rules, principles and concepts, to look at its embedded elements such as the legal histories, the culture-specific language, and the justifications for a legal rule. Comparative lawyers should also support the need for legal education within universities to rethink law in terms of legal pluralism, and they should endorse John Bell's comments that the skills necessary even for the practising lawyer need to go beyond those skills that have traditionally been taught in universities.

All the same, the process of legal interpretation – the interpretative method and arguments – remains at the core of the comparative enquiry. Sacco's 'formative elements', the statutory rules, scholarly legal writing and decisions of judges crystallise the 'living law',[7] a dynamic reality of competing policies, principles, rules and values balanced by the courts and legal doctrine to accommodate new social and economic realities. A process of interpretation is required to arrive at one rule at a point in time, and any enquiry into the rational justification of an interpretive choice extends to the context of statutory interpretation.[8] A comparative enquiry, we submit, is a case of practical reasoning: it is an attempt to consider legal developments as 'competing, always incomplete, versions of what the law is on a particular matter within a country',[9] and it seeks to provide a rational justification for what the law is and how it has developed within the framework of the prevailing legal order.[10] These are 'competing, always incomplete, versions' at the very least because an account of any rule and its development engages different participants – judges, practitioners, civil servants, police or probation officers.[11] Justifications for legal decisions by reference to sources of law thus constitute 'an appeal to the best interpretation of what the legal community accepts as the reference points for correct legal argument in that particular area of law'.[12]

[6] G. Samuel, Chapter 2 in this volume.

[7] R. Sacco, 'Legal Formants: A Dynamic Approach to Comparative Law' (Installment I of II) (1991) 39 *American Journal of Comparative Law* 1, 22.

[8] Bell, 'Studying Statute Law'.

[9] J. Bell, 'The Argumentative Status of Foreign Legal Arguments' (2012) *Utrecht Law Review* 8, 9.

[10] Bell, 'Sources of Law'.

[11] J. Bell, *French Legal Cultures* (London: Butterworths, 2001).

[12] Bell, 'Sources of Law'.

Drawing these points together, one may stand back and reflect what we should expect to see in fair comparative legal research. We should expect authors to detail what they expected to gain from adopting a comparative perspective, how they sought to analyse the evolution of legal concepts and how their findings may have differed from their initial expectations, depending on what turned out to be the wider influences on legal development in the relevant jurisdiction. Various other themes arise. We will list just four of them here, and readers will find illustrations of all of them at various points within the essays in this volume.

First, bearing in mind that authoritative statements about the law do not simply result from authoritative acts, our contributors have extended their enquiry to the overarching legal, political, socio-economic and historical structures of each legal system considered. A good example is the contributing role of insurance in the development of modern vicarious liability. Second, the scrutiny of legal sources and their interpretation addresses the manifest sensibilities in, and the manifold connections between, the use of the legal sources and the sorts of circumstances within which they may be used. Third, comparative legal research seeks to understand the way in which the legal community in another legal system, as well as its wider community, describes, explains, represents or otherwise engages in practical actions about the law. Immersion in another legal system is, however, not necessarily a search for uniformity. The application of broad principles may be understood differently before different institutions or groups such as legislatures, courts, administrations and the legal professions. Our contributors have studied many types of claims to what the 'law' is in another jurisdiction – a striking example would be the recent introduction of citations of *les précédents* within the judgments of the Cour de cassation in important cases.

Fourth, a whole variety of reasons will often embed justifications for a specific rule and limit the ability of foreign legal solutions to provide practical solutions to specific problems. The process of diffusion of foreign legal ideas and their relevance to legal change within domestic law, e.g. 'borrowing and imitation', is a matter of lively debate within comparative law. So is the notion of path dependence, the 'pressure of established ways of dealing with issues',[13] which may then close down legal change. It makes us mindful of the past in shaping legal change, and invites us to acknowledge the importance of some internal dynamic of

[13] J. Bell, 'Path Dependence and Legal Development' (2013) 87 *Tulane Law Review* 787, 788.

the law.[14] Issues of translation and transposition are rife. Reasons for both the circulation of ideas and the domestic law reception mechanisms are discussed throughout this volume.

Our first author, Geoffrey Samuel, has more to say on comparative methodology. He calls for practitioners and academics working within the legal discipline to promote the 'enquiry paradigm', to question the textual authority of statutes and court decisions much more than currently happens in law faculties. Samuel argues that a more challenging approach would enable law graduates to gain a proper understanding of the epistemological tensions that underpin legal reasoning and legal learning.[15] Only then, argues Samuel, will legal knowledge be valuable not just to judges and practitioners, but also to other social scientists and those working in the humanities. Samuel gives the example of applying social science epistemological thinking to legal reasoning and legal interpretation to gain insights into how judges arrive at their decisions and why they may differ between themselves, still a non-standard approach in research on legal reasoning and statutory interpretation. In this regard, the work by comparatists is promising, contributing 'not just to movement within the discipline of law but to a recognition by those in other disciplines that comparative lawyers may have something to offer social scientists'.[16]

Samuel's contribution will remind many of the reductionist perspective of law studies as they are traditionally understood, and the impact that this can have on comparative legal research. A commitment to methods and theories seems particularly necessary for the increasing awareness of cultural issues affecting legal thinking and aspects of legal practice. However, expanding the boundaries of legal knowledge with comparative legal studies isn't a claim for grand-scale comparisons in order to avoid the pitfalls of fragmented knowledge of the law in another jurisdiction. Instead, we suggest that the expansion of disciplinary boundaries through a comparative enquiry is an invitation to adopt a sectoral approach, with layers of justifications added or overlapping with each other, to give altogether a richer picture of the object of legal research.

[14] Ibid.

[15] G. Samuel, 'Can Social Science Theory Aid the Comparative Lawyer in Understanding Legal Knowledge?' (2019) 14 *Journal of Comparative Law* 311.

[16] G. Samuel, Chapter 2 in this volume.

## 1.2 Overarching Structures and Underlying Values or Ideas

A comparative enquiry will then need to look into the incremental and experimental legal formulations developed over time over one issue, as they build towards a more settled view of the law.[17] Significantly, to understand legal change, we must also identify the institutional values explicitly or implicitly influencing the application of legal concepts in different jurisdictions. Taking John Bell at his word, Paula Giliker in Chapter 3 identifies how the Australian, English and French legal systems apply the notion of 'risk' as a justification for modern vicarious liability in Australia, France and the United Kingdom in different ways and to different degrees. Ideas of risk, notably 'enterprise risk', have provided a justification for strict liability, ensuring victim compensation and in turn encouraging employers to engage in accident prevention. There are five intertwined factors influencing the understanding of 'risk' in this area: the extent of a desire to compensate victims; the availability of state-based compensation; the extent to which the courts are willing to actively shape principles of tort law; the extent to which the courts are willing to embrace matters of social and moral policy; and the availability of insurance. These factors come into the interpretation of the rules, making sense of each rule in the context of the law as a whole and its purposes.[18] These factors also orient legal developments without having by themselves, in the abstract, any identifiable outcome.[19]

Giliker shows precisely the dynamic relationship between legal reasoning and the five factors mentioned earlier; in spite of a seemingly common legal framework, different values explain a different scope of application and results. Thus, even though the Australian test for the course of employment betrays some affiliation to notions of risk and confines vicarious liability to the scope or course of employment as in English law, the wording of 'course of employment' is applied and interpreted in a variety of ways in each jurisdiction. The same goes for the meaning of 'risk' in French law. Here, a common enterprise across jurisdictions – such as the recognition of the role of risk in shaping vicarious liability – justifies a comparative analysis, but this comparison best serves the purpose of offering 'a reflecting mirror to observe our own

[17] Bell, 'Sources of Law'.
[18] Ibid., 51.
[19] Ibid.

system and the options it has for development'.[20] On this view too, legal change must be firmly grounded in domestic law to be effective and legitimate; foreign solutions operate within a combination of reasons, and these reasons will add force to reasons that exist within the system.[21]

Indeed, in the Western world, borrowing (with adaptation) has been said to be 'the usual way of legal development'.[22] It speeds up the process of finding legal solutions to similar problems,[23] and imitating rules from other legal systems has been central to legal change.[24] However, as will be familiar to comparative lawyers and legal historians alike, something of the original meaning will be lost in the process of translation, and nuances or some description of that meaning are likely to be needed. David Ibbetson's tour de force, in Chapter 4, is a case in point. Ibbetson traces the trajectory of development, over the centuries and all over the world,[25] of the Aristotelian-Stoic principle that no one should be enriched at the expense of another. The reception and operation of Roman law ideas on the enrichment remedy added to the range from which later legal systems could choose. Shifts in terminology and meaning across jurisdictions can be quite subtle, but some of them are still having consequences today on our understanding of the enrichment remedy. Savigny and others reoriented the law in the 1794 Prussian Code in direction of unjustified enrichment based on the Roman *condictio sine causa* (enrichment without lawful cause), and Savigny's model then spread around the world. Ibbetson shows how the 'absence of basis', grounded on the Romans' *condictio sine causa* and channelled through Savigny, forms one of the two approaches to the enrichment remedy that have successfully sifted over the centuries. The other approach is that the enrichment is 'unjust' or 'wrongful', based on the narrower Pomponius principle of D.50.17.206, and both approaches might independently justify remedies in different, if overlapping, situations.

20 Bell, 'The Argumentative Status', 17.

21 Ibid.

22 Watson, *Legal Transplants: An Approach*, 7.

23 D. Nelken, 'Legal Transplants and Beyond: Of Disciplines and Metaphors', in A. Harding and E. Örücü (eds.), *Comparative Law in the 21st Century* (London: Kluwer, 2002), p. 26.

24 Watson, *Legal Transplants: An Approach*, p. 7; R. Sacco, 'Legal Formants: A Dynamic Approach to Comparative Law' (1991) 39 (Installment II of II) *American Journal of Comparative Law* 293, 394.

25 David Ibbetson considers the development of the remedy of unjust(ified) enrichment in France, Germany, Belgium, Luxembourg, Italy, Switzerland, Spain, Portugal, Romania, England and the United States, South and Central America as well as Japan and China.

Ibbetson's main point is that, behind terminology and sometimes high-level abstractions, these are the underlying rules today and we should not lose sight of them. Based on a set of texts, norms and social practices within a legal community, legal histories and comparative studies demonstrate their ability to go beyond concepts, across jurisdictions and over time, to reconstruct what the law is on a sectoral issue.

## 1.3 Legal Sources and Interpretation

Paying tribute to John Bell's influential work on legal sources and interpretation,[26] Joanna McCunn cuts to the chase in Chapter 5 with the portrait of William Fulbecke, an Elizabethan scholar who somehow bears comparison with John Bell: deeply acquainted with continental legal thinking, Fulbecke taught students that, to fully appreciate their meaning and significance, English legal sources needed to be read in their wider context. Fulbecke understood that common law methods were embedded in the broader intellectual context of his time, and he drew upon his knowledge of civil law and rhetoric to introduce the concept of circumstances into the common law of interpretation. In this rhetorical tradition, the circumstances of an action were its key features, and the scholar must consider the circumstances of the action so as to describe it and formulate arguments about it. The analysis of legal sources cannot be detached from the specific circumstances of their use.

Comparative lawyers will find here further evidence that foreign legal ideas do not directly transplant into another system unless they integrate with, or provide, a local solution. Although Fulbecke distinguished between rhetoric and law, he saw rhetorical techniques as universally applicable tools of interpretation which could be used by common lawyers to understand the general principle beyond the many cases considered. Interpretive methods from other jurisdictions and disciplines stimulate legal method and argument locally.

John Bell would underline that the sources relied on in legal justification go beyond the confines of an actual civil code or a constitution. They extend to 'the accumulated wisdom developed within the legal tradition (and even outside)' as to the meaning of legal enactments.[27] In Chapter 6,

[26] See Appendix and, for example, J. Bell, 'The Acceptability of Legal Arguments', in D. N. MacCormick and P. Birks (eds.), *The Legal Mind* (Oxford: Oxford University Press, 1986), pp. 45–65.

[27] Bell, 'Sources of Law'.

Solène Rowan delves into the 'accumulated wisdom' on the French doctrine on contractual interpretation as it illustrates a deeply embedded attachment to interpretation as a subjective enquiry. She analyses the 2016 reform of French contract law,[28] the first overhaul of the French Code civil on contractual interpretation since 1804, and she shows a debate still framed in very different terms to that in English law. Unlike in England, there is generally little doctrinal discussion of contractual interpretation in France, and the French reform maintains a traditionally subjective approach to the intention of the parties. Even when the French reform formally recognises the role of objective considerations where the subjective intention of the parties cannot be ascertained, this does not, Rowan suggests, bring French law closer to English law (and to its emphasis on an objective approach at all times). Rather, she explains, there are important procedural consequences in French law to this deep theoretical attachment to interpretation as a subjective enquiry.

It also follows from the French subjective approach that issues of interpretation are questions of fact decided by the lower courts, which, as we know, say little about their reasons in their judgments. By comparison, the objective approach taken in England renders issues of interpretation closer to questions of law, with a concurring detailed reasoning. Here, Rowan is critical of the Cour de cassation, which is unlikely to disturb the lower courts' findings on interpretation for as long as they rely on the search for a subjective intention of the parties. Rowan's conclusion that neither the French nor English approach seems unarguably more attractive than the other follows from understanding each system in its own terms: French and English contract law are characterised by some distinct theoretical underpinnings and law-making role allocated to the courts in this area. Comparative lawyers will there recognise the need to identify legal situations and actions by reference to the criteria lawyers engaged in that legal system refer to as adequate or appropriate. In this way, we can also understand the factors that shape the character of national legal systems.

## 1.4 Path Dependence

If we approach another legal system on its own terms, how do we then weigh the competing factors which affect its evolution of ideas and legal

[28] *Ordonnance no 2016-131 du 10 février 2016 portant réforme du droit des contrats, du régime général et de la preuve des obligations*, JORF no 0035 of 11 February 2016, translation by John Cartwright, Bénedicte Fauvarque-Cosson and Simon Whittaker.

changes? A first difficulty is the level of generality in which the comparison is couched. In Chapter 7, Colm McGrath identifies that conclusions on convergence and divergence between legal systems will be different when we apply a 'big picture' of comparison or a detailed examination of the rules in operation to the same set of narratives. To analyse legal change, he argues, the comparative researcher must identify and justify the most relevant level of abstraction for comparative research. By McGrath's account, a more granular analysis of medical liability in England and Germany between 1850 and 2000 – a hint that any comparative enquiry is hardly a short-term enquiry – shows a long-settled deferential approach to medical error in England, at least until the decision of *Bolam*.[29] This is contrasted with John Bell and David Ibbetson's account of a judicially driven deferential shift towards medical practitioners encapsulated, they say, in the decision in *Bolam*. McGrath explains the difference in his conclusions by a closer look at medical practice, itself prompted by a comparison with German law on the same issue. At the time of *Bolam*, German courts, unlike those in England, had gradually come to define their own view of acceptable medical conduct, distinct from medical views and shifting towards a pro-patient interpretation. In both McGrath's and Bell and Ibbetson's accounts, however, the elucidation of differences matters as much as the elucidation of similarities, because the comparison primarily seeks to clarify the background assumptions and conceptions that inform the law in each jurisdiction.

Although the three authors ultimately share similar broad conclusions – i.e. the locus of change in England and Germany is the interpretation of the fault rule – the difference in argument turns on weighing differently the influence of competing considerations on the observed patterns of liability. Clarifying one's own level of scrutiny is therefore key to solving the first difficulty of balancing competing factors in relation to legal change, as this balance will naturally influence the comparison that follows.

Another answer to our question about weighing different considerations behind a rule lies in examining the range of reasons in its support from different parts of the law or from outside the law. In this respect,

[29] *Bolam* v. *Friern Hospital Management Committee* [1957] 1 WLR 582, 587; Bolam laid down the standard of care in relation to skilled professionals with the principle that 'A doctor is not guilty of negligence if he has acted in accordance with a practice accepted as proper by a responsible body of medical men skilled in that particular art' to avoid liability in negligence, ibid., 587.

Matthew Dyson, in Chapter 8, suggests ways to manage forms of reasoning, what he calls a network of connected pathways of thought. Dyson's 'roundabout reasoning' consists in a process to resolve potential conflict between two or more ways of thinking about a legal issue, by sequencing their consideration and stripping these issues of some of their background. Dyson links the development of a legal solution within a legal system to the route, direction or even speed adopted for its circulation. For example, the Human Rights Act 1998, implementing the European Convention of Human Rights (ECHR) in English law, provides under section 3, the duty to interpret legislation in line with the ECHR to the extent that it is possible to do so. Applying 'roundabout reasoning' to section 3, we see priority given to individual judges to manoeuvre through the junction between the ECHR and domestic law without a centralised authority; and we also see the existence of a 'neutral' space, an interpretative duty so that national law and the ECHR can integrate, rather than a direct comparison of rules or merits assessment between the ECHR and domestic law.

One may object that a prior difficulty lies in creating such a neutral 'space' or fertile soil for legal change, by stripping the 'formants' out of a legal issue. Still, Dyson's 'roundabout reasoning' adds to the recurrent discussion on path dependence in legal development, on how far known forms of reasoning and solutions are closing down the routes into and out of legal change, and how the order in which alternative legal solutions are considered, or the path by which they are selected, shapes the outcome.

As ideas and models circulate across jurisdictions, their circulation leads to a degree of mutual adjustment: the idea transposed into a legal system needs adjustment but still opens the path for legal change in the recipient system.[30] Cristián Banfi, in Chapter 9, illustrates such a circulation of ideas by analysing the merits of an English perspective in the case of the Chilean tortious (extracontractual) liability for pure economic loss caused by unfair commercial practices. In the context of unfair competition, as Chilean courts enforce tortious liability for interference with contracts, Banfi argues in favour of adopting the more conservative English approach to economic torts when balancing the third party's freedom to compete with the claimant's contractual rights. Tortious liability between commercial rivals should then be reformed and limited through the requirement of intention or gross negligence – and, importantly, he argues that this would be consistent with

[30] G. Teubner, *Law as an Autopoietic System* (Oxford: Blackwell, 1993), see e.g. pp. 61, 95–7.

existing social policy in Chile. His references to English law demonstrate ways in which this can be achieved: in respect of unfair competition, the mental element of intention, more stringent than mere carelessness, is crucial for counteracting the risk of limitless liability and litigation arising from negligence-based liability for pure economic loss.

Banfi's contribution illustrates the search for some 'institutional fit' of the English approach into Chilean law, in that, to turn into an imported standard, any foreign illustration must be consistent with principles within the existing domestic legal order. There is, he argues, enough similarity in the broad direction of the law between England and Chile to make his arguments plausible, though it is a matter of debate whether the actual reasoning he recommends will be found to be coherent within existing national legal principles. Here, the reference to a foreign illustration triggers an internal enquiry about one's own system and constitutes a contributing reason for the development of Chilean law. On this understanding, a comparative enquiry acts as a constraint to developing one's own domestic law in a way that is both consistent internally and coherent within the objectives identified externally.

## 1.5 Immersive Approach

Path dependence is also more likely to occur when a special rule is underpinned by structural or organisational aspects of the system, because of the difficulty in changing institutional arrangements, whether they concern organisations, procedures, personnel or ethos.[31] Institutions play a prominent part in John Bell's comparative enquiry: governmental institutions, Parliament and the judiciary – particularly the judiciary – require special treatment alongside the analysis of judicial decisions themselves, given the 'enduring effects'[32] – the demarcating effects – they have on the scope of action of legal actors. Only a full immersion in how lawyers within a legal system think will clarify the role of these institutions in the way legal rules are formulated, interpreted and applied at domestic and supranational level.

In Chapter 10, Mitchel Lasser shows the benefits of an immersive approach. An internal perspective on legal rules will get closer to the unstated and unconscious assumptions on which those within this other

[31] Bell, 'Path Dependence', 799.

[32] J. Bell, 'Researching Globalisation: Lessons from Judicial Citations' (2014) 33 *Cambridge Journal of Comparative and International Law* 961, 962.

legal system operate, leading to any predefined set of questions likely to be revised in light of the discoveries made. Lasser revisits the intricate link between the judicial style of reasoning and the role of the judiciary. His discussion of the French and European highest courts – the European Court of Human Rights (ECtHR) and the Court of Justice of the European Union (CJEU) – 'in their own terms' shows how judicial reforms have empowered the French Supreme courts further to engage self-consciously, overtly and effectively in policy-making initiatives. A long series of interlocking reforms of the CJEU and the ECtHR has also attempted to enhance judicial legitimacy in contemporary Europe. In this context of increased judicial power, Lasser demonstrates how the judicial authority has moved past the interpretive, to the normative, to the political, and to the constitutional levels, and that these courts are also fully cognisant of this new state of affairs. This matters as Lasser, like John Bell, looks at the way in which a judge comes to a decision not merely as an explanation of their judicial reasoning, but also as a justification of the legal norm produced by judges. There is no better illustration than the recent shift of the Cour de cassation towards citing *les précédents* in its judgments, with a major shift in procedural, institutional and constitutional presuppositions and consequences. Behind the iconic syllogism of the traditional Cour de cassation or Conseil d'Etat judgment, there has then been a major shift, over a decade, of French judicial legitimacy towards a more discursive model. Lasser once more breaks down any reductionist perspective on the French judicial discourse that would artificially exclude from the picture the deeper components of its authority.

The context in which judicial decisions are made – e.g. via specific court procedures and mechanisms for judicial selection – further shapes the judicial role and the level of judicial creativity. According to John Bell, four factors prominently shape the character of a judiciary:[33] the historical development of the judiciary as an institution, its allocated judicial role and organisational structure and the values that shape the judiciary. Taken together, these factors give a full picture of the assumptions and values about the judiciary, and about the legal practices that reinforce, supplement or nuance the former, e.g. on the issues of independence, appointments and judicial decision making.[34] Expanding on these four factors, in Chapter 11 Elaine Mak proposes a methodology to

[33] J. Bell, *Judiciaries in Europe* (Cambridge: Cambridge University Press, 2006), p. 351.
[34] Ibid., 2.

study a European judicial culture, with an understanding of 'legal cultures' as a learning process – thereby seeing comparative law as an enquiry into legal change. Attitudes and values aren't static, hence the four factors above should be seen as part of the 'mental software' of judges in member states of the European Union, a 'programming of the mind', as termed by Smits,[35] in a constant process of individual learning within a specific community.

Mak is concerned with 'top-down' supranational, as well as 'bottom-up' transnational influences on judicial functions. She acknowledges different legal cultures within one jurisdiction or cross-nationally – judges may both apply a domestic conception of 'good faith' in contract law and connect with a cross-border conception of a 'fair trial' under the European Convention on Human Rights. Normative changes under the influence of external or EU legal sources are subject to some historically developed views and practices regarding the flexibility of the constitution and its interpretative standards. This collective view remains subject to dynamics between professional and societal expectations regarding the judiciary, in relation to developing domestic laws but also in their alignment of practices towards a shared European standard for a sound and fair administration of justice. In the latter context, Mak's contribution reminds us of the importance of identifying different judicial communities in relation to law, and the dynamic exchanges locally and transnationally. Comparative legal research plays an instrumental role towards a possible process of alignment of domestic judiciaries within the European Union, and John Bell's framework for the comparative analysis of judiciaries finds ready application in a transnational or global context.

## 1.6 Reasons and Context

From John Bell, we learn that comparative arguments should aim to be compelling, and they should weigh competing considerations from within and outside the law. The conclusions need not be uncertain even though they remain defeasible. The structure through which to think about legal development further requires commentators to look at the law's roots in society. A comparative legal enquiry should yield justifications about what has been an obstacle to or has facilitated certain courses

[35] J. Smits, 'Legal Culture as Mental Software', in Th. Wilhelmsson, E. Paunio and A. Pohjolainen (eds.), *Private Law and the Many Cultures of Europe* (Alphen aan den Rijn: Kluwer Law International, 2007), pp. 141–51.

of legal development. This will then enable a discussion as to why, in different settings, similar concepts have different meanings, and why heterogenous words and concepts may still resemble one another through their specific uses.

John Bell has led the way in constructing comparative legal research as an endeavour to question and renegotiate the boundaries of law; we hope that these essays in his honour do justice to his many contributions.

2

# What Can Law Schools Offer Other Disciplines?

GEOFFREY SAMUEL

John Bell's contributions to comparative law, to public law, to legal reasoning and to legal theory are so well known that they hardly need mentioning. But he has also made an important contribution to legal education. It is in relation to this latter contribution that this chapter is offered to Professor Bell, although the influence of his other writings will also become evident. The question to be investigated in this homage to Professor Bell is this: What is the role of a law school within the university community in terms of what it might offer, intellectually, to other disciplines within this academe? This is a question that has now become more urgent in light of the professional qualification reforms introduced by the Solicitors Regulation Authority.

***

In his principal contribution to legal education, Professor Bell posed the question about the purposes of a law school and he noted that the 'literature on legal education has not contributed significantly to the broad debates about the purposes of university education in general'.[1] In saying this, he had in mind law student learning within the context of a university education. He was, however, writing at the beginning of this present century and so it is pertinent to ask if eighteen or so years later the position has changed. Professor Bell certainly looked forward to the generation of further literature.[2] But, despite an increasing amount of writing about legal education, it is arguable that there is still much uncertainty surrounding the question of the purposes of a law school within the context of the academic community. It is clear that other

[1] J. Bell, 'Legal Education', in P. Cane and M. Tushnet (eds.), *The Oxford Handbook of Legal Studies* (Oxford: Oxford University Press, 2003), pp. 901, 904.

[2] Ibid., 917.

disciplines have contributed, and are contributing, to law, but does law have anything to contribute in return?

Writing in 2002–3, Professor Bell was looking to the future. But, before considering this future, it might be useful to look back from 2002 and examine the position of law schools towards the end of the twentieth century. In 1996 the late Peter Birks convened a series of seminars that resulted in the publication in 1996 of a collection entitled *What Are Law Schools For?*[3] The question as to what law schools might offer to other disciplines was not directly addressed in that collection, but there were many indirect observations and assertions that remain of relevance. However, many of these observations are not particularly positive (with regard to the question). Peter Goodrich, for example, asserted that in the past the 'English Bar had always seemed derivative, parochial and unlearned to outsiders' and that not much seems to have changed today.[4] 'In terms of scholarship', he wrote, 'the English law school labours under the fantasm of certainties that other disciplines have long eschewed and repeats traditional patterns of formal instruction or transmission of information which have for long lacked any educational justification'.[5] Indeed, he concludes that legal education is a matter of 'isolation from scholarship and the scholarly community'.[6] Stuart Toddington was not much more encouraging. Focusing on legal skills, he asserted that they were narrowly professional and that this was 'inhibiting the development of an imaginative and critical conception of not only the essential nature and wide importance of legal skills, but of the very idea of legal education'.[7]

The position from outside law was also not particularly encouraging. For example, in France, since 1996 a series of works by social scientists have been produced examining a range of epistemological questions such as what constitutes a discipline,[8] whether or not social science knowledge

[3] P. Birks (ed.), *Pressing Problems in the Law: Volume 2: What Are Law Schools For?* (Oxford: Oxford University Press, 1996).

[4] P. Goodrich, 'Of Blackstone's Tower: Metaphors of Distance and Histories of the English Law School', in Birks, *Pressing Problems*, 64.

[5] Ibid., 64–5.

[6] Ibid., 67.

[7] S. Toddington, 'The Emperor's New Skills: The Academy, The Profession and the Idea of Legal Education', in Birks, *Pressing Problems*, 69.

[8] J. Boutier, J.-C. Passeron and J. Revel (eds.), *Qu'est-ce qu'une discipline?* (Paris: Éditions de l'École des Hautes Études en Sciences Sociales, 2006).

is cumulative[9] and distinctions between academic and popular knowledge.[10] In none of these collective works is there a chapter from law. Worse, perhaps, is a major work on social science epistemology published in 2001 in which the editor suggests that one reason there is no contribution from law is that this discipline has little that is original to offer to the topic.[11] The exclusion of law from these collections is arguably regrettable, for it is clear that even in 1996 there were a number of jurists from both civil and common law jurisdictions who could have provided sophisticated chapters.[12] However, the isolation of law schools, especially in the civil law world, from other social and human science disciplines seems to have been perceived by all in the academy. In other words, it might well be argued that in 1996 legal scholarship had little to offer to other disciplines. One reason for this position is no doubt to be found in the late Professor Birks' Preface, where he asserts that he would find it difficult 'not to hold fast to the notion that everything done in law schools bears ultimately on decision-making in the courts'. Should it be otherwise, the institution 'would have defined itself out of existence as a law school'.[13] According to this outlook, it would seem that law schools are more closely linked to the law in practice than to other disciplines within the university. One might add that in France interdisciplinary research and scholarship would count as non-doctrinal work (*la doctrine*) and thus dangerous for the career of an aspiring legal academic.[14]

But is this position changing? Indeed, can it – and should it – be changed? One immediate response to this question is that the position is changing because, if for no other reason, since 1996 the Research Assessment Exercises have forced a rethink as to what counts as acceptable scholarship.[15] This change is an evolving one in that the assessment exercises themselves have evolved, one contemporary requirement being the importance of impact. It would seem inevitable that impact will

9 B. Walliser (ed.), *La cumulativité du savoir en sciences sociales* (Paris: Éditions de l'École des Hautes Études en Sciences Sociales, 2009).

10 B. Walliser (ed.), *La distinction des savoirs* (Paris: Éditions de l'École des Hautes Études en Sciences Sociales, 2015).

11 J.-M. Berthelot (ed.), *Épistémologie des sciences sociales* (Paris: Presses Universitaires de France, 2001), p. 12.

12 See e.g. C. Atias, *Épistémologie juridique* (Paris: Presses Universitaires de France, 1985) and *Épistémologie du droit* (Paris: Presses Universitaires de France, 1994).

13 P. Birks, Editor's Preface, in Birks, *Pressing Problems*, ix.

14 P. Jestaz and C. Jamin, *La doctrine* (Paris: Dalloz, 2004), pp. 172–6.

15 F. Cownie, *Legal Academics* (Oxford: Hart, 2004), pp. 135–41.

encourage at least some within the legal research community to produce work that will be of interest and importance to those outside both the academic community and the legal world. Certainly, at the level of research skills and method this change in outlook is becoming evident;[16] and an increasing awareness of cultural issues affecting legal thinking – and indeed aspects of legal practice – is bringing together law and social science researchers.[17] Interestingly, even in France, where legal academics are not (at least not as yet) subject to research assessment exercises, a change, however small, can be perceived. There is a growing interest in epistemological issues affecting law and legal studies and this is giving rise to a literature that is moving beyond the traditional doctrinal textbooks and monographs.[18] It would perhaps be speculative to assert that this movement towards epistemological issues has been stimulated by a revolution within comparative law.[19] But there is no doubt – as in fact Professor Bell anticipated[20] – that work by comparatists is contributing not just to movement within the discipline of law but to a recognition by those in other disciplines that comparative lawyers may have something to offer social scientists.[21] Finally, mention must be made of the changes to professional qualifications issued by the Solicitors Regulation Authority. Whatever one may think about these changes, in freeing law schools from the Qualifying Law Degree requirement (at least with regard to solicitors), law schools will no longer have the excuse of having a curriculum in part imposed on them from outside.[22]

## 2.1 Resisting Change: Epistemological Conditions

This change (prompted by research assessment exercises) with respect to legal scholarship is not something that has been happening since 1996. It

16 See e.g. D. Watkins and M. Burton (eds.), *Research Methods in Law*, 2nd ed. (London: Routledge, 2018).

17 See e.g. R. Provost (ed.), *Culture in the Domains of Law* (Cambridge: Cambridge University Press, 2017).

18 See e.g. M.-L. Mathieu, *Les représentations dans la pensée des juristes* (Paris: IRJS Éditions, 2014).

19 See e.g. P. Legrand, *Le droit comparé*, 5th ed. (Paris: Presses Universitaires de France, 2015).

20 Bell, 'Legal Education', 917–18.

21 See e.g. C. Vigour, *La comparaison dans les sciences sociales: pratiques et méthodes* (Paris: Éditions La Découverte, 2005).

22 R. Bower, 'Regulatory Threats to the Law Degree: The Solicitors Qualifying Examination and the Purpose of Law Schools' (2019) 30 *Law and Critique* 117.

long predates the Birks collection and in part has its immediate roots in the Realist movement of the early part of the last century. Accordingly Gareth Jones, in his contribution defending traditional legal scholarship, noted that in 'the United States the younger generation of law teachers is dismissive of traditional legal scholarship'. And he continued:

> The doctrinal sceptics include some, but not all critical legal scholars, and some of the *law and*' school, for example, law and philosophy, law and political science, law and economics, law and the social sciences, law and literature, law and anthropology, who come equipped into the law schools with PhD's in such disciplines. They also include some feminist and race scholars. The legal historian is now the historian, not of substantive law, but of the constitution and racial and gender discrimination.[23]

Gareth Jones did not condemn as such this movement in the United States but, after quite a long discussion of the law and economics school, he felt that some aspects of this scholarship should have little part in the life of the law faculty. He 'would not discourage their *cautious* pursuit, provided the legacy of the past is not lost'.[24] According to Jones, the 'formulation of legal doctrine is a challenging task which demands rigorous analytical skills',[25] and he ended his contribution quoting a question posed by Mary Ann Glendon, herself quoting Charles Fried. 'So what is it', she asked, 'that lawyers and judges know that philosophers and economists do not?'[26]

No doubt Gareth Jones thought that the Fried and Glendon question supported his personal thesis about traditional legal scholarship. Yet the question is perhaps more nuanced than he may have thought. This is because the response set out by Glendon, and thus presumably endorsed by Jones, is 'the law', but this response has less depth than one might think since it simply begs a range of further questions. What is it to have knowledge of the law? What knowledge is being transmitted by law schools? How is such knowledge validated? What are the methods associated with such knowledge? There are, of course, seemingly easy answers to these further questions and so, for example, Peter Birks implied that it is a matter of studying official source texts such as cases

[23] G. Jones, '"Traditional" Legal Scholarship: A Personal View', in Birks, *Pressing Problems*, 12 (emphasis in original).
[24] Ibid., 14 (emphasis in original).
[25] Ibid.
[26] Ibid., 15. And see M. A. Glendon, *A Nation under Lawyers* (New York: Farrar, Straus & Giroux, 1994), p. 104.

organised ('given direction') by textbooks.[27] As regards legislation, the role of the law school is 'the identification of deficiencies in the law, agitation for change and critical commentary on the legislator's earlier efforts'. This may all sound noble. But, as Stuart Toddington pointed out, the 'values which shape commentary and analysis in legal journals may have more intellectual merit than those which motivate the owners and publishers of *The Daily Sport*, but this is not explained by the mere fact that they appear in legal journals and are espoused by academics'.[28] As for the 'rigorous analytical skills' supposedly taught by law schools, Toddington warned that 'to write about the contextual issues "critically" is to describe the simple "legal" facts and then sprinkle moral or political comment over the top of them like so much icing sugar'.[29] No doubt he had in mind only the mediocre textbooks, articles and case notes, but law schools might still be directing students towards this kind of scholarship – at least that would appear to be the case if one examines catalogues from the publishers of law books.

Another issue with regard to 'the law' response is Glendon's assertion that favouring philosophy, economics and other subjects over the teaching of law means neglecting, inter alia, the history of law.[30] Yet one of the oddities about legal education in many of the world's law schools is that there is very little emphasis on legal history. How many students graduate with a knowledge of the works of Gaius, Ulpian, Azo, Bartolus, Baldus, Doneau, Domat, Leibniz, Savigny and so on? The common lawyer might respond by saying that these jurists are civilians and thus irrelevant, but this would be a somewhat inaccurate assertion because many of these jurists have had a profound indirect influence on the common law, especially during the nineteenth century.[31] This is not to suggest that there is an absence of jurists working on such material in law schools (there is not) or that a knowledge of such material is essential if legal scholarship is going to contribute to knowledge in other disciplines (although it certainly could in many ways). But it is to suggest, perhaps, that an epistemological understanding of law as knowledge has not been a major concern in many law faculties. It seems very strange that if one asks what is special about legal knowledge when compared to philosophy,

[27] Birks, *Pressing Problems*, vii.
[28] Toddington, 'The Emperor's New Skills', 74.
[29] Ibid.
[30] See Jones, '"Traditional" Legal Scholarship', 15.
[31] See J. Gordley, *The Jurists: A Critical History* (Oxford: Oxford University Press, 2013).

if not other disciplines, one somehow arrives at a conclusion that excludes a serious diachronic appreciation of the subject. What has law been? Surely this is a vital epistemological question? Of course it can be argued that law is like the sciences and that one does not need a knowledge of the history of science and mathematics to be a good scientist and mathematician. Yet any sophisticated appreciation of legal knowledge ought to lead to a realisation that law is not like the sciences. The kind of models that it constructs are not models of some external object; and even if one focuses simply on mathematics – one science that does not have an external object – history itself ought to confirm that the *mos mathematicus* legal approach was not ultimately a successful project. Yet turning towards the interpretation of language (*ars hermeneutica*) as the methodological foundation of legal knowledge does not provide a means of escape from the diachronic perspective, for most of the foundational work was done by Renaissance jurists.[32] In short, there is an extremely rich body of texts on legal knowledge stretching back over two millennia, knowledge of which remains outside the vision of many law teachers in Western law schools.

There is a further point to be made about the Glendon comment. Philosophy, economics and other subjects are, she wrote, 'useful adjuncts' to law even if they ought not to be a substitute for a traditional legal training. But is law a 'useful adjunct' to philosophy, economics and other subjects? One would think that it ought to have a major contribution to make both to economics and to philosophy, if not to other subjects; for example, notions such as interest, ownership and contract are fundamental concepts in both law and economics.[33] Yet in 1996, and indeed in 2003, it was unclear that law schools were supplying a steady stream of scholarship and teaching that was of direct use in other social science and humanity disciplines. There was some input in the past. In particular, jurists once made important contributions to history and to political theory – one thinks of the medieval jurists to political theory and the Renaissance jurists to historical method.[34] Yet not only does this not

[32] See I. Maclean, *Interpretation and Meaning in the Renaissance* (Cambridge: Cambridge University Press, 1992).

[33] See e.g. K. Renner, *The Institutions of Private Law and Their Social Functions* (London: Routledge & Kegan Paul, 1949; trans. A. Schwarzschild; reprint 1976).

[34] See e.g. W. Ullmann, *Law and Politics in the Middle Ages: An Introduction to the Sources of Medieval Political Ideas* (London: Hodder and Stoughton, 1975); B. Tierney, *Religion, Law, and the Growth of Constitutional Thought 1150–1650* (New York: Cambridge University Press, 1982); J. Canning, *The Political Thought of Baldus de Ubaldis* (New

seem to be the case today – no doubt because law is no longer the 'social science' discipline it once was[35] – but the work of legal historians such as Walter Ullmann and Donald Kelley hardly seem to feature on the reading lists in many law schools (at least if the law catalogues are to be believed). Indeed, it is perhaps to be regretted that this aspect of the law school's scholarship was not developed further in the 1996 collection (although Peter Goodrich's contribution does touch upon some of the relevant texts).

## 2.2 Comparative Studies

One jurist, and legal historian, in more recent times who did have an influence beyond the discipline of law was Henry Maine (1822–88). He taught Roman law in the Cambridge faculty and in the Inns of Court but his books – especially *Ancient Law* (1861) – had an appeal well beyond the law school. It might perhaps be difficult to defend his writings today as works making a major contribution to anthropology via the use of Roman law (and to some extent the common law), but his focus on legal evolution 'can be regarded as a species of the theories of social evolution which became popular in the 1850s and 1860s'.[36] Moreover, 'legal evolution fitted into the vogue for thinking in terms of biological evolution, which followed the publication of Darwin's *Origin of Species* in 1859'.[37] This said, Maine does have his defenders.[38] More importantly, his whole approach to history, to society and to law was of a kind that was something more than a jurist importing social science into the legal discipline. Maine was offering to the social and human sciences insights, however defective some of them might appear today, from law and its evolution far beyond mere black-letter learning.

Maine equally championed the 'comparative method'. Quite what he meant by this is never explained, but in looking at the histories of different legal traditions, the 'method' permitted him to make a number

York: Cambridge University Press, 1987); D. Kelley, *Foundations of Modern Historical Scholarship* (New York: Columbia University Press, 1970).

[35] See D. Kelley, *The Human Measure: Social Thought in the Western Legal Tradition* (Cambridge, MA: Harvard University Press, 1990).

[36] P. Stein, *Legal Evolution: The Story of an Idea* (Cambridge: Cambridge University Press, 1980), p. 99.

[37] Ibid., 100.

[38] Ibid., 105–6. And see generally R. Cocks, *Sir Henry Maine: A Study in Victorian Jurisprudence* (New York: Cambridge University Press, 1988).

of generalisations that became celebrated because they seemingly had a certain ring of truth to them. One thinks of his assertion 'that substantive law has at first the look of being gradually secreted in the interstices of procedure',[39] which, when applied both to early Roman and to pre-eighteenth-century common law, seems to sum up their developments.[40] Again, with his most well-known aphorism about the movement from status to contract, there appeared to be an evolutionary reality about this progression.[41] Another historical generality which also has a ring of truth is his lesser known observation that the sixteenth- and seventeenth-century reform of the law meant reform of the law books.[42] What Maine was highlighting here, through his 'comparative method', was the important epistemological gulf between what amounted to legal knowledge in the past and what amounted to such knowledge in his century. In the past, it was legal taxonomy (and the search for coherence) that preoccupied the minds of the Renaissance jurists.[43] And even Bentham (1748–1832) 'instead of speculating on the possibility of transforming the law into conformity with the greatest happiness of the greatest number, or with any other principle, speculated rather on the possibility of rearranging it in new and more philosophical order'.[44] In Maine's time, it was legislation used to achieve institutional and social reform that became more influential; that is to say, law as a functional instrument rather than law as a formalised conceptual structure. And this orientation towards a functional approach came to eclipse taxonomical thinking for much of the twentieth century.[45] However, one does not need to be a comparatist to appreciate that this tension between the functional approach and the formalism of taxonomical precision has by no means disappeared and by 1996 classification of law thinking was beginning to enjoy a revival thanks mainly to Peter Birks himself.[46]

39 H. Maine, *Early Law and Custom* (London: John Murray, 1890 edition), p. 389.

40 On Roman law, see A. Schiavone, *Ius: L'invenzione del diritto in Occidente*, 2nd ed. (Turin: Einaudi, 2017); on the common law *see First Report of Her Majesty's Commissioners for Inquiring into the Process, Practice and System of Pleading in the Superior Courts of Common Law*, PP, 1851, xxii 567, p. 31.

41 H. Maine, *Ancient Law* (London: John Murray, 1861), chapter V.

42 Maine, *Early Law*, 363.

43 On which see Gordley, *The Jurists*.

44 Maine, *Early Law*, 362–3.

45 See e.g. F. Cohen, 'Transcendental Nonsense and the Functional Approach' (1935) 35 *Columbia Law Review* 809.

46 See P. Birks (ed.), *The Classification of Obligations* (Oxford: Oxford University Press, 1997).

Whether such scholarship, whatever its value to jurists, has much to offer other disciplines is an interesting question. Certainly, Birks' own attempt to fashion a science of taxonomy displayed a certain epistemological naivety.[47]

Returning to the 'comparative method' itself, it is perhaps surprising that Maine, and those influenced by his work, has (or have) not received more attention from comparatists.[48] He is recognised as being part of the now discredited legal evolution movement, but Maine and his successors in the historical jurisprudence school could well be seen as laying the foundations for the important renaissance of comparative legal studies that was just getting underway when Birks' *What Are Law Schools For?* was published and Professor Bell's contribution appeared in the *Handbook*.[49] Of course, much of this work by Maine and his successors was rather colonialist in its orientation, yet there was equally a recognition that law was the reflection of a nation's 'spirit and history'.[50] And while the 'comparative method' is not as such defined in any analytical detail, there does appear to have been an orientation towards the importance of culture and law. Structural approaches were also evident in the emphasis on Roman law and common law and here some of Maine's successors felt that English law would progressively become more like Roman law.[51] This is a theme that Peter Birks took up in arguing that Justinian's (and Gaius') *Institutes* provides a universal map of the law.[52] Moreover, it is a theme that was to underpin one of the major comparative law programmes of the last decade of the twentieth century and the first decade of the present one, namely the harmonisation of private law in Europe.[53] This programme is of importance in itself, but perhaps its

[47] Discussed in G. Samuel, 'Can Gaius Really Be Compared to Darwin?' (2000) 49 *International and Comparative Law Quarterly* 297; G. Samuel, 'English Private Law: Old and New Thinking in the Taxonomy Debate' (2004) 24 *Oxford Journal of Legal Studies* 335.

[48] But see generally A. Diamond (ed.), *The Victorian Achievement of Sir Henry Maine* (Cambridge: Cambridge University Press, 1991).

[49] J. Cairns, 'Comparative Law in England', in M. Reimann and R. Zimmermann (eds.), *The Oxford Handbook of Comparative Law* (Oxford: Oxford University Press, 2006), pp. 135–8.

[50] Ibid., 137.

[51] Ibid., 135.

[52] See e.g. P. Birks, 'Definition and Division: A Meditation on *Institutes* 3.13', in Birks, *Classification of Obligations*.

[53] See A. Hartkamp et al. (eds.), *Towards a European Civil Code*, 3rd ed. (Nijmegen: Kluwer/ Ara Aequi Libri, 2004); R. Zimmermann, 'Comparative Law and the Europeanization of Private Law', in Reimann and Zimmermann, *Oxford Handbook of Comparative Law*, 539.

major contribution to comparative law is in the reaction that it stimulated, which in turn led to a much more sophisticated focus on the comparative method.[54]

Few of these developments are to be found in the comparative law contributions in *What Are Law Schools For?* In fact, there is only one contribution that can properly be described as dedicated to comparative law – that by Basil Markesinis[55] – as the other contribution is restricted to a discussion of legal education in Germany.[56] Professor Markesinis' contribution does make some valid points about having an understanding of foreign law and foreign cultures in legal education and, importantly, it stresses the role of legal histories in the understanding of legal cultures. But there is very little on comparative theory and methodology and thus not much that would be of interest to academics outside the discipline of law. Indeed, in 1996 there was not much in the comparative law literature that could be said to be sophisticated with regard to theory and method (a point made before 1996).[57] However, one of the leading textbooks on comparative law, which was to come out in its third edition in 1998 but whose first appearance in English translation was in 1977, did stress the role of the functional method.[58] Whatever the merits of this assertion by the two German authors, it did stimulate a debate that since 1996 has resulted in work by comparatists that ought, probably, to be of interest to social scientists in general. Thus Pierre Legrand's work on comparative legal studies and culture, offering a very different approach to functionalism, is cited in works from other disciplines.[59] There is also Ralf Michaels' exhaustive analysis of what is meant by the functional method, which may well attract readers from outside law.[60] These examples are perhaps quite rare though, and much work in comparative law relies on academic imports. Take the textbook just mentioned. The two authors assert that the functional method is 'the basic methodological principle of all comparative

[54] This harmonisation issue is developed further in G. Samuel, *Law of Obligations* (Cheltenham: Edward Elgar, 2010), pp. 312–33.

[55] B. Markesinis, 'The Comparatist (or a Plea for Broader Legal Education)', in Birks, *Pressing Problems*, 107.

[56] H. Leser, 'Legal Education in Germany', in Birks, *Pressing Problems*, p. 91.

[57] P. Legrand, 'Comparative Legal Studies and Commitment to Theory' (1995) 58 *Modern Law Review* 262.

[58] K. Zweigert and H. Kötz, *An Introduction to Comparative Law*, 3rd ed. (Oxford: Oxford University Press, 1998; trans. T. Weir), pp. 36–47.

[59] See e.g. Vigour, *La comparaison*.

[60] R. Michaels, 'The Functional Method of Comparative Law', in Reimann and Zimmermann, *Oxford Handbook of Comparative Law*, 339.

law',[61] yet they provide no information whatsoever on other methodological approaches; in order to discover the alternatives one had to look outside law.[62]

So, can comparative law offer a way towards law becoming an exporter? Certainly Professor Legrand's work on the problems of translation – how, for example, does one translate the term 'equity' into French? – is seen as being of value to comparison in the social sciences in general.[63] And the insistence by many comparative lawyers that one should presume difference rather than similarity has implications that go well beyond law.[64] But comparative law is hardly a mainstream subject in law schools and thus for most law students the epistemological issues that are inherent in this domain are not likely to be brought to their attention.[65] Certainly, the methods and theories have important implications for what might be called mainstream positive law and so, for example, applying social science epistemological thinking to legal reasoning and legal interpretation can provide important insights into how judges arrive at their decisions and why they may differ between themselves.[66] Yet the standard textbooks on legal reasoning and statutory interpretation seem, on the whole, little interested in examining the works of Hans Gadamer or Jacques Derrida and so are hardly likely to be of much interest to those studying social science epistemology or hermeneutical philosophy.[67]

## 2.3 Authority and Enquiry Paradigms

One reason there is little interest in writers from outside the discipline of law in many of the standard legal textbooks is that the work by such

[61] Zweigert and Kötz, *An Introduction to Comparative Law*, 34.

[62] See G. Samuel, 'Dépasser le fonctionnalisme', in P. Legrand (ed.), *Comparer les droits, résolument* (Paris: Presses Universitaires de France, 2009), p. 405.

[63] Vigour, *La comparaison*, 141.

[64] Ibid., 263.

[65] Brexit will probably provide little encouragement for students to pursue comparative law modules in English university law schools.

[66] See further G. Samuel, *Rethinking Legal Reasoning* (Cheltenham: Edward Elgar, 2018), pp. 273–7; G. Samuel, 'Does One Need an Understanding of Methodology in Law before One Can Understand Methodology in Comparative Law?', in M. van Hoecke (ed.), *Methodologies of Legal Research: Which Kind of Method for Which Kind of Discipline?* (Oxford: Hart, 2011), p. 177.

[67] Derrida is mentioned in W. Twining and D. Miers, *How to Do Things with Rules*, 5th ed. (Cambridge: Cambridge University Press, 2010), p. 372.

writers is not law. Such writers are not authoritative.[68] The problem, if indeed it is a problem, is not just one of methodology but equally of paradigm orientation. Legal writing has in the Western tradition been largely governed by what might be called the authority paradigm.[69] Such an orientation can be contrasted with an enquiry paradigm in which the goal of research is to furnish as far as possible an explanation of the phenomenon under investigation. If the facts do not, in the end, conform to the theory, then the latter has to change; indeed, the change might be so dramatic that it amounts to what Thomas Kuhn has famously called a scientific revolution.[70]

The authority paradigm has texts, not facts, as the phenomenon under investigation. This is not to say that factual situations have no role as such. One only needs to look at Justinian's *Digest* to appreciate the Post-Glossators' comment that law arises out of fact (*ex facto ius oritur*).[71] Yet such facts produce the 'law' because they are categorised and manipulated internally by a legal model that sees the world in terms of persons, things, actions, fault, consent, damage, interest and so on. In turn, these 'virtual' facts are injected with a normative dimension through the application of a structural model consisting of normative notions such as ownership, right, duty, obligation and the like.[72] It is not the model that has to change if the facts prove awkward; it is the facts themselves.[73] The model itself is founded in various texts, the most important of which – legislation and judgments (as organised by jurists in their writings)[74] – cannot be challenged in terms of their absolute authority by those commenting on them. They can be criticised of course, and, as

[68] For the situation in France see P. Jestaz and C. Jamin, *La doctrine* (Paris: Dalloz, 2004), pp. 172–4.

[69] See generally G. Samuel, 'Interdisciplinarity and the Authority Paradigm: Should Law Be Taken Seriously by Scientists and Social Scientists?' (2009) 36 *Journal of Law and Society* 431.

[70] T. Kuhn, *The Structure of Scientific Revolutions*, 2nd ed. (Chicago, IL: University of Chicago Press, 1970).

[71] The comment is usually attributed to Baldus commenting on D.9.2.52.2, but the expression is used by Bartolus and other commentators.

[72] R. Esposito, *Les personnes et les choses* (Paris: Éditions Mimésis, 2018; trans. C. Marchetti), p. 46. And see generally Samuel, *Rethinking Legal Reasoning*. This legal model was developed by the Romans and its long historical elaboration is analysed in Schiavone, *Ius: L'invenzione del diritto in Occidente*.

[73] Samuel, *Rethinking Legal Reasoning*, 143–96.

[74] Thus legal taxonomy was largely the work of civilian jurists from Gaius up to codification: see e.g. A.-S. Chambost (ed.), *Histoire des manuels de droit* (Paris: LGDJ, 2014); R. Cabrillac (ed.), *Qu'est-ce qu'une introduction au droit?* (Paris: Dalloz, 2017).

with all texts, they are open to interpretation through the application of a hermeneutical scheme of intelligibility.[75] But, like theological texts, they are an authoritative 'given' which can be approached only through 'approved' methods.[76] One finds, therefore, statutory interpretation governed not by hermeneutical principles fashioned by the likes of Gadamer and Derrida, but by rules formulated by those who have the authority to formulate the law.

Does this authority paradigm, in the end, prevent law schools from contributing very much to the academy in general? In posing this question, it must be said at once that the question has to be understood in a particular way. It is not implying that there are few people in law schools contributing to the academy. Indeed, the opposite is becoming the case. There are many legal academics whose interdisciplinary learning is producing scholarship of value to those in other disciplines. Law academics are, then, contributing to the social and human sciences in general. What is being posed is a question about law itself. Does legal learning – the learning of legal concepts, categories, positive rules and so on – have in itself something to say to those outside law? As we have suggested, it clearly did in the past, even if that past is now becoming more distant. But the 'construction' (to use the expression of Jean-Michel Berthelot) of disciplines such as sociology in the nineteenth century has eclipsed legal thought as the primary model for viewing society as a political and social entity.[77] Donald Kelley has talked of law being transcended by philosophy, subverted by economics, surpassed by anthropology and overpowered by sociology.[78] As he went on to observe:

> By the end of the nineteenth century, however, jurisprudence, which had once boasted of being a bridge between nature and culture, played an increasingly minor role in these debates. In his discussion of the 'contest

[75] Dialectical analysis is also important in that legal categories and concepts are presented as dialectical alternatives: public or private; contract or tort; person or thing; substantive or procedural; and so on. Indeed, as Roberto Esposito has noted, '[e]ach category is never defined in itself but only in relation to one that is different from it': Esposito, *Les personnes*, 50. For an excellent English example of this kind of thinking see *Birmingham CC* v. *Oakley* [2001] 1 AC 617.

[76] On which see J. Bell, 'The Acceptability of Legal Arguments', in N. MacCormick and P. Birks (eds.), *The Legal Mind: Essays for Tony Honoré* (Oxford: Oxford University Press, 1986), p. 45.

[77] J.-M. Berthelot, *La construction de la sociologie*, 6th ed. (Paris: Presses Universitaires de France, 2005).

[78] Kelley, *The Human Measure*, 252–75.

> of faculties' Kant had cast doubt on the claim of the law to constitute a rational science, arguing that jurists, in contrast to the philosophers, look to the Code rather than to reason.[79]

In other words, the authority paradigm as expressed through the legislative text (and no doubt other authoritative texts such as recorded precedents) had confined law to its own prison within the academy.

What might be called the Kant critique remains in evidence not just since 1996 but since Professor Bell's chapter in 2003 as well. In a work on the goals of private law published in 2009, one of the contributors talked of the legal academy, along with the legal profession, providing 'a significant institutional constraint by *policing* (in textbooks and scholarly literature) consistency, coherence and doctrinal stability, and by scrutinising and criticising assumptions made by the judges about the potential social and economic consequences of particular rules'.[80] This idea of *policing* is both revealing and ambiguous. It is revealing in the way that it appears to set quite narrow limits of what is expected from the legal academy, limits investigated, as we have seen, in Stuart Toddington's and Peter Goodrich's contributions to the 1996 collection. Since this date, however, there have been further investigations into what is expected from legal scholarship, and perhaps one of the most disturbing is Mathias Siems' essay questioning what might be lost if law professors disappeared from the world.[81] This discussion by Siems has many strengths, one of which is its wide-ranging research revealing some pretty negative remarks that have been made about law schools for well over a century now. Legal education has been compared to a driving school where students learn to drive from a detailed manual of the car and then allowed to drive in traffic.[82] Indeed, as early as 1848 a German jurist 'claimed legal research to be worthless because it did not aim to establish general truths but merely to support the current legal system'.[83] And

79 Ibid., 277.

80 A. Robertson, 'Constraints on Policy-Based Reasoning in Private Law', in A. Robertson and T. H. Wu (eds.), *The Goals of Private Law* (Oxford: Hart, 2009), p. 269 (emphasis added). The remark to some extent recalls the observations made in Peter Birks' Preface to Birks, *Pressing Problems*.

81 M. Siems, 'A World without Law Professors', in M. van Hoecke (ed.), *Methodologies of Legal Research: Which Kind of Method for Which Kind of Discipline?* (Oxford: Hart, 2011), p. 71.

82 Ibid., 72. Professor Bell would see this as a focus on knowing how rather than knowing that: Bell, 'Legal Education', 908.

83 Siems, 'A World without Law Professors', 78.

Siems himself says that in Germany and England, 'legal training is not very sophisticated from an epistemological perspective'; it is 'predominantly knowledge transmission'.[84]

More pertinent to the question pursued in this chapter, Professor Siems proposes what he calls the dinner party test. Can law professors convince academics from other disciplines that their research is worth pursuing?[85] Siems does not think that German law professors would score well;[86] but, more generally, he feels that that there could be problems with the type of knowledge that law would bring to social scientists. It would not have much value in itself.[87] This is a pretty devastating conclusion, but it needs to be seen in the wider context of the relationship between professional practitioners and university law schools. It may be a little unfair to compare law schools to schools of fencing or dancing,[88] yet practitioner law is subject to the authority paradigm and thus by definition is epistemologically limited in its scope.[89] What Siems describes as good legal research (no doubt governed by the enquiry paradigm) is certainly possible, but such research will be interdisciplinary and will thus, if he is right about social scientists being little interested in legal knowledge itself, be 'importing' rather than 'exporting' knowledge. Good legal academics could, therefore, move to other faculties while the teaching of practical law is left to practitioners.

Has the position improved since the publication of Siems' chapter in 2011? Certainly there has been institutional change in that obtaining outside funding for law research has become of much greater importance than was the case in 1996. And, as Van Gestel and Lienhard point out, 'legal research proposals are assessed not by legal scholars, but by panels of social scientists, economists, political scientists, historians and so on'.[90]

[84] Ibid., 75. And see Bell, 'Legal Education', 906–8.

[85] Siems, 'A World without Law Professors', 82.

[86] Ibid., 83.

[87] Ibid., 84.

[88] Ibid., 72.

[89] This said, Professor Bell makes the important point that practitioner skills are in the process of undergoing quite important, if not radical, changes which may well require law graduates to be more critical in their approaches: Bell, 'Legal Education', 910. Indeed, Bell suggests that they may have to develop 'the ability to unlearn established ways of looking at things' (910).

[90] R. Van Gestel and A. Lienhard, 'Conclusion and Discussion', in R. Van Gestel and A. Lienhard (eds.), *Evaluating Academic Legal Research in Europe* (Cheltenham: Edward Elgar, 2019), p. 447.

This has not been positive, it would seem, for law academics in some countries such as Italy.[91] One problem 'seems to be that they have great difficulties in explaining their scholarly methods and how they approach theory building to reviewers from other disciplines'.[92] Another problem is that 'funding for legal research is increasingly monitored and evaluated according to the rules and criteria of other disciplines, which for law as a discipline implies a gradual shift from qualitative indicators and assessments methods towards more quantitative approaches'.[93] This gives rise to a paradoxical situation. If law is to make a contribution to disciplines outside law, it would appear that legal scholars will need to impress academics from these other disciplines; in other words, they will need to participate in an upgraded version of Siems' dinner party test. Yet to impress these academics, they will need to shift towards more quantitative approaches – approaches that are proving highly controversial even to comparative lawyers and legal epistemologists sensitive to interdisciplinarity.[94] This could provide an opportunity for jurists. If they are to make an impact, however, jurists will have to confront the fact 'that legal scholars are not particularly good at reflecting on their own discipline'.[95] They may argue that 'law is different', but they will need to 'explain how and why'.[96] Moreover, if university law teachers cannot explain their methods to other academics, it does not bode well for law students, who will remain similarly unenlightened.

## 2.4 Back to the Future?

Indeed, if the idea of policing is to become the research aim of juristic scholarship, the outlook certainly does not look good. Policing is also ambiguous because the conceptual model that underpins it – 'consistency, coherence and doctrinal stability' – was once regarded as the very essence of legal science.[97] On this point it may be worth returning to Henry Maine.

91 Ibid.
92 Ibid.
93 Ibid., 448.
94 For a general overview see M. Siems, *Comparative Law*, 2nd ed. (Cambridge: Cambridge University Press, 2018), pp. 180–228; cf. H. Muir Watt, 'Les réactions françaises à "Doing Business"', in J.-F. Gaudreault-DesBiens, E. Mackaay, B. Moore and S. Rousseau (eds.), *Convergence, Concurrence et Harmonisation des Systèmes Juridiques* (Montréal: Éditions Thémis, Université de Montréal, 2009), p. 67.
95 Van Gestel and Lienhard, 'Conclusion and Discussion', 449.
96 Ibid.
97 And see Bell, 'Legal Education', 908.

This jurist's view of legal education was influenced by the 1846 House of Commons Select Committee Report on legal education in England and Ireland, which was, to say the least, somewhat negative in its conclusions.[98] There was no legal education worthy of the name. The reason was one that can be directly related to Mathias Siems' reflections on what the academy would be like if there were no law professors. This of course was exactly the situation in England before the 1846 report; there were virtually no law faculties teaching the common law and those that did exist found it difficult to attract students.[99] It was this situation, together with the report's conclusions that the elements of jurisprudence (or legal science) taught in law schools should form part of a lawyer's education, that seems to have, at least in part, motivated Maine.[100] Now, as Peter Stein pointed out, although English law has remained relatively free of Roman law, 'English jurisprudence has traditionally turned for inspiration to the current continental theories, necessarily based on Roman law'.[101] Roman law thus became, in the hands of people like Maine, the basis of the general elements of jurisprudence to be taught to aspiring common lawyers.[102] Indeed, Maine went further and claimed that ignorance of Roman law impacted beyond the discipline of law itself, for moral philosophy and aspects of the English language were informed by the Roman legal sources.[103]

However, much of this Roman law was not really Roman as such because it was being perceived through the scholarship of the German nineteenth-century Pandectists, who 'had categorized and conceptualized it into a coherent system'.[104] Indeed, they had gone further and had created a closed conceptual system which was perceived as having no gaps and endowed with a methodological purity; it was positivism in its most essential and hardened form.[105] These positivists did not ascribe to the idea that the concepts were part of a natural law, but they did see them as being anchored in texts with legal authority. 'A jurist's conclusions were to follow from authoritative texts rather than immutable principles', writes James Gordley,

98 Report of the Select Committee on Legal Education, 1846, House of Commons Proceedings. And see P. Stein, 'Maine and Legal Education', in Diamond, The Victorian Achievement of Sir *Henry Maine*, 195–6.

99 Stein, 'Maine', 196.

100 Ibid. See also W. Twining, 'Maine and Legal Education: A Comment', in Diamond, *The Victorian Achievement of Sir Henry Maine*, 210.

101 Stein, *Legal Evolution*, 123.

102 Stein, 'Maine', 200.

103 Ibid., 201–2.

104 Ibid., 200.

105 O. Jouanjan, *Une histoire de la pensée juridique en Allemagne (1800–1918)* (Paris: Presses Universitaires de France, 2005), p. 224.

'yet they must follow deductively or they would not have the same authority as the texts.'[106] The American Realists were subsequently to denounce much of this as transcendental nonsense, or at best 'jargon', adopting instead a functionalist view of law.[107] The authority paradigm was to some extent loosened by these realists.[108] In turn, this escape from conceptual and axiomised jurisprudence, based on the long history of Roman law in Europe, was to result in the erosion of Roman law not just from many law schools but from jurisprudence (legal theory) courses as well.[109] Historical jurisprudence of the kind associated with Maine fell out of fashion.[110] Nevertheless, while functionalism gradually took over from conceptualism during the last century, conceptual positivism remained alive in the minds of jurists such as Peter Birks. As far as this jurist was concerned, the 'Realists and post-realists have done a good job of debunking legal science' and in the 'United States where Jerome Frank and his intellectual successors did their most serious damage, it has never recovered and now lets in floods of law and economics in the hope of filling the broken vessel'.[111] Rather oddly, Professor Birks went on to state 'that a rational science of the law has not been tried and found wanting but has merely been found difficult and left untried'.[112] This is surely an odd comment given the history of the civil law. Legal science was the dominant epistemological orientation – the *mos mathematicus* – from the seventeenth to the twentieth century and in the end it simply failed to convince.[113] As a leading French writer on legal reasoning has put it, law and legal reasoning cannot be reduced to a set of mathematical equations; there is a multiplicity of principles, ideas, methods and so on in play other than those founded on mathematical logic.[114] And it would be ridiculous to say that this conclusion is based on anything other than experience.

[106] Gordley, *The Jurists*, 214.

[107] J. Frank, *Law and the Modern Mind* (London: Stevens & Sons, 1949), p. 97.

[108] See in particular Frank, *Law and the Modern Mind*. This author talked of 'the image of the father hidden away in the authority of the law' (at 252); such authority, thought Frank, needs to be cast off.

[109] Twining, 'Maine', 215–16.

[110] C. Woodard, 'A Wake (or Awakening?) For Historical Jurisprudence', in Diamond, *The Victorian Achievement of Sir Henry Maine*, 217.

[111] P. Birks, 'Equity in the Modern Law: An Exercise in Taxonomy' (1996) 26 *University of Western Australia Law Review* 1, 4.

[112] Ibid.

[113] See generally Gordley, *The Jurists*.

[114] J.-L. Bergel, *Théorie générale du droit*, 5th ed. (Paris: Dalloz, 2012), pp. 307–8.

Nevertheless, Professor Birks' view seems to have survived his untimely death. As Professor Steve Hedley puts it, 'there is a developing school of radical internalists who are prepared to deny any validity at all to the external viewpoint, and have been quite explicit that externalists should either be deprived of influence within the law school or even to be run out of it (on the argument that externalists are not really 'doing law' at all)'.[115] Professor Hedley subsequently points out that this development is rather odd, for if one reads the scholarship of these new internalists, it 'merely repeats the views of leading law teachers circa 1880'.[116] This is odd, he says, because in any other discipline 'academics would be embarrassed at using much the same theories and attitudes as were advanced a century and a half ago, with nothing to show for the work of the intervening period except some minor updating'.[117] In fact, another jurist, Stephen Waddams, has suggested that the internalists (as Hedley calls them) have themselves misinterpreted the Victorian cases, which were, says this author, as much about policy considerations (functionalism) as legal principle.[118] If Professor Hedley is right – although it must in fairness be pointed out that he is aiming his critique primarily at law of obligations specialists – there emerges a pretty bleak picture of what a law school has to offer others in the academy. Law has nothing more to offer than what was offered by the German Pandectists of the nineteenth century (and which so impressed the Parliamentary Commissioners in the 1840s). Again, the point must be made that one is not saying that legal academics are providing no input into the academy in general. Indeed, there is another development headed by other legal academics embracing inter-disciplinarity and producing stimulating work on law and history, law and gender studies, law and culture and so on.[119] What is being asserted is that what might be called non-interdisciplinary legal knowledge – black-letter or doctrinal law – is of little epistemological interest to other social

[115] S. Hedley, 'Looking Outward or Looking Inward? Obligations Scholarship in the Early 21st Century', in A. Robertson and T. H. Wu (eds.), *The Goals of Private Law* (Oxford: Hart, 2009), p. 194. A legal externalist is one, says Hedley, who looks at law from an external point of view in order to discover what is going on; an internalist looks at law only from the internal mind of the lawyer. Thus the first approach would embrace functionalist reasoning while the second would not because 'it is not law'.

[116] Ibid., 199.

[117] Ibid., 199–200.

[118] See in particular S. Waddams, *Principle and Policy in Contract Law: Competing or Complementary Concepts?* (New York: Cambridge University Press, 2011).

[119] Not that this would have necessarily pleased the late Gareth Jones, as has been seen.

scientists. It need not have been like this, but the authority paradigm means that the kind of scholarship being offered by the internalists, or neo-formalists, is likely to be of little interest to those outside of law. Internalist contemporary legal thought is little more than pastiche.[120]

## 2.5 Concluding Remarks

What, then, have law schools to offer other disciplines? As we have said, the question has been confined to what might be termed doctrinal or 'black-letter' legal knowledge, usually regarded as a conceptual structure of rules, principles and concepts organised into a coherent system (or relatively coherent, depending upon the legal tradition). Is knowledge of this doctrinal knowledge in itself of value to those in the academy outside of the law school? Although the question was not directly tackled in the 1996 collection edited by Peter Birks, the picture which nevertheless emerges from this collection is, to say the least, rather negative. Indeed, not only is a negative picture portrayed by Peter Goodrich and Stuart Toddington, but the subsequent chapter by Mathias Siems just adds to the gloom. Again, one has insisted that this situation is to be kept distinct from the question whether high-quality research and scholarship is emerging from law schools. Here the position is very positive and has surely improved since 1996, probably in part as a result of the research assessment (now excellence) exercises, in which traditional doctrinal knowledge has not scored highly since 1996. However, much of this good-quality research is founded on jurists who have a high degree of interdisciplinary learning. Law schools, in other words, have imported rather than exported knowledge, although of course the high-quality research just mentioned is of considerable value to other disciplines (re-exported one might say).

This said, John Bell's view in his contribution was that there are a number of agendas for research. What is needed are 'the skills and knowledge necessary to operate as a person using the law professionally (not necessarily in conventional legal professions), the appropriate range of perspectives for studying the law in a pluralistic society, and the pedagogical strategies required, as well as measured for their effectiveness'.[121] These are agendas that might seem, at first sight, fairly modest, but they present huge challenges. Rethinking law in terms of legal

[120] See further G. Samuel, 'Is Legal Neo-Formalism Nothing but Pastiche?' (2020) 15 *Journal of Comparative Law* 347.

[121] Bell, 'Legal Education', 918.

pluralism will require something of a rethink about the kind of legal theory that underpins much doctrinal law.[122] And, surely, his view that the skills necessary even for the professional lawyer need to go beyond those skills that have traditionally been taught in universities should encourage us to rethink the very idea of legal education – as Stuart Toddington's contribution to the Birks 1996 collection made clear.

More generally, and from a diachronic viewpoint, the position was once very different, with law perhaps being the oldest social science.[123] But the position changed in the nineteenth century, as Donald Kelley (among others) has shown: law became eclipsed by other disciplines. Can traditional legal knowledge reassert itself so that it becomes of value to others in the academy? If Siems is to be believed, possibly not. Yet perhaps an approach to the basic sources of doctrinal legal knowledge that is far more challenging to students than the approach inherent in the neo-formalists agenda could be a stimulus for change. Such a challenge might aim to produce graduates who become highly skilled in understanding the epistemological tensions that underpin legal reasoning and legal learning, and this skill might be adapted so as to be valuable to other social scientists and those working in the humanities.[124] However, the culture is not encouraging at the moment and those jurists following very much in the Gareth Jones tradition will probably produce scholarship that is, on the whole, of little interest to those in the academy outside of the law school.[125] In fairness, though, it might be of great value to the judiciary and to the profession as a whole. Or, in the end, as Professor Bell implied, it might not.

[122] See e.g. R. Provost (ed.), *Culture in the Domains of Law* (Cambridge: Cambridge University Press, 2017).

[123] W. T. Murphy, *The Oldest Social Science? Configurations of Law and Modernity* (Oxford: Oxford University Press, 1997).

[124] See further G. Samuel, 'Can Social Science Theory Aid the Comparative Lawyer in Understanding Legal Knowledge?' (2019) 14 *Journal of Comparative Law* 311.

[125] See for example Samuel, 'Is Legal Neo-Formalism Nothing but Pastiche?'

# 3

# Examining Vicarious Liability Comparatively

## A Risky Business?

PAULA GILIKER

Vicarious liability (or, in French, *fait d'autrui*[1]) is a topic that might be described as 'the cuckoo in the nest'[2] of the law of torts. If we take as our starting point that the law of civil wrongs imposes liability for wrongful behaviour, then a doctrine that imposes strict liability on an innocent party for the torts of another will trouble traditional notions of corrective justice. Weinrib, a leading corrective justice theorist, argues that 'the unity of the plaintiff–defendant relationship lies in the very correlativity of doing and suffering harm'.[3] Vicarious liability, then, to a corrective justice or rights theorist can only be justified if the employer can in some sense be regarded as the doer of the harm, for example, by imputation or attribution.[4] However, looking across legal systems, we can discern a common idea that there *should* be situations where an innocent party be held strictly liable for the torts of another employee in the course of activities assigned to them.[5] This chapter will focus on employers' vicarious liability for the torts of their employees in three systems – one civil (France), two common law (England and Wales; Australia) – where there has been recent case law on vicarious liability and an active discussion of the basis for liability, notably from the perspective of risk. In 2017, the French Ministry of Justice published proposals to reform its law of

[1] Liability for the act of another.

[2] P. Giliker, *Vicarious Liability in Tort: A Comparative Perspective* (Cambridge: Cambridge University Press, 2010), p. xli.

[3] E. J. Weinrib, *The Idea of Private Law* (Oxford: Oxford University Press, 2012), p. 73.

[4] Ibid., 186. See also R. Stevens, *Tort and Rights* (Oxford: Oxford University Press, 2007), chapter 11.

[5] While German law does not on its face (§831 BGB) have a doctrine of vicarious liability, commentators have noted that, in practice, there are a number of means by which employers can be held liable for the torts of their employees: see Giliker, *Vicarious Liability in Tort*; B. S. Markesinis, J. Bell and A. Janssen, *Markesinis's German Law of Torts*, 5th ed. (Oxford: Hart, 2019), chapter 5.

tort,[6] which included consolidating case law on *fait d'autrui* based on risk-centred reasoning.[7] Recent decisions of the UK Supreme Court and High Court of Australia (HCA) have also actively engaged in this debate.[8]

In all three of the systems surveyed in this chapter, the courts have moved from early ideas of presumed fault – if the employer had taken reasonable care, the harm would not have occurred – to strict liability. While all systems continue to favour some limitation on the doctrine – confining it to certain relationships, primarily that of an employee committing a tort whilst engaged in tasks assigned by the employer – the scope of vicarious liability has expanded from the late nineteenth century onwards. This has been due to two factors: economic growth, notably influenced by the Industrial Revolution, which dramatically increased the number of personal injury victims, and the development of the insurance industry.[9] These two factors have had a significant impact on the willingness of the courts to impose strict(er) liability. Fleming James Jr, for example, declared in 1952 that, 'with the growth of vicarious liability and of liability insurance, [tort law] has become, in effect, a modified form of enterprise liability'.[10] While not all lawyers would go this far, the willingness of the courts over the last century to extend vicarious liability to cover a wider category of relationships, including public and charitable bodies, and to broaden the types of situation where liability will occur has rendered ideas based on presumed fault, control or implied command of limited validity. Instead, courts

[6] For clarity, the word 'tort' will be used generally throughout this chapter to designate the French law of 'extra-contractual liability'. This is for ease of reference only. The concepts are distinct.

[7] *Projet de réforme du droit de la responsabilité civile* (Ministère de la Justice, 2017): www.textes.justice.gouv.fr/textes-soumis-a-concertation-10179/projet-de-reforme-du-droit-de-la-responsabilite-civile-29782.html. For an English translation, see www.textes.justice.gouv.fr/textes-soumis-a-concertation-10179/projet-de-reforme-de-la-responsabilite-civile-traduit-en-anglais-30553.html. This translation will be used throughout the text.

[8] See e.g. *Various Claimants* v. *Morrison Supermarkets* [2020] UKSC 12, [2020] AC 989; *Various Claimants* v. *Barclays Bank* [2020] UKSC 13, [2020] AC 973; and *Prince Alfred College* v. *ADC* [2016] HCA 37, (2016) 258 CLR 134.

[9] See J. Bell, 'Convergence and Divergence in the Development of Fault Liability', in J. Bell and D. Ibbetson (eds.), *European Legal Development: The Case of Tort* (Cambridge: Cambridge University Press, 2014), p. 174; G. E. White, 'The Emergence and Doctrinal Development of Tort Law, 1870–1930' (2014) 11 *University of St Thomas Law Journal* 463; A. Tunc, *La responsabilité civile* (Paris: Economica, 1981).

[10] F. James, 'Social Insurance and Tort Liability: The Problem of Alternative Remedies' (1952) 27 *New York University Law Review* 537, 560.

have turned to ideas of risk, notably 'enterprise risk', as a justification for strict liability that ensures victims are compensated and employers 'encouraged' to engage in accident prevention.

Risk, then, has been the justification *du jour* for vicarious liability, providing judges with a means to develop tort law more proactively to assist claimants. John Bell's work on vicarious liability addresses this development and indeed was cited favourably by the UK Supreme Court in support of its view that vicarious liability could be justified where the defendants had, in the exercise of their mission or enterprise, placed the tortfeasor in a position where the commission of the tort was an inherent risk of the activities assigned.[11] Yet John's work, as a leading comparative law scholar and one I have had the great fortune to work with as both a student and a collaborator, urges us to go further and engage with the underlying values that underpin this legal analysis. In this chapter, then, I will critically examine the use of 'risk' in the law of England and Wales, Australia and France, but also, using comparative law analysis, identify the factors that explicitly (or implicitly) influence legal reasoning. I will also address the apparent backlash to the expansive power of risk in recent decisions of the UK Supreme Court. Following John's example, therefore, the aim of this chapter is to gain not only a clearer understanding of how 'risk' is used by the courts as a justification for vicarious liability but also a deeper understanding of the operation of modern vicarious liability across legal systems.

## 3.1 Vicarious Liability: Finding a Framework for Comparative Analysis

### *3.1.1 A Common Formula?*

Examining vicarious liability comparatively, three common features can be identified across legal systems: first, the need for a relationship, usually that of employer/employee; second, the commission of a wrong causing damage; third, that the wrongful act is committed by the employee in the course of duties allocated. For the common lawyer, this manifests itself traditionally in three conditions: (i) an employer will be held strictly liable, (ii) for the torts of their employee, (iii) provided that they take place in the course of employment. We see a similar approach in civilian systems influenced by the French Civil Code, which states at Article 1242

[11] *Cox* v. *Ministry of Justice* [2016] UKSC 10, [2016] AC 660, at [31] per Lord Reed.

(5): 'Masters and employers [are strictly liable] for the damage occasioned by their servants and employees in the exercise of the functions in which they are employed.'[12]

Such similarities should not, however, lead us to assume that the application of these legal tests achieves the same results. Apparent similarities may mask differences in practice, and it is dangerous to assume that similar source material will automatically lead to parallel forms of reasoning. Only by examining the operation of the law, going beyond legal rules per se, can we identify whether similarities of policy and principle do in fact exist. While we may *predict* that legal systems at equivalent levels of economic development with political and social ties such as the United Kingdom and France (until recently, fellow EU members) and the United Kingdom and Australia (fellow Commonwealth countries) reach similar solutions,[13] this needs to be tested. We should therefore examine the goals, purposes and ends that lawmakers in each jurisdiction are trying to achieve.[14] While a comparative study will not necessarily identify the 'right' answer to a particular social problem (here to what extent employers should be liable for the torts of their employees),[15] it is seeking to gain a more meaningful understanding of the values that underlie legal systems.[16] Differences are not a problem if they can help us to gain a clearer insight into the operation of the law and the reasoning of the courts.[17]

Looking, then, at the three common features identified, we can see key definitional decisions facing the courts: What do we mean by the term

[12] Formerly Article 1384(5). Reforms in 2016 to the Code civil led to a renumbering of its articles. Translation courtesy of Légifrance: www.legifrance.gouv.fr/Traductions/en-English/Legifrance-translations.

[13] B. S. Markesinis, 'Learning from Europe and Learning in Europe', in B. S. Markesinis (ed.), *The Gradual Convergence* (Oxford: Clarendon Press, 1993); J. Gordley, 'The Universalist Heritage', in P. Legrand and R. Munday (eds.), *Comparative Legal Studies: Traditions and Transitions* (Cambridge: Cambridge University Press, 2003). For a dissenting view, see P. Legrand, 'European Legal Systems Are Not Converging' (1996) 45 *International and Comparative Law Quarterly* 52.

[14] See J. Gordley, 'Comparison, Law and Culture: A Response to Pierre Legrand' (2017) 65 *American Journal of Comparative Law* 133.

[15] Gordley argues that comparative lawyers should recognise and respect the purposes that members of different societies pursue: ibid., 180.

[16] M. Van Hoecke, 'Deep Level Comparative Law', in M. Van Hoecke (ed.), *Epistemology and Methodology of Comparative Law* (Oxford: Hart, 2004).

[17] G. Dannemann, 'Comparative Law: Study of Similarities or Differences?', in M. Reimann and R. Zimmermann (eds.), *Oxford Handbook of Comparative Law*, 2nd ed. (Oxford: Oxford University Press, 2019).

'employee'? Do we use the definition found in labour law (contracts of employment; *contrats de travail* involving *salariés*) or do we adopt a looser definition designating someone we 'employ' to do tasks for us, even if they are unpaid volunteers or agency staff? Equally, we might question how a court would interpret a test of acting in the course of employment or one's functions. During our working days, we talk to our work colleagues, check our phones for messages, pop out for lunch and so on. These are not strictly activities linked to our work, but are part of our working lives. If we take into account, therefore, that a worker delivering petrol in the 1940s was likely to smoke during the working day[18] or that a barman might lose his temper and throw broken glass at a drunken customer,[19] then we are already creating a more flexible view of this test.

The starting point in any discussion must be the cases themselves in England and Wales, Australia and France. These will enable us to identify the policy choices taken by the courts in interpreting these tests.

### *3.1.2 The Employee/*Préposé

Both the English and French courts adopt generous tests for 'employees' that are not linked to labour law definitions, but rather focus on the nature of the relationship between the tortfeasor and their employer. In *Cox* v. *Ministry of Justice*,[20] therefore, prisoners working in a prison kitchen were deemed 'akin to employees' in that their work, under the direction of prison staff, was integrated into the operation of the prison and carried out as an integral part of its enterprise. In contrast, the medical practitioner in *Various Claimants* v. *Barclays Bank*[21] was an independent contractor when, as a minor part of his practice, he undertook health checks for prospective employees of the bank. He had been paid a fee per examination and had not been on a retainer. Objectively, held the court, he was not anything close to an employee.[22]

Similarly, in France the term used is *préposé* (appointee or officer) rather than *salarié* (paid employee), which indicates a broader *lien de préposition* (employment relationship). While the test remains one

18 *Century Insurance* v. *NI Road Transport Board* [1942] AC 509.

19 *Petterson* v. *Royal Oak Hotel Ltd* [1948] NZLR 136; *Contrast Deatons Pty Ltd* v. *Flew* (1949) 79 CLR 370.

20 *Cox* v. *Ministry of Justice*. See also *Armes* v. *Nottinghamshire CC* [2017] UKSC 60, [2018] AC 355 (foster parents were 'akin to employees' of local authority).

21 [2020] UKSC 13, [2020] AC 973.

22 Ibid., [28] per Baroness Hale.

whereby the employer is someone with the right to give the employee orders or instructions on how to do the work they are employed to do,[23] modern French law accepts that the power to give instructions need not have a contractual or legal basis but may simply exist as a matter of fact. Equally, it is no longer necessary to prove that such a power has been exercised, provided that the employer (again more loosely termed *commettant* [principal]) is deemed to possess some degree of authority over the employee. In both cases, then, the courts have come to the view that they should look beyond the confines of employment law to the nature of the relationship that links tortfeasor and employer/*commettant*. Both adopt a broad notion of employee.

The English approach may be contrasted with that of the Australian courts, which adhere to a stricter notion of employee and reject the inclusion of relationships 'akin to employment'.[24] In the controversial case of *Trustees of Roman Catholic Church* v. *Ellis*,[25] for example, the NSW Court of Appeal argued that Catholic priests were not employees in that no contract of employment was involved.[26] While the High Court of Australia indicated in *Hollis* v. *Vabu*[27] that it would look at the notion of employment 'in the round', the 'akin to employment' test has been rejected as a step too far.

For the comparative lawyer, this creates a conundrum: Why is Australia following a different approach? What has dictated this reluctance to extend the employment relationship?

### 3.1.3 Course of Employment/In the Exercise of One's Functions

The tests confining vicarious liability/*fait d'autrui* to the scope/course of employment or the 'functions' for which one is employed are equally comparable between the jurisdictions studied. Again, however, on closer examination, differences may be found in application and the courts have

[23] F. Terré et al., *Droit Civil: Les Obligations*, 12th ed. (Paris: Dalloz, 2019), No. 1060. See Civ 4 May 1937 (*Veuve Meyer*) DH 1937.363.

[24] H. Luntz et al., *Torts: Cases and Commentary*, 8th ed. (Chatswood, NSW: LexisNexis, 2017), 17.2.1–14.

[25] [2007] NSWCA 117; (2007) 70 NSWLR 565. Confirmed in *Day* v. *Ocean Beach Hotel Shellharbour Pty Ltd* [2013] NSWCA 250; (2013) 85 NSWLR 335.

[26] Priests are office holders, not employees. Contrast the English case of *JGE* v. *English Province of Our Lady of Charity* [2012] EWCA Civ 938; [2013] QB 722 (Diocesan Trust vicariously liable for parish priest's child sexual abuse).

[27] [2001] HCA 44, (2001) 207 CLR 21. See also *Stevens* v. *Brodribb Sawmilling Co. Pty Ltd* [1986] HCA 1, (1986) 160 CLR 16.

adopted a number of different formulations. From an English perspective, the courts have moved from the classic Salmond test, which includes unauthorised modes of doing something you were authorised to do,[28] to the *Lister* v. *Hesley Hall* test, whereby an employer would be held liable for the torts of their employees if the commission of the tort was *so closely connected* to the employment that it would be fair and just to hold the employer vicariously liable.[29] The test was revised again in 2016 in *Mohamud* v. *Morrison Supermarkets*:

> The first question is what functions or 'field of activities' have been entrusted by the employer to the employee, or, in everyday language, what was the nature of his job ... Secondly, the court must decide whether there was sufficient connection between the position in which he was employed and his wrongful conduct to make it right for the employer to be held liable.[30]

While the 'field of activities' test seemed on its face more generous than the *Lister* test,[31] the Supreme Court in the later decision of *Morrison Supermarkets* v. *Various Claimants* sought to address any misunderstandings to this effect.[32] This was not, it said, the intention of Lord Toulson in that case. Read 'in context', his Lordship had merely 'restated' the *Lister* test in the simplest terms.[33] The court firmly rebutted any suggestion that *Mohamud* meant that any temporal or causal connection would satisfy the close connection test.[34] That said, it redirected courts back to the earlier *Lister* test as reformulated by Lord Nicholls in *Dubai Aluminium*: The wrongful conduct had to be *so closely connected* with acts the employee was authorised to do that, for the purposes of the liability of the employer to third parties, it might *fairly and properly* be regarded as done by the employee while acting in the ordinary course of their employment.[35] The motivation of the Supreme Court in *Morrison* was clear – to return to a stricter version of the 'close connection' test. If

[28] J. W. Salmond, *The Law of Torts*, 1st ed. (London: Stevens and Haynes, 1907), p. 83.
[29] [2001] UKHL 22; [2002] 1 AC 215, [28] (Lord Steyn).
[30] *Mohamud* v. *Morrison Supermarkets* [2016] UKSC 11, [2016] AC 677, [44]–[45] (Lord Toulson).
[31] Described as 'broad and evaluative' by Langstaff J at first instance in *Various Claimants* v. *Morrisons Supermarkets*: [2017] EWHC 3113 (QB) [195].
[32] [2020] UKSC 12, [2020] AC 989, [1] (Lord Reed).
[33] Ibid., [17].
[34] Ibid., [31].
[35] *Dubai Aluminium Co. Ltd* v. *Salaam* [2002] UKHL 48; [2003] 2 AC 366, [23] (Lord Nicholls).

this meant rewriting the past, so be it. The *Lister/Dubai Aluminium* test is nevertheless still fairly liberal. A close connection may be shown, for example, where a carer or parish priest has sexually abused a child or an employee has assaulted a customer.

In contrast, Australia proved more reluctant to follow the 'close connection' test, and in *New South Wales* v. *Lepore*[36] the High Court of Australia offered a dizzying selection of approaches that could be taken, with one judge (McHugh J) basing his judgment on the imposition of a non-delegable duty.[37] Reviewing the situation in 2016, the High Court in *Prince Alfred College* v. *ADC (PAC)*[38] favoured an approach that considered whether the employer had assigned to the employee any special role that placed the employee in contact with the victim, whereby the apparent performance of this role could be said to give the 'occasion' for the wrongful act. In applying the 'occasion' test, which stresses the vulnerability of the victim, courts were advised to consider whether the role gives the employee authority, power, trust, control and the ability to achieve intimacy[39] with the victim or if the employee had taken advantage of their position.

The above analysis demonstrates that the mere wording of 'course of employment' has no special magic but can be interpreted in a variety of ways. It will come as no surprise, therefore, that the French formulation of the 'exercise of the functions' in which the tortfeasor is employed has raised similar interpretative problems.[40] Famously, the criminal and civil chambers of the French Supreme Court between 1960 and 1988 struggled to resolve how this phrase should be interpreted, despite attempts by its plenary assembly to find a means of reconciling the different applications of the same test.[41] This debate was only resolved in 1988 and offers yet another formulation.[42] Liability for the acts of others will be presumed to exist *unless* the act of the employee is:

36 [2003] HCA 4; (2003) 212 CLR 511.

37 Contrast Kirby J, ibid., [277], who argued for a consistent common law approach.

38 *Prince Alfred College* v. *ADC* [2016] HCA 37, (2016) 258 CLR 134, [81].

39 A factor regarded as especially important.

40 See, in more detail, Giliker, *Vicarious Liability in Tort*, 181–8.

41 See, for example, Cass (Ch réunies) 9 March 1960, D 1960.329 note R. Savatier; Cass (Ass plén) 10 June 1977, D 1977.465 note C. Larroumet; Cass (Ass plén) 17 June 1983, JCP 1983 II 20120 concl P. A. Sadon; Cass (Ass plén) 15 November 1985, D 1986.81 note J.-L. Aubert.

42 Cass (Ass plén) 19 May 1988, D 1988.513 note C. Larroumet (liability where *préposé* had defrauded a client whilst advising her on insurance policies on behalf of the defendant company).

(i) without authorisation (*sans autorisation*);
(ii) for their own ends (*à des fins étrangères à ses attributions*); and
(iii) outside the normal duties of their job (*hors de ses fonctions*).

While this formula did not find immediate acceptance, it now represents the law.[43] Its operation may be usefully compared to the common law tests explained above. In a French case of May 2011, Mr X had been subjected to violence while being ejected from a disco by three bouncers employed by the club. Such acts amounted to intentional criminal misconduct, but the Cour de cassation overturned the view of the Court of Appeal that the employer would not be liable and criticised the court for not applying the 1988 test.[44] The tortious conduct had taken place during the bouncers' professional activities at the club and at their place of work. French law would thus find vicarious liability in this context: the presumption of liability had not been rebutted. In the English case of *Mattis* v. *Pollock*,[45] the claimant had similarly been stabbed by a nightclub doorman following an altercation between his group of friends and the doorman. Despite the fact that the doorman had gone to his own flat 500 metres away and then returned with his knife to avenge himself, the Court of Appeal found the act within the course of his employment. The attack was closely connected to his job as doorman to keep order and discipline in the nightclub, he was still in his working hours and the attack was related to an incident taking place on the premises. Interestingly, the Australian 'occasion' test would reach the same result here on the facts, namely that the club had given the doorman a special role of maintaining order in the club and given him authority to act, rendering the 'revenge' aspect less important. In such a case, vicarious liability should follow.[46]

Where the Australian courts would differ, however, is on the facts of *Mohamud*. Here a racist attack on a customer by a petrol kiosk attendant was regarded within the 'field of activities' for which he was employed,

[43] Terré et al., *Droit Civil*, No. 1065.
[44] Civ (2) 12 May 2011, Bull civ 2011, II, No. 110. See also Civ (2) 22 January 1997, Bull civ 1997, II, No. 21 (baggage handlers stealing from luggage) and Civ (2) 17 March 2011, Bull civ 2011, II, No. 69 (sexual abuse by music teacher).
[45] [2003] EWCA Civ 887; [2003] 1 WLR 2158.
[46] Contrast *Deatons Pty Ltd* v. *Flew* [1949] HCA 60; (1949) 79 CLR 370.

namely to attend to customers and to respond to their inquiries.[47] In its review of the *Mohamud* test, the court in *Morrison* agreed that there had been a close connection between the defendant's capacity as a sales attendant and the assault on the victim, whom the attendant had ordered to stay away from the premises.[48] A French court equally would be likely to find that the acts were within the normal duties of his job, so defined. For the High Court, this would not pass the 'occasion' test.[49] No special role was assigned to the employee and the test, for the court, amounted to no more than identifying a causal link between the tort and the employee's job.

We are left with an unanswered question. Why are the English and French courts willing to adopt a broader approach and why is that not followed in Australia? Studying the decisions in cases will only get us so far. A comparative lawyer needs to dig deeper to understand the reasoning underlying the application of these tests, identifying factors that influence judicial decision making.

## 3.2 Risk and Vicarious Liability

> [T]he ultimate justification of vicarious liability is really the risk which an employer creates for those who encounter his business or enterprise.[50]

> [C]ivil liability acts as an agent for the distribution of losses throughout a community. This function is in fact fulfilled either when liability is imposed on an enterprise which can pass on the cost to the public or quite simply through the channel of civil liability insurance.[51]

The first statement by Bell in 2010 highlights the significance of risk-based reasoning in shaping modern vicarious liability law. In particular, this quotation from the *Cambridge Law Journal* highlights the importance of the notion of 'enterprise risk' – the idea that an employer's strict liability can be justified by the fact that they have put into the community an enterprise carrying with it certain risks and when those risks materialise and cause injury it is fair that, having created the enterprise and the risk, the employer should bear the loss. Equally, Viney in 1976 recognised the role that strict liability can play in redistributing the risks of tortious injury via enterprise liability, supported by the existence of a vibrant

47 *Mohamud* v. *Morrison Supermarkets*, [47].

48 *Morrison Supermarkets* v. *Various Claimants*, [28].

49 *Prince Alfred College* v. *ADC* [2016] HCA 37, (2016) 258 CLR 134, [83].

50 J. Bell, 'Vicarious Liability for Child Abuse' (2010) 69 *Cambridge Law Journal* 440, 442.

51 G. Viney, 'Réflexions sur la responsabilité civile' (1976) 28 *Revue Internationale de Droit Comparé* 581, 587 (my translation).

insurance industry. In this section, I will examine the role of risk in shaping modern vicarious liability law in England and Wales, France and Australia and the extent to which it can provide an explanation and justification for the law stated above.

### *3.2.1 Risk in Common Law Jurisdictions: England and Wales*

Reference to risk as a justification for vicarious liability may be traced back to early nineteenth-century authority such as *Duncan* v. *Findlater*, which relied on the simple logic that 'by employing him I set the whole thing in motion, and what he does, being done for my benefit and under my direction, I am responsible for the consequences of doing it'.[52]

Atiyah, writing in 1967, found it persuasive to rationalise vicarious liability on the basis that the employer 'ought to be liable for all those torts which can fairly be regarded as reasonably incidental risks to the type of business he carries on'.[53] He tied this argument to ideas of loss distribution; insurance here facilitating the spread of liability, the management of risks and the compensation of victims injured by virtue of these risks.[54] As Lord Hobhouse explained in *Lister* v. *Hesley Hall*, the general idea is that a person who employs another for their own ends inevitably creates a risk that the employee will commit a legal wrong. If the employer's objectives cannot be achieved without a serious risk of the employee committing the kind of wrong which they have in fact committed, the employer ought to be liable.[55] Liability, in his and Atiyah's view, should arise if the risk is one that *common experience shows* is inherent in the nature of the business.[56]

The Supreme Court of Canada in *Bazley* v. *Currie*,[57] a case cited favourably by the House of Lords in *Lister*, utilised similar reasoning when, influenced by US writings on law and economics,[58] it set out enterprise risk as the justification for vicarious liability:

52 (1839) 6 Cl & Fin 894, 910; (1839) 7 ER 934, 940. See also *Hall* v. *Smith* (1824) 2 Bi 156, 160; (1824) 130 ER 265; and A. Bell, 'Scope of Employment: Connecting Closely with the Past' (2021) 137 *Law Quarterly Review* 254, 275: 'inherent risk is an unavoidable core of the ideas emerging'.

53 P. S. Atiyah, *Vicarious Liability in the Law of Torts* (London: Butterworths, 1967), p. 171.

54 Ibid., 172.

55 [2001] UKHL 22; [2002] 1 AC 215, [66]

56 Ibid. See also Atiyah, *Vicarious Liability*, 172.

57 (1999) 174 DLR (4th) 45. See also *Jacobi* v. *Griffiths* (1999) 174 DLR (4th) 71; *Blackwater* v. *Plint* (2005) 258 DLR (4th) 275.

58 The literature is enormous but see, generally, *Faragher* v. *City of Boca Raton* [1998] USSC 84; (1998) 524 US 775; A. O. Sykes, 'The Economics of Vicarious Liability' (1984) 93 *Yale*

> The employer puts in the community an enterprise which carries with it certain risks. When those risks materialize and cause injury to a member of the public despite the employer's reasonable efforts, it is fair that the person or organisation that creates the enterprise and hence the risk should bear the loss ... It must be possible to say that the employer *significantly* increased the risk of the harm by putting the employee in his or her position and requiring him to perform the assigned tasks.[59]

Thus interpreted, vicarious liability has, it is argued, associated normative effects, notably acting as a deterrent, inducing employers to exercise a greater degree of care in relation to the appointment and supervision of employees, and ensuring 'fair and *efficient*' compensation for wrongs.[60]

Reading *Lister*, we can identify tension between the *Bazley* version of 'enterprise risk' and the looser formulation of Atiyah. While borrowing the 'close connection' test from *Bazley*, the court avoided adopting its policy reasoning.[61] Lord Millett indeed regarded Atiyah's argument as the 'unspoken rationale' of the course of employment test.[62] Later cases did, however, take *Bazley* more seriously. By 2012, Lord Phillips was able in the influential case of *Catholic Child Welfare Society* v. *Various Claimants (CCWS)*[63] to identify five policy reasons underlying modern vicarious liability:

(i) The employer is more likely to have the means to compensate the victim than the employee and can be expected to have insured against that liability (the deeper pockets argument);
(ii) The tort will have been committed as a result of activity being taken by the employee on behalf of the employer (delegated task argument);
(iii) The employee's activity is likely to be part of the business activity of the employer (enterprise liability);

*Law Journal* 1231; W. M. Landes and R. A. Posner, 'Joint and Multiple Tortfeasors: An Economic Analysis' (1980) 9 *Journal of Legal Studies* 517.

59 *Bazley* v. *Curry* (1999) 174 DLR (4th) 45, [31] and [42].

60 Ibid., [46]. See, further, A. O. Sykes, 'The Boundaries of Vicarious Liability: An Economic Analysis of the Scope of Employment Rule and Related Legal Doctrines' (1988) 101 *Harvard Law Review* 563, 577–8.

61 '[I]t is unnecessary to express views on the full range of policy considerations examined in those decisions': [2001] UKHL 22; [2002] 1 AC 215, [27] (Lord Steyn).

62 Ibid., [65]–[66].

63 [2012] UKSC 56; [2013] 2 AC 1.

(iv) The employer, by employing the employee to carry on the activity will have created the risk of the tort committed by the employee (enterprise risk);

(v) The employee will, to a greater or lesser degree, have been under the control of the employer (control argument).[64]

Enterprise liability and risk (note the distinction) were therefore by 2012 regarded as two-fifths of the justifications for vicarious liability law, but this is an understatement. Looking at the reasoning of the court in relation to claims of historic sexual abuse, risk-based reasoning stands out as highly influential. Vicarious liability, held the court in *CCWS*, is imposed 'where a defendant, whose relationship with the abuser put it in a position to use the abuser to carry on its business or to further its own interests, has done so in a manner which has created or significantly enhanced the risk that the victim or victims would suffer the relevant abuse'.[65] As Bell commented, again in the *Cambridge Law Journal*, in terms of policy, factors 2 (delegation of task); 3 (enterprise liability) and 4 (risk creation) 'are woven together into a theory of enterprise liability for helpers, whether they are employed or not'.[66] This view is supported by Lord Reed in *Cox* v. *Ministry of Justice*,[67] who believed that of the five factors mentioned by Lord Phillips, it was these three that were the most significant and were interrelated: 'the risk of an individual behaving negligently, or indeed committing an intentional wrong, is a fact of life, anyone who employs others to carry out activities is likely to create the risk of their behaving tortiously within the field of activities assigned to them'.[68] While in the later case of *Armes* v. *Nottinghamshire CC*[69] Lord Reed seemed to modify his position, allowing for weight to be attached to all *five* of the Phillips policy reasons,[70] the significance of risk, notably enterprise risk, as an explanatory and justificatory device seemed unquestionable.

The impact of such reasoning is evident in a series of decisions which broadened both the relationship and course of employment elements of vicarious liability law. In *Cox*, the Supreme Court was prepared to impose vicarious liability on prison authorities for the torts of prisoners

[64] Ibid., [35].
[65] Ibid., [86].
[66] J. Bell, 'The Basis of Vicarious Liability' (2013) 72 *Cambridge Law Journal* 17, 20.
[67] *Cox* v. *Ministry of Justice* [20]–[21].
[68] Ibid., [23].
[69] [2017] UKSC 60, [2018] AC 355.
[70] Ibid., [56].

working in its kitchens where they were integrated into the operation of the prison and placed in a position where there was a risk that they might commit a variety of negligent acts within the field of activities assigned to them. Equally, in *Armes*, the local authority's placement of children into foster care was found to create a situation where the children were particularly at risk of abuse in circumstances where the carers were an integral part of the local authority's organisation of its childcare services. In *Mohamud*,[71] liability arose because it was the employee's job to attend to customers and respond to their inquiries, giving rise to a risk that he might use violence and foul language in dealing with them. The position in these cases could therefore be summed up by the statement: 'The risk of an employee misusing his position is one of life's unavoidable facts.'[72]

However, the status of risk-based reasoning has now been called into question following two decisions of the UK Supreme Court in 2020. While not overturning the decisions mentioned above, the court indicated a change of approach. Less emphasis would be placed on policy. A more 'principled' approach would be adopted. In *Barclays*, therefore, the relationship test focused on the details of the parties' relationship: on the facts, was the tortfeasor an independent contractor carrying out his own business? Only in doubtful cases should resort be made to the Phillips policy concerns to identify whether the relationship was sufficiently analogous to employment to make it fair, just and reasonable to impose vicarious liability.[73] Equally, in *Morrison* the court emphasised that the Phillips policy factors were not concerned with the close connection test, but rather the test for akin to employment.[74] The court advocated incrementalism, advising lower courts to seek guidance from decided cases on a basis which is principled and consistent.[75] One significant caveat was made – policy would continue to be relevant to the application of the close connection test in relation to the sexual abuse of children, which would be regarded as a special case.[76]

Overt reference to risk-based reasoning, therefore, is now confined to cases of sexual abuse and relationships 'akin to employment'. The inference is that too much reliance on enterprise risk threatens to destabilise the law, creating legal uncertainty. A risky business indeed.

[71] *Mohamud* v. *Morrison Supermarkets*.
[72] Ibid., [40] (Lord Toulson).
[73] *Various Claimants* v. *Barclays Bank*, [27].
[74] *Morrison Supermarkets* v. *Various Claimants*, [31].
[75] Ibid., [24] (Lord Reed).
[76] Ibid., [23], [36].

### 3.2.2 *Risk in Common Law Jurisdictions: Australia*

Australian courts, in contrast, have long been sceptical of the magic of the 'enterprise risk' argument. In its leading 2016 judgment in *Prince Alfred College* v. *ADC (PAC)*,[77] the High Court of Australia held that: '[P]rinciples [that] depend upon policy choices and the allocation of risk ... are matters upon which minds may differ. They do not reflect the current state of the law in Australia and the balance sought to be achieved by it in the imposition of vicarious liability.'[78] On this basis, in a case involving sexual abuse of a minor, the HCA preferred a more orthodox route and adopted an incremental approach based on established case law. That this turned it against its English and Canadian counterparts made little impression. In particular, the HCA took the view that despite the quasi-scientific appearance of 'enterprise risk', at heart lay a decision whether it would be 'fair and just' to impose liability.[79] Risk-based reasoning had equally not appealed to the majority of the HCA in the earlier case of *New South Wales* v. *Lepore*[80] and the HCA approved the more conservative views of Gleeson CJ, and Gummow and Hayne JJ in that case. In favouring an alternative test based on whether the employee's apparent performance of the job could be said to give the 'occasion' for the wrongful act, the court drew on Australian case law, notably *Deatons Pty* v. *Flew*,[81] and regarded *Mohamud* as wrongly decided.

The Australian position is informative in two ways. First, by rejecting 'enterprise risk' as a justification of vicarious liability, the court adopts an incremental approach which rejects a broad discussion of the policy justifications for vicarious liability in favour of certainty and consistency in the law. In the words of the court:

> [T]he orthodox route [considers] whether the approach taken in decided cases furnishes a solution to further cases as they arise. This has the advantage of consistency in what might, at some time in the future, develop into principle. And it has the advantage of being likely to identify factors which point toward liability and by that means provide explanation and guidance for future litigation.[82]

[77] [2016] HCA 37, (2016) 258 CLR 134.
[78] Ibid., [45]
[79] Ibid., [68].
[80] [2003] HCA 4; (2013) 212 CLR 511. Kirby J, however, did find enterprise risk analysis as explained by the Supreme Court of Canada in *Bazley* 'persuasive': [303].
[81] [1949] HCA 60, (1949) 79 CLR 370.
[82] *PAC*, [46]. See also S. Kiefel CJ, 'The Adaptability of the Common Law to Change', Brisbane, 24 May 2018. On the importance of consistency for the HCA, see A. Fella, 'The

The 'occasion' test therefore represents an alternative test to that of *Mohamud/Bazley*. It permits controlled expansion of the course of employment test, while the test for employment stated in *Hollis* v. *Vabu*[83] remains unchanged. It reflects a desire to approach the expansion of vicarious liability more cautiously.

Second, the mixed reception of the Australian approach highlights the difficulties of articulating a principled test, free of policy concerns.[84] We might question, in particular, whether the 'occasion' test is, as the High Court seems to assume, completely divorced from risk-based liability given its focus on vulnerability.[85] While it rejects a law and economics approach, the test does examine whether the employer had assigned to the employee any special role which placed the employee in contact with the victim, giving rise to the ability to achieve intimacy with the victim. These will inevitably be occasions where there is a particular *risk* of harm to the victim. Is it possible, then, to expand vicarious liability without resorting to some notion of risk?

### 3.2.3 *Understanding Common Law Risk Reasoning: Enterprise Risk, Orthodox Legal Reasoning and Incrementalism*

Examining English and Australian responses to risk-based reasoning before 2020, we see a clear split in the common law world. Enterprise risk seemed to be on the increase in England but was treated with suspicion in Australia as giving rise to illegitimate judicial law making. *Barclays* and *Morrison*, however, suggest the UK Supreme Court becoming more hesitant about relying on such reasoning.

Two reasons can be identified. The first is the fact that enterprise risk has never been wholeheartedly endorsed by the UK courts. Even its strongest advocates have conceded that it does not fully explain vicarious liability, the doctrine being at best a flawed form of enterprise liability in that it permits the employer (in theory at least) to shift liability back to

Concept of Coherence in Australian Private Law' (2018) 41 *Melbourne University Law Review* 1160.

83 [2001] HCA 44; (2001) 207 CLR 21.

84 For criticisms of the 'occasion' test, see e.g. D. Ryan, 'From Opportunity to Occasion: Vicarious Liability in the High Court of Australia' (2017) 76 *Cambridge Law Journal* 14, 17; J. Goudkamp and J. Plunkett, 'Vicarious Liability in Australia: On the Move?' (2017) 17 *Oxford University Commonwealth Law Journal* 162, 167.

85 See A. Gray, 'Liability of Educational Providers to Victims of Abuse: A Comparison and Critique' (2017) 39 *Sydney Law Review* 167.

the actual tortfeasor as a joint tortfeasor at law.[86] The enterprise risk argument also goes too far. It fails to explain why social risks – for example, of physical or sexual abuse – are borne by the employer rather than society as a whole. It is also unclear why proof of a tort (rather than simply the fact that an employee has caused harm to the victim) is required. Enterprise risk also threatens the distinction between employees and independent contractors that lies at the heart of vicarious liability. If liability is triggered by a person harming another while acting on behalf of the risk-creating employer, there is no reason why vicarious liability should not apply to independent contractors.[87] As McIvor argues, enterprise risk logically extends liability to any risk-producing activity traditionally covered by insurance.[88] Full endorsement of enterprise risk would therefore require the courts to reshape vicarious liability. This has not occurred. As seen in *CCWS*, the UK courts have never argued that enterprise risk should be the sole policy justification of vicarious liability, although it comes close in sexual abuse cases.

The second reason relates to the courts' reluctance to be seen as overt policy makers. In moving from the common-sense logic of Atiyah to the more complex reasoning of *Bazley*, the courts were being drawn into a policy debate. Such a view is at odds with the current position in negligence law where the UK Supreme Court has actively sought to limit resort to policy arguments in favour of a more incremental approach which takes guidance from previous cases.[89] The courts, declared Lord Mance in 2018, are not a law commission.[90] References to 'social justice'[91] in *Mohamud* and whether it would be 'fair and just' to impose vicarious liability highlighted the role being played by policy in setting the parameters for the doctrine. As Burns' work has shown, reference by judges to common sense and intuition create fertile ground for accusations of cognitive bias in tort judging.[92] This leaves the courts open to

[86] See S. Deakin, 'The Evolution of Vicarious Liability', 2017 Allen and Overy Lecture, Cambridge University, p. 7.

[87] D. Brodie, 'Enterprise Liability: Justifying Vicarious Liability' (2007) 27 *Oxford Journal of Legal Studies* 493.

[88] C. McIvor, 'The Use and Abuse of the Doctrine of Vicarious Liability' (2006) 35 *Common Law World Review* 268.

[89] See *Robinson* v. *Chief Constable of West Yorkshire Police* [2018] UKSC 4; [2018] AC 736.

[90] Ibid., [84].

[91] *Mohamud* v. *Morrison Supermarkets*, [45] (Lord Toulson).

[92] K. Burns, '"In This Day and Age": Social Facts, Common Sense and Cognition in Tort Law Judging in the United Kingdom' (2018) 45 *Journal of Law and Society* 226.

criticism of engaging in unprincipled extension of the law (as seen in *PAC*). The Supreme Court in *Barclays* and *Morrison* clearly sought to rebut any such accusations. While not expressly hostile to risk-based reasoning, the court emphasised that orthodox common law reasoning should be the starting point. Policy would provide a fallback should such reasoning fail.[93] Baroness Hale in *Barclays* was critical of a tendency to elide the policy reasons for the doctrine with the application of the law.[94] We can also identify some implicit criticism of risk-based reasoning. *Barclays*, for example, made it very clear that the conventional distinction between employees/those analogous to employees and independent contractors should stand, despite the fact that it conflicts with pure notions of enterprise risk.[95]

Nevertheless, it is important to read the 2020 judgments carefully. The Supreme Court did not overturn any of its previous decisions, including *Mohamud*. Sexual abuse cases are acknowledged as applying 'a more tailored version of the close connection test'.[96] However, it is clear that the court expects a more principled approach in future. One noticeable omission from both judgments is reference to *PAC*. Nevertheless, it was arguably there in spirit, reasoning for a more principled 'orthodox' approach which avoids any signs of unlimited judicial discretion.

### 3.2.4 *Risk in Civil Law Jurisdictions: France*

In contrast, in France, risk is accepted as a dominant justification for its doctrine of liability for the acts of others in tort (*fait d'autrui*). What is interesting is that, in contrast to the common law, which confines this debate to vicarious liability, this policy is reflected across the whole of tort law. From the late nineteenth century,[97] French tort law has moved towards objective theories of fault and explaining liability on the basis of

93 Lord Reed clarified, for example, that in *Mohamud* Lord Toulson was not suggesting that all that was involved was social justice: *Morrison Supermarkets* v. *Various Claimants*, [26].

94 *Various Claimants* v. *Barclays Bank*, [16].

95 Ibid., [24], rejecting suggestions to the contrary in the Court of Appeal.

96 *Morrison Supermarkets* v. *Various Claimants*, [36].

97 The works of Saleilles (*Les accidents du travail et la responsabilité civile* (Paris: Librairie Nouvelle de droit et de jurisprudence, 1897)) and Josserand (*De la responsabilité du fait des choses inanimées* (Paris: Librairie Nouvelle de droit et de Jurisprudence, 1897)) were influential. Legislation in 1898 also supported the idea of risk as a justification for liability: see the *loi*, 9 April 1898 (creating a special compensation regime for victims of workplace accidents).

ideas of risk, be it, on a sliding scale, *risque-autorité, risque-profit, risque-crée* (liability for those over whom you have authority, profit from or whose actions on your behalf create risks).[98] Certain authors such as Starck have gone further still, stating that civil liability is not founded on fault or risks, but a guarantee of essential rights to individuals: *la théorie de la garantie.*[99] Risk remains the dominant force, although, it may be noted, it takes a number of forms – a fact openly recognised by theorists – justifying varying degrees of judicial intervention. For commentators such as Viney and Tunc, risk-based reasoning is needed to satisfy the essential object of extra-contractual liability: the compensation of harm.[100]

The courts have been assisted in legal development by the broad wording of Article 1242(5) of the Civil Code: 'Masters and employers [are strictly liable] for the damage occasioned by their servants and employees in the exercise of the functions in which they are employed.' Abandoning early ideas of presumed fault,[101] risk provides an explanation and justification for expanding liability. More recently, reliance has been placed on ideas of *risque-crée* (risk creation), tied, as in English law, to notions of loss distribution via insurance and accident prevention/deterrence.[102] For Moréteau, it represents a move from the individualist system of 1804, where victims had to bear their own losses in the absence of proof of fault, to one where the victim occupies centre stage.[103] Borghetti, in his survey of French tort law culture, notes also the influence of academics such as Viney in adopting a strong pro-victim stance which seeks to expand the boundaries of tort law yet further.[104] All agree that 'French

[98] See Terré et al., *Droit Civil,* No. 905-8, 'La faute et le risque'; P. Giliker, 'France (1850–2000)', in P. Mitchell (ed.), *The Impact of Institutions and Professions on Legal Development* (Cambridge: Cambridge University Press, 2012).

[99] B. Starck, 'Domaine et fondement de la responsabilité sans faute' (1958) 56 *Revue trimestrielle de droit civil* 475. See also B. Starck, *Obligations* (Paris: Litec, 1972), No. 58–90. Starck argues that the law provides an individual right to safety (droit à la sécurité) and so any unauthorised harm to one's person or property should give rise to strict liability.

[100] See G. Viney, *Introduction à la responsabilité*, 3rd ed. (Paris: LGDJ, 2008), generally No. 33–56.

[101] See P. Le Tourneau, *La responsabilité civile* (Paris: Presses Universitaires de France, 2003), p. 9.

[102] C. Thibierge, 'Avenir de la responsabilité, responsabilité de l'avenir' (2004) 4 *Recueil Dalloz (Chroniques)* 577; J. Bell and D. Ibbetson, *European Legal Development – The Case of Tort* (Cambridge: Cambridge University Press, 2012), pp. 155–6.

[103] O. Moréteau, 'France: French Tort Law in the Light of European Harmonization' (2013) 6 *Journal of Civil Law Studies* 759, 761.

[104] J.-S. Borghetti, 'Culture of Tort Law in France' (2012) 3 *Journal of European Tort Law* 158, 176. This is not unanimous, however, and other writers, e.g. Terré, have been more concerned to strike a balance between various stakeholders.

law adopts organic and flexible ways to ensure compensation, at least in part as a result of a world view where risks should be borne by their creator or beneficiary'.[105]

Support for the 'socialisation' of risk in French law rests on a number of bases: (i) a moral sense that society should ensure that victims are compensated for injuries caused by the risks created by, in this case, enterprises; (ii) acceptance that this will be funded by widespread insurance;[106] and (iii) recognition that liability in tort complements an interventionist state which provides social security and specialist funds to support victims – most famously the *loi Badinter* creating a special no-fault compensation regime for traffic accidents in 1985.[107] Borghetti has commented that tort law in France is thus best understood 'as an element of a wider set of compensation and insurance mechanisms which include social security, direct insurance and liability insurance'.[108]

The impact of these policies is obvious if we examine how the courts apply Article 1242(5). As seen above, the relationships giving rise to liability are interpreted generously to help distribute risk throughout society. Equally, there is a presumption that the *préposé* is acting in the course of their employment unless the *commettant* can satisfy the three-fold rebuttal test. Risk-based reasoning has further encouraged the courts to restrict the *commettant*'s right to an indemnity: the *préposé* should not have to bear the burden of liability (either directly or by indemnifying the *commettant*) unless, without authorisation, they acted for purposes alien to their attributions.[109] The fact that this expansion relies heavily on the existence of insurance is underscored by Article L121–2 of the Insurance Code, which provides that the insurer shall cover the losses and damage caused by persons for whom the insured is legally liable, pursuant to Article 1242, Civil Code, regardless of the nature and seriousness of such

[105] M. Dyson, 'What Does Risk-Reasoning Do in Tort Law?', in M. Dyson (ed.), *Regulating Risk through Private Law* (Cambridge: Intersentia, 2017) p. 457.

[106] Viney, Introduction à la responsabilité, No. 29; G. Viney, *Le déclin de la responsabilité individuelle* (Paris: LGDJ, 1965).

[107] *Loi* 5 July 1985, no. 85-677. See also *loi* 4 March 2002, no. 2002-303 (on public health), discussed in S. Taylor, 'Medical Accidents and Pharmaceutical Product Liability in France', in M. Dyson (ed.), *Regulating Risk through Private Law* (Cambridge: Intersentia, 2017) and, generally, J. Knetsch, *Le droit de la responsabilité et les fonds d'indemnisation* (Paris: LGDJ, 2013).

[108] Borghetti, 'Culture of Tort Law in France', 167.

[109] Cass ass plén, 25 February 2000 Bull Ass plén No. 2; JCP 2000 II 10295 note M. Billiau. Later case law has clarified that an indemnity may still be obtained in case of criminal fault: Ass plén 14 December 2001 Bull Ass plén No. 17; JCP 2002 II 10026 note M. Billiau.

persons' faults. This is treated as having the status of *d'ordre public* and so cannot be modified by agreement. Here legislator and judge work hand in hand to ensure victims are compensated for injuries caused by the torts of others.

One particular development serves to highlight the true impact of risk-based reasoning in French law. Article 1242(1) was intended to be an introductory section and states simply that '[o]ne is liable not only for harm caused by one's own acts but also for that caused by persons for whom one is responsible'. Nevertheless, the courts have taken this general statement to justify imposing strict liability outside the categories specifically listed in Article 1242. Strict liability for the acts of others now arises with respect to bodies responsible for organising and controlling third parties – e.g. a privately run care centre for the acts of mentally handicapped individuals under its care,[110] or even a sports club where one of its members injures a fellow competitor during a sporting event.[111] Here we are beyond the *préposé/commettant* relationship and in the general sphere of risk-based liability.[112]

Nevertheless, even Viney has noted that, despite changes attributable to risk-based reasoning, French law retains an ongoing attachment to the idea of fault.[113] Fault-based liability remains at the core of the tort provisions of the French Civil Code (Article 1240) and its prominence has been retained in the 2017 reform proposals. Risk-based reasoning can therefore only ever be *part* of French tort law. There has also been criticism of the current position – it should not be assumed that risk-based reasoning receives universal acclaim. Borghetti, for example, has questioned whether expansion of strict liability on the basis of risk-based reasoning is always beneficial and whether judges consider its consequences, both to the insurance industry and society in general.[114] There is, indeed, a sense that liability cannot be extended indefinitely and recognition is needed of possible adverse effects on the French economy and on service provision.

110 Ass plén 29 March 1991 D 1991.324 note C. Larroumet.

111 See e.g. Civ 2, 22 May 1995 Bull civ II No. 155; JCP 1995 II 22550 note J. Mouly.

112 See M. Josselin-Gall, 'La responsabilité du fait d'autrui sur le fondement de l'article 1384 (1): Une théorie générale est-elle possible?' *JurisClasseur Périodique* (JCP) 2000.I.2011 (Article 1242(1) was previously numbered 1384(1)).

113 Viney, *Introduction à la responsabilité*, No. 56-1.

114 J.-S. Borghetti, 'Les intérêts protégés et l'étendue des préjudices réparables en droit de la responsabilité civile extra-contractuelle', in *Etudes offertes à Geneviève Viney* (Paris: LGDJ, 2008), pp. 145–6.

This attitude is reflected in the 2017 proposals for reform. Fault-based liability is listed as the first basis for tortious liability: Article 1241. Harm caused by another person is dealt with under Articles 1245–9, and what is noticeable about these provisions is that they seek to control the extent of liability. Article 1245 states that '[a] person is liable for harm caused by another person in the cases and subject to the conditions laid down in articles 1246 to 1249'. Notably, the expansive treatment of Article 1242(1) of the current Code (discussed above) is given a statutory framework and divided into those charged by judicial or administrative decision with organising and controlling the way of life of a minor[115] or adult[116] on a permanent basis, and those who take on by way of their business or profession contractual obligations to supervise or organise and control another person.[117] It is also made clear at Article 1245(2) that liability rests on proof of a tort by the direct author of the harm, overturning authority that, in relation to parental vicarious liability, it was unnecessary to show that the child had been at fault.[118] In terms of employers' vicarious liability (Article 1249), again we may note an attempt to establish a statutory framework to 'confine' liability.[119] While consolidating the case law discussed earlier, notably the May 1988 and February 2000 decisions of the French Supreme Court, the aim is not to provide a platform for further extension of liability – quite the opposite.

Our study of French law tells us three things. First, even a system that for over 100 years has openly embraced risk-based reasoning retains 'fault-based' liability at its core. Second, there is not a universal consensus as to the merits of risk-based reasoning, especially in its broadest form of *risque crée*. Third, recent legislative proposals indicate a finding that liability based on risk can take the law too far. The reforms refuse to endorse the logical end point of *risque crée* reasoning, which would be to

[115] Article 1246(3). Parental responsibility may be found at Article 1246(1).

[116] Article 1247.

[117] Article 1248 is broad and intended to cover the sports club cases and importantly is subject to a rebuttable presumption of fault. For criticism, see B. Häcker, '*Fait d'autrui* in Comparative Perspective', in J.-S. Borghetti and S. Whittaker (eds.), *French Civil Liability in Comparative Perspective* (Oxford: Hart, 2019), pp. 157–9.

[118] Cass Ass Plén 13 December 2002 Bull Ass plén No. 4, p. 7; JCP 2003 II 10010 note A. Hervio-Lelong.

[119] Article 1249(1): An employer is liable strictly for harm caused by his employee. An employer is a person who has the power to give orders or instructions to his employee in relation to the performance of his functions.

remove the need for tortious behaviour and extend the relationship to any situation where one person has supervision of another. In so doing, the French legal system indicates that risk should not be the sole justification for vicarious liability.

### 3.3 Understanding Vicarious Liability and Risk Comparatively

Risk-based reasoning is part of the modern law of tort. It has facilitated a broader notion of vicarious liability/*fait d'autrui* in English and French law. While Australian law has resisted its lure, its test for course of employment nevertheless does betray a certain affiliation to notions of risk. What, as comparative lawyers, do we make of this situation? Three observations may be made.

First, while all three systems use similar rules and adopt a common legal framework, in application we see differences. To understand the rules in question, we must dig below the surface. As Van Hoecke states, '[c]onceptual frameworks are one thing, the content of the law (values, principles, rules) and the attitude towards the law are another'.[120] By adopting a comparative approach which focuses not just on rules but on the underlying values and policies of tort law, we gain an insight into the operation of vicarious liability within the legal system.

Second, risk-based reasoning has no single meaning. A court may take a purist law and economics approach or alternatively favour more of a 'gut' feeling that enterprises should be held responsible for incidental risks that eventuate in the pursuit of profit. Equally, a system may adopt a more theoretical approach (as seen in France) identifying different types of risk or a more instrumental approach which uses the idea of enterprise risk to promote ideas of social justice. While the UK Supreme Court in 2020 seemed less supportive of risk-based reasoning, it should be noted that, in refusing to overturn existing case law, it retained extensions to the doctrine of vicarious liability which are hard to justify without some resort to notions of risk. Equally, Australian law, in tying liability to occasions where the employee has authority, power or control over the victims, arguably betrays an underlying affiliation to notions of risk-based reasoning. All systems therefore use risk, but in different ways and to different degrees.

[120] M. Van Hoecke, 'Methodology of Comparative Legal Research' (2015) 12 *Law and Method* 5.5.2.

Third, and perhaps most important, comparative studies of this kind cast light on *why* legal systems adopt different approaches to risk. From the above analysis, it is possible to identify five factors as influential:

(i) The desire to compensate victims;
(ii) The availability of state-based compensation;
(iii) The extent to which the courts are willing to actively shape principles of tort law;
(iv) The extent to which the courts are willing to embrace matters of social and moral policy;
(v) The availability of insurance.

These five interrelated factors provide a means by which we can seek to explain the current differences of approach between our three jurisdictions. Examining vicarious liability/*fait d'autrui* in England and Wales and in France, we can see the influence of all five of these factors. English law, in particular, has been motivated by (i), to assist victims of sexual abuse (see *Lister*, *CCWS*, *Armes*) who would find it difficult otherwise to obtain compensation. Such concerns also affect French law, albeit in relation to tort law generally. On this basis, both systems have been willing to rely on judicial intervention to shape the rules of tort liability (iii) and accept that courts are making decisions based on social policy (England and Wales/France) and to a certain extent matters of moral policy (France) (iv).[121] Fundamental to both systems has been insurance (v), although an important difference may be noted. Academic writers such as Viney openly advocate legal development funded by insurance. This is general acceptance across French society that insurance should be obtained as a matter of course. In contrast, English law has traditionally sought to downplay the role of insurance in tort law.[122] However, by relying on arguments of 'enterprise risk', or even the broader logic of Atiyah, the English courts are implicitly accepting an extension of liability founded on the assumption of insurance cover. For (ii), we can note interesting divergence. French law has long accepted that state-based compensation funds should supplement judicial-made law and that such schemes reflect an understanding that French law should be open to

[121] Borghetti has noted the Christian ideology of many French tort lawyers including Viney and Tunc: Borghetti, 'Culture of Tort Law in France', 173–4.

[122] See, for example, *Hunt* v. *Severs* [1994] 2 AC 350; J. Stapleton, 'Tort, Insurance and Ideology' (1995) 58 *Modern Law Review* 820, but contra R. Merkin and J. Steele, *Insurance and the Law of Obligations* (Oxford: Oxford University Press, 2013).

strict liability approaches to ensure victim compensation. In contrast, in England and Wales, it is the *absence* of a state-based approach to compensation that has provoked the courts to intervene in abuse cases. For example, the Criminal Injuries Compensation Scheme offers limited financial support for victims of abuse.[123] Lord Hope commented in 2013 that there is 'a heavy responsibility on our legal system to deal as fairly and justly as it possibly can with the consequences [of child sexual abuse]'.[124] In both cases, the (non-)availability of state compensation funds have influenced the finding of vicarious liability, albeit for different reasons.

Will *Barclays/Morrison* require a recalibration of the English response? While (i) remains, notably for abuse victims, the Supreme Court now seems far more reticent in relation to (iv) (social and moral policy), and warns against the non-incremental development of tort law: (iii). On this basis, subsequent case law *should* adopt a more restrictive approach post-2020, despite the fact that technically none of the previous authority has been overturned. Subsequent case law indicates, however, that a generous approach is still being adopted in relation to sexual abuse claims.[125]

In contrast, the High Court of Australia in *PAC* made it very clear that it was not for the courts to embrace matters of social and moral policy (upon which minds may differ) and that judicial activism in this area has created uncertainty (iii, iv). In advocating the incremental approach, the High Court was conscious of the need to compensate victims of sexual abuse (i) and, while not embracing the English/Canadian approach, some adjustments were made. Two other factors are important here, however. First, *PAC* was decided in 2016. In 2013, the Australian Royal Commission into Institutional Responses to Child Sexual Abuse was established and reported in 2017.[126] Two years earlier, the Commission published its *Redress and Civil Litigation Report*,[127] recommending the provision of effective redress for survivors of abuse through the establishment, funding and operation of a single national redress scheme and

[123] See D. Miers, 'Historic Sexual Offices and the Criminal Injuries Compensation Scheme' [2019] *Personal Injuries and Quantum Reports* 277.

[124] Lord Hope, 'Tailoring the Law on Vicarious Liability' (2013) 129 *Law Quarterly Review* 514, 525.

[125] *Trustees of the Barry Congregation of* Jehovah's *Witnesses* v. *BXB* [2021] EWCA Civ 356; [2021] 4 WLR 42.

[126] Royal Commission, *Final Report: Preface and Executive Summary* (Commonwealth of Australia, 2017).

[127] Australian Royal Commission into Institutional Responses to Child Sexual Abuse, *Redress and Civil Litigation Report* (Commonwealth of Australia, 2015).

statutory intervention to assist survivors bringing claims against institutions. The High Court, unlike in England and Wales and in France, was working alongside a proposed state-based response to the issue of historic sexual abuse (ii). Where the state itself fills the gap in victim protection, there is a diminished need for judicial intervention. Second, in relation to (v), Australia still bears the scars of its insurance crisis in the 2000s, when the collapse of two large insurance providers and sudden large increases in premiums led to calls for a more restrictive approach to tort liability.[128] The Ipp report,[129] commissioned by the Federal Government, made recommendations which led to statutory reform of negligence law in Australia limiting liability and damages for negligence.[130] There remains ongoing reluctance to place large compensatory burdens on defendants, notably in the field of public authority liability. From an Australian perspective, then, insurance cover is *not* the indisputable answer to the question of victim compensation. Insurance cover at a reasonable premium cannot be taken for granted. On this basis, the cautious reaction of the Australian courts in *PAC* is entirely predictable.

## 3.4 Conclusions

Comparative analysis helps us not only to identify legal rules, but the key values and policy arguments that shape the application of the law. It also forces us to question our assumptions: if we advocate 'risk-based' reasoning, what does that mean? What role should it play in legal reasoning? Is risk being used as an economic concept, instrumentally to justify compensation, or in combination with a number of different factors? This chapter has demonstrated that there is not one meaning of 'risk' and, in reality, a number of different factors influence how the courts approach vicarious liability in tort. Factors such as insurance and state-based responses to compensation will either encourage intervention by the courts (England and Wales; France) or indeed the opposite (Australia). Risk, it would seem, cannot be analysed in isolation, but needs to be considered in its broader context.

[128] See R. Davis, 'The Tort Reform Crisis' (2002) 25 *University of New South Wales Law Journal* 865; P. Cane, 'Reforming Tort Law in Australia: A Personal Perspective' (2003) 27 *Melbourne University Law Review* 649.

[129] Commonwealth of Australia, *Review of the Law of Negligence: Final Report* (Canberra, 2002).

[130] B. McDonald, 'The Impact of the Civil Liability Legislation on Fundamental Principles and Policies of the Common Law of Negligence' (2006) 14 *Torts Law Journal* 268.

Engaging in such comparative analysis is not easy. As Bell has advised, we must seek a true understanding of legal principle and look beyond black-letter law to obtain a deeper understanding of the operation of the law. In engaging in a comparative study of vicarious liability, we must dissect a seemingly common legal framework to ascertain differences in application and legal reasoning. By identifying the values influencing the courts, this chapter provides an insight not only into the theoretical underpinnings of vicarious liability/*fait d'autrui* and the motivation of the courts, but crucially of the weaknesses (and strengths) of risk-based reasoning.

As comparative lawyers, then, we must face head-on the risks of misunderstanding, mistranslation and misconception.[131] The key, as any comparative lawyer knows, is to appreciate these risks and adopt a methodology which addresses these issues. As John Bell's work has shown:

> [T]he important driving force for legal thinking is not the self-perpetuating logic of the legal concepts, but the values which the law is trying to enforce and lawyers to implement. The legal concepts are the building blocks which are used to present arguments, but the values determine the kind of building which is constructed.[132]

Values can also change over time. Comparative scholars must be alert to this. Studying risk is indeed a risky business. The role of the comparative scholar is to monitor and appraise legal change. The insights we gain make us better critical legal scholars.

[131] J. Stapleton, 'Benefits of Comparative Tort Reasoning: Lost in Translation' (2007) 1(3) *Journal of Tort Law* 1.

[132] J. Bell, 'English Law and French Law – Not So Different?' (1995) 48 *Current Legal Problems* 63, 98.

# 4

# What's in a Name?

## Historical Foundations of Unjust(ified) Enrichment

DAVID IBBETSON

Legal historians and comparative lawyers have much in common. Unlike those who specialise in the current law of their own legal system, both comparatists and historians cannot fail to be conscious of the contingency of legal ideas. Other places and other times may order things differently, even when they reach the same result. So far as private law is concerned, perhaps nowhere is this contingency better illustrated than by the area of law known in England as unjust enrichment, in continental Europe as unjustified enrichment.

### 4.1 Roman Law and Its Development

Roman law is the inevitable starting point.[1] In his brilliant little book *Roman Law in European History*, Peter Stein observed that Roman law served as a supermarket of legal ideas from which later legal systems could pick and choose what they wanted.[2] So it did, and over the centuries new products appeared on the supermarket shelves, derived

Earlier versions of this chapter were delivered at seminars in Frankfurt and Oxford, and I am grateful to participants for their comments. Thanks are due to Alex Iordache, Astrid Bolea, Akiko Ohta, Yasunori Kasai, Matthew Mirow, Charles Donahue, Stefan Vogenauer, Guido Rossi, Paulo Canelas de Castro, Li Tang, Michael Loewe, Çağrı Gürkanlı, Helen Scott and Matt Dyson.

Most of this chapter has perforce been written during the period when the ordinary conditions for research were impossible, so these thanks are more than conventional; without them, for better or worse, the chapter would not have been written. Gratitude is especially due to David Wills and Lizz Edwards Waller of the Squire Law Library, who dealt cheerfully and efficiently with my sometimes wholly unreasonable demands.

[1] For all of what follows see the pioneering work of J. P. Dawson, *Unjust Enrichment* (Boston: Little, Brown, 1951) and R. Zimmermann, *The Law of Obligations* (Cape Town: Juta & Co., 1990), pp. 834–901.

[2] P. Stein, *Roman Law in European History* (Cambridge: Cambridge University Press, 1999), p. 2.

from the earlier ideas but adding to the range from which later legal systems could choose.

At least four ideas from it have influenced the development of the law in this area in Europe. We may list them.

- The general principle attributed to Pomponius appearing twice in the Digest in slightly different forms derived from Aristotle via the Stoics, that none should be enriched, or enriched wrongly, at the expense of another:

  D.12.6.14

  > Nam hoc natura aequum est neminem cum alterius detrimento fieri locupletiorem.
  >
  > For it is fair by nature that no one should be made richer to the detriment of another.

  D.50.17.206

  > Iure naturae aequum est neminem cum alterius detrimento et iniuria fieri locupletiorem.
  >
  > By the law of nature it is fair that no one should wrongfully be made richer to the detriment of another.

- The remedy known as *condictio*, a claim to money or a thing which ought to be handed over to the claimant, by the time of Justinian subdivided into a number of categories.[3] Two of these were of principal importance to the future: the *condictio indebiti*, where money had been paid over in the erroneous belief that it was due;[4] and the *condictio sine causa*, where property had been conveyed or an obligation contracted without an underlying *causa* recognised by law, and which was potentially wide enough to subsume all the Roman *condictiones* as well as giving a remedy in some situations where no other *condictio* would apply.[5] One text in the Digest, D.12.1.32, attributed to Celsus, was to

[3] D. Liebs, 'The History of the Roman Condictio up to Justinian', in N. MacCormick and P. Birks (eds.), *The Legal Mind* (Oxford: Oxford University Press, 1986), p. 163.

[4] D.12.6.

[5] D.12.7. Later lawyers would distinguish between the *condictio sine causa specialis*, covering the instances of liability which did not fit elsewhere, and the *condictio sine causa generalis* which could be seen as the basis of all *condictiones*.

prove particularly influential, since it justified the reversal of enrichment where there had not been a defective transfer from plaintiff to defendant:

> [Q]uia pecunia mea ad te pervenit, eam mihi a te reddi bonum et aequum est.
>
> Because my money came to you, it is just and fair that you restore it to me.

- The category of obligations *quasi ex contractu* in Justinian's institutes.[6] These included the *condictio indebiti* and the situation where one person had administered another person's affairs other than pursuant to a contract, *negotiorum gestio*. But more generally their unifying feature was that there was an obligation similar to one which might have arisen out of a contract, but where there was in fact no agreement.
- The *actio de in rem verso*, where a slave's master or a *paterfamilias* had gained a benefit under a contract made by his slave or family member, but where he was otherwise not liable.[7]

These were overlapping to some extent – but only to some extent. Quasi-contractual obligations included the *condicto indebiti*, for example. But at the most general level, the central issue was the tension between the two different formulations of the Pomponius principle. That of D.12.4.16, that enrichment at the expense of another was contrary to the law of nature, could serve as a background justification for rules, explaining for example the rescript of Antoninus Pius that a minor who had borrowed money without a tutor's authority should be liable to the extent of their enrichment;[8] but it was too wide to operate as a general rule rather than an *ex post facto* justification. On the other hand, D.50.17.206, focusing on 'wrongful' enrichment, expressed a principle which could be applied generally but was too narrow in its sphere of application, depending as it did on the defendant's conduct having been independently wrongful.

The medieval lawyers developed these elements, while remaining more or less faithful to the texts. Some manuscripts of the Digest indicate a

6 Inst 3.27.

7 D.15.3. C.4.26.7.3 suggests that this extended to the contracts of free people in Justinian's law. See A. M. Honore, 'Third Party Enrichment' (1960) *Acta Juridica* 236, 237–8. Medieval lawyers regarded this as wholly heterodoxical and struggled to reinterpret it.

8 D.26.8.1.pr. See generally, W. W. Buckland, *Textbook of Roman Law*, 3rd ed. (Cambridge: Cambridge University Press, 1963), pp. 158–9.

generalising trend in terms of the reversal of enrichment,[9] but the dominant view of the glossators enshrined in the Accursian gloss was more conservative, essentially seeing the principle as no more than a justification for specific actions. One important feature of the Roman texts was picked up, their rooting in *aequitas*, or equity, helped by the Celsus text.[10]

It should be emphasised that all of this took place in the medieval universities. Legal practice might be different. Texts influenced by the learned civil and canon laws reflected the Roman base.[11] In thirteenth-century Spain, for example, the *Siete Partidas* contained the *condictio indebiti* of Roman law as well as the general rule against wrongful enrichment at the expense of another,[12] without any suggestion that they might be related; unsurprisingly there is little trace of anything like a generalisation of the Roman ideas in legal practice. England provides a very good parallel. *Bracton* has a section on quasi-contractual obligations which is taken straight from the Institutes of Justinian,[13] but there is nothing of this in the law of the courts. All we have there is a degree of plasticity in the operation of ideas of property and contract without any suggestion of the application of any general principle.[14]

Although the medieval law was generally faithful to the Roman texts, there were two developments that had consequences for later law. First, probably insignificant at the time but with a baleful future ahead of it, was the gradual emergence of a substantive quasi-contract, typically in the form *obligatio ex quasi contractu*, slipping from the Roman *obligatio quasi ex contractu*.[15] The linguistic shift made it seductively attractive to look for the essence of quasi-contracts as an independent source of

[9] J. Hallebeek, 'Developments in Medieval Roman Law', in E. J. H. Schrage (ed.), *Unjust Enrichment: The Comparative Legal History of the Law of Restitution* (Berlin: Duncker & Humblot, 1995), pp. 59, 64.

[10] Gl *pervenit*, ad D.12.1.32; Bartolus, Commentary ad D.12.6.15 (14) no. 1; see too ad D.12.6 rubric no. 19.

[11] For the general principle in Canon law, see VI.12.De Reg Iur 48: Locupletari non debet aliquis, cum alterius iniuria vel jactura.

[12] P.5.14.28; P.7.34.17.

[13] Henry de Bracton, *De Legibus et Consuetudinibus Angliae*, ed. G. E. Woodbine, trans. S. E. Thorne (Cambridge, MA: Harvard University Press, 1968–77), 2.20.

[14] D. Ibbetson, 'Unjust Enrichment in England before 1600', in Schrage, *Unjust Enrichment*, 121.

[15] Gl *igitur* ad Inst. 3.27.1 (and in England *Bracton* 2.295; *Fleta*, ed. G. O. Sayles (72 Selden Soc) 198). The Byzantines had already made this move. See *Theophili Antecessoris Paraphrasis Institutionum*, ed. J. H. A. Lokin, R. Meijering, B. H. Stolte and N. van der Wal (Groningen: Chimaira, 2010), 710 : 'το QUASICONTRACTON'.

obligation unified by some sort of common feature. Second, a greater role was given to *aequitas*, either in the form of a *condictio sine causa ex aequitate* based on D.12.1.32, an *actio negotiorum gestorum in factum ex aequitate*, or, as the Orléans professor Jacques de Révigny preferred, a *condictio ex aequitate* based on C.4.26.7 (extending the *actio de in rem verso*).[16] It may be that behind these formulations was an elision between the idea of *aequitas* as fairness or justice, the dominant sense of the word in the writings of the glossators, and a subordinate sense of *aequitas* as *aequalitas*, equality, or in this context analogy.[17] All this fed into the work of the commentators of the fourteenth century, most notably Baldus, for whom there was a general equity (*aequitas*) arising out of the maxim that none should be enriched at the expense of another, which equity grounded a general action, a *condictio certi*.[18] Equity could have a creative function going beyond the specific Roman rules of the *condictiones*.

## 4.2 Thomas Aquinas

Another source feeding into later law was Thomas Aquinas' treatment of the obligation to make restitution.[19] Its most influential form was found in the *Summa Theologiae* II.II 62,[20] but its clear rooting in Aristotle is most explicit in his commentary on Aristotle's *Nicomachean Ethics* V.4.[21] The making of restitution was an aspect of the virtue of commutative justice, arising out of inequality. Its object was not so much that the person who had been enriched should disgorge his gain as that the person who had been impoverished should be restored.[22] The obligation

[16] Hallebeek, 'Developments', 103–6, with the important qualification of R. Feenstra, 'Grotius' Doctrine of Unjust Enrichment as a Source of Obligation', in Schrage, *Unjust Enrichment*, 197, 215 n. 115. For mediaeval jurists' treatment of the *condictio sine causa* as the general remedy, see A. Söllner, 'Die Kausa im Kondiktionen- und Vertragsrecht des Mittelalters bei den Glossatoren, Kommentatoren und Kanonisten' (1960) 77 ZSS (RA) 182, esp. at 189–212.

[17] L. Maniscalco, *Equity in Early Modern Legal Scholarship* (Leiden: Brill, 2020), pp. 13–43.

[18] Ad C.4.51.1 ('*actio ex generali aequitate*', based on D.12.1.32), D.12.1.32, C.3.32.3

[19] J. Hallebeek, *The Concept of Unjust Enrichment in Late Scholasticism* (Nijmegen: Gerardt Noodt Inst., 1996), pp. 7–16.

[20] *Summa Theologiae*, ed. T. Gilby (Cambridge: Cambridge University Press, 1975), vol. 37, pp. 102–26.

[21] *Commentary on Aristotle's Nicomachean Ethics*, trans. C. I. Litzinger (Notre Dame, IN: Dumb Ox Books, 1964), pp. 293–6.

[22] *ST* II.II 62 art. 6 resp ad 1. Hence the person who has gained without causing loss, as by taking advantage of light from another's candle, is not obliged to restitution.

to make restitution could be subdivided: *ratione rei*, where one person had property which ought to be handed over to another; and *ratione acceptionis*, where he had taken another's thing or wrongfully ceased to have it. In the former, the obligation depended on the continued holding of the property; in the latter it did not. Importantly, 'restitution' here included giving compensation for losses for personal injury and injuries to reputation or honour; in Roman legal terms it encompassed most of the law of delict.

We can hardly think of the Thomistic analysis in terms of 'unjust enrichment'. Injustice only had a part to play in so far as any violation of equality could be regarded as unjust,[23] and in voluntary transactions like deposit there would only be an obligation to restitution *ratione acceptionis* if there had been an *iniuria*, if the depositee had been at fault.[24] Enrichment too had a part to play, but only if the causation of loss without gain, as in burning down another's house,[25] could be strait-jacketed into a notion of enrichment.

## 4.3 The Spanish Scholastics

These medieval streams began to come together in the works of the sixteenth-century Spanish scholastics, primarily at the University of Salamanca.[26] Their dominant framework was that of Thomas Aquinas, with its division into restitution *ratione rei* and restitution *ratione acceptionis*, typically found in commentaries on justice and law, *De Justitia et Jure*. Though the framework was Thomistic and hence based on the restoration of equality, there was a strong move towards the assimilation of this with civil and canon law. Significantly, their analysis was strongly skewed in the direction of restitution *ratione acceptionis*, largely covering the ground which a lawyer would have channelled into the law of delict, with an increasing stress on the wrongfulness of the defendant's conduct.[27] Restitution *ratione rei* was given far less emphasis, a bridge between property and wrongdoing, and commonly fragmented into a number of standard situations, such as the restoration of property or

23 *Commentary on Nicomachean Ethics*, esp. p. 296; *ST* II.II 62 resp ad art. 2.

24 *ST* II.II 62 resp ad art. 6; Aristotle, *NE* V.4.1132.

25 *ST* II.II 62 resp ad art. 4. In this he reflects Aristotle, *NE* V.4 1132a12, where such cases are treated in terms of gain, 'perhaps inappropriately'.

26 Hallebeek, *Concept of Unjust Enrichment*, 47–85.

27 J. Sampson, *The Historical Foundations of Grotius' Analysis of Delict* (Leiden: Brill, 2018), pp. 164–82, 208–25.

fruits to an owner by a *bona fide* or *mala fide possessor*. Here there was no focus at all on wrongfulness; the obligation to restore was strict.[28]

This realignment involved the drawing of a sharper distinction between restitution *ratione acceptionis* and restitution *ratione rei*. The former was focused on the defendant's wrongful conduct and the loss suffered by the victim; no longer was there any reason to think of there being an equivalent gain to the wrongdoer, as there had been, uncomfortably, for Aristotle.[29] The latter, on the other hand, could be seen to be based on the defendant's enrichment, liability to restitution *ratione rei* arising only when there was a genuine enrichment to be reversed.

## 4.4 Grotius and the Early Modern Development of Ideas

It was with Hugo Grotius that these distinctions came to be clearly delineated. In his best-known work, *De Iure Belli ac Pacis* (*The Law of War and Peace*), he quoted the source of the Pomponius enrichment principle in Cicero's *De Officiis* and footnoted the juristic use of the idea in D.50.17.206, a principle imbued with *aequitas* alongside other features of Roman law such as the liability of a master for the acts of a slave to whom he entrusts his business.[30] His footnotes and sidenotes point to his having been influenced more by scholastic writers of the sixteenth century who had commented on the *Summa Theologiae* than by Roman law.[31] His focus here, importantly, is on an extended notion of property, *dominium*, treating the *condictio* as, or as equivalent to, a claim *in rem*. More transparently obligational was his *Inleidinge tot de Hollandsche Rechtsgeleerheid* (*Introduction to the Law of Holland*).[32] His principal division of obligations here was between those derived from contract and those derived from inequality; the latter category – the scholastics' restitution – was further subdivided into those stemming from '*baet-*

28 Ibid., 168.

29 See Section 4.1.

30 *De Iure Belli ac Pacis*, ed. B. J. A. de Kanter-van Hettinga Tromp, with additional notes by R. Feenstra and C. E. Persenaire (Leiden 1939, Aalen 1993), 2.10.2.1–2 (pp. 321–2).

31 R. Feenstra, 'Grotius' Doctrine of Unjust Enrichment as a Source of Obligation', in Schrage, *Unjust Enrichment*, pp. 197, 207–19.

32 Ibid., 200–7. There are convenient English translations of the relevant Dutch texts in R. W. Lee, *Jurisprudence of Holland* (Oxford: Clarendon Press, 1926). I have used the edition of the *Inleidinge* by F. Dovring, H. F. W. D. Fischer and E. M. Meijers, 2nd ed. (Leiden: Universitaire Pers, 1965), which includes some manuscript annotations in Grotius' own copy of the text, found in Lund.

*trecking*' (profit-making, enrichment) and those stemming from wrongdoing.[33] It is the former sub-category in which we are interested here, dealt with in *Inleidinge* III.30. The examples given are largely stock Roman examples: the *condictio indebiti*; the *condictio causa data causa non secuta*; the *condictio ob turpem causam*; ending with the *condictio sine causa* as a general remedy where property had been transferred without an antecedent gift or promise,[34] giving as his example what appears to be a reference to Celsus' D.12.1.32, providing a remedy in all cases where one person's property had come to the hands of another without any valid *causa*. The concluding section, drawing together all situations of enrichment, perhaps points towards a conception of a general remedy: [T]he question is not so much whether one man has caused another to have less than he had before (though often this is involved) as rather whether he has been enriched by the other's property.'[35] Whether this is a general remedy whenever there is enrichment or rather a generalisation of the reason for the granting of the specific remedies is less clear.[36] But there are hints elsewhere that Grotius recognised this as an expansive principle: a letter he wrote to his younger brother in 1616, and an addition found in his own copy of the *Inleidinge* giving a remedy, and not merely a defence (which was orthodox Roman law), to a possessor of land against the owner whose land he had improved.[37] But Grotius had made one major step forward: he had elevated the enrichment principle to a third basis of obligation alongside contract and wrongdoing. However, we cannot yet see it as a principle of 'unjust' or 'unjustified' enrichment: neither in the *De Iure Belli ac Pacis* nor in the *Inleidinge* is there any hint that Grotius was explicitly thinking in terms of any specific limit on the enrichment principle.

A slightly different line is found in the commentary on the Institutes by Grotius' younger contemporary, Arnold Vinnius. In his commentary on Inst. 3.14.2, after noting Justinian's fourfold division of obligations he adds that there was a residuary set of obligations, including Celsus' D.12.1.32, which were based solely on *aequitas*.[38] As Feenstra points out, 'Inspiration by Grotius is not obvious'.[39] The reference to *aequitas*

[33] *Inleidinge*, III.1.9, 14–18.
[34] Ibid., III.30.18.
[35] Ibid., III.30.19.
[36] Feenstra, 'Grotius' Doctrine', 205–6, with refs at n. 58.
[37] Ibid., 219–22.
[38] A. Vinnius, *Institutionum Imperalium Commentarius*, ad Inst 3.14.2 no. 3.
[39] Feenstra, 'Grotius' Doctrine', 223.

takes us back to Révigny and Baldus,[40] but the fact that D.12.1.32 is just one of a list of disparate situations where an obligation *ex sola aequitate* is given strongly suggests that Vinnius is not providing any general *condictio* whenever one is required by equity.

An alternative approach, more remedial than taxonomic, was to develop the scope of the Roman law *actio de in rem verso*, which, it will be remembered, had lain where a master or a paterfamilias had gained under a contract made by his slave or family member and where no other action was available. Some German writers in the seventeenth century were willing to extend this beyond the case of slaves and subordinate family members, first to spouses and then allowing the action against any person who had benefited under a third party's contract at the expense of the other contracting party, describing it as *hodiernis moribus*, according to modern usage.[41] This position was reached in Heinrich Hahn's notes on Wesenbeck's commentary on the Digest.[42] Hahn's approach found followers in Germany, and it was incorporated into the eighteenth-century Austrian *Codex Theresianus*.[43] Alongside this, though, weight was coming to be placed by some writers on *aequitas*, generating a *condictio* or *actio in factum ex aequitate* building on Celsus' D.12.1.32.[44]

The different strands came together in the *Praelectiones Iuris Romani et Hodierni* of the Frisian Ulrik Huber.[45] Here, after a more or less conventional treatment of the *actio de in rem verso* (with Hahn's extension into all third-party contracts) Huber said that this was not simply a matter of modern practice but also of Roman law, based on D.12.1.32, linking this with Grotius' *baet-trekking* of the *Inleidinge*. It seems clear that, although the context is the *actio de in rem verso*, the thrust of Huber's words is focused on Grotius' general enrichment remedy. However, it is no less clear that his route to the application of the general remedy is through the *actio de in rem verso* and not, as Grotius himself

[40] See Section 4.1.

[41] Feenstra 'Grotius' Doctrine', 224.

[42] H. Hahn, *Observata Theoretico-practica ad Matthaei Wesenbecii in L. Libros Digestorum Commentarios* (Helmstedt: Henning Müller, 1668) ad D.15.3 no. 4: B. Kupisch, *Die Versionsklage, Ihre Entwicklung von der Gemeinrechtlichen Theorie des 17 Jahrhunderts bis zum Österreichischen Allgemeinen Bürgerlichen Gesetzbuch* (Heidelberg: Universitätsverlag Winter, 1965), p. 17.

[43] B. Kupisch, 'Ungerechtfertigte Bereicherung', in Schrage, *Unjust Enrichment*, 237, 249–52 (greater detail in Kupisch, *Versionsklage*; *Codex Theresianus* 3.20.5 nos. 35, 37.

[44] Kupisch, *Versionsklage*, 252–60.

[45] *Praelectiones Iuris Romani et Hodierni* (Franeker, 1689) ad D.15.3, pp. 520–1.

might have favoured, through the *condictio sine causa*: Huber's commentary on the *condictio sine causa* (D.12.7) does no more than reproduce the conventional division between the *condictio sine causa generalis* and the *condictio sine causa specialis*, both of which had at their heart the reversal of a defective transfer, without any elaboration. A generation later, however, Voet transposed the reference to D.12.1.32 together with *Inleidinge* III.30.18 into his commentary on the *condictio sine causa*.[46] The same was the case for Johann Gottlieb Heineccius, who was at various times professor in Franeker, Frankfurt and Halle and whose works were widely read throughout Europe; for him, the main vehicle was the *condictio sine causa*; this lay whenever *aequitas* did not permit one person to be enriched at the expense of another.[47]

Dutch law, after Huber, has clear signs of a move in the direction of a general remedy arising out of equity alone, with no concern to identify any formal action. This idea lies behind a series of cases in the Hoge Raad, the Supreme Court of Holland, Zeeland and West Frisia. Pomponius' text gives the legal grounding for a series of decisions reported by van Bijnkershoek and Pauw described as arising *ex sola aequitate*.[48]

Similar ideas are found elsewhere in Europe, though without their source always being visible. In France in the late seventeenth century, Jean Domat hints at a general remedy when he says that a person who 'finds himself' with another's property without just cause is bound to return it;[49] and in England the judgment of Lord Mansfield CJ in *Moses* v. *Macferlan*,[50] allowing the action for money had and received when it was just and equitable to do so, is strongly reminiscent of civilians' *condictio ex aequitate*.[51]

46 J. Voet, *Commentarius ad Pandectas*, ad D.12.7 no. 2.

47 Johann Gottlieb Heineccius, *Elementa Iuris Civilis Secundum Ordinem Pandectarum*, ad D.12.7 s. 62. His analysis of the *actio de in rem verso* is more muted; although built on a foundation of *aequitas*, whose ratio applied equally to benefits received under contracts of free persons as to contracts of family members and slaves, it is on the *condictio* that he focuses: cf. ad D.15.4 s. 191. See too his *Syntagme Antiquitatum Romanorum*, IV.7 s. 31, where the *condictiones* are said to be based on agreements or to arise *ex sola aequitate*.

48 Feenstra, 'Grotius' Doctrine', 228–35.

49 *Les Loix Civiles dans leur Ordre Naturel*, 2.7.1.10. For further references to France, see J.-M. Augustin, 'Introduction Historique à l'Enrichissement Sans Cause en Droit Français', in V. Mannino and C. Ophèle (eds.), *L'Enrichissement sans cause: la classification des sources des obligations* (Poitiers: Université de Poitiers, 2007), pp. 31, 33–4.

50 (1765) 3 Burr 1665, 1 W Black 219.

51 D. Ibbetson, 'Unjust Enrichment and Lord Mansfield', in M. Schermaier, H. Dondorp and B. Sirks (eds.), *De Rebus Divinis et Humanis* (Göttingen: V & R Unipress, 2019), p. 193, where I suggest Mansfield's source might have been Heineccius.

Although the focus of these tentative extensions of liability was on the *actio de in rem verso* and the *condictio sine causa*, both of which depended on money or property having come into the defendant's hands, the general enrichment remedy of Grotius' *Inleidinge*, and in its wake of Domat, Mansfield and the eighteenth-century Hoge Raad, was not so limited: a person might have to disgorge the enrichment stemming from the receipt of some service without a contract or donative intent.[52] Behind these tentatives were two repeated themes: a justification for liability, either generally or in a particular case, in *aequitas*; and a description of the enrichment having been *sine causa*, lacking (legal) justification.

## 4.5 Quasi-contract

None of this cut across the quasi-contractual analysis of commentators, however. Huber, for example, though very clearly supportive of Grotius' general enrichment remedy, was happy to deal with quasi-contractual obligations in the part of his *Praelectiones Iuris Romani et Hodierni* commenting on the Institutes, following Vinnius in saying that not all obligations fitted into Justinian's fourfold classification and expressly giving Celsus' D.12.1.32 as one example of a situation falling outside it.[53] The same is true of Heineccius[54] and Voet (this time in the context of his comment on D.44.7), unhesitatingly dealing with quasi-contractual obligations independently of any general enrichment remedy.[55] A multiplicity of further examples could be cited. An occasional writer insists on the importance of the Roman terminology of *obligationes quasi ex contractu*.[56] Some, like Huber, note that the Institutes read *quasi ex contractu* and not *ex quasi contractu* but say that the terminological shift is insignificant;[57] but most writers simply use the substantive quasi-

[52] See in particular W. Pauw, *Observationes Tumultuariae Novae* 12 (1743), discussed by J. Scholtens, 'The General Enrichment Action That Was' (1966) 83 *South African Law Journal* 391, 397–401; and Feenstra, 'Grotius' Doctrine', 231–2, where the judges stressed the availability of the general enrichment action notwithstanding that the facts might have grounded an *actio negotiorum gestorum*.

[53] *Praelectiones Iuris Romani et Hodierni*, ad Inst 3.28.

[54] *Elemena Iuris Civilis secundum Ordinem Institutionum*, ad Inst 3.14 s. 778.

[55] *Commentarius ad Pandectas*, ad D.44.7.1 no. 5.

[56] See for example the rant (I can think of no better word) of D. G. van der Keessel, *Dictata ad Justiniani Institutiones*, ad Inst 3.28 no. 1, ed. B. Beinart and P. van Warmelo (Amsterdam: Balkema, 1967), 2.123.

[57] U. Huber, *Praelectiones Iuris Romani et Hodierni*, ad Inst 3.28.pr (Franeker, 1689); similarly Vinnius, *Institutionum Imperialium Commentarius*, ad Inst 3.14.2 no. 2

contract without comment. A major consequence of this was that it was easy to slip into the assumption that the underlying cause of the obligation was something like a contract; not a genuine contract, it is true, but an implied, presumed or tacit contract.[58]

Two writers' approaches to quasi-contract were particularly influential, William Blackstone in England and Robert-Joseph Pothier in France.

Some writers before Blackstone had discussed quasi-contract from a Roman standpoint,[59] but Blackstone's starting point was not Roman law but the English action of assumpsit. This was primarily a contractual action but for procedural reasons had come to be based upon an implied promise to perform the contract; and it had been all too easy to move from the language of implied promise to speaking of an implied contract.[60] His list of situations in which an action of assumpsit would lie where there had been no genuine contract owed nothing to Roman law: it included the payment of taxes, the performance of a judgment of an inferior or foreign court, a few cases of misperformance of office.[61] But it also included the action for money had and received, and so incorporated Lord Mansfield's analysis of *Moses* v. *Macferlan* as rooted in equity. It followed that the principal English vehicle for an enrichment remedy was now categorised as based upon an implied contract.

In his *Traité des Obligations*, Pothier expressly rejected others' views that quasi-contracts might be based on any tacit agreements – though he does not say who saw them in this way – stressing that they are not based on agreement but are derived from a law (*loi*) or natural equity.[62] None the less, he slanted quasi-contractual liability in the direction of contractual. Hence the payment of money by mistake, giving rise to the *condictio indebiti* in Roman law, was treated as an adjunct to the contract of loan (*mutuum*), and

(Elzevir, 1642), slips from *obligationes quasi ex contractu* to *obligationes ex quasi contractu* without comment.

58 P. Birks and G. McLeod, 'The Implied Contract Theory of Quasi-Contract: Civilian Opinion Current in the Century before Blackstone' (1986) 6 *Oxford Journal of Legal Studies* 46.

59 Ibid., 77–8.

60 D. Ibbetson, *Historical Introduction to the Law of Obligations* (Oxford: Oxford University Press, 1999), pp. 137–40, 269–73.

61 W. Blackstone, *Commentaries on the Laws of England* (Oxford: Clarendon Press, 1765–9), 3.158–66.

62 *Traité des Obligations* (Paris, 1761) 1.1 s. 114; see too *Coutumes des Duché, Bailliage et Prévoté d'Orléans* (Paris, 1772), Introduction s. 115.

*negotiorum gestio* was treated as an adjunct to the contract of mandate.[63] Nowhere was there any suggestion that these might be related to any form of enrichment remedy deriving from Pomponuis' principle.

## 4.6 Codifications and Their Consequences

The years around 1800 saw three major codifications of private law: Prussia in 1794, France in 1804 and Austria in 1811.

Those of Prussia and Austria included *condictiones*, together with the expanded *versio in rem*.[64] This latter had become generalised in the German *usus modernus*, to the extent that it could potentially encompass all the *condictiones* as well as *negotiorum gestio*, indeed any situation where the most expansive version of Pomponius' or Grotius' enrichment principle could be justified on the grounds of *aequitas*, *billigkeit*. The codes' provisions were expressed more narrowly in terms of property having come to the defendant, but still retained some of the elasticity of the *actio de in rem verso* of the *usus modernus*. A generation later, this was re-characterised by Savigny in terms of the *condictio sine causa generalis*, where one person had been enriched *ohne Grund* at the expense of another.[65] There was perhaps an ambiguity in Savigny's analysis, between enrichment without cause (*ohne Grund*) and enrichment without lawful cause (*ohne rechtlichen Grund*), but any possible ambiguity was resolved in favour of the latter by his pupil, Friedrich Puchta.[66]

The French *Code Civil* took a different line following Pothier. Its section on quasi-contract covered just two situations, *negotiorum gestio* and the payment of something that was not due,[67] though in the legislative tribunal Tarrible stated that the same principles lay behind other provisions on the code distributed among their proper titles.[68] Nowhere was there any suggestion that behind these situations there lay any idea of the reversal of enrichment. This focus on quasi-contract, following the *Code Civil*, became a second paradigm in the nineteenth century.

[63] Traité du Quasi-Contrat appelé Promutuum; et de l'Action Condictio Indebiti, in *Traité du Prêt de Comsomption*, part 3; Du Quasi-contrat Negotiorum Gestorum, in *Traité du Contrat de Mandat*, Appendice (both Paris, 1766).

[64] Prussia: ALR 1.13 Arts. 262–72; Austria: ABGB Art. 1071.

[65] F. C. von Savigny, *System des Heutigen Römischen Recht* (Berlin: Veit, 1841), 5.523–7.

[66] F. Puchta, *Lehrbuch der Pandekten* (Leipzig: Johann Ambrosius Barth, 1838), s. 299.

[67] Arts. 1376–81.

[68] J. G. Locré, *La Législation Civile, Commerciale et Criminelle de la France* (Paris: Imprimerie Nationale, 1828), 13.50–1.

The third paradigm, or perhaps just an outlier, was the common law's explanation in terms of implied contracts. Lord Mansfield soon backtracked from his approach to the action for money had and received in *Moses v. Macferlan*, where he had suggested that it should lie whenever equity required someone to disgorge money,[69] and by the start of the nineteenth century the situations in which the action would lie had been reduced to a list without any abstract principle at its base.[70] As English law began to crystallise its theory of contract around a model of agreement stemming from the meeting of minds of the parties, inspired by Pothier, cases where there had been no meeting of minds were marginalised. Since they were invariably formally actionable in the same way as contracts were, by an action of assumpsit brought on an implied promise to perform, they could be treated as near-contractual. The implied promise mutated into an implied contract, with the well-known baleful consequences. The sheer awfulness of this form of analysis is very well illustrated by Frederick Pollock's textbook on contract law published in 1876:

> It does not follow that because there is no true contract, there may not be cases falling within this general description in which it is just and expedient that an obligation analogous to contract should be imposed upon the person receiving the benefit. In fact there are such cases: and as the forms of our law do not recognise quasi-contracts in any distinct manner, these cases are dealt with by the fiction of an implied previous request, which often has to be supplemented (as in the action for money had and received) by an equally fictitious promise. The promise, actual or fictitious, then relates back to the fictitious request, so that the transaction which is the real foundation of the matter is treated as forming the consideration in a fictitious contract of the regular type.[71]

## 4.7 European Developments

### 4.7.1 *The German Model*

The development of the German model is the easiest to describe. The generalised form of the *actio de in rem verso* was already established in the codes of Prussia and Austria, and Savigny and Puchta had reoriented

[69] See Section 4.4.

[70] W. D. Evans, *The Action for Money Had and Received* (Liverpool: Merritt and Wright, 1802), conveniently reprinted in (1998) 6 *Restitution Law Review* 1.

[71] F. Pollock, *Principles of Contract at Law and Equity* (London: Stevens and Sons, 1876), p. 29.

the law in the direction of unjustified enrichment based on the Roman *condictio sine causa*. The model of unjustified enrichment, based on a receipt without (lawful) cause, came to prevail. It explicitly formed the basis of liability in the *Bürgerliches Gesetzbuch* (BGB), *ungerechtfertigte Bereicherung*.[72]

Beyond this, the Austrian Civil Code was widely adopted in central and eastern Europe, reflecting the spread of the Austrian Empire: Hungary and Transylvania; Galicia; Czechoslovakia; Serbia; Moldavia; Croatia; Bosnia.[73] Elsewhere, Savigny's influence was clearly visible: in the civil codes of the Baltic States;[74] of the German-speaking Swiss canton of Zurich (from where it was borrowed by other German-speaking cantons);[75] of Saxony.[76] All of these were strongly rooted in the Roman law of the *usus modernus*.

### *4.7.2 France*

French law formed the dominant model in much of western continental Europe, and its development is a central theme. We have seen that the *Code Civil* followed Pothier's treatment of quasi-contract with its focus on *negotiorum gestio* and undue payment. Within only a few years of the enactment of the code, the *actio de in rem verso* was being relied on to justify a decision, expanding the scope of the enrichment remedy.[77] Other cases followed along this route too,[78] and it gradually found its way into commentaries. The Belgian Laurent, in the 1870s, incorporated it into his analysis of *negotiorum gestio*, though noting that most authors simply included it without any comment; he doubted whether it was consistent with the *Code* but accepted that it had been '*consacrée par la tradition*'.[79] This was not the only early expansion or generalisation

[72] Art. 812. Zimmermann, *Obligations*, 887–8.
[73] G. Hamza, *Wege der Entwicklung des Privatrechts in Europa* (Passau: Schenk Verlag, 2007), 132, 150, 153, 167, 171, 181, 183.
[74] Liv-, est- und curlaendisches Privatrecht, Arts. 3680–9.
[75] *Privatrechtliches Gesetzbuch für den Kanton Zürich*, Arts. 1216–34.
[76] *Bürgerlich Gesetzbuch für das Königreich Sachsen*, Arts. 1519–33 (*condictio indebiti*). See the text and related materials edited by Christian Hattenhauer and Frank Schäfer, www.juris.de/jportal/portal/t/10wi/bs/22/page/sammlung.psml/action/controls.sammlung .ChangeNavigation?nid=root
[77] Rep Dalloz, XIII tit. Contrat de Mariage 1014 n. 3. See generally D. Deroussin 'Répétition de l'Indu et Enrichissement sans Cause en France 1804–1950' (2020) 4 *Tribonien* 78.
[78] Dawson, *Unjust Enrichment*, 177 n. 102, citing D.52.2.193 and D.69.2.213.
[79] F. Laurent, *Principes de Droit Civil* (Paris: Toullier – Sociètè Typographique Belge, 1876), 20.361 s. 333ff. Quote at p. 364, s. 337.

redolent of Roman law. Toullier got close to saying that the quasi-contracts were held together by a general principle that one person should not be enriched at the expense of another without the will of the other,[80] close though not identical to enrichment *sine causa*. Around the middle of the century, the translation into French of Savigny's *System* in 1855 began the process whereby French law came to be based around causeless enrichment. The terminology was still unstable though. We do occasionally find *enrichissement sans motifs*, but the dominant term, so far as I can see, was *enrichissement illégitime*. *Enrichissement injuste* is also found, from the same period, but it seems largely to have been used in a non-technical sense.[81] *Enrichissement illégitime* is close to Savigny, but is skewed in the direction of Pomponius' principle of wrongful enrichment in D.50.17.206. The same is perhaps true of *enrichissement injuste*, though this borrows more clearly the idea of the reversal of enrichments which are contrary to *aequitas*. Some thirty years later there is a shift of emphasis towards *enrichissement sans cause*, far closer to Savigny's original idea. The trigger for this looks to have been German law, more accurately the draft *Burgerliches Gesetzbuch*. The popularity of the terminology dates from the appearance of Raymond Saleilles' French commentary on the proposed German law,[82] and it was then consolidated in the *Boudier* case in 1892.[83] Here the Cour de cassation caught up with commentators and with lower courts, recognising the legitimacy of the *actio de in rem verso* despite its absence from the code. Labbé's note on the case went a step further, explaining the general principle on which all was based as the defendant's *enrichissement sans juste cause*.[84] Finally, a century or so later, in 2016, it was incorporated into the new *Code Civil* in the form of *enrichissement injustifié*, appended to the pre-existing provisions on undue payment and *negotiorum gestio*.[85]

[80] C.-B.-M. Toullier, *Le Droit Civil Français suivant l'Ordre du Code*, Book 4 title 3 chapter 1 (see summary at 4.3.1 s. 112). I have used the edition published in Brussels by Bruyland-Christophe in 1838, where it appears as vol. 6, pp. 9–44.

[81] I base these suggestions on a study of the terms from those texts in gallica.bnf.fr. This is, of course not comprehensive.

[82] R. Saleilles, *Étude sur les Sources de l'Obligation dans le Projet du Code Civil Allemand* (Paris: Cotillon, 1889).

[83] D.1892.1.596, S.1893.1.281.

[84] S.1893.1.281

[85] *CC* 2016, Art. 1303.

### 4.7.3 Belgium, Luxembourg, Italy

In Belgium and Luxembourg, where the French *Code Civil* applied as it stood, law and practice followed France, though authors, in particular the Belgian Laurent, played a major part in liberalising the application of the law of the *Code Civil*, adopting the shift towards *enrichissement sans cause* after 1892.

The story in Italy was not dissimilar to that in France. Pre-unification codes mimicked the French *Code Civil*, as did the general *Codice Civile* of 1865.[86] A degree of expansiveness was found by borrowing from Roman law the *actio negotiorum gestorum utilis* and the *actio de in rem verso*, until, in the very last years of the century, the superior courts recognised a general principle behind quasi-contractual liability, a generalised form of the *actio de in rem verso*.[87] Terminology might have been unstable – in 1898 it is referred to as *ingiusta locupletazione*, unjust enrichment[88] – but, following the French model, *arricchimento senza causa* came to be preferred. When the code was redrafted in 1942, it included the remedy in this form, following the draft Italo-French obligations code of 1932.[89]

### 4.7.4 Holland

Dutch law had been precocious in its recognition of a general enrichment remedy.[90] As a result of this, the first draft codes of the nineteenth century included a general clause.[91] However, the influence of French law was too strongly felt and the *Burgerlijk Wetboek* of 1838 simply included provisions equivalent to the *Code Civil*.[92] Dutch law did not follow the widening of French law, from the *actio de in rem verso* to *enrichissement sans cause*, but stayed more or less within the boundaries of the 1838 code, and it was not until the early twentieth century that opinion began to shift. Two men stand out in particular. M. H. Bregstein argued on historical and policy grounds, and on the basis of French scholarship, that the law should (and did) recognise a general claim for

86 *CC*, Art. 1140–50.

87 P. Gallo, *L'Arricchimento Senza Causa* (Padua: CEDAM, 1990), pp. 137–8. The first case identified by Gallo was in December 1897.

88 Il Foro Italiano 1898.I.321, 325 (Florence, *Corte de Cassazione*).

89 *CC* Art. 2041.

90 See Section 4.4.

91 E. J. H. Schrage, 'The Law of Restitution: The History of Dutch Legislation', in Schrage, *Unjust Enrichment*, 323.

92 *BW*, Arts. 1390–400.

causeless enrichment, first in his thesis on unjustified enrichment in 1927 and then in an article in 1948;[93] and E. M. Meijers argued in a note in 1935 that the code could be interpreted to generate a general provision.[94] The Hoge Raad disagreed.[95] By this time, though, a new Civil Code was in preparation under the auspices of Meijers. Parliament was asked to determine whether there should be a general principle or specific remedies. They followed his view in recommending the former, based on the equivalent provisions in the codes of Japan, Germany, Switzerland, Italy and Greece (and undoubtedly French law); in due course, this was incorporated into the new *Burgerlijk Wetboek* of 1992, expressed in terms of unjustified (*ongerechtverdigt*) enrichment, as a supplement to the pre-existing *negotiorum gestio* and undue payment.[96]

### *4.7.5 Switzerland*

For most of the nineteenth century the Swiss cantons' laws were based on either the Austro-German or the French model, depending on their linguistic group.[97] It codified its unified law of obligations in 1881, three decades before it had a general civil code. It is well known that the draft of the German Civil Code was very influential here, and this is clearly visible in the German version of the text, where the enrichment action is generalised as *ungerechtfertigte Bereicherung* and the derivation from the *condictio sine causa*, and hence from Savigny, is very marked. The text of the French version is unsurprisingly similar, but after some debate its heading was the then-orthodox *enrichissement illégitime*.[98] The terminology of the French stuck, but the Germanised content of the provisions, and indeed the title of the heading in the German version, prevented the focal meaning of the French exercising any real gravitational force on the application of the law. Linguistic conservatism was a

93 M. H. Bregstein, 'Ongegronde Vermogensvermeerdering', in *Verzameld Werk* (Zwolle: Tjeenk Willink, 1960), 1.265.

94 Note on H. R. 9 November 1935, NJ 1936, no. 239, cited by Bregstein, 'Ongegronde Vermogensvermeerdering', 279.

95 *Quint* v. *de Poel*, HR 30 January 1959, NJ 1959 48.

96 *NBW* 6.212.

97 See Sections 4.7.1 and 4.7.2; J. P. Dunand, 'Le Géant et les Nains: Le Code Napoléon comme Modèle des Codes Civils des Cantons Suisses Romands' (2005) *Forum Historiae Iuris*, https://forhistiur.net/2005-10-dunand/

98 *Code des Obligations / Obligationenrecht*, Arts. 70–5 (amended 1911 and renumbered as Arts. 62–7).

strong counter-force holding off the terminological shift to *enrichissement sans cause* common in France after 1892, which would have been substantively redundant. Whatever the language, Swiss law was framed in terms of unjustified enrichment. Moreover, its multilingual quality, and the inherent quality of the code which had the flexibility to integrate different regional customs, meant that it could all the more easily influence other systems: it was, for example, transplanted into Turkey in 1926, translated rather inelegantly into Turkish but retaining something like the idea of wrongfulness of the French version of the Swiss code[99] – though in time it followed the inevitable trend and mutated into causeless enrichment, *Sebepsiz zenginleşme.*[100]

### 4.7.6 *Spain*

Although superficially wholly dependent on a French model of quasi-contract, in the *Código Civil* of 1889,[101] the Spanish reality was somewhat different. As with Holland, Spain had an indigenous tradition to build on. This was the *Siete Partidas* of the mid-thirteenth century, itself very highly Romanised but recognised as a formal source in Spanish law. There, right at the end of the final *Partida*, was a Spanish version of Pomponius' principle in its less generalised form, that none should be enriched wrongfully – *tortizeramente* – at the expense of another.[102] It is effectively a straight translation of this text of Pomponius, and Lopez's standard gloss on the *Partidas* does no more than cross-refer to the Latin of this text. So far as I know, the text exercised no influence on Spanish law for the next 600 years. Whatever the explanation, it began to play a part in the decisions of the *Tribunal Supremo* from the 1850s, and alongside D.50.17.206 was cited as justification for various provisions in the commentaries on the

[99] E. Örücü, 'A Legal System based on Translation: The Turkish Experience' (2013) 6 *Journal of Civil Law Studies* 445. According to V. H. Velidedeoglu, 'enrichissement illégitime' was translated in six distinct ways in the civil and obligations codes: 'De Certains Problèmes provenant de la Réception du Code Civil Suisse en Turquie' (1956) 5 (6) *Annales de la Faculté de Droit d'Istanbul* 99, 108. I am grateful to Eray Bulut and Çağrı Gürkanlı for help in understanding the Turkish texts.

[100] Code of Obligations 2011, Art. 77.

[101] *Código Civil*, Arts. 1888–94.

[102] P.7.34.17.

draft code of 1851 and the code of 1889.[103] A piece published around seventy years later by Antoni Maria Borell i Soler[104] studied 120 decisions where the relevant text from the *Siete Partidas* formed part of the argument. In most of these cases the principle of wrongful enrichment based on the *Partidas* played only a subsidiary part, providing a partial justification for a decision reached on more orthodox grounds, but in two cases Borell i Soler argued that the decision would not have been reached without application of the principle, and there was no doubt that it could potentially be applied where there were gaps in the range of application of existing rules.

Borell i Soler's paper attempted to give shape to the legal principles, focused on when one might be lawfully enriched at another's expense. Its basis is revealing, showing how history could play a major part. The law it describes is relatively conservative and almost exclusively Spanish. The influence German law was having on the law of France and elsewhere by this time is nowhere to be seen. Thirdly, though the structure of the analysis is very clearly a structure of wrongful enrichment, by which was meant enrichment that was in some sense legally wrongful, at least at a rhetorical level this legal wrongfulness is treated as equivalent to injustice. In other words, there is some underpinning of morality, strengthened by the similarity to the canon law principle. We should notice too what is not there. Grotius' principle of enrichment, which had lain behind the pre-1838 Dutch developments, had been based substantially on the thought of Thomas Aquinas and his sixteenth-century Spanish commentators; nowhere do we find a reference to any of these.

But the Spanish approach, as described by Borell i Soler, was perhaps too close to Savigny's approach to survive any rethinking by Spanish scholars. This rethinking occurred with the appearance of Nuñez Lagos' monograph, *Enriquecimiento sin Causa*, in 1934.[105] Lip service was paid to the fact that this area of law had a long history in Spain and had been recognised by the *Tribunal Supremo*, but the rest of the book after this very brief nod to history was firmly based on German and French scholarship dealing with unjustified enrichment: Spanish law fell into the Franco-German, or more accurately Germano-French, line.

[103] J. B. Grandon, 'Enriquecimiento Injustificado y Codificación', in P. Del Olmo Garcia and X. Basozabal (eds.), *Enriquecimiento Injustificado en la Encrucijada* (Navarra: Aranzadi, 2017), pp. 49, 94–118.

[104] (1925) 32 *Revista Jurídica de Catalunya* 10.

[105] R. Nuñez Lagos, *Enriquecimiento sin Causa* (Madrid: Reus, 1934).

### 4.7.7 *Portugal*

As in most other places, Portugal's medieval laws had no general category covering enrichment remedies, but under the influence of natural and Roman law thinking in the eighteenth century, its institutional literature knew a category of quasi-contracts based on presumed or fictitious agreement, based on a number of 'very equitable' principles, including the principle that none should be enriched at the expense of another.[106] There was, however, nothing similar in the *Código Civil* of 1867, despite the familiarity of the drafter with the French code and its commentators and with Savigny's *System*.[107] The Portuguese turning point came in the middle of the twentieth century, in a series of cases from the 1940s to 1960s.[108] This led to the incorporation into the Code of 1966 of a section dealing with causeless enrichment.[109]

### 4.7.8 *Romania*

Romania was, of course, completely different from the countries of western Europe in terms of its history, politics and culture, but the trajectory of development of its enrichment remedy was identical. The starting point was the Civil Code of 1864, introduced after a degree of unification had been achieved in 1858, which was closely modelled on the French *Code Civil*. Unsurprisingly, its provisions on quasi-contract were those of the *Code Civil*, divided into *negotiorum gestio* and undue payment.[110] Around the start of the twentieth century, the influence of the French – and to a lesser extent German – developments began to be felt.[111] Romanians wrote theses in Paris on *enrichissement sans cause*, and this began to trickle back into scholarship in Romania too, largely based on the French writings. At first the courts were unwilling to go beyond the provisions of the *Code Civil*, but in 1922 the *Curte de Casaţie* recognised a general remedy for enrichment

[106] P. de Melo Freire, *Instituições de Direito Civil Portugues* (Lisbon: Regalis Academiae Scientiarum, 1789), IV.4.
[107] M. A. Domingos de Andrade, 'Em Memoria do Visconde de Seabra' (1952) 28 *Boletim da Faculdade de Direito da Universidade de Coimbra* 270, 295 n. 33.
[108] A. Menezes Cordeiro, *Tratado de Direito Civil Portugues, II* (Lisbon: Almedina, 2010), vol. 3, pp. 188–92.
[109] *Código Civil*, Arts. 473–82 ('enriquecimento sem causa').
[110] *Codul Civil*, Arts. 986–97.
[111] See L. Pop, 'Îmbogăţirea fără justă cauză în reglementarea noului Cod civil' (2013) 7 *Dreptul* 13

without just cause, expressed as a principle of equity and natural law.[112] Eventually this was incorporated in the revised Civil Code of 2011.[113]

### *4.7.9 Russia*

The power of the Germano-French model is well illustrated by the development of the enrichment remedy in Russia.[114] There was no formal provision covering enrichment before the enactment of the Civil Code of 1923, but by then it had become recognised in judicial practice that none should be enriched at the expense of another, described as unlawful enrichment.[115] Scholarly writing had moved in the same direction, following the law of the West (essentially the Prussian ALR) and with clear reference to Roman law in the description of the remedy as a *condictio* (*kondiktsia*).[116] Commentary on the draft of these provisions of the Civil Code refers to the law of Germany (by now the BGB), Saxony, Zurich, Switzerland, Austria, France and the Baltic States.[117] Explicitly claiming to follow the German, Swiss and Baltic codes, the language of unlawful enrichment, rather than simply causeless enrichment, was preferred.[118] The 1923 Civil Code itself, though, shifted its language away from unlawfulness in the direction of the BGB, incorporating a series of articles on causeless enrichment.[119]

From here the provision spread into other legal systems within the former Soviet bloc, notwithstanding the tension between the enrichment remedy and Marxist–Leninist theory.

[112] Înalta Curte de Casaţie, secţia I, deciziunea nr. 1344 din 12 decembrie 1922, în 'Jurisprudenţa română', anul X, 1923, no. 1–2, pp. 277–8, quoted by Pop, 'Îmbogăţirea fără justă cauză', 19.

[113] *Codul Civil*, Arts. 1345–8.

[114] G. E. Glos, 'The Doctrine of Unjust Enrichment in Soviet Law' (1961) 3 *University of Malaya Law Review* 46.

[115] I. M. Tiutriumov, *Zakony Grazhdanskie* (Riga: Izdanie knigoizdatel'stva i knizhnago magazina Davida Gliksmana, 1923), Art. 574 ss. 16–37.

[116] Ibid., Art. 574 ss. 30–5.

[117] Ibid., Art. 574 s. 36.

[118] Ibid., Art. 574 s. 37. The Russian text describes it in German as '*ohne rechtlichen Grund*'.

[119] Arts. 473, 474. For this code, see A. Oistroukh, 'Russian Society and Its Civil Codes: A Long Way to Civilian Civil Law' (2013) 6 *Journal of Civil Law Studies* 373.

### 4.7.10 *England and the United States*

In the late nineteenth century there appeared a third model alongside the quasi-contract of the Code Civil and the unjustified enrichment of the Germano-French line traceable back to Savigny. This appeared, seemingly fully formed right from the start, in the common law world in 1888, in a historical article by the American James Barr Ames in the *Harvard Law Review*. Rejecting the ubiquitous analysis of implied contracts, he identified one principle behind actions of assumpsit where there was no genuine contract as one of unjust enrichment.[120] While Ames and his immediate successors recognised other bases of quasi-contract, following Blackstone,[121] within a generation unjust enrichment was being seen as the only element within quasi-contract.[122] It is probable, though there is no direct evidence, that a twisted version of Savigny lay behind this.[123] In his *Obligationenrecht* he had placed *grundlose Bereicherung* as the source of non-contractual remedies where there was no wrongdoing, but in the French translation of 1863 this appears as *enrichissement injuste.*[124]

England continued with its implied contract analysis until the publication of the First American Restatement of Restitution in 1937, whose focus was unjust enrichment, by now seen as the content of the older quasi-contract. The language of restitution was relatively unfamiliar and open to criticism,[125] but it took hold, concealing the underlying basis of liability. English lawyers in the 1930s, prominent among them

[120] 'The History of Assumpsit: Implied Assumpsit' (1888) 2 *Harvard Law Review* 53, 64. Proof of a negative is of course impossible, but the database of journals in *Hein Online* and the database of books in *The Making of Modern Law* reveal no earlier use of the phrase, though Ames had used similar phrases the year before: A. Kull, 'James Barr Ames and the Early Modern History of Unjust Enrichment' (2005) 25 *Oxford Journal of Legal Studies* 297.

[121] See Section 4.5. See W. Keener, *Treatise on the Law of Quasi-Contracts* (New York: Baker, Voorhis & Co., 1893).

[122] F. C. Woodward, *The Law of Quasi-Contracts* (Boston: Little, Brown, 1913).

[123] Ames is known to have spent a year in Germany before starting to teach at Harvard, though history does not reveal where in Germany he went.

[124] *Das Obligationenrecht als Theil des heutigen römischen Rechts* (Berlin: Veit, 1851), 1.25, 26; *Le Droit des Obligations* (Paris: A. Durand, 1863), 1.38, 39

[125] E. W. Patterson, 'The Scope of Restitution and Unjust Enrichment' (1936) 1 *Missouri Law Review* 223. See further E. V. Abbot, 'Keener on Quasi-Contracts' (1896) 1 *Harvard Law Review* 209, 479; Learned Hand, 'Restitution or Unjust Enrichment' (1897) 11 *Harvard Law Review* 249.

comparative lawyers and legal historians, picked up on these ideas, though with considerable adjectival instability: we find unjust, unjustified and unjustifiable enrichment, as well as restitution. Eventually restitution was adopted as the general category, and after the appearance of Peter Birks' *Introduction to the Law of Restitution* it came to be explained in terms of unjust enrichment, analysed in terms of discrete 'unjust factors', though in its second edition Birks made a move towards thinking in terms of unjustified enrichment on the Germano-French model.[126]

### *4.7.11 South and Central America*

Both paradigms of liability in the early nineteenth-century European codes could be seen to be rooted in Roman law, and both could be reinforced by the rhetoric of equity or reference to the moral principle of Pomponius that none should be enriched at the expense of another. The interplay between these models is very clearly visible in South and Central America, where a movement for legal codification inspired by the Enlightenment came about in the wake of the increasing independence from colonial rule.[127] In so far as there was a previous legal tradition, this was the law of the colonial power, and with independence there was no pressing reason to retain this. On the contrary, especially in those states which had been under Spanish or Portuguese domination, it was possible to point to Spanish or Portuguese law as being feudal or monarchical, not to mention repetitive and disorganised, with no code appropriate to a modern independent state. Although some argued for the creation of a new code based on the relatively familiar Spanish law, greater favour attached to the adoption of the *Code Civil*, either in whole or substantially. The French code was preferred to the German for many reasons: in

[126] For the difference between the two models see K Barker, 'Responsibility for Gain: Unjust Factor or Absence of Legal Ground?', in C. Rickett and R. Grantham (eds.), *Structure and Justification in Private Law* (Oxford: Hart, 2008), p. 47; S. Meier, 'Restitución de Pagos Indebidos: "Factores Injustos" vs "Sine Causa"', in Basozabal and del Olmo, *Enriquecimiento Injustificado*, 199.

[127] A. Guzmán Brito, 'La Influencia del Código Civil Francés en las Codificaciones Americanas' (2005) 2005 *Cuadernos de Análisis Juridico* 25; with greater detail in *Historia de la Codificación Civil en Iberoamérica* (Santiago: Editorial Jurídica de Chile, 2000); M. C. Mirow, *Latin American Law* (Austin: University of Texas Press, 2004), pp. 133–42.

particular, it was written in a language that was more or less easily understood and it had been enacted in a post-revolutionary republican state rather than within an absolutist monarchy.

Hence in 1808 Louisiana, ceded to the United States in 1803, adopted a code that was largely modelled on the French. This, it was said, was better than the alternative of descending into the 'horrible chaos' of the common law.[128] Quasi-contracts consisted of all voluntary acts generating an obligation other than those based on agreement; excluded were the obligations of tutors appointed by law and of neighbours (dealt with elsewhere), since they were not undertaken voluntarily, leaving only *negotiorum gestio* and undue payment.[129] Other early codes straightforwardly following the *Code Civil* on this point were those of Haiti (1825), Bolivia (1831) and Peru (1838, adopting that of Bolivia). After the middle of the century codes may have copied the *Code Civil* less slavishly but were nonetheless very strongly influenced by it, with the Roman law base sometimes showing through. The Chilean *Código Civil* of 1855 is transparent. The draft of 1847 specified that there were two principal quasi-contracts, following the *Code Civil*; that of 1853 added common ownership and neighbourhood, while the final form recognised three principal forms: *negotiorum gestio*, undue payment and common ownership. The annotations of the draftsman, the polymath Andres Bello, reveal its underpinnings: the first two cross-refer to the equivalent provisions of the *Code Civil* and their parallels in the *Siete Partidas*, the third cross-refers to Pothier.[130] A similar trajectory of development is visible in the new Peruvian code of 1852, where the section on quasi-contract is prefaced by the Pomponius principle and quasi-contract is defined as being based on presumed consent, before dealing with *negotiorum gestio* and undue payment in a thoroughly French way.[131] In Peru, co-ownership and joint heirship were treated as analogous but not equivalent to quasi-contracts, though in Guatemala twenty-five years later common ownership was incorporated into the Peruvian list, along the lines of the Chilean code; the French influence is still visible but it is attenuated.[132]

[128] 'el horrible caos del *common law*': quoted by Guzmán Brito, 'Influencia', 39.

[129] *Digest of the Civil Laws now in Force in the Territory of Orleans* (New Orleans: Bradford & Anderson, 1808), pp. 318–20.

[130] *Código Civil*, Arts. 2284–313; in P. L. Urquieta (ed.), *Obras Completas de Andres Bello, XIII* (Caracas: Ediciones del Ministerio de Educación, 1955), pp. 893–905; Grandon, 'Enriquecimiento Injustificado', 75–93.

[131] *Código Civil* 1852, Arts. 2110 ff.

[132] *Código Civil* 1877, Arts. 2249–75.

Alongside this, from around 1850 the influence of Savigny began to be felt.[133] It is present in the Chilean code (though not in the section on quasi-contract),[134] and it was given wider currency in the *Esboço del Código Civil* of the Brazilian Teixeira de Freitas (1860–4), for whom the principle that one should not be enriched at the expense of another without just cause was the main basis of the category of non-contractual obligations derived from voluntary acts, though the component elements (undue payment, *negotiorum gestio*) were individually justified on the grounds of presumed intention.[135] From here it was incorporated into the Argentine code of 1869,[136] passing thereafter into that of Paraguay in 1876.[137] Still, there was no general treatment of quasi-contract or unjustified enrichment, and it was not until well into the twentieth century that there was explicit recognition of enrichment without cause. In Brazil, for example, although its code of 1916 was largely based on German law, a general clause reversing *enriquecimento sem causa* was rejected as a pure pandectist innovation.[138] Nonetheless, the idea was present in South America early in the twentieth century. It was recognised in case law in Argentina from 1918 that, expressly following French doctrine, the *actio de in rem verso* should be given a wide scope, and soon this was formulated in terms of *enriquecimiento sin causa*.[139] In Chile the 'immutable principle of law that none should be enriched at the expense of another' was being given an expansive force, and soon this too was being explained as enrichment *sin causa*;[140] the same development occurred in Colombia, first basing liability

[133] N. A. Pizarro, 'El Código de Prussia y Savigny (su influencia en la doctrina y la legislación)' (1944) 31 *Revista De La Universidad Nacional De Córdoba* 1059, 1077, 1089–90.

[134] G. Brito, *Codificación del derecho civil e interpretación de las leyes. Las normas sobre interpretación de las leyes en los principales códigos civiles europeo-occidentales y americanos emitidos hasta fines del siglo XIX* (Madrid: Iustel, 2011), p. 175.

[135] A. Teixeira de Freitas, *Esboço del Código Civil*, Art. 3.400, 3.405–6.

[136] For the sources used in the code, see Mirow, *Latin American Law*, 139–40.

[137] Guzman Brito, *Codificacion*, 296–302.

[138] J. D. Harke, 'Pandectística e sua Recepção no Direito Brasiliero' (2017) 473 *Revista de Instituto Historico e Geografico Brasileiro* 31, 46–8. The more limited provision of Arts. 964–71 were said to be modelled on the Austrian code of 1811.

[139] R. C. Casad, 'Unjust Enrichment in Argentina: Common Law in a Civil Law System' (1974) 22 *American Journal of Comparative Law* 757, 764, based on the explanatory note to Art. 499 of the Argentine code. See Banco de Londres y Bresil c. Gobierno Nacional, in *Jurisprudencia de los Tribunales Nacionales* (December 1918), 21, 26.

[140] J. Fabrega, *El Enriquecimiento sin Causa* (Bogotá: Plaza & Janés, 1996), pp. 43–4. The first case quoted where *enriquecimiento sin causa* is expressly relied upon dates from 1931.

on the *actio de in rem verso* and then formulating it in terms of *enriquecimiento sin causa*;[141] and alongside – earlier than – the generalisation in case law, doctoral theses on the subject began to appear.[142] Soon, too, the analysis is found in newly drafted civil codes.[143]

### 4.7.12 *Japan and China*

After the Meiji restoration and Japan's opening to the West in the middle of the nineteenth century, it was resolved to have a 'modern' civil code.[144] The first draft, by the Frenchman Gustave Boissonade, owed a great deal to the *Code Civil*. Articles 381–9 were based on the general principle that a person enriched *sans cause légitime* should be required to disgorge the enrichment, exemplified by undue payment and *negotiorum gestio*, as well as two or three other examples which had been dotted around the *Code Civil*. The heading of the section in the original French, 'De l'Enrichissement Indû ou des Quasi-Contrats', again mirrored orthodox nineteenth-century French terminology;[145] in his commentary on the sections, Boissonade said that this was an improvement on the French and Italian codes, whose undefined 'quasi-contract' gave no hint of any unifying feature.[146] Boissonade's draft was rejected, and a new code prepared incorporating elements of many modern Western systems; this became the Civil Code of 1898. The enrichment provisions here (Articles 703–8, distinct from the immediately preceding *negotiorum gestio*) owed more to the German model than the French, but the Japanese heading of the section was identical to that of Boissonade, though appearing as 'unjust enrichment' in the contemporaneous English translation (edited by a German), where it is described as covering the ground of the Roman *condictiones*.[147]

141 See the cases printed in ibid., 183–93.

142 M. L. Stabile de Nucci, *Enriquecimiento sin Causa* (Buenos Aires: Valerio Abeledo, 1921); E. Caffarena Morice, *El Enriquecimiento sin Causa a Expensas de Otro en El Derecho Civil Chileno* (Santiago: Establecimientos Gráficos de Balcells, 1926).

143 Mexico: *Código Civil Federal* (1928), Art. 1882.

144 I am grateful to Michael Loewe, Akiko Ohta and Li Tang for help with the Japanese and Chinese texts.

145 See Section 4.7.2.

146 G. Boissonade, *Projet de Code Civil pour l'Empire du Japon*, 2nd ed. (Tokyo: n.p., 1883), 2.248.

147 L. Lönholm, *The Civil Code of Japan* (Tokyo: Maruya & Co., 1898), p. 183.

Qing China, and the Republic which followed it, also followed German law;[148] its provisions on unjust(ified) enrichment (the Chinese text does not clearly translate as unjust or unjustified) in the draft Civil Code of 1911 (drafted by Wu Teng-Fang, the first Chinese called to the English bar) were yet more closely modelled on Germany than the Japanese had been, though it retained the Japanese hiatus between *negotiorum gestio* and undue payment. Political circumstances prevented the code being brought into force immediately, but an abbreviated form was enacted in 1929. The provisions are retained in the same form in the Civil Code of 2021.[149]

## 4.8 Some Concluding Thoughts

The development of this area of law over the last 2,000 years illustrates perfectly Peter Stein's observation that Roman law provided a supermarket of ideas, ideas that have spread all over the world. Behind all of this history lies the Aristotelian-Stoic principle that no one should be enriched at the expense of another, a principle that could justify concrete rules but was too wide to offer new solutions to specific problems. Along the way we see two dead ends which have been explored: an apparently fruitful, though insufficiently specific, line that a remedy should be given when justified by equity; and a clearly inadequate explanation dependent on implied or presumed contract.[150] We are left with two distinct approaches. First is the 'absence of basis', grounded on the Romans' *condictio sine causa* and channelled through Savigny. Second is that the enrichment is 'unjust' or 'wrongful', based on the narrower Pomponius principle of D.50.17.206. But there is no good reason to see these as alternative justifications of a third head of obligations alongside contract and wrongdoing, a hare set running by Grotius; they might independently justify remedies in different, if overlapping, situations.

[148] Xiaiqun Liu, *Heaven Has Eyes: A History of Chinese Law* (Oxford: Oxford University Press, 2020), pp. 107–17. More specifically, see S. Gallagher, Lin Siyi and L.-C. Wolff, 'The History of a Mystery: The Evolution of the Law of Unjust Enrichment in Germany, England and China' (2020) 3 *International Comparative Politics and Ethics Law Review* 337, 362–4.

[149] Arts. 979–84 ('*negotiorum gestio*' in the official English translation), Arts. 985–8 ('unjust enrichment' in the official translation, though closer to 'profit obtained without legal basis' in the Chinese text).

[150] That said, French law and the many systems influenced by the *Code Civil* still bear the scars of the dalliance with quasi-contract in their retention of specific rules of undue payment and *negotiorum gestio*.

At risk of overextending the metaphor of the supermarket, over time the shelves can be filled with very similar products which at first sight look to be identical but which have subtle differences. In nineteenth-century Germany, for example, we have *ohne Grund*, *ohne rechtlichen Grund* and *ungerechtfertigte Bereicherung*. French is yet more prodigal: *enrichissement sans cause*, *sans juste cause*, *illégitime*, *injuste*, *sans motifs*, *injustifiée*. Foreign products are imported, typically following the latest fashion, be it Dutch, French, German or American. Something of the meaning can be lost, or gained, in translation, especially when transplanted onto foreign shelves. None of this, of course, need matter. It is the underlying rules that are significant, not the high-level abstractions – until, that is, taxonomically minded scholars begin to take them seriously.

# 5

# 'An Art Obscured with Difficult Cases'

## Interpretation and Rhetoric in Fulbecke's Direction

JOANNA MCCUNN

John Bell has contributed much to the study of legal interpretation, perhaps most notably as editor of Cross's *Statutory Interpretation.*[1] He has also written helpfully about learning and teaching principles of interpretation.[2] Unsurprisingly, John brought his considerable expertise in comparative law to bear on this issue. In one article, he lamented that 'few books in the common law have dwelt at length on the jurisprudential aspects of statutory interpretation – what interpretation involves and how the choice of interpretations is rationally justified'.[3] Comparing practices and theories of interpretation across jurisdictions, he suggested, will generate valuable insights into the nature of interpretation itself,[4] as well as its interaction with legal institutions, values and practices more broadly.[5] Elsewhere, John has discussed the ways in which legal arguments and methods develop,[6] and how they are influenced by those of other jurisdictions.[7]

I am grateful to Andrew Bell, Adolfo Giuliani and Ian Williams for their very helpful comments. My thanks also go to Lorenzo Maniscalco and Jane Sancinito for their invaluable assistance with Latin texts. Original spelling has been retained in quotations, but punctuation has occasionally been modernised to aid comprehension.

1 J. Bell and Sir G. Engle (eds.), *Cross: Statutory Interpretation*, 2nd ed. (London: Butterworth, 1987); J. Bell and Sir G. Engle (eds.), *Cross: Statutory Interpretation* 3rd ed. (Oxford: Oxford University Press, 1995).

2 See, for example, J. Bell, 'Studying Statute Law' (1993) 13 *Oxford Journal of Legal Studies* 130; J. Bell, 'Teaching Statutory Interpretation' [2009] Statute Law Society paper, www.statutelawsociety.co.uk/teaching-legislation/background-notes/

3 Bell, 'Studying Statute Law', 130.

4 Ibid.

5 Ibid., 131.

6 See, for example, J. Bell, 'The Acceptability of Legal Arguments', in N. MacCormick and P. Birks (eds.), *The Legal Mind: Essays for Tony Honoré* (Oxford: Oxford University Press, 1986).

7 See, for example, J. Bell, 'The Argumentative Status of Foreign Legal Arguments' (2012) 8 *Utrecht Law Review* 8.

In England, detailed scholarly discussions of legal interpretation date back to the sixteenth century;[8] pedagogic materials on the subject have almost as long a history, as do those that draw on methods and arguments from outside the common law. Perhaps the first to write a student primer on legal interpretation was the Elizabethan lawyer William Fulbecke. Like John, Fulbecke looked beyond the common law to understand the process of interpretation. His book demonstrates the impact of arguments and methods from other jurisdictions and disciplines on the nascent common law of interpretation. One particularly influential source of ideas was rhetoric, the art of speech and persuasion, which had been studied since ancient times and was revered by the humanist scholars of Fulbecke's day.

The extent to which the early modern common law was susceptible to such influence has been the subject of much debate. John Baker argues that English law was 'manifestly' not influenced by 'humanist scholarship in a narrow technical sense', but acknowledges that 'certain attitudes of thought' may have been shared by humanists and common lawyers.[9] Lorna Hutson has fewer reservations, claiming that 'humanist rhetoric had a transformative effect' on English legal argument in the sixteenth and seventeenth centuries.[10] She explains that a lawyer of this period, having received a humanist education, would naturally have understood the common law in the context of the rhetoric he had been taught.[11] Thus, while humanist rhetoric did not alter the substantive common law, it may well have affected lawyers' approaches to legal method and argument.

Recent scholarship has discussed some points of connection between the early modern common law and the rhetorical tradition. However, the crucial link between rhetoric and legal interpretation has not yet been explored. This chapter fills that gap, arguing that rhetorical ideas did influence common lawyers' attitudes to interpretation in the sixteenth century. It focuses on Fulbecke's discussion of interpretation, intended for law students approaching the subject for the first time. The links between rhetoric and the common law are particularly clear in Fulbecke's work, which aimed to set out a clear method of interpretation for beginners. Finding the common law

[8] S. Thorne (ed.), *A Discourse upon the Exposicion & Understandinge of Statutes* (San Marino: Huntington Library, 1942), p. 3.

[9] J. H. Baker, *The Oxford History of the Laws of England, Vol. VI: 1483–1558* (Oxford: Oxford University Press, 2003), p. 17.

[10] L. Hutson, 'Rhetoric and Early Modern Law', in M. J. Macdonald (ed.), *The Oxford Handbook of Rhetorical Studies* (New York: Oxford University Press, 2017), p. 399.

[11] Ibid., 402.

lacking in order and method, Fulbecke instead drew heavily on terminology from the rhetorical tradition, which would have already been familiar to his students. Fulbecke's work is therefore a vital source for understanding the connections between the common law and rhetoric in this period. However, Fulbecke was not alone: many of his contemporaries were also exploiting the resources of rhetoric. Ultimately, this chapter demonstrates the importance of John's call to understand English law and its history in their wider intellectual context.

## 5.1 Fulbecke's Direction and Legal Interpretation

Little is known about Fulbecke himself. Born in Lincoln around 1560, he took his BA from the University of Oxford in 1581 and his MA in 1584.[12] He then embarked on his legal studies at Staple Inn and Gray's Inn and was called to the Bar in 1591.[13] Anthony Wood wrote that Fulbecke was reputed to have obtained a doctorate in civil law at a continental university,[14] but evidence of this has never been uncovered. Later in his life, Fulbecke took holy orders: in 1603 he became the rector of Waldershare in Kent, where he died in 1616.[15] Much about his life is now a mystery.

What is clear, however, is that Fulbecke was a man of varied interests and a prolific writer. Indeed, he observed that one advantage of 'champing upon the unpleasant barke of the studie of the Law' was that it allowed him to 'afford some leasurable time to the divulging of an historie'.[16] While a student at Gray's Inn, he wrote *A Booke of Christian Ethicks* (1587)[17] and contributed to *The Misfortunes of Arthur*, a masque performed for Queen Elizabeth in 1588.[18] He later published a book of Roman history,[19] as well as a number of pioneering legal texts. *A Direction or Preparative to the*

[12] D. R. Woolf, 'William Fulbecke', in H. C. G. Matthew and B. Harrison (eds.), *Oxford Dictionary of National Biography* (Oxford: Oxford University Press, 2004).

[13] R. J. Terrill, 'The Application of the Comparative Method by English Civilians: The Case of William Fulbecke and Thomas Ridley' (1981) 2 *Journal of Legal History* 169, 174.

[14] A. Wood, *Athenae Oxonienses*, vol. 1 (London: Thomas Bennet, 1691), p. 274.

[15] W. Prest, 'William Fulbecke (1560–1616)' (1982) 3 *Journal of Legal History* 173.

[16] W. Fulbecke, *An Historicall Collection of the Continuall Factions, Tumults and Massacres of the Romans and Italians* (London: William Ponsonby, 1601), dedication (unpaginated).

[17] W. Fulbecke, *A Booke of Christian Ethicks or Moral Philosophie* (London: Richard Jones, 1587).

[18] Woolf, 'William Fulbecke'; see Th. Hughes, *Certaine Devises and Shewes Presented to Her Majestie by the Gentlemen of Grayes-Inne* (London: Robert Robinson, 1587).

[19] Fulbecke, *An Historicall Collection of the Continuall Factions*; later reissued as W. Fulbecke, *An Abridgement, or Rather, A Bridge of Roman Histories* (London: Richard More, 1608).

*Study of the Lawe* (1600) was a book of advice for law students.[20] *A Parallele or Conference of the Civill Law, the Canon Law, and the Common Law*, published in two volumes in 1601 and 1602,[21] was the richest existing treatment of comparative law by an English writer.[22] Fulbecke's final book, *The Pandectes of the Law of Nations* (1602),[23] was the first international law treatise written in English.[24]

However, Fulbecke's writing has, to a large extent, fallen into obscurity. Modern scholars have described his books, variously, as 'quaint',[25] 'eclectic',[26] 'eccentric,'[27] 'florid'[28] and 'hilarious'.[29] When Fulbecke's guide for law students, the *Direction*, was republished in 1987, Peter Birks suggested that it would 'now be read by many lawyers simply for amusement'.[30] It is true that many of Fulbecke's most pressing concerns seem idiosyncratic to a modern reader. He devoted, for example, significant portions of the book to discussing which astrological signs are the most auspicious for aspiring lawyers (none in particular);[31] warning law students not to stay up too late (in case 'their native humiditie dried up');[32] and establishing the best time of day for studying law (the morning, before the air is 'corrupted with contagious exhalations' that 'pierce into the braine').[33]

These picturesque diversions have perhaps served to disguise the fact that Fulbecke's *Direction* also contains much sophisticated discussion of legal method and theory. David Ibbetson, for example, has recently argued that the *Direction* provides the first real theory of authorities in

20 W. Fulbecke, *A Direction or Preparative to the Study of the Lawe* (London: Thomas Wight, 1600).

21 W. Fulbecke, *A Parallele or Conference of the Civill Law, the Canon Law, and the Common Law of This Realme of England* (London: Thomas Wight, 1601); W. Fulbecke, *The Second Part of the Parallele, or Conference of the Civill Law, the Canon Law, and the Common Law of This Realme of England* (London: Thomas Wight, 1602).

22 D. R. Coquillette, 'Legal Ideology and Incorporation I: The English Civilian Writers, 1523–1607' (1981) 61 *Boston University Law Review* 1, 88.

23 W. Fulbecke, *The Pandectes of the Law of Nations* (London: Thomas Wight, 1602).

24 'Fulbecke's Pandectes' (1920) 149 *Law Times* 361.

25 Ibid.

26 Prest, 'William Fulbecke (1560–1616)', 173.

27 Coquillette, 'Legal Ideology and Incorporation I', 34.

28 P. Birks, 'Introduction', *Fulbeck's Direction, or Preparative to the Study of the Law* (Upper Saddle River, NJ: Gregg International, 1987), p. iv.

29 Ibid., vi.

30 Ibid., v.

31 Fulbecke, *A Direction or Preparative to the Study of the Lawe*, 10v–11v.

32 Ibid., 19.

33 Ibid., 18.

the common law, much of which was 'quite explicitly drawn from the writings of modern civilians'.[34] Most obviously, however, Fulbecke gave 'a great deal of space' to instructing law students in principles of legal interpretation.[35]

Fulbecke's preoccupation with the law of interpretation was not unusual for his time: this was also a major concern for many of his contemporaries. Shortly before Fulbecke began his legal studies, Edmund Plowden's law reports, the *Commentaries*, had brought questions of interpretation to the forefront of legal thought.[36] These questions were frequently discussed by the leading lawyers of Fulbecke's day, including Edward Coke,[37] Francis Bacon[38] and Thomas Egerton.[39] However, those lawyers were generally concerned only to address specific interpretive questions as they arose in cases, or to compile jumbled collections of interpretive maxims.[40] Only a few writers had sought to offer more systematic instruction on principles of interpretation, generally focusing mainly or exclusively on statutes: they included Christopher St German,[41] Plowden[42] and the authors of a

[34] D. Ibbetson, 'Authority and Precedent', in M. Godfrey (ed.), *Law and Authority in British Legal History, 1200–1900* (Cambridge: Cambridge University Press, 2016), pp. 73–4.

[35] Birks, 'Introduction', xii.

[36] L. W. Abbott, *Law Reporting in England 1485–1585* (London: Athlone Press, 1973), p. 238. The Commentaries were published in two volumes in 1571 and 1579.

[37] In Coke's *Reports*, about a third of the cases involve a point of interpretation. Coke also discussed interpretation in the prefaces to his *Reports*, and in his *Commentary upon Littleton*: Sir Edward Coke, *The First Part of the Institutes of the Laws of England, or, A Commentary upon Littleton* (London: The Societie of Stationers, 1628).

[38] Bacon collected Latin maxims, including many relating to interpretation: J. Spedding, R. L. Ellis and D. D. Heath (eds.), *The Works of Francis Bacon*, vol. 7 (Cambridge: Cambridge University Press, 2011), pp. 327–87. He also wrote about interpretation more generally: see, for example, J. Spedding, R. L. Ellis and D. D. Heath (eds.), *The Works of Francis Bacon*, vol. 4 (Cambridge: Cambridge University Press, 2011), pp. 61–2.

[39] Egerton's manuscripts and printed books, held by the Huntington Library, are filled with notes on interpretation. He possessed two copies of the first English treatise on legal interpretation, *A Discourse upon the Exposicion & Understandinge of Statutes* (Hunt MS El 496 and Hunt MS El 2565). William Fleetwood probably wrote the original text: J. H. Baker, *The Reinvention of Magna Carta 1216–1616* (Cambridge: Cambridge University Press, 2017), pp. 323–7. However, Egerton produced an abbreviated and updated version: Thorne, *A Discourse*, 97–9.

[40] See, for example, Coke, *The First Part of the Institutes of the Laws of England*, 36; Spedding, Ellis and Heath, *The Works of Francis Bacon*, vol. 7, 325–6; Hunt MS El 496 (unpaginated).

[41] Ch. St German, *Doctor and Student* (T. F. T. Plucknett and J. L. Barton eds., Selden Society, 1974). This treatise seems first to have been printed in 1528.

[42] Plowden appended lengthy notes on interpretation to two of his case reports: *Eyston* v. *Studd* (1574) Plow 459; and *Nichols* v. *Nichols* (1575) Plow 477.

handful of sixteenth-century treatises.[43] Fulbecke's treatment of interpretation, however, was exceptional. Not only did he address himself specifically to law students, but he was also uniquely ambitious, attempting to lay down a comprehensive method for solving all kinds of interpretive difficulty in all kinds of legal text.[44]

The advice that Fulbecke offered on interpretation was, characteristically, somewhat meandering. He began by observing that law students 'must not vary or depart from the proper sense & signification of the words' of the law, 'unles therby some absurditie, inconvenience, or iniustice may appeare'.[45] A few pages later, he advised students to 'follow the literall sense' of a covenant or devise when it is 'cleare and manifest'. However, 'when the words be obscure, or when some thing is omitted . . . wee imagine that more was spoken then written, and more intended, then uttered'.[46]

If it was clear that the literal meaning of the words should not be followed, the student had to determine which meaning was most 'probable'. Fulbecke suggested a number of techniques for doing so: '[F]irst, by the common use of speech, secondly, by comparing the consequent with the antecedent, thirdly, by the circumstances of a mans actions, fourthly, by the concordance or agreement with the law, because every one is intended to conforme his will according to lawe.'[47] Fulbecke then reiterated that 'there ought to be no departing from the words . . . unlesse there bee apparent proofe of an other meaning'. If this were indeed the case, 'the words onely . . . are not to be regarded, but wee must consider what was meant by the person, quantitie, qualitie, place, time, precedents, consequents, and other circumstances'. Thus, he concluded, 'the speech

[43] Thorne, *A Discourse*, composed c. 1565 (see n. 39 above); *A Treatise Concerning Statutes, or Acts of Parliament, and the Exposition Thereof* (London: Tonson, 1677), composed c. 1575 and usually attributed to Christopher Hatton; and Edward Hake, *Epieikeia: A Dialogue on Equity in Three Parts* (D. E. C. Yale ed., New Haven, CT: Yale University Press, 1953), composed at the end of the sixteenth century.

[44] Fulbecke's principles applied both to 'the law' and to private legal documents: see, for example, Fulbecke, *A Direction or Preparative to the Study of the Lawe*, 33v. Hake also dealt with the interpretation of a variety of legal texts, but his treatise was narrowly focused on the operation of equity as an interpretive principle. Equity in this sense was distinct from the equity of the Chancery: see D. Ibbetson, 'A House Built on Sand: Equity in Early Modern English Law', in E. Koops and W. J. Zwalve (eds.), *Law & Equity: Approaches in Roman Law and Common Law* (Leiden: Martinus Nijhoff, 2014).

[45] Fulbecke, *A Direction or Preparative to the Study of the Lawe*, 29v.

[46] Ibid., 33v.

[47] Ibid.

of a man is not alwayes the touchstone of the minde, but the concurrence of circumstances'.[48]

Having introduced the relevance of circumstances to interpretation, Fulbecke now expanded on their significance. He explained that 'a mans speech doth consist of words and meaning, even as a man himselfe doth consist of bodie and soule, or to make the matter more plaine, the words are but the *superficies* [surface], and the intent or meaning is the substance. And the lawe traceth the meaning of a man by the circumstances'. Thus, he continued, 'such an intendment must be taken, as the words being compared with circumstances may yeeld. For words are not by violence to be racked, but by circumstance to be ruled'.[49] He concluded that it was not just words that could express a man's intention, but also 'the circumstances before the acte, in the acte, and after the acte'.[50]

Fulbecke, then, had some key principles in mind for his law students. Their starting point should be the 'true propertie' of the words of the text.[51] However, if these words proved unsatisfactory, they must identify the writer's meaning in another way. In particular, they must examine the circumstances. But what were these circumstances, and how did Fulbecke expect his students to use them?

## 5.2 The Rhetorical Circumstances

Fulbecke's references to circumstances would have held a particular meaning for his readers. Ancient rhetoricians such as Hermagoras of Temnos, Cicero and Quintilian had developed a theory of circumstances that remained influential in Fulbecke's period.[52] In this rhetorical tradition, the circumstances of an act were its key features. A speaker must consider the circumstances of the act so that he could describe it and formulate arguments about it. As Hutson explains, 'circumstances were the topics that made any human action intelligible and able to be narrated and enquired into'.[53]

48 Ibid., 34.
49 Ibid., 34v.
50 Ibid., 35.
51 Ibid., 34.
52 R. Copeland, *Rhetoric, Hermeneutics, and Translation in the Middle Ages: Academic Traditions and Vernacular Texts* (Cambridge: Cambridge University Press, 1991), pp. 67–8.
53 L. Hutson, *Circumstantial Shakespeare* (Oxford: Oxford University Press, 2015), p. 2.

In order to discuss an act, the rhetorician would first identify its circumstances, including its 'motive, time, place, opportunity, means, method and the like'.[54] He would then construct arguments based on these features. Rhetoric traditionally focused on arguments relating to law,[55] and, for lawyers, circumstances were an aid to inventing convincing arguments on behalf of their clients. For example, a relevant circumstance in a murder trial might be that the accused was found after the murder with a blood-stained sword.[56] It has been demonstrated that sixteenth-century common lawyers adopted the terminology of circumstances both in their law of evidence[57] and in their approach to legal argument.[58]

However, rhetoricians were also very interested in questions of interpretation. After all, the meaning of a legal document was a fact that could be relevant to the outcome of a client's dispute.[59] Thus, for example, Cicero's *De inventione* offered guidance on attacking some standard interpretive problems, such as ambiguous words, contradictory texts, and discrepancies between a writer's words and his intentions.[60] Circumstances did not form part of this interpretive scheme: they were used to invent 'artificial proofs', while legal documents were considered separately, as a kind of 'inartificial proof'.[61] However, Kathy Eden observes that classical rhetoricians recognised the close links between the circumstances and their interpretive techniques.[62]

These links only became more pronounced in late antiquity. Questions of interpretation became increasingly important in post-classical law,[63]

54 Ibid.

55 H. Hohmann, 'Ciceronian Rhetoric and the Law', in V. Cox and J. O. Ward (eds.), *The Rhetoric of Cicero in Its Medieval and Early Renaissance Commentary Tradition* (Leiden: Brill, 2006), p. 193.

56 Cicero, *De Inventione* 2.viii.43.

57 B. Shapiro, 'Classical Rhetoric and the English Law of Evidence', in L. Hutson and V. Kahn (eds.), *Rhetoric & Law in Early Modern Europe* (New Haven, CT: Yale University Press, 2001).

58 Hutson, 'Rhetoric and Early Modern Law', 405–6.

59 K. Eden, 'Forensic Rhetoric and Humanist Education', in L. Hutson (ed.), *The Oxford Handbook of English Law and Literature, 1500–1700* (Oxford: Oxford University Press, 2017), p. 27.

60 Cicero, *De Inventione*, 2.xl.116–2.li.154. These standard problems were known as the *status legales*.

61 Eden, 'Forensic Rhetoric and Humanist Education', 27. Here, 'artificial' means that they were produced by the art of the rhetorician.

62 K. Eden, *Hermeneutics and the Rhetorical Tradition: Chapters in the Ancient Legacy & Its Humanist Reception* (New Haven, CT: Yale University Press, 1997), pp. 26–7, 41.

63 C. Humfress, *Orthodoxy and the Courts in Late Antiquity* (Oxford: Oxford University Press, 2007), pp. 27–8, 121–7.

and rhetorical devices, such as the use of circumstances, were channelled towards the reading of texts. They were no longer simply used as 'strategies of composition', but also as 'strategies of reading, taxonomy and interpretation'.[64] Circumstances had been used by rhetoricians to explain the key features of a human act. Since the writing of a text was an act like any other, it could be understood, like any other, through its circumstances.[65] Thus, a reader could successfully interpret a text by investigating the circumstances of its composition.[66]

This dual function of circumstances was recognised, for example, by the Church Fathers. St Augustine of Hippo, who had trained as a rhetorician,[67] recommended the use of rhetoric both to compose sermons and to interpret Scripture.[68] He wrote that ambiguous passages in the Bible could usually be understood by examining 'the circumstances', which 'demonstrate the intention of the writer'.[69] Medieval grammarians and commentators also used the rhetorical circumstances to understand the composition of texts, asking who had composed them; where, when and why they had been written; and so on.[70]

Classical works of rhetoric were 'influential and popular' throughout late antiquity and the Middle Ages.[71] However, their influence reached its peak during the Renaissance.[72] Carl Springer writes that Renaissance humanists accorded Cicero 'a kind of respect we can now scarcely imagine'.[73] Many of these Renaissance writers continued to emphasise the use of circumstances for interpretation. Erasmus, for example, was

[64] Copeland, *Rhetoric, Hermeneutics*, 64.
[65] Ibid., 69.
[66] Ibid., 64.
[67] Eden, *Hermeneutics and the Rhetorical Tradition*, 42.
[68] Copeland, *Rhetoric, Hermeneutics*, 154.
[69] Augustine, *De Doctrina Christiana* 3.iv.8; see Eden, *Hermeneutics and the Rhetorical Tradition*, 55–6.
[70] Copeland, *Rhetoric, Hermeneutics*, 66, 161–6.
[71] Th. Wilson, *The Art of Rhetoric (1560)* (P. E. Medine ed., University Park: Pennsylvania State University Press, 1994), p. 10; Th. J. Keeline, *The Reception of Cicero in the Early Roman Empire: The Rhetorical Schoolroom and the Creation of a Cultural Legend* (Cambridge: Cambridge University Press, 2018), p. 338, fn. 4; C. P. E. Springer, *Cicero in Heaven: The Roman Rhetor and Luther's Reformation* (Leiden: Brill, 2018), pp. 29–32.
[72] J. O. Ward, 'Cicero's De Inventione and the Rhetorica Ad Herennium', in V. Cox and J. O. Ward (eds.), *The Rhetoric of Cicero in Its Medieval and Early Renaissance Commentary Tradition* (Leiden: Brill, 2006), p. 53.
[73] Springer, *Cicero in Heaven*, 35.

profoundly influenced both by classical rhetoric and by St Augustine's work.[74] In his *Ratio Verae Theologiae* (1518), he argued that, to understand Scripture, we must investigate the circumstances in which it was written: the meaning of a text 'depends on who is speaking, to whom, when, on what occasion, with what words, and in what frame of mind; what precedes the passage in question and what follows it'.[75]

Lutheran reformers also emphasised the teaching of rhetoric,[76] and their example was duly imitated across northern Europe.[77] The first manual of rhetoric to be published in English, Leonard Cox's *Arte or Crafte of Rhethoryke*, was substantially a translation of Philip Melanchthon's *Institutiones Rhetoricae* (1521),[78] which itself drew heavily on Cicero and Quintilian.[79] Melanchthon also wrote about the use of circumstances, explaining that, to understand an ambiguous text, it was necessary to identify 'the circumstances and the mind of the author'.[80]

Any schoolboy in Fulbecke's period would have been well aware of the significance of circumstances. In the fifteenth century, English education began to be remodelled along humanist lines.[81] By the mid-sixteenth century, rhetoric was taught in grammar schools across the country,[82] largely based on the works of Cicero and Quintilian.[83] Humanist educators encouraged their pupils to use circumstances both to construct and to construe texts. Cox, for example, advised on the use of circumstances to compose a text.[84] 'Arguments', he explained, could be identified from 'the circumstances of the cause, that is to saye, the tyme, the place, the

[74] Eden, *Hermeneutics and the Rhetorical Tradition*, 66.

[75] Quoted in ibid., 74. See also K. Eden, 'Equity and the Origins of Renaissance Historicism: The Case for Erasmus' (1993) 5 *Yale Journal of Law and the Humanities* 137, 138–9.

[76] Springer, *Cicero in Heaven*, 101.

[77] Ibid., 123.

[78] L. Cox, *Arte or Crafte of Rhethoryke* (Frederic Ives Carpenter ed., Chicago, IL: University of Chicago Press, 1899), p. 30. This work was first published around 1530: ibid., 12.

[79] Springer, *Cicero in Heaven*, 136.

[80] P. Melanchthon, 'Institutiones Rhetoricae', in W. P. Weaver, S. Strohm and V. Wels (eds.), *Philipp Melanchthon, Opera Omnia: Opera Philosophica, vol. II: Principal Writings on Rhetoric* (Berlin: De Gruyter, 2017), p. 229.

[81] Eden, 'Forensic Rhetoric and Humanist Education', 24.

[82] Q. Skinner, *Reason and Rhetoric in the Philosophy of Hobbes* (Cambridge: Cambridge University Press, 1996), p. 23.

[83] The pseudo-Ciceronian *Rhetorica ad Herennium* was another popular text: Eden, 'Forensic Rhetoric and Humanist Education', 25.

[84] In this part of his treatise, Cox was drawing heavily from Cicero as well as from Melanchthon: Cox, *Arte or Crafte*, 22, fn. 1.

doers, the thyng it selfe, the meanes whereby it shulde be done' and so on.[85] Similarly, in the *Art of Rhetoric* (1553), Thomas Wilson drew on Quintilian to explain the use of circumstances in composing oratory: 'Who, what, and where, by what help, and by whose / Why, how, and when, do many things disclose.'[86] In his 1612 manual for grammar school teachers, John Brinsley wrote that pupils should set 'downe all the circumstances' of their subject matter when composing an essay.[87]

These writers also discussed circumstances as aids to interpretation.[88] Cox, for example, advised that, to understand an ambiguous text, the reader 'must declare the wryters mynde by circumstaunces'.[89] For Wilson, it was important that laws be 'well weighed and considered according to their circumstances'.[90] Brinsley, too, explained that, when construing a text, pupils should 'consider wel of all the circumstances of each place … That is, who speaks in that place, what he speaks, to whom he speakes, upon what occasion he speaks, or to what end, where he spake, at what time it was, what went before in the sentences next, what followeth next after'.[91] Brinsley added that a pupil should 'alwaies thinke of [this] in his construing. It is a very principall rule for the understanding of any Author or matter whatsoever'.[92]

Cox's treatise was aimed at 'yonge studientes', including those who aimed to be 'advocates and proctoures in the lawe'.[93] Indeed, an Elizabethan law student could hardly have completed his education without a thorough soaking in rhetorical techniques. After grammar school, many would have studied at university, where literature, rhetoric and dialectic formed major components of the curriculum.[94] By Fulbecke's period, over half of those called to the Bar had a university

[85] Ibid., 70–1.
[86] Wilson, *The Art of Rhetoric*, 60.
[87] J. Brinsley, *Ludus Literarius: Or, the Grammar Schoole* (London: Thomas Man, 1612), p. 180.
[88] P. Mack, *Elizabethan Rhetoric* (Cambridge: Cambridge University Press, 2002), p. 19.
[89] Cox, *Arte or Crafte*, 85.
[90] Wilson, *The Art of Rhetoric*, 129.
[91] Brinsley, *Ludus Literarius*, 123.
[92] Ibid.
[93] Cox, *Arte or Crafte*, 41.
[94] See generally L. Jardine, 'The Place of Dialectic Teaching in Sixteenth-Century Cambridge' (1974) 21 *Studies in the Renaissance* 31; P. Mack, 'Rhetoric and Pedagogy in the Renaissance', in M. J. Macdonald (ed.), *The Oxford Handbook of Rhetorical Studies* (New York: Oxford University Press, 2017).

education.[95] While rhetoric does not seem to have been explicitly taught at the Inns of Court, study there obviously involved rhetorical skills.[96] Thomas Elyot described students' moots as 'a shadowe or figure of the auncient rhetorike', explaining that law students must be skilled in a range of rhetorical techniques.[97]

Common lawyers were also reading rhetorical treatises. Coke's library included sixty-two works on philosophy, rhetoric, grammar and logic, subjects he hailed as 'handmaids to the knowledge of laws'.[98] Wilson's *Art of Rhetoric* was described as 'the daily bread of our common pleaders & discoursers' in the Inns of Court,[99] while Elyot's *The Governour* (1531) devoted a chapter to the rhetorical techniques used by lawyers.[100] To such an audience, saturated in rhetoric, Fulbecke's references to circumstances would have been immediately recognisable.

## 5.3 Rhetoric and Law

Fulbecke would also have encountered rhetorical circumstances in his studies of the *ius commune*. As we have seen, he was reputed to have studied law in continental Europe, and certainly had 'an unusually substantial knowledge of the civil law'; Ibbetson describes the *Direction* as 'shot through with civilian learning'.[101] To students wishing to study the civil law, Fulbecke was able to recommend a wide range of authors, including Bartolus, Baldus, Philip Decius, Andreas Alciatus, Ulrich Zasius, Gulielmus Budaeus, Franciscus Duarenus and Hugo Donellus.[102] He singled out Alberico Gentili for especial praise, describing him as one with 'the judgement of a great state-man: the soundnes of a deep Philosopher,

95 W. R. Prest, *The Rise of the Barristers: A Social History of the English Bar 1590–1640* (Oxford: Clarendon Press, 1991), p. 112.

96 D. S. Bland, 'Rhetoric and the Law Student in Sixteenth-Century England' (1957) 54 *Studies in Philology* 498, 498; R. J. Schoeck, 'Lawyers and Rhetoric in Sixteenth-Century England', in J. J. Murphy (ed.), *Renaissance Eloquence* (Berkeley: University of California Press, 1983), pp. 280–1.

97 Sir T. Elyot, *The Boke Named the Governour* (London: Thomas Berthelet, 1531), p. 56v.

98 W. O. Hassall, *A Catalogue of the Library of Sir Edward Coke* (New Haven, CT: Yale University Press, 1950), pp. 59–64.

99 See Wilson, *The Art of Rhetoric*, 9; R. J. Schoeck, 'Rhetoric and Law in Sixteenth-Century England' (1953) 50 *Studies in Philology* 110, 120.

100 Elyot, *The Boke Named the Governour*, 53v–59v.

101 Ibbetson, 'Authority and Precedent', 74.

102 Fulbecke, *A Direction or Preparative to the Study of the Lawe*, 26v.

and the skill of a cunning Civilian'.[103] Fulbecke may in fact have known Gentili personally: the two men overlapped at Oxford and at Gray's Inn.[104]

These civilian writers also used the rhetorical circumstances as aids to textual interpretation. As Adolfo Giuliani explains, jurists of the *ius commune* regarded the intention of the writer of a private document as a matter of fact. As such, it fell into the province of rhetoric, and could be identified, like any other fact, through an examination of the circumstances. Statutory interpretation was treated separately, as a question of law.[105] However, rhetorical ideas were still relevant to statutes, since it was a commonplace that equity required general laws to be tailored to the circumstances of each case.[106]

All students of the *ius commune* would have received training in rhetoric,[107] and they derived their theories of interpretation primarily from rhetorical treatises.[108] For example, Giuliani argues that the frame of reference for Alciatus' influential treatise on interpretation, *De verborum significatione* (1530), 'was not law but classical rhetoric'.[109] Alciatus grappled with the same problems, in the same terms, as classical rhetoricians: for example, what should be done when the words of a text did not express the writer's meaning?[110] Like rhetoricians, he recommended the use of circumstances to identify the writer's intentions in such cases. Sometimes, he explained, it should be presumed that a writer had not intended a general rule to be applied in a specific case: for example, if the thing in dispute were trivial, or if the person to be penalised were of high rank.[111]

103 Ibid.

104 Coquillette, 'Legal Ideology and Incorporation I', 14 n. 34; 'Fulbecke's Pandectes', 361.

105 A. Giuliani, 'From Presumption to Interpretation', in F. Treggiari (ed.), *Giuristi dell'Università di Perugia* (Rome: Aracne, 2010), pp. 452–3. This divide began to break down in the late sixteenth century. In contrast, ancient rhetoricians had viewed questions about the meaning of any legal document as questions of fact: Humfress, *Orthodoxy and the Courts*, 117; Giuliani, 'From Presumption to Interpretation', 461.

106 See, for example, Baldus, *In Primam Digesti Veteris Partem Commentaria* (Venice, 1577) ad D.1.1.1.pr n. 5; M. Salamonius, *Commentarioli in librum I Pandectarum* (Rome, 1525) 4v. For English writers adopting this definition, see, for example, St German, *Doctor and Student*, 95; William West, *The Second Part of Symboleography* (London: Thomas Wight, 1601), p. 174v.

107 P. Mack, *A History of Renaissance Rhetoric 1380–1620* (Oxford: Oxford University Press, 2011), p. 278.

108 Giuliani, 'From Presumption to Interpretation', 453.

109 Ibid., 460.

110 Ibid. This was one of the *status legales* commonly discussed by rhetoricians.

111 A. Alciatus, *De verborum significatione libri quatuor* (Lyons, 1530), p. 96.

Gentili, Fulbecke's contemporary, also wrote a treatise on interpretation, which drew frequently on Alciatus' work. Like Fulbecke, Gentili argued that a writer's meaning was more important than the literal sense of his words.[112] Gentili made explicit reference to rhetorical ideas to substantiate his points. He wrote, for example, that 'meaning comes before words ... as rhetoricians always conclude in those treatises on ambiguous meaning and writing'.[113] Elsewhere, he linked these to Alciatus' work, referring to 'the most serious and solemn discussions of rhetoricians about writing and meaning, of which Alciatus reminds us'.[114] Unsurprisingly, Gentili also used the rhetorical circumstances – place, time, person and so on – to structure his analysis of legal texts.[115]

Civilian jurists also referred to circumstances when they discussed equity, which was closely linked to the interpretation of statutes.[116] For example, Johann Oldendorp wrote in 1529 that 'the circumstances of persons, things, places and times' must be used to ascertain what was equitable.[117] A statute, he explained, could be equitable in one place or time, but not another.[118] He therefore advised his readers, when applying a written law, to consider 'when, where and by whom' the law had been established.[119] In a later treatise, Oldendorp focused even more closely on the circumstances, following Melanchthon, a fellow Lutheran whose concept of equity he had adopted.[120] Similarly, Claudius Cantiuncula wrote that, although legislators must be presumed to act equitably, their laws could not be fully understood without considering the circumstances in which they were made.[121] Like Oldendorp, Cantiuncula was very familiar with the rhetorical tradition: he corresponded with Erasmus and wrote a manual of legal dialectic for students, which combined legal and rhetorical sources.[122]

112 V. Vadi, *War and Peace: Alberico Gentili and the Early Modern Law of Nations* (Leiden: Brill, 2020), pp. 102–3.
113 A. Gentili, *De verborum significatione* (Hanau, 1614), p. 20.
114 Ibid., 19.
115 See, for example, ibid., 9.
116 L. Maniscalco, *Equity in Early Modern Legal Scholarship* (Leiden: Brill 2020), p. 122.
117 J. Oldendorp, 'Was Billig Und Recht Ist', in E. Wolf (ed.), *Quellenbuch zur Geschichte der deutschen Rechtswissenschaft* (Frankfurt: Klostermann, 1949), p. 64.
118 Ibid.
119 Ibid., 68.
120 Maniscalco, 'Equity in Early Modern Legal Scholarship', 77–83.
121 C. Cantiuncula, *De Officio Iudicis Libri Duo* (Basel, 1543), p. 66.
122 Mack, *A History of Renaissance Rhetoric*, 279.

Lawyers of the *ius commune*, then, referred to circumstances when interpreting both statutes and private documents. English lawyers were well aware of these developments. The English canon lawyer Henry Swinburne wrote that, to interpret a will, the testator's 'mind and purpose must be proved by circumstances',[123] citing the work of Jacobus Menochius. Fulbecke was also familiar with this approach: in the *Parallel*, his book of comparative law, he observed that, in the civil law, a testator's 'meaning is . . . to be examined by circumstances'.[124]

Indeed, much of Fulbecke's discussion of interpretation in the *Direction* bore a strong resemblance to theories developed in the *ius commune*. For example, Bartolus and Baldus had similarly stressed that an interpreter ought to follow the literal meaning of a text, unless this would lead to injustice or otherwise infringe the purpose of the law.[125] Civilian writers also advised that an interpreter should examine the 'consequents and antecedents' of a text,[126] avoid absurdity[127] and conform his interpretation to the law.[128] Fulbecke even drew a distinction between the interpretation of statutes and contracts, explaining that 'in bargains and contracts wee must not respect so much that which was meant, as that which is spoken, because bargaines do properly consist in *facto*'.[129] This was not a distinction known to English law, but mirrored arguments made by civil lawyers. Alciatus, for example, had written that, unlike statutes, contracts must be interpreted according to the proper meaning of their words.[130]

Fulbecke's treatment of interpretation was stuffed with references to civilian sources. Most of his citations on this topic were to continental writers, both ancient and contemporary. Fulbecke's discussion of circumstances, for example, was concentrated in his fourth chapter, on 'Rules to be observed of the Student in the reading of his bookes'. In this chapter, Fulbecke referenced the Digest about thirty times.[131] He cited many

123 H. Swinburne, *A Briefe Treatise of Testaments and Last Willes* (London: John Windet, 1590), p. 8v.

124 Fulbecke, *A Parallele or Conference of the Civill Law*, 46.

125 S. Vogenauer, *Die Auslegung von Gesetzen in England und auf dem Kontinent: Eine Vergleichende Untersuchung der Rechtsprechung und ihrer Historischen Grundlagen* (Tübingen: Mohr Siebeck, 2001), p. 467.

126 Ibid., 447–8.

127 Ibid., 460–1.

128 Ibid., 449–50.

129 Fulbecke, *A Direction or Preparative to the Study of the Lawe*, 31.

130 Giuliani, 'From Presumption to Interpretation', 465.

131 Fulbecke, *A Direction or Preparative to the Study of the Lawe*, 29–38.

jurists of the *ius commune*, including Baldus,[132] Bartolus,[133] Alciatus,[134] Gentili,[135] Decius,[136] Marius Salamonius,[137] Andreas Tiraquellus,[138] Petrus Loriotus[139] and Jean Bodin,[140] and referred to ancient writers, philosophers and rhetoricians such as Horace,[141] Plato,[142] Cicero,[143] Quintilian[144] and Polybius.[145] His only English authorities were seven cases drawn from the Year Books and Plowden's *Commentaries*.[146]

Fulbecke was also heavily reliant on tropes borrowed from rhetoricians and civil lawyers. For example, we saw earlier that Fulbecke described speech as consisting of 'words and meaning, even as a man himselfe doth consist of bodie and soule'. The words were merely the '*superficies*', while the meaning was the 'substance', and was to be identified 'by the circumstances'.[147] These metaphors were common currency in the *ius commune*. Gratian's *Decretum*, a twelfth-century canon law text, had advised that the meaning of a text must govern its words, just as the soul governed the body.[148] As Stefan Vogenauer explains, this language was then borrowed by a range of civilian jurists, including Panormitanus and Alciatus.[149] The *Decretum* had also described words as the '*superficies*', this time referring to the words of the Gospel.[150] Again, the metaphor was adopted by later jurists: Baldus, for example, argued that the meaning of the law was more important than the 'surface of the words'.[151]

132 Ibid., 34, 35v, 36, 36v.
133 Ibid., 34v, 37.
134 Ibid., 31v, 32v, 34, 36.
135 Ibid., 32, 32v.
136 Ibid., 30v.
137 Ibid., 33v.
138 Ibid., 34.
139 Ibid., 34v.
140 Ibid., 35.
141 Ibid., 31v, 35v.
142 Ibid., 32.
143 Ibid.
144 Ibid., 34.
145 Ibid., 35v.
146 Ibid., 29v, 30v, 36, 37.
147 Ibid., 34v.
148 Vogenauer, *Die Auslegung von Gesetzen*, 468.
149 Ibid., 468–9.
150 Ibid., 471. This metaphor derived from the work of St Jerome.
151 Ibid.

In his next passage, Fulbecke wrote that

> the lawe traceth the meaning of a man by the circumstances, even as the hunter traceth the hare by the print of his foote. Yet I would not that a mans deede or act in the countrie be made frustrate by some Jewish or misticall interpretation: but such an intent must be taken, as the words being compared with circumstances will yeeld.[152]

The metaphor of the hunter had been used by rhetoricians since the classical period: they imagined themselves hunting in the circumstances of the case, seeking arguments as their quarry.[153] Bacon compared a rhetorician inventing arguments to 'a hunter pursuing a hare',[154] and Wilson to 'the hontesman in huntyng the foxe'.[155] Lawyers used the metaphor to refer specifically to the hunt for a writer's intention. The English canonist Swinburne, for example, wrote that, when interpreting a will, 'the meaning of the testator … ought to bee sought for as earnestly as the hunter seeketh his game'.[156] Meanwhile, the anti-Semitic slur ultimately derived from the works of the Church Fathers: St Augustine described literal interpretation as 'a miserable kind of spiritual slavery' that had afflicted the Jewish people.[157] This language was adopted by civil lawyers from Baldus to Charles Dumoulin,[158] who disparagingly associated literal interpretation with Judaism and argued that a less rigid approach to interpretation had been sanctioned by the Christian God.[159] As St Paul wrote, 'the letter killeth, but the spirit giveth life'.[160]

Later in the *Direction*, Fulbecke provided an example of proper interpretive technique at work. 'Very often', he explained, 'the principall sense of Lawe doth differ from the litterall sense'. He gave the example of 'a law

[152] Fulbecke, *A Direction or Preparative to the Study of the Lawe*, 34v.

[153] C. R. Miller, 'The Aristotelian Topos: Hunting for Novelty', in A. G. Gross and A. E. Walzer (eds.), *Rereading Aristotle's Rhetoric* (Carbondale: Southern Illinois University Press, 2000), pp. 138–40; M. C. Leff, 'The Topics of Argumentative Invention in Latin Rhetorical Theory from Cicero to Boethius' (1983) 1 *Rhetorica* 23, 24.

[154] Spedding, Ellis and Heath, *The Works of Francis Bacon*, vol. 4, 437.

[155] T. Wilson, *The Rule of Reason* (London: Richard Grafton, 1552), p. 74v.

[156] Swinburne, *A Briefe Treatise*, 9v.

[157] Augustine, *De Doctrina Christiana*, 3.v.9–vi.10; see Eden, *Hermeneutics and the Rhetorical Tradition*, 55–60.

[158] Vogenauer, *Die Auslegung von Gesetzen*, 470, fn. 300; I. Maclean, *Interpretation and Meaning in the Renaissance: The Case of Law* (Cambridge: Cambridge University Press, 1992), p. 142, fn. 190.

[159] Vogenauer, *Die Auslegung von Gesetzen*, 469–70.

[160] 2 Corinthians 3:16. Eden argues that Paul himself was drawing on rhetorical traditions in this passage, adapting the terminology to suit his Jewish audience: Eden, *Hermeneutics and the Rhetorical Tradition*, 57.

amongest the Romanes': a stranger who climbed the city walls must be put to death. Suppose that 'certaine enemies did scale the wall and a straunger did ascende to beate them backe'. In this case, Fulbecke argued, 'the litterall sense of the Law' should clearly not apply.[161]

Fulbecke left it to his students 'to endeavour amongst themselves' to explain this result.[162] However, they would likely have been familiar with it already: the case of the city walls was a 'standard hypothetical' amongst rhetoricians.[163] Cicero had referred to it as a 'simple' prompt for student debates,[164] while Quintilian and, later, St Thomas Aquinas used it to illustrate the workings of equity.[165] It was also deployed by contemporary English rhetoricians. Cox, for example, discussed 'a law in Caleys that no straunger may go uppon the towne walles on payne of dethe'. In order to properly interpret this law, he argued, we 'must declare the wryters mynde by circumstaunces, what straunger he dyd forbyd, and what tyme, and after what maner, and in what intent he wolde nat have any straunger to come on the walles, & in what intent his mynde might be understanden to suffre an alien to go upon the walles'.[166] It would be concluded, thought Cox, that the lawmaker 'was nat so undiscrete & unreasonable that he wolde have no maner of excepcion' to the law, if that was to the benefit of the town.[167] Fulbecke must have been hoping that his students would reason along similar lines.

Earlier in the *Direction*, Fulbecke seemed to have discounted the importance of rhetorical learning. He warned that 'wise and grave common weale men learned in the Lawe are not to be censured by Grammarians, and Rhetoricians' for their lack of polish and other 'frivilous vanities'.[168] This has led some scholars to argue that Fulbecke saw 'rhetoric and classical knowledge' as 'superfluous to the proper business of legal study'.[169] However, it is clear from context that Fulbecke was not

161 Fulbecke, *A Direction or Preparative to the Study of the Lawe*, 43.
162 Ibid.
163 H. W. Baade, 'The Casus Omissus: A Pre-History of Statutory Analogy' (1994) 20 *Syracuse Journal of International Law and Commerce* 45, 81.
164 Cicero, *De Oratore* 2.xxiv.100.
165 Quintilian, *Institutio Oratoria* 7.vi.6–7; Thomas Aquinas, *Commentary on the Nicomachean Ethics* 5.xvi.
166 Cox, *Arte or Crafte of Rhethoryke*, 85. While Cox used Cicero and Melanchthon as his main sources, he added the 'law of Caleys' illustration himself: ibid., 112.
167 Ibid., 85.
168 Fulbecke, *A Direction or Preparative to the Study of the Lawe*, 20.
169 J. McBain, '"Attentive Mindes and Serious Wits": Legal Training and Early Drama', in L. Hutson (ed.), *The Oxford Handbook of English Law and Literature, 1500–1700* (Oxford: Oxford University Press, 2017), p. 90.

here speaking of rhetoric as a whole. Rather, he was concerned with questions of style.[170] In particular, he was addressing the common complaint that legal language was 'harshe and obscure',[171] and that lawyers lacked, as Elyot put it, 'Eloquution, and Pronunciation, two the principall partes of rhetorike'.[172] Fulbecke riposted that such complaints were suitable for 'the Theater or dauncing Schoole', but not when 'matters of weight' were debated by lawyers.[173]

When it came to questions of interpretation, however, it is clear that 'rhetoric and classical knowledge' had profoundly influenced Fulbecke's perspective. He was a prolific user of tropes from the rhetorical tradition, which had leaked steadily into the legal, philosophical and theological writings of his day. Fulbecke's treatment of interpretation fell squarely into this broad intellectual milieu. Indeed, much of his advice to aspiring common lawyers would not have looked out of place in a book directed at contemporary students of civil law, rhetoric or theology.

## 5.4 A Cosmopolitan Common Law

That is not to say, however, that Fulbecke was seeking to import new ideas into the common law. As we have seen, he sharply criticised those who failed to distinguish between the proper spheres of rhetoric and law. Common lawyers, he warned, must be allowed to speak 'in their owne dialect and language proper to their Art';[174] it was 'not good to have the interpretation' of their words 'from any other than the Lawyers themselves'.[175] He also defended common lawyers against logicians who criticised their lack of method.[176] There was not one method 'in all sciences alike to be used', he explained, 'but in every science things are so to be ordred and digested, as the subiect or matter doth require'.[177]

In fact, few of Fulbecke's ideas or reference points were new to the common law. Many sixteenth-century common lawyers had already drawn on similar sources to support their arguments about interpretation.

170 Fulbecke, *A Direction or Preparative to the Study of the Lawe*, 20–4.

171 Ibid., 20; see D. C. Smith, *Sir Edward Coke and the Reformation of the Laws: Religion, Politics and Jurisprudence, 1578–1616* (Cambridge: Cambridge University Press, 2014), p. 120.

172 Elyot, *The Boke Named the Governour*, 57.

173 Fulbecke, *A Direction or Preparative to the Study of the Lawe*, 21v–22.

174 Ibid., 22v.

175 Ibid., 23.

176 Ibid., 23v–25.

177 Ibid., 82v–83. Fulbecke's argument was drawn from Aristotle: Aristotle, *Nicomachean Ethics* i.7.

Plowden, for example, explicitly attributed his account of equitable interpretation to Aristotle,[178] and elsewhere mentioned Cicero as an authority on interpretation.[179] When discussing statutes, he used similar metaphors to Fulbecke, comparing the words and meaning of the text to a 'body and soul', or to 'a shell and a kernel within'.[180] He also cited the civilian maxim, '*qui haeret in litera haeret in cortice*', or 'he that sticks to the letter, sticks to the outside of the law'.[181] Later lawyers, including Coke and Egerton, followed Plowden's lead.[182]

The case of the city walls appeared twice in Plowden's *Commentaries*: once in Sjt Pollard's argument in *Reniger* v. *Fogossa* (1550),[183] and once in a note appended to *Eyston* v. *Studd* (1574). Here, Plowden used the case as an example of equity at work, crediting it to Geraldus Odonis' commentary on Aristotle.[184] Plowden proposed that the case could be resolved by imagining the answer that the lawmaker, 'being an upright and reasonable man, would have given' if confronted by the question,[185] a strategy devised by Aristotle and adopted by rhetoricians and theologians.[186] Again, Plowden's work was influential: Edward Hake borrowed the city walls case for his *Dialogue on Equity*, crediting it to both Plowden and Cicero.[187]

Fulbecke's contemporary, Thomas Egerton, meanwhile, observed that many principles of interpretation had 'been drawn out of some writers of the civil law'.[188] He himself frequently quoted theologians and canon lawyers as authorities on interpretation. In one draft argument, he quoted *dicta* from

178 *Eyston* v. *Studd*, 465, 466.

179 *Throckmerton* v. *Tracy* (1555) Plow 145, 161.

180 *Eyston* v. *Studd*, 465.

181 Ibid., 467; *Nichols* v. *Nichols*, 488. This maxim was derived from the canonist Panormitanus: Vogenauer, *Die Auslegung von Gesetzen*, 770.

182 See, for example, *The Lord Mountjoy's Case* (1589) 5 Co Rep 3b, 4b; *Powlter's Case* (1610) 11 Co Rep 29a, 34b; Coke, *The First Part of the Institutes of the Laws of England*, 365v; for Egerton, *Saunders & Starkey* v. *Stanfourde* (undated) Hunt MS El 482 f70, f72.

183 *Reniger* v. *Fogossa* (1550) Plow 1, 18.

184 *Eyston* v. *Studd*, 466.

185 Ibid., 467.

186 Aristotle, *Nicomachean Ethics* v.10; Eden, *Hermeneutics and the Rhetorical Tradition*, 77.

187 Hake, *Epieikeia*, 17–18. The case had previously been mentioned in a treatise by the fifteenth-century common lawyer, John Fortescue: Sir J. Fortescue, *De Natura Legis Naturae* (London: Clermont, 1864), pp. 28–9. A similar illustration appeared in *Doctor and Student*: St German, *Doctor and Student*, 96–9. This, slightly different, case had been discussed by Cicero and by Aquinas: Cicero, *De Inventione*, 2.xlii.123; T. Aquinas, *Summa Theologica* I–II.96.vi.

188 L. Knafla, *Law and Politics in Jacobean England: The Tracts of Lord Chancellor Ellesmere* (New York: Cambridge University Press, 1977), p. 229.

St Augustine, St Bernard of Clairvaux and Panormitanus;[189] in others, he cited St Hilary of Poitiers[190] and St Anselm of Canterbury.[191] Meanwhile, 'virtually all of the Latin-language maxims on interpretation' from Coke's *Reports* and *Institutes* 'are readily traced to' the *ius commune*,[192] and Bacon explicitly attributed his interpretive maxims to the 'civilians'.[193]

Other common lawyers were also drawing on the rhetorical circumstances as aids to interpretation. This trend seems to have gathered steam in the second half of the sixteenth century, precisely when university-educated men were first called to the Bar in significant numbers.[194] In 1567, for example, Sjt Barham explained that where a will 'is obscure in words it will be expounded by the circumstances',[195] noting in particular that 'time is a good circumstance to know the truth'.[196] Similarly, in his notes from the 1580s, Egerton argued that the courts should 'seek diligently the true intent and plain meaning of the parties, as far as the words will bear, or as may be collected by other circumstances'.[197] They should depart from 'the literal sense' of a document's words 'when the intent and meaning, or the circumstance of the matter' indicated that they should do so.[198] In 1594, the King's Bench judges declared that they would seek 'circumstances to guide the intent of the devisor' when interpreting a will.[199]

Fulbecke was not, then, introducing new ideas to the common law. Nor was he aiming to do so. Like his contemporaries, he simply saw rhetorical techniques as universally applicable tools of interpretation. They could be used by common lawyers to understand texts, just as they were used by everyone else, from Church Fathers to Elizabethan schoolboys. Fulbecke believed that these principles already formed part of the common law, and, as such, could be illustrated using common law sources.

Thus, for example, Fulbecke cited Celsus' dictum on interpretation: 'to know the Law is not to know the wordes of the law, but the force and

[189] *Saunders & Starkey* v. *Stanfourde*, f72, f76v. These arguments likely date to the 1580s.
[190] *Scott* v. *Scott* (undated) Hunt MS El 482 f116, f119.
[191] *Englande's Case* (undated) Hunt MS El 482 f53, f57.
[192] Baade, 'The Casus Omissus', 92. See Vogenauer, *Die Auslegung von Gesetzen*, 766–72.
[193] Spedding, Ellis and Heath, *The Works of Francis Bacon*, vol. 7, 336.
[194] Prest, *The Rise of the Barristers*, 110–13.
[195] *Le Serjaunts Case* (1567) Hunt MS El 482 f3, f11v.
[196] Ibid.
[197] *Saunders & Starkey* v. *Stanfourde*, f73v.
[198] Ibid., f76v.
[199] *Portman* v. *Willis* (1594) Moore 352, 352.

property of the wordes'.[200] He linked this to an argument made by Sjt Saunders in Plowden's *Commentaries*: that 'words, which are no other than the verberation of the air, do not constitute the statute, but are only the image of it, and the life of the statute rests in the minds of the expositors of the words, that is, the makers of the statutes'.[201] Similarly, he paired his analysis of the case of the city walls with a recent English case, drawn from Dyer's reports: '[A] Maid servant did conspire with a bad fellow to robbe her Mistres, and in the night shee opened the doore and brought the fellow to the bed of her Mistres, who did kill the Mistres, the Maid holding the candle, but saying nothing.'[202] Fulbecke argued that 'by the letter of the Law' the servant was guilty as a principal, but 'by the intent of the law' she was merely an accessory.[203] He then offered another case from Dyer to the students as an exercise for 'argument on the one side upon the letter of the Law, and on the other side upon the meaning of the Law'.[204]

Fulbecke, then, was well-versed in the common law, and able to draw precepts of interpretation from recent cases. However, he consistently used civilian and rhetorical texts as his main authorities on interpretation, adding English cases only to illustrate his points. Here, Fulbecke's approach contrasted sharply with that of other contemporary common law treatise-writers who discussed interpretation.

For example, in the first part of his *Dialogue on Equity*, covering 'Equity in General', Hake referred to a wide variety of sources: they included Plato,[205] Aristotle,[206] Cicero,[207] Horace,[208] St Augustine,[209] Melanchthon,[210] Johann Wild,[211] the Bible[212] and both Roman[213] and

[200] Fulbecke, *A Direction or Preparative to the Study of the Lawe*, 29v. See D.1.3.17.
[201] *Partridge* v. *Strange & Croker* (1553) Plow 77, 82. See also Fulbecke, *A Direction or Preparative to the Study of the Lawe*, 30v and 37, linking the writings of Decius and Bartolus with Year Books cases.
[202] Fulbecke, *A Direction or Preparative to the Study of the Lawe*, 43.
[203] Ibid., 43–43v. See *Anon* (1556) Dyer 128a; *Saunders* v. *Browne* (1574) Dyer 332a.
[204] Fulbecke, *A Direction or Preparative to the Study of the Lawe*, 43v. See *Parker's Case* (1560) Dyer 186a.
[205] Hake, *Epieikeia*, 25.
[206] Ibid., 7, 10, 22, 25, 27, 44.
[207] Ibid., 17–18, 27.
[208] Ibid., 36.
[209] Ibid., 27.
[210] Ibid., 14.
[211] Ibid., 8, 56.
[212] Ibid., 37.
[213] Ibid., 26.

canon law.[214] However, this was balanced by his lengthy discussions of common law sources, including Bracton,[215] St German,[216] Plowden,[217] Coke,[218] various statutes[219] and over thirty cases from the Year Books.[220] Furthermore, in part two of his treatise, Hake moved on to discuss 'the Equity of the Common Lawe'. Here, he focused specifically on English case law, with few references to continental sources of any kind.[221] Similarly, the author of the *Discourse on Statutes* referred almost exclusively to English statutes, cases and treatises. He was clearly aware of practice 'amonge the cyvilians'[222] and 'logycians',[223] and may have drawn some of his ideas from civilian writers,[224] but his focus was primarily on English concerns.

These writers, then, took a very different approach to Fulbecke. Their aim was to explain English law; their references to continental writers were limited to establishing points of general theory, pithily summarising common law rules, or ornamenting their texts with displays of learning.[225] In contrast, Fulbecke used civilian and rhetorical sources as authorities for the substantive practical advice he gave to law students. His focus was on explaining the interpretive methods laid down in these works, with English law mentioned only briefly to illustrate his points. Fulbecke stands out, not because he was the only common lawyer to know and use these continental sources, but because he chose to emphasise them at the expense of the common law.

214 Ibid., 16–27.
215 Ibid., 11, 24, 38.
216 Ibid., 7, 13, 17.
217 Ibid., 7, 9–10, 17, 33.
218 Ibid., 23, 32.
219 Ibid., 24.
220 Ibid., 19–20, 32–6, 40–2.
221 Ibid., 45–118.
222 Thorne, *A Discourse*, 128.
223 Ibid., p. 129.
224 Vogenauer, *Die Auslegung von Gesetzen in England*, 768–9.
225 This was typical for the period: see D. Ibbetson, *Common Law and Ius Commune* (London: Selden Society, 2001), p. 16; J. H. Baker, 'Roman Law at the Third University of England' (2002) 55 *Current Legal Problems* 123, 146–7; I. Williams, 'The Role of Rules: Legal Maxims in Early-Modern Common Law Principle and Practice', in M. Del Mar and M. Lobban (eds.), *Law in Theory and History: New Essays on a Neglected Dialogue* (Oxford: Hart, 2016), p. 190.

## 5.5 Law and Pedagogy

Why did Fulbecke choose this approach? After all, he could have given similar advice to his law students while relying, like Plowden or Hake, primarily on common law sources. The answer lies in Fulbecke's stated aim for the *Direction*: to set out 'a certaine art and science of the Law, generall rules & preceptes, and convenient discourses' for students to learn.[226]

At the end of the sixteenth century, the common law was experiencing a crisis of confidence. David Chan Smith argues that the law had become a victim of its own success: its 'sixteenth-century fluorescence' had brought about intellectual transformation,[227] but also led to fears that it was becoming confused and uncertain.[228] A deluge of new legal texts had left many floundering, unable to keep up with the vastly increased flow of information.[229] Bacon wrote that 'the uncertainty of the law' was 'the principal and most just challenge that is made to the laws of our nation at this time',[230] while Abraham Fraunce described the common law as 'confusedly scattered and utterly undigested'.[231] Even the king lambasted the 'uncertainty' of the law.[232]

Many lawyers responded by advocating improvements to common law methods. As Wilfrid Prest puts it, they 'insisted that the apparent chaos of English law was a mere surface phenomenon'.[233] It was not the law itself that was at fault, they explained, but those who had failed to understand it properly.[234] This prompted a trend for a new kind of legal text, one which laid out a clear and rational method for understanding the common law's vast literature.[235] Coke's *Reports*[236] and Bacon's collection of maxims[237] were both examples of this trend. Many such writers

226 Fulbecke, *A Direction or Preparative to the Study of the Lawe*, 4v.
227 Smith, *Sir Edward Coke*, 1.
228 Ibid., 14.
229 Ibid., 144.
230 Spedding, Ellis and Heath, *The Works of Francis Bacon*, vol. 7, 322.
231 A. Fraunce, *The Lawier's Logike* (London: William How, 1588), 3v.
232 King James VI and I, *Political Writings* (J. P. Sommerville ed., Cambridge: Cambridge University Press, 1995), p. 211.
233 W. Prest, 'The Dialectical Origins of Finch's Law' (1977) 36 *Cambridge Law Journal* 326, 327.
234 See, for example, *The Reports of Sir Edward Coke*, vol. V (London: Joseph Butterworth and Son, 1826), 10 Co Rep xxx.
235 Prest, 'The Dialectical Origins of Finch's Law', 328.
236 Smith, *Sir Edward Coke*, 143–4.
237 Ibid., p. 159.

borrowed methods from the rhetorical tradition to structure and map the disorderly common law;[238] Ramism, a logical method beloved of Renaissance humanists, was particularly influential.[239]

Fulbecke's *Direction* also formed part of this trend. In his introductory chapter, Fulbecke addressed critics of the common law directly: those who saw it as 'an art obscured with difficult cases, shadowed with conceited termes, and as it were, covered with cloudes, and wrapped in darknes'.[240] It was true, he accepted, that 'the weaknes of mans memorie cannot tollerate the multitude of particular lawes'. However, the law was 'bounded by certaine rules & limits' and could be 'comprehended and delivered in certaine generale preceptes'.[241] There was nothing in it that could 'not be reduced unto some universall theoreme, which may easily be conceyved and remembred, because it is generall'.[242] Law professors might multiply examples of particular cases, but if the student understood the general principle, he could apply it to any case that might arise. Thus, he need not be troubled 'that the Law bookes are so huge, & large, and that there is such an ocean of reportes, and such a perplexed confusion of opinions, because the science it selfe is short and easie to one that is diligent'.[243]

Consequently, an in-depth treatment of common law sources was ill-suited for Fulbecke's pedagogic purposes. He complained that 'it is not enough to have a great heape of things that are to be read, unlesse the use or order and manner of reading them be well understoode'.[244] Students could not learn by reading many examples without rules to guide them, just as 'a man cannot make a shooe by a number of lastes, but hee must have instruction of one that is skilfull in the trade'.[245] Fulbecke's aim in

[238] R. J. Ross, 'The Memorial Culture of Early Modern English Lawyers: Memory as Keyword, Shelter, and Identity, 1560–1640' (1998) 10 *Yale Journal of Law and the Humanities* 229, 275–85.

[239] Prest, 'The Dialectical Origins of Finch's Law'; Knafla, *Law and Politics in Jacobean England*, 40–2; I. Williams, 'A Medieval Book and Early-Modern Law: Bracton's Authority and Application in the Common Law c. 1550–1640' (2011) 79 *Tijdschrift voor Rechtsgeschiedenis* 47, 77–9. Fulbecke, like many others, was sceptical of pure Ramism: Fulbecke, *A Direction or Preparative to the Study of the Lawe*, 82v; Ross, 'The Memorial Culture of Early Modern English Lawyers', 286, fn. 199.

[240] Fulbecke, *A Direction or Preparative to the Study of the Lawe*, 4–4v.

[241] Ibid., 4v.

[242] Ibid., 5.

[243] Ibid.

[244] Ibid., 83.

[245] Ibid., 82v.

writing the *Direction* was to lay out the rules of the common law, not to give examples of their application. Indeed, he rebuked himself for presenting too many sample cases on legal interpretation, writing that 'my meaning was in this treatise rather to drawe the lineaments of things, than to discusse them to the full'.[246]

Fulbecke believed that presenting 'a great heape' of case law to his readers would only confuse them. Before reading cases on legal interpretation, students should first be instructed in a basic interpretive method. They could then identify this method at work when they graduated to reading cases. Fulbecke recognised that the interpretive methods used by rhetoricians, civil lawyers and theologians could equally be applied to the common law. His immersion in this broad intellectual tradition enabled him to set out a clear method for students to follow, borrowing terminology and tropes from writers in other disciplines.[247]

As we have seen, writers like Hake and the author of the *Discourse on Statutes* were also influenced by the rhetorical tradition. However, their aim in writing was not to set out a method for beginners, but to explain the common law's rules in detail. As a result, they tended to get bogged down in minutiae that Fulbecke could skate over. Hake, for example, did not simply wish to explain what equity was, but also to show how it worked within the common law.[248] This required him to multiply examples of cases where he saw equity at work, discussing, for example, the technicalities of limiting an estate in a will,[249] or the availability of the action on the case.[250] Similarly, much of the *Discourse* was directed at explaining how key English statutes were interpreted. For example, after proposing that 'statutes that take awaie doubtes at the commen lawe' should be taken by equity, the author gave examples of relevant provisions in Magna Carta, the Statutes of Westminster I and II, and the Statute of Gloucester.[251] In contrast, Fulbecke stripped away such details, and focused on presenting a general method for his readers to follow.

[246] Ibid., 43v.
[247] Fulbecke took a similar approach elsewhere in the *Direction*. He used the rhetorical technique of analysis to demonstrate how students should break down the cases and treatises they came across in their reading: ibid., 84–95; see Ross, 'The Memorial Culture of Early Modern English Lawyers', 281, fn. 179.
[248] Hake, *Epieikeia*, 5.
[249] Ibid., 57–60.
[250] Ibid., 106–7.
[251] Thorne, *A Discourse*, 145.

Rhetoric had been taught and studied for centuries, and there was a proliferation of well-established texts that could introduce new students to its principles.[252] Indeed, the production of rhetorical handbooks was fundamental to the practice of rhetoric.[253] In contrast, common lawyers were yet to establish a helpful programme for beginners. Students were simply expected to read their way through the case law and other legal literature, observe the courts at work, and take part in learning exercises at the Inns of Court.[254] Arriving at the Inns, many were shocked at the difference between this programme and their previous rhetorical education. They despaired at common lawyers' 'uncouth method' of learning,[255] or objected that there seemed to be no method to the law at all.[256] Fulbecke was attempting to bridge this gap. Since English legal literature was too chaotic for beginners, he turned instead to guidance from established traditions external to the common law, traditions with which new law students would have already been familiar.

## 5.6 Conclusion

What, then, can we learn from Fulbecke's odd little work of legal pedagogy? Firstly, it confirms that at least some early modern common lawyers made the connection between rhetorical theories of interpretation and common law practice. Fulbecke clearly understood common law methods as they were embedded in the broader intellectual context of his time. Drawing on his knowledge of civil law and rhetoric, he was able to integrate the rhetorical concept of circumstances into the common law of interpretation.

[252] For a discussion of texts used in the Renaissance, see P. Mack, 'Rediscoveries of Classical Rhetoric', in E. Gunderson (ed.), *The Cambridge Companion to Ancient Rhetoric* (Cambridge: Cambridge University Press, 2009).

[253] T. Habinek, *Ancient Rhetoric and Oratory* (Oxford: Blackwell Publishing, 2005), pp. 44–5.

[254] Coke, *The First Part of the Institutes of the Laws of England*, 70–70v; see W. Prest, *The Inns of Court under Elizabeth I and the Early Stuarts, 1590–1640* (London: Longman, 1972), pp. 115–32. Fulbecke prescribed a lengthy reading list for his students and advised them to take part in moots: Fulbecke, *A Direction or Preparative to the Study of the Lawe*, 26v–29, 41.

[255] Ross, 'The Memorial Culture of Early Modern English Lawyers', 304.

[256] Fraunce, *The Lawier's Logike*, 3v.

Fulbecke was in some ways exceptional: not many common lawyers had such an extensive knowledge of civilian sources. However, all would likely have been introduced to rhetorical techniques at school or university. They would have understood these techniques as tools that they could use to analyse any kind of text, including legal documents.[257] This new breed of law student would have 'understood and assimilated their legal training in relation to previous study at university',[258] including their study of rhetoric. Fulbecke could therefore assume that his readers would understand rhetorical terminology, and, indeed, many other lawyers of his period frequently deployed it. Fulbecke was not exceptional in relying on the rhetorical tradition; he was simply more explicit about it than most of his contemporaries.

The common law of interpretation was absorbing the interpretive methods of other disciplines and jurisdictions. As Ibbetson has suggested, it is not in the substantive law but in legal method and argument that we see 'the clearest point of influence of continental legal thinking on the common law in the early modern period'.[259] Fulbecke's work, which bears the hallmarks of this influence, teaches us to read English legal sources in their wider context in order to fully appreciate their meaning and significance. In particular, it demonstrates that, as John has suggested, an understanding of other legal systems and intellectual traditions can help us to clarify the interpretive methods used in our own jurisdiction.[260] At a key point in its history, we find that the common law of interpretation could be situated in the mainstream of European intellectual thought.

Finally, Fulbecke's work reminds us how rewarding the study of law can be. At the beginning of his textbook, he wrote that students should be inspired by those who came before them, since 'nothing is a greater spurre to the student of any Arte or Science, then the just reward of fame and commendation, which belongeth to those, who by labor attaine

[257] Hutson, 'Rhetoric and Early Modern Law', 402.

[258] McBain, '"Attentive Mindes and Serious Wits"', 81.

[259] D. Ibbetson, 'The Arguments in Calvin's Case (1608)', in T. L. Harris (ed.), *Studies in Canon Law and Common Law in Honor of R. H. Helmholz* (Berkeley, CA: Robbins Collection Publications, 2015), p. 214.

[260] Though John would likely disapprove of Fulbecke's free-wheeling approach to different kinds of interpretation: see Bell, 'Studying Statute Law', 133.

to perfection in any praiseworthie science. For as nature rewardeth the Bee with hony, so Art recompenseth the painfull student with riches, praise or honor'.[261]

John has certainly inspired many students throughout his career, and well deserves the 'fame and commendation' he has earned from his labour.

[261] Fulbecke, *A Direction or Preparative to the Study of the Lawe*, 1.

# 6

# Observations on the Reform of the French Law on Contractual Interpretation

SOLÈNE ROWAN

Professor John Bell has been instrumental in developing my interest in comparative law and in my career generally. He taught me comparative law when I was an LLM student at the University of Cambridge and then became the supervisor of my doctoral thesis on comparative English and French contract law. Although many of his writings focus on public law, the breadth of his knowledge in comparative private law is immense. His kindness and generosity with his time has continued after I finished my PhD and as I spread my wings as an academic. He has quite simply always been there to guide and support me, something for which I am very grateful.

***

After more than 200 years of being almost completely untouched, the entire section of the French Civil Code on contract law was revised in October 2016.[1] This was the first re-examination of French contract law since the Code was enacted as long ago as in 1804. It marked the culmination of several attempts at reform that began more than 100 years previously and intensified over the last 15 years.[2] The result is that

My thanks go to Gregg Rowan and the participants to the workshop in Cambridge in honour of Professor John Bell (September 2019) for their feedback.

1 *Ordonnance no 2016-131 du 10 février 2016 portant réforme du droit des contrats, du régime général et de la preuve des obligations*, JORF no 0035 of 11 February 2016. The Ordonnance was translated by John Cartwright, Bénedicte Fauvarque-Cosson and Simon Whittaker: www.textes.justice.gouv.fr/art_pix/THE-LAW-OF-CONTRACT-2-5-16.pdf. Many of the translations of the new articles used in this chapter are based on their excellent work.

2 Avant-Projet de Réforme du Droit des Obligations (Art. 1101 à 1386 du Code civil) et du Droit de la Prescription (Art. 2234 à 2281 du Code Civil) under the direction of P. Catala, 22 September 2005 (Paris: Documentation française, 2006) translated into English by Professors John Cartwright and Simon Whittaker: www.justice.gouv.fr/art_pix/rapportca

French contract law is now governed by a more comprehensive body of over 150 new articles.[3] In many respects, these articles simply codify rules that had been developed and applied in cases over the previous two centuries but, in a number of others, there are real innovations.[4]

A key reason for the 2016 reforms was that many articles of the original 1804 Code had, over their 200-year lifetime, been developed so extensively by judicial interpretation as no longer to state the law applied by French courts with any degree of accuracy. There was also a perception that French contract law was falling in influence overseas and attractiveness to international businesses as a possible governing law to be chosen for their contracts. One of the main aims of the reforms was to reverse this trend. They were meant to signal the beginning of a new era and establish a modern framework for contractual relationships that would be more attuned to the challenges of the twenty-first century and a globalising world. Other objectives included making French contract law more certain, predictable, attractive to business and credible as an alternative to the major common law systems, but also fairer. This chapter considers whether, in the context of contractual interpretation, which requires the court to ascertain the meaning of the contract, these lofty objectives have been achieved.

Perhaps surprisingly, the topic of contractual interpretation has generally drawn little attention in France. For one French academic lawyer, 'the articles of the Civil code on interpretation are without a doubt those that have left commentators most indifferent'.[5] For another, 'these articles are well-known but seldom used and relatively little studied'.[6] This apparent lack of interest did not, however, deter the authors of the 2016 reforms, who identified the prevailing French approach to interpretation

tatla0905-anglais.pdf; see also Ministère de la Justice, Projet de réforme du droit des contrats, July 2008; and the new version from 2009; lastly F. Terré, *Pour une réforme du droit des contrats* (Paris: Dalloz, 2008).

[3] Arts. 1101–1231-7 relate to contract law but there have also been reforms in other areas (the 'general legal regime of obligations' and the 'proof of obligations'); in total 353 new articles were introduced. The focus of this chapter is solely on the new rules on contractual interpretation.

[4] See S. Rowan, 'The New French Law of Contract' (2017) 66 *International & Comparative Law Quarterly* 805.

[5] P. Simler, 'Art 1188 à 1192 – Fasc 10: Contrat – Interprétation du contrat – L'instrument: notion, normes, champ d'application', *JCL*, 4 May 2017, [3].

[6] O. Deshayes, 'Les directives d'interprétation du Code civil: la cohérence des textes', *RDC* 2015.159, 159.

as requiring significant overhaul.[7] A key purpose was to 'clarify the rules relating to interpretation ... and abandon articles which have been seldom or never used by the courts and whose usefulness has not been demonstrated'.[8] This overhaul has resulted in the number of articles on interpretation in the Code being reduced from nine to five. New Articles 1188–92 replace Articles 1156–64 of the original 1804 Code.[9] A number of the reforms were inspired by various international contract instruments including the Principles of European Contract Law[10] and the Unidroit Principles.[11]

In this chapter, consideration will be given to four principal aspects of the law of contractual interpretation that were affected by the 2016 reforms. These are the dichotomy between the subjective and objective approaches to interpretation; the codification of the *dénaturation* power of the Cour de cassation to quash interpretations of lower courts that have the effect of distorting the clear and precise meaning of a contract term (*dénaturation des clauses claires et précises*); the relationship between 'creative interpretation' (*interprétation créatrice*) and 'explanatory interpretation' (*interprétation explicative*); and the application of the *contra proferentem* rule in the specific context of the interpretation of standard-form contracts.

My view is that the reforms that relate to contractual interpretation are positive and should be welcomed. Certain innovations in particular are an improvement upon the previous set of rules. These include the formalisation of the long-established practice of the courts taking account of subjective and objective considerations as aids to interpretation; the clarification of the relationship between creative and explanatory interpretation; and the introduction of a rule for standard-form contracts that seeks to bring uniformity to the way in which they are interpreted. Each of these developments has drawn a line under debates

[7] See paragraph 5 of Art. 8, *Loi d'habilitation de l'ordonnance n°2016-131 portant réforme du droit des contrats du 10 février 2016.*

[8] *Rapport au Président de la République relatif à l'Ordonnance no 2016–131 du 10 février 2016 portant réforme du droit des contrats, du régime général et de la preuve des obligations*, *JORF* no. 0035 of 11 February 2016.

[9] Old Arts. 1158, 1159, 1160, 1163 and 1164 have not been kept in the new Code.

[10] O. Lando and H. Beale (eds.), *Principles of European Contract Law Parts I and II* (The Hague: Kluwer, 2000); and O. Lando, E. Clive, A. Prüm and R. Zimmermann (eds.), *Principles of European Contract Law Part III* (The Hague: Kluwer, 2003).

[11] UNIDROIT Principles of International Commercial Contracts (PICC) 2016 (Italy, UNIDROIT, 2016).

and controversies that were live before the reforms. However, there are some issues that the reforms stopped short of addressing. One notable such issue is the uncertainty that is inherent in the French approach as a consequence of interpretation being a question of fact in which the Cour de cassation has historically been reluctant to intervene. This has the effect that whatever decision is made by the lower courts is likely to survive any appeal, provided that, in reaching its determination, the court ostensibly searched for the subjective intention of the parties.

## 6.1 The Tension between Subjective and Objective Interpretation

Whilst French law has traditionally taken a subjective approach to contractual interpretation, the 2016 reforms have formally recognised that the courts can have regard to both subjective and objective considerations when interpreting a contract. As a result, French law can now be said to take a mixed approach to interpretation, although there is clearly a deeply entrenched attachment to identifying the subjective intention of the parties as the primary approach, which has a number of consequences.

### *6.1.1 The Starting Point: The Subjective Intention of the Parties*

In the first paragraph of new Article 1188 of the reformed Civil Code, it is stated that 'a contract is to be interpreted according to the common intention of the parties rather than stopping at the literal meaning of its terms'.[12] This amounts to a clear rejection of literalism as the exclusive method of interpretation, which French commentators have sought to explain as a manifestation of the principle of good faith.[13] This would be defeated in the event that contracting parties were able to rely upon a literal interpretation in order to escape from the intended effect of a provision.[14] As will be shown, a more contextual and purposive approach to interpretation has long been taken by the courts. They willingly depart from the literal meaning where, from an examination of the context in

[12] This is almost identical to old Art. 1156 of the 1804 Code.

[13] The principle of good faith is now formally recognised at new Art. 1104 of the Code.

[14] M.-H. Maleville, *Pratique de l'interprétation des contrats: étude jurisprudentielle* (Rouen: PU de Rouen, 1995), at [281]; P. Simler, 'Art 1188 à 1192 – Fasc 20: Contrat – Interprétation du contrat – La mise en oeuvre: rôle respectif des juges du fond et de la Cour de cassation', *JCL*, 4 May 2017 at [23]–[24]; M. Fabre-Magnan, *Droit des obligations, Contrat et engagement unilatéral* (Paris: PUF, 2019), at p. 485.

which the term was agreed, it is apparent that such an interpretation would not accurately reflect what the parties intended to achieve.

In the search for the common intention of the parties, at least as a starting point, the French courts take a subjective approach. The aim of the exercise is to ascertain their real and actual intention at the time of the formation of the contract.[15] This is based on the theory of party autonomy (*théorie de l'autonomie de la volonté*), which is central to French contract law.[16] Contractual obligations are born out of the consent of the parties, who ought only to be bound if, and to what, they truly intended to be bound.[17]

This subjective approach to interpretation is regarded as being fairer and achieving better outcomes than simply ascertaining the declared intention of the parties. One important difference is that it seeks to eliminate the possibility of obligations that do not reflect their actual intention and to which they did not agree being imposed on them. This search for the actual intention has been described as the most fundamental and essential principle of interpretation[18] and its effect as being that the court is the 'servant of the will of the parties'.[19]

A corollary of the exercise of interpretation being focused on the common subjective intention of the parties is that, unlike in other legal systems, a good example being England, French law does not have any formal and separate doctrine of rectification.[20] To the extent that there

[15] Ass Plén 12 May 1989, *JCP* 1989.II.21322 noted by G. Lyon-Caen; Civ 1, 2 March 1982, GP 1982. 2. Pan. 245. Of course, it is questionable whether there can ever be a 'subjective' intention of both of the contracting parties as opposed to a subjective intention of one party. If there is no actual common intention, the law on mistake can become relevant if one party wants to get out of the contract. If a party has made a mistake that 'bears on the essential qualities of the act of performance owed or the other contracting party', this is a ground of nullity. However, the mistake cannot be about 'mere (subjective) motive' or the value of the pact of performance (Arts. 1132–6).

[16] F. Terré, P. Simler, Y. Lequette and F. Chénédé, *Droit civil, Les obligations*, 12th ed. (Paris: Dalloz, 2018), p. 606.

[17] A. Bénabent, *Droit des obligations*, 15th ed. (Paris: LGDJ, 2018), p. 281.

[18] Maleville, *Pratique de l'interprétation*, 272; B. Gelot, *Finalité et méthodes objectives d'interprétation des actes juridiques* (Paris: LGDJ, 2003); Simler, 'Art 1188 à 1192 – Fasc 10', [24].

[19] Terré et al., *Droit civil*, 606.

[20] Maleville, *Pratique de l'interprétation*, 310 ff. and 544 ff.; S. Vogenauer, 'Interpretation of Contracts: Concluding Observations', in A. Burrows and E. Peel (eds.), *Contract Terms* (Oxford: Oxford University Press, 2007), pp. 136–42; N. Jansen and R. Zimmermann (eds.), *Commentaries on European Contract Laws* (Oxford: Oxford University Press, 2018), pp. 750–1; C. Valcke, 'On Comparing French and English Contract Law: Insights from Social Contract Theory' (2009) 4 *Journal of Comparative Law* 69.

are mistakes in the language of the contract or in how the intended terms are recorded in it, this can be corrected through interpretation. Where French courts give effect to the contractual intention in a way that would be regarded by an English lawyer as rectification, they characterise the exercise as one of interpretation and refer in their judgments to the articles of the Code on interpretation.[21] Provided that the subjective intention of the parties is clear, the scope for the court to correct the language that they have used in the contract is unfettered.

The evidence that can be admitted to assist the court in ascertaining the common subjective intention of the parties is similarly without any limitation.[22] It can include what the parties said or did before[23] or after[24] the contract was formed, whether between themselves or to third parties. Any pre-contractual correspondence,[25] even if only containing subjective statements of intent, is admissible. This is also true of other contracts between the parties[26] and contracts made by one of them with a third party,[27] and of documents that were generated by the parties themselves or third parties at the time that the contract was formed. Indeed, the Cour de cassation positively encourages reliance on evidence of the pre- and post-contractual conduct of the parties in the interest of painting the fullest possible picture of their subjective intention.[28] This is regarded as being probative to the meaning that should be given to the terms that they used, achieving a more precise form of justice than would otherwise be achievable.

[21] Vogenauer, 'Interpretation of Contracts', 136–42.

[22] This is subject to the relatively narrowly confined new Art. 1359 (old Art. 1341) of the Civil Code, which does not apply to commercial contracts and concerns evidence that the contract has been entered into but not evidence as to the extent of the obligations agreed by the parties.

[23] Civ 1, 18 February 1986, No. 84-12.347; Bull civ I, No. 31.

[24] Civ 1, 9 November 1993, Bull civ I No. 317.

[25] Com 15 May 1972, *JCP* 1974.II.17864; Civ 1, 21 April 1976 Bull I No. 135, p. 108.

[26] Aix 18 April 1978, Bull Aix 1978/2, p. 60.

[27] Com 8 December 1987 Bull IV No. 262, p. 97; Maleville, *Pratique de l'interprétation*, 409.

[28] See the cases cited in Maleville, *Pratique de l'interprétation*, 403; T. Ivainer, 'La lettre et l'esprit de la loi des parties', *JCP* 1981.I.3023; Simler, 'Art 1188 à 1192 – Fasc 10', [2]. I am grateful to Professor Whittaker for commenting that there is a key irony in that whilst French courts seek to identify the actual intentions of the parties rather than what was written, the courts in practice do not take direct evidence of this intention. There are no witness statements by the parties as to what one or other (or both) intended. Civil decisions are made on the basis of a *dossier* of documents. In other words, the nature of the French civil process leads to a fundamentally objective set of evidence of intention.

### *6.1.2 Objective Methods of Interpretation to Ascertain the Parties' Common Intention*

When interpreting a contract, the approach of French courts, where it is not possible to ascertain the common subjective intention of the parties, has for a long time been to take account of objective considerations. Such considerations can include the nature of the contract,[29] commercial usage, and practices and customs in the relevant trade or profession.[30] The articles on interpretation in the Civil Code itself refer to the following objective factors: the purpose of the contract; other terms of the contract; and common sense. Paragraph 1 of new Article 1189 provides that 'terms should be interpreted in the light of the other terms of the contract and in a way that is consistent with the spirit and purpose of the contract as a whole'.[31] This principle is stated in paragraph 2 also to apply where 'several contracts contribute to a single operation'. They are to be interpreted by reference to the 'purpose of the whole operation'. Similarly, new Article 1991 provides that 'where a term is capable of bearing two meanings, a meaning which gives the term some effect should be preferred over one which does not'.[32] The principles of coherency and effectiveness are integral to both of these articles and the interpretation given to the contract must be coherent, make sense, render the words used by the parties effective and accord with their purpose.[33]

This is neatly illustrated by a case involving a non-compete clause, by which the director of a business agreed not to take 'similar employment' in a competing business in a specific region for a period of one year. The Cour de cassation affirmed the lower court decision that this meant he could not take the same position in a company that he had newly set up. In order to give full effect to the purpose of the clause, the court held that

[29] *CA* Paris 30 September 1983, *GP* 1984.1 Som 176; *CA* 2 December 1985, *GP* 1986.1.214 noted by A. Piedelièvre.

[30] Com 9 February 1976, *JCP* 1977.II.18598. See also the relationship between the articles on interpretation and new Art. 1194 (old Art. 1135) of the Code in the section below on *Interprétation créatrice* and *Interprétation explicative*.

[31] Reproducing Art. 1161 of the 1804 Code.

[32] See Art. 1157 of the 1804 Code.

[33] For illustrations of the application of these factors, see Com 29 November 1965, Bull III No. 612, p. 550.1; *CA* Paris 2 December 1985; Soc 5 January 1984, *BRDA* 1984/7, p. 12, and, for further examples, Gelot, *Finalité et méthodes objectives d'interprétation*, 147–8 and 157.

the word 'employment' should not be interpreted narrowly so as to apply only where the individual was 'employed by a third party business'.[34]

Another illustration is a case concerning a loan agreement that contained a term providing for 'an exemption (*franchise*) of one year' from the payment of interest. A dispute arose as to whether interest was payable in respect of that year. It was argued by the borrowers that the effect of the term was that no interest was due in respect of that year at all. This was resisted by the bank, which argued that interest accrued during the year in the usual way but only became payable following the end of the year. The Paris Court of Appeal found in favour of the bank. It reasoned that, from the perspective of the bank, the very purpose of the loan was to generate revenue, which it did by charging interest. That being the case, it could not realistically have been expected by the borrowers that no interest would be charged.[35]

### 6.1.3 *Recognition in the 2016 Reforms of Objective Considerations in the Interpretation Process*

Whilst it is common for French courts to take account of objective considerations such as the purpose of the contract, other clauses of the contract and common sense, in many instances when doing so, they have characterised them not as objective considerations but instead as going to the parties' subjective intention.[36] This relies upon a usually unspoken presumption that the parties would have intended to achieve coherency and effectiveness in their contract. Through the device of this presumption, the courts claim to search for the subjective intention of the parties while actually looking beyond it.[37]

Commentators had, prior to the 2016 reforms, railed against the artificiality of these judicial denials that objective considerations are

[34] Soc 5 January 1984, *BRDA* 1984/7, p. 12.

[35] *CA* Paris 2 December 1985. For other examples, see Gelot, *Finalité et méthodes objectives d'interprétation*, 147–8. Note the relationship with the 'essential qualities of the act of performance' in the context of mistake (Arts. 1132–6 of the Code) or the 'essential obligation' of the substance of a term (Art. 1170 of the Code) and the 'main-subject of the contract' (Art. 1171) in the context of unfair terms.

[36] See the cases referred to in Gelot, *Finalité et méthodes objectives d'interprétation*, 1–19; Maleville, *Pratique de l'interprétation*, 443 ff.; Deshayes, 'Les directives d'interprétation', 163–5; Simler, 'Art 1188 à 1192 – Fasc 10', [29].

[37] See previous note.

taken into account.[38] Their criticisms were heeded by the drafters of the reforms, who gave formal recognition to the role of objective considerations. Newly inserted paragraph 2 of Article 1188, immediately following the statement of principle at paragraph 1 that the court should ascertain the common intention of the parties, provides that, 'where the intention cannot be discerned, a contract is to be interpreted in the sense which a reasonable person placed in the same situation would give it'. This is a clear statement that, in circumstances where the subjective intention of the parties cannot be ascertained, the contract should be interpreted objectively.[39]

This is a welcome addition to the Code, achieving greater coherency and alignment with the long-standing practice of the courts. There is no longer any need for the courts somewhat unconvincingly to disclaim having taken account of objective considerations and it should bring an end to debate about the artificiality of the French approach. The practical reality that the subjective approach to interpretation does not always work and therefore sometimes needs to be supplemented by objective analysis is now openly recognised. Similarly, the fiction that in all cases the parties have a common intention that is capable of ascertainment can be abandoned. It is inevitable that, where a subjective approach falls short, there will be a need to draw upon objective factors and this occurs on a regular basis. Denying that this is happening makes no sense, and formally recognising that the approach to interpretation in French law draws upon a combination of subjective and objective factors can only serve to mean greater transparency and certainty, which were two of the avowed aims of the reforms.

### 6.1.4 *The Influence of International Contract Law Instruments and a Rapprochement with English Law?*

Some commentators consider that new paragraph 2 of Article 1188 was inspired by, and brings the French approach to interpretation closer to, English law,[40] where the objective intention of the parties must be

[38] Gelot, *Finalité et méthodes objectives d'interprétation*, 1–19; N. Martial-Braz, 'L'objectivation des méthodes d'interprétation: la référence à la 'personne raisonnable' et l'interprétation *in favorem*', *RDC* 2015.193.

[39] G. Chantepie and M. Latina, *Le nouveau droit des obligations* (Paris: Dalloz 2018), p. 503.

[40] E.g. Martial-Braz, 'L'objectivation des méthodes d'interprétation', 2: 'ce standard du raisonnable . . . est directement importé de nos amis anglo-saxons'.

ascertained and given effect. In ascertaining this intention, the English courts seek to establish what a reasonable person in the position of the parties would have understood by the disputed term.[41] The search for this meaning is undertaken by reference to the intention that can be distilled from the contract, rather than any enquiry into their real intention as in France. It is fundamentally objective in nature[42] and believed to bring about greater predictability and consistency; the absence of any attempt to ascertain what the parties actually meant is said to give rise to greater certainty as to how the contract will be interpreted. One incidental advantage is that third-party assignees who come to the contract after its formation and therefore were not privy to what the parties truly intended should nonetheless be able to ascertain its meaning.[43]

Factors balanced in each case to determine reasonable intention include the natural and ordinary meaning of the disputed term, the context, facts and circumstances known to the parties when the contract was formed, other terms of the contract, the overall purpose of the term and the contract, and business common sense.[44] The weight to be given to these factors depends on the nature, formality and quality of the drafting, and in particular whether the contract has been negotiated and drafted by skilled professionals who have carefully considered the words used.[45]

A corollary of the objective approach to interpretation is that evidence of subjective intention is seen as irrelevant to ascertaining the intention of the parties. This means that the courts do not have regard to evidence of pre-contractual negotiations.[46] It is considered that such evidence is 'unhelpful'[47] since only in the final agreement is the common intention of the parties recorded.[48] Other justifications for the exclusion include that taking pre-contractual negotiations into account would add to the cost of litigation since negotiations generate a significant volume of

[41] *Investors Compensation Scheme* v. *West Bromwich Building Society* [1998] 1 WLR 896, 912–13 (Lord Hoffmann); *Deutsche Geonossenschaftbank* v. *Burnhope* [1995] 1 WLR 1580 at 1587 (Lord Steyn).

[42] *Deutsche Geonossenschaftbank* v. *Burnhope*, 1587 (Lord Steyn).

[43] Ibid., 40 (Lord Hoffmann).

[44] *Investors Compensation Scheme* v. *West Bromwich* [1998] 1 WLR 896; *Rainy Sky SA* v. *Kookmin Bank* [2010] EWCA Civ 582; *Arnold* v. *Britton* [2015] UKSC 36, [2015] AC 1619; *Wood* v. *Capita* [2017] UKSC 24, [2017] AC 1173.

[45] *Wood* v. *Capita* [2017] UKSC 24, [2017] AC 1173, [10]–[13] (Lord Hodge).

[46] *Chartbrook Ltd* v. *Persimmon Homes Ltd* [2009] UKHL 38, [2009] 1 AC 1101.

[47] *Prenn* v. *Simmonds* [1971] 1 WLR 1381 at 1384 (Lord Wilberforce).

[48] Ibid.

potentially relevant documentation that might need to be reviewed by the parties' solicitors and before the court.[49] The admissibility of pre-contractual negotiation evidence is also perceived as creating uncertainty. It would be more difficult for practitioners to advise on what a reasonable outside observer would take to have been the intentions of the parties.[50]

In reality and as openly acknowledged by the drafters, new paragraph 2 of Article 1118 was directly 'inspired by the Principles of European Contract Law, the Draft Common Frame of Reference and the Unidroit Principles'.[51] It is in almost identical terms to these instruments. This is exemplified by Article 4.1 of the Unidroit Principles, which provides that:[52]

> (1) A contract shall be interpreted according to the common intention of the parties.
> (2) If such an intention cannot be established, the contract shall be interpreted according to the meaning that reasonable persons of the same kind as the parties would give to it in the same circumstances.

These instruments establish a hierarchy between the different approaches to interpretation.[53] Priority is given to ascertaining the actual intention of the parties. In this way, their subjective intention takes precedence. If this cannot be ascertained, only then does the court turn to objective factors.

This hierarchy, and more generally the perceived tension between the objective and subjective approaches to interpretation, is regarded by some commentators as having no real practical significance. Vogenauer, for instance, has said that 'the conflict between [the objective and subjective approaches] rarely matters in practice . . . it is more or less irrelevant once it is acknowledged that the same interpretative criteria must be employed in establishing the "subjective" intention of the parties as well as the "objective" understanding of reasonable persons'.[54] For him, 'the priority rule [of article 4.1(1) of the Unidroit Principles is confined to a very narrow group of cases [where] . . . both parties . . . intend to employ words in a distinctive sense which does not correspond

49 *Chartbrook Ltd* v. *Persimmon Homes Ltd* [2009] 1 AC 1101, [41] (Lord Hoffmann).
50 Ibid., [39] and [41] (Lord Hoffmann).
51 *Rapport au Président de la République.*
52 Art. 5:101 of PECL and Art. II. 8:101 of the DCFR.
53 Official Comments to Art. 4.1; see S. Vogenauer (ed.), *Commentary on the UNIDROIT Principles of International Commercial Contracts (PICC)*, 2nd ed. (Oxford: Oxford University Press, 2015), pp. 578 ff.
54 Vogenauer, *Commentary*, 580, [15].

to the meaning which the words reasonably bear . . . the application of Art. 4.1(2) is the rule, whilst Art. 4.1(1) is the exception'.[55]

Whilst it is true that, in many cases, both the subjective and objective methods would lead to the same outcome, that is, to the interpretation of ambiguous terms in the same way, the differences of approach remain relevant in several respects. First, the formal bias in France towards the subjective approach explains why French law has a wide conception of 'interpretation' that covers not only the ascertainment of express terms but also rectification and, as will be explained shortly,[56] the implication of terms in fact. Giving meaning to, correcting and supplementing the express terms of the contract all form part of a single, unified exercise that strives to ascertain and give effect to the actual intention of the parties, whether expressed or otherwise. The search for this intention is the common thread running through these processes. Second, the difference in approach helps explain why evidence of pre- and post-contractual behaviour is admissible in French law but not in some systems that adopt an objective approach, including English law. The exclusion of such evidence in England has been said to follow 'from the objective character of all contractual construction. The course of the negotiations cannot tell us what the contract objectively meant. It can tell us only what one or other or both of the parties subjectively thought or assumed or hoped that I meant'.[57] Third, and as will be explained in the next section, it follows from the predominantly subjective approach in French law that issues of interpretation are questions of fact, whereas the objective approach taken in England renders them questions of law.

More generally, there is a deep theoretical attachment amongst French lawyers to interpretation as a subjective enquiry. A number of commentators have opined that new paragraph 2 of Article 1188 respects this attachment and serves to entrench the primacy of the actual intention of

[55] See also Vogenauer, 'Interpretation of Contracts': 'mere programmatic points of departure from which European legal systems attempt to develop solutions that are predictable and . . . fair'; H. Kötz, *European Contract Law*, 2nd ed. (Oxford: Oxford University Press, 2017), pp. 109–10 and 112: 'hardly matters at all today'. H. Beale, B. Fauvarque-Cosson, J. Rutgers and S. Vogenauer, *Ius Commune Casebook on European Contract Law*, 3rd ed. (Oxford: Hart, 2019), p. 727: the distinction is 'largely irrelevant, particularly since it is well established that the same criteria must be employed in establishing both the "subjective" intention of the parties and the "objective" understanding of reasonable persons'.

[56] See Section 6.3 on *Interprétation créatrice* and *Interprétation explicative*.

[57] Lord Sumption, 'A Question of Taste: The Supreme Court and the Interpretation of Contracts' (2017) 17 *Oxford University Commonwealth Law Journal* 301, 309–10.

the parties over their declared intention.[58] The simple requirement in old Article 1156 for the court to establish the subjective common intention of the parties did not have any greater importance than the other principles of interpretation in the 1804 Code. In contrast, the drafters of the reforms have symbolically positioned its successor, new Article 1188, as the first article in the section of the Code on interpretation and as overarching all of the others.[59]

There has not been any suggestion that new paragraph 2 of Article 1188 casts doubt on the primacy of the subjective approach. On the contrary, French commentators have variously remarked that 'to abandon the subjective approach of interpretation . . . which has an essential role, has never seriously been considered';[60] 'nothing has supplanted the classical search for the subjective intention of the parties';[61] 'the search for the common intention continues to reign . . . and this is not to be regretted';[62] 'Article 1188 gives real primacy to the search for the common intention of the parties . . . this hierarchy would not make sense if the court could freely choose his preferred method of interpretation'.[63] The subjective approach has even been described as 'sacrosanct'[64] and the 'one and only mandatory principle' of interpretation.[65] Whilst it might be contended that French lawyers 'cling to the ideal of autonomy

[58] O. Deshayes, T. Génicon and Y.-M. Laithier, *Réforme du droit des contrats, du régime général et de la preuve des obligations*, 2nd ed. (Paris: LexisNexis, 2018), pp. 417–19; Chantepie and Latina, *Le nouveau droit des obligations*, 502–3; Terré et al., *Droit civil*, 608.

[59] Ibid.

[60] Simler, 'Art 1188 à 1192', [3] and [9].

[61] Ibid., [24].

[62] Deshayes, 'Les directives d'interprétation', 162: see also C. Grimaldi, 'Paradoxes autour de l'interprétation des contrats', *RDC* 2008.207; A. Cermolacce 'L'article 1159 du Code civil', *RLDC* 2004/7 No. 302.

[63] Terré et al., *Droit civil*, 607 ff.; A. Etienney-de Sainte Marie, 'Les principes, les directives et les clauses relatives à l'interprétation', *RDC* 2016.384 at 388.

[64] P. Simler, 'Propos introductifs – A la recherche des frontières de l'interprétation' *RDC* 2015.146; Deshayes, 'Les directives d'interprétation', 165; D. Mazeaud, 'L'encadrement des pouvoirs du juge: l'efficacité des clauses relatives à l'interprétation', *RDC* 2015.187.

[65] Gelot, *Finalité et méthodes objectives d'interprétation*, 315; Deshayes, 'Les directives d'interprétation', 163–5; A. Etienney-de Sainte Marie, 'Les principes'; D. Mazeaud, 'L'encadrement des pouvoirs du juge'; Deshayes et al., *Réforme du droit des contrats*, 417–19. E. Rawach, 'La portée des clauses tendant à exclure le rôle des documents précontractuels dans l'interprétation du contract', *D* 2001.223 14–16. Supporting this view: Civ 1, 20 January 1970 Bull civ I. No. 24.

of the will',[66] which sits uneasily with what happens in practice, it confirms the importance that they attach to this subjective conception.[67] To dismiss this attachment and its consequences as irrelevant is to deny the French conception of the interpretation process.

## 6.2 Rewriting Contracts and Distorting Terms

Another novel feature in the 2016 reforms is the inclusion of an express provision relating to *dénaturation*. This is the power of the Cour de cassation to review on appeal the decision of a lower court on contractual interpretation that distorts the meaning of a term or terms which are clear and precise. In practice, however, the Cour de cassation rarely exercises this review power, which has the effect of leaving the final determination of issues of interpretation almost exclusively in the hands of lower courts. It will be shown that the limited intervention of the Cour de cassation, and corresponding latitude that lower courts enjoy in the interpretation process, can be a source of uncertainty and has been the subject of criticism. One step that would have been conducive to greater certainty, particularly for commercial parties, would have been to give formal recognition to 'interpretation clauses', which are terms included in the contract by the parties for the purpose of directing the court as to how to construe its terms. Regrettably the drafters of the reforms opted not to do so.

### 6.2.1 *The Codification of Dénaturation by the 2016 Reforms*

Ascertaining the subjective intention of the parties is a factual question,[68] and is a matter for the courts of first instance and lower appeal courts. The Cour de cassation does not review findings of fact. Its appellate jurisdiction is confined to ensuring that legal principles have been applied properly. Therefore, as long as the aim of a lower court is to ascertain the actual intention of the parties (which is almost invariably the case), the manner in which it goes about applying the principles of interpretation in the Civil Code and its resulting determinations on the meaning of the words that

[66] Vogenauer, 'Interpretation of Contracts', 127; Valcke, 'On Comparing French and English Contract Law', 87.

[67] Valcke, 'On Comparing French and English Contract Law'.

[68] 'Une question de fait tranchée souverainement par les juges du fond': Terré et al., *Droit civil*, 616.

they have used are seldom overturned on appeal. It is for this reason and due to the absence of any defining decisions or significant guidance from the Cour de cassation on the principles on interpretation[69] that the subject has not generated nearly the same interest in France as in common law jurisdictions.[70]

Only where a lower court interprets a contract term in a way that distorts a meaning that is clear and precise (*dénaturation des clauses claires et précises*) will the Cour de cassation exercise its jurisdiction and review the decision. New Article 1192, which was introduced by the 2016 reforms, codifies this jurisdiction in the following words: 'clear and unambiguous terms are not subject to interpretation as doing so would risk their distortion'. Such terms are regarded as being in no need of interpretation since the intention of the parties is self-evident and admits of no other meaning. It is not for the court to seek to interfere with the way that the parties have allocated risk or impose a different bargain to the one that they intended.[71] The jurisdiction of the Cour de cassation protects against any decision that strays into this terrain, thereby giving the parties greater confidence that the clear and unambiguous meaning of the terms that they have used will be given effect.[72]

However, the Cour de cassation very rarely exercises the jurisdiction to quash lower court decisions.[73] In most cases that come before court, some degree of ambiguity can be identified, particularly when regard is had to the context, surrounding circumstances and other clauses of the contract. As a consequence, only occasionally is the power engaged.[74] This is likely to mean that the impact of the codification of *dénaturation* is minimal.

It is difficult to know whether and to what extent lower courts take advantage of the Cour de cassation's narrow remit in order to rewrite or distort contract terms. Any proper analysis is prevented by interpretation issues ultimately turning on the subjective intention of the parties, which is very much fact-specific and hard to second-guess from the brief

[69] Cass, sect réun, 2 February 1808, S chron, *GAJC*, t 2, No. 160; D. Tricot, 'Le juge: le contrôle de dénaturation et la liberté d'interprétation des conventions', *RDC* 2015.149.

[70] See, however, the series of papers on 'L'interprétation: une menace pour la sécurité des conventions?' in *RDC* 2015.1.

[71] Vogenauer, 'Interpretation of Contracts', 131; Simler, 'Art 1188 à 1192 – Fasc 10', [5].

[72] *Rapport au Président de la République*; Civ 4 May 1942 dc 1942.131, noted by J. Besson; see also the many cases cited by Maleville, *Pratique de l'interprétation*, 241–3.

[73] Simler, 'Art 1188 à 1192 – Fasc 20', [51].

[74] Ibid., [61]–[72].

judgments that are given by French courts. This itself can give rise to uncertainty and has been the subject of criticism.[75] Some have called for the Cour de cassation to be more vigorous in its use of the *dénaturation* jurisdiction to review lower court interpretation decisions[76] but, at least prior to the reforms, this had not caused any change of approach.[77] Perhaps more powerfully, the calls were echoed by the drafters of the reforms[78] in their comments on the new interpretation articles, which must raise at least a slight prospect that they will be heeded.

### 6.2.2 *Interpretation Clauses to Provide Commercial Certainty?*

A possible means of enhancing transparency and certainty in the interpretation process in French law would be for contracting parties to be able to contract out of, or adapt, the principles of interpretation in the Civil Code. This would be effected through the insertion into the contract of an interpretation clause to direct or influence how the words used are understood and applied.[79]

It is clear from decisions of the Cour de cassation that the interpretation principles contained in the Code do not bind but instead serve as 'mere advice to judges ... without mandatory character and not imposing absolute rules';[80] they should be seen as akin to a 'tool box',[81] there to assist the court in identifying what the parties sought to achieve.[82] It is therefore not open to the Cour de cassation to quash a decision simply because the lower court has failed to apply or incorrectly applied the

[75] See Tricot, 'Le juge: le contrôle de dénaturation', and other papers in a special issue on 'L'interprétation: une menace pour la sécurité des conventions?' in *RDC* 2015.1.

[76] E.g. Tricot, 'Le juge: le contrôle de dénaturation', 150–1 and 153.

[77] Ibid.

[78] F. Ancel, B. Fauvarque-Cosson and J. Gest, *Aux sources de la réforme du droit des contrats* (Paris: Dalloz, 2017), pp. 33–6.

[79] See Rawach, 'La portée des clauses'; Mazeaud, 'L'encadrement des pouvoirs du juge'; Gelot, *Finalité et méthodes objectives d'interprétation*, 258 ff.; C. Helleringer, 'Quand les parties font leur loi. Réflexion sur la contractualisation du pouvoir judiciaire d'interprétation', in M. Xifaras and G. Lewkowics (eds.), *Repenser le contrat* (Paris: Dalloz, 2009), p. 277; B. Fauvarque-Cosson, 'Les Nouvelles règles du Code civil relatives à l'interprétation des contrats: perspective comparative et internationale', *RDC* 2017.363.

[80] Req 18 March 1807, S 1807, 1, 367; Req 16 February 1892, S 1893.1.409; Civ 1 19 December 1995, Bull civ 1995, I, No. 466.

[81] P. Simler, 'Propos introductifs – A la recherche des frontières de l'interprétation', *RDC* 2015.146.

[82] C. Grimaldi 'La valeur normative des directives d'interprétation', *RDC* 2015.154 at [4].

principles.[83] One perceived benefit of enabling the parties to contract out of the principles of interpretation of the Code and include interpretation clauses is that it would enable the broad powers of the lower courts over the interpretation process to be limited or even excluded. This would curtail the court's scope to depart from the meaning intended by the parties.[84]

The reforms to the Civil Code are silent in relation to interpretation clauses. There should not, however, be any fundamental objection to their use or enforceability, given that they are simply an expression of the will of the parties and, after all, the process of interpreting a contract is but a search for their intentions. Any other analysis would be at odds with the fundamental principle of freedom of contract.

The academic discussion in France has focused mainly on two types of interpretation clause. First, the entire agreement clause (*clauses d'intégralité*), which typically provides that the obligations of the parties are entirely contained in the contractual document, excluding any collateral or oral agreements or pre-contractual statements from having contractual or any other effect. The aim is to stop evidence of such agreements or statements from being taken into account in ascertaining the obligations of the parties. Second, the so-called priority clause (*clauses de priorité*), which seeks to create a form of hierarchy between the terms of the contract and/or other documents between the parties whether from before, during or after the formation of the contract. Such clauses can be particularly helpful in the context of complex contracts or other instruments that have legal effect where there is an increased risk of terms being in contradiction. By establishing an order of priority, they direct the court as to how the contradiction should be resolved.

There has been little coverage of priority clauses in the case law but in a few cases they have been held to be valid.[85] Seemingly only in one case – a decision of the Paris Court of Appeal – has consideration been given to the impact of an entire agreement clause on the interpretation. In that case, it was held that, in order to be effective, the clause must contain an express exclusion of evidence of pre-contractual negotiations and other extraneous documents from being admissible to *interpret* the

[83] Simler, 'Art 1188 à 1192 – Fasc 20', [37].

[84] Mazeaud, 'L'encadrement des pouvoirs du juge'.

[85] CA Paris 15 June 2005, RTD civ 2006 p. 111 noted by J. Mestre; see also the cases cited by Mazeaud, 'L'encadrement des pouvoirs du juge'; and Rawach, 'La portée des clauses'; Gelot, *Finalité et méthodes objectives d'interprétation*, 258 ff.

contract. A statement that they are excluded from evidencing the *content* of the contract is not sufficient as this does not necessarily disqualify them from being used in the interpretation process.[86]

This silence of the 2016 reforms in relation to interpretation clauses is in contrast with the international contract law instruments that have served as the inspiration for some of the other articles on interpretation in the 2016 reforms. An example is Article 2:105 of PECL, which states that:[87]

> (1) If a written contract contains an individually negotiated clause stating that the writing embodies all the terms of the contract (a merger clause), any prior statements, undertakings or agreements which are not embodied in the writing do not form part of the contract. . . .
> (3) The parties' prior statements may be used to interpret the contract. This rule may not be excluded or restricted except by an individually negotiated clause.

Under this provision, unless there is an express exclusion, evidence of pre-contractual negotiations is admissible in the interpretation process, which achieves a similar effect to the Paris Court of Appeal decision.

It is regrettable that the 2016 reforms did not tackle interpretation clauses and bring an end to the doubt as to their enforceability.[88] This would have been conducive to transactional certainty[89] and, as regards entire agreement clauses, which are commonly incorporated in international commercial contracts,[90] it would have helped to fulfil one of the stated objectives of the reforms of increasing the attractiveness of French law to the international business community. As it is, the uncertainties that existed before the reforms persist, and this can only be regarded as a missed opportunity.

### 6.3 *Interprétation explicative* and *Interprétation créatrice*

The 2016 reforms also addressed the distinction between 'creative interpretation' (*interprétation créatrice*) and 'explanatory interpretation'

[86] CA Paris 4 March 1980, Expertises, No. 17, April 1980, p. 8.
[87] See also Art. 2.1.17(2) and Art. II.4:104(3)(2) *DCFR*.
[88] Terré et al., *Droit civil*, 603; A. Bénabent, *Droit des obligations*, 15th ed. (Paris: LGDJ, 2018), p. 284; Deshayes et al., *Réforme du droit des contrats*, 417–19.
[89] Mazeaud, 'L'encadrement des pouvoirs du juge'; and B. Fauvarque-Cosson, 'L'interprétation du contrat: observations comparatives', *RDC* 2007.481.
[90] Ibid.

(*interprétation explicative*).[91] In essence, *interprétation explicative* involves ascertaining the meaning of terms that are unclear and *interprétation créatrice* is the process of filling gaps where the contract does not address a significant issue.

It has traditionally been understood in France that what English lawyers would consider as implying terms 'in fact' and 'in law'[92] is not a distinct exercise[93] but instead is part of a broader process of interpretation in which the unifying purpose is to ascertain and give effect to the common subjective intention of the parties. This is because both interpretation and implication share the common purpose of ascertaining this intention.[94] Where a term that the parties have agreed upon is unclear, that process is confined to ascertaining their intended meaning for that term. If, however, the parties have not addressed an issue at all, such that there is no relevant term capable of being interpreted, it is open to the court to consider whether or not to imply one. In doing so, the court must determine their hypothetical common intention or alternatively the intention that they would have formed in the event that they had addressed their minds to the issue.

There has been no real debate in France on whether it is appropriate for what an English lawyer would consider as the implication of terms 'in fact' to be regarded as part of a broader exercise of contractual interpretation. It has, however, been contended by a number of commentators that, where terms are implied 'in law', this is not truly in the nature of interpretation and must instead be seen as a distinct process. Some commonly cited

[91] Ibid.; A. Etienney-de Sainte Marie, '"L'interprétation créatrice": l'interprétation et la détermination du contenu du contrat', *RDC* 2015.166.

[92] French lawyers do not distinguish between the express and implied terms of the contract in the way that English lawyers do. As summarised by Professor Whittaker, 'while from time to time French lawyers do distinguish between the express and implied agreement of the parties, this is not as pervasive a distinction as is found in English law in relation to express and implied contract terms nor does it have the latter's significance', in J. Bell, S. Boyron and S. Whittaker, *Principles of French Law*, 2nd ed. (Oxford: Oxford University Press, 2008), p. 329.

[93] Terré et al., *Droit civil*, 608–14.

[94] Ibid., 608–14; P. Malaurie, L. Aynès and P. Stoffel-Munck, *Droit des obligations*, 10th ed. (Paris: LGDJ, 2018), p. 772; Professor Whittaker added that, 'instead, the French starting point in determining the effects of a contract is to look into what was the common ("subjective") intention of the parties and in this respect no distinction needs to be drawn between what they expressly and what they impliedly agreed. Questions of what the parties agreed are treated as ones of interpretation, whether this relates to determining what was included within their agreement or what meaning should be attributed to words which they clearly did include': Bell et al., *Principles of French Law*, 329.

examples are the implication of an obligation of safety (*obligation de sécurité*) in contracts for transportation and the obligation of information (*obligation d'information*) in the context of contracts for professional services.[95] On no view can the implication of these obligations be attributed to any common subjective intention of the parties, and indeed the process does not involve ascertaining the meaning of terms that they have chosen.[96] To the contrary, it is usually indisputable that the parties did not intend or even think about such obligations, which are implied for policy reasons and often based on fairness. The exercise of implying such obligations is also entirely objective in nature. It has even been described as 'forcing the contract' (*forçage du contrat*),[97] reflecting that it occurs independently of the subjective intentions of the parties.

One reason that the implication of terms in law has been understood as a species of interpretation is that that some provisions in the section on interpretation in the 1804 Civil Code dealt with *interprétation créatrice*. One often-cited example is old Article 1160, which provided that 'the contract must be supplemented by clauses which comply with usages'. Whilst this could be linked to the parties' intention, in substance this amounts to the implication of terms.

The objection that *interprétation créatrice* should be regarded as a distinct process was heeded as part of the 2016 reforms with the removal of reference to *interprétation créatrice* from the section of the Code on interpretation.[98] The five surviving articles in that section relate principally to *interprétation explicative*. It is later in the Code that references to usages can be found and that *interprétation créatrice* is addressed. Article 1194 provides that 'contracts create obligations not merely in relation to what they expressly provide, but also to all the consequences which are given to them by equity, usage or legislation'.[99] This is consistent with the approach in a number of international contract law instruments such as

[95] Terré et al., *Droit civil*, 614 ff.

[96] Etienney-de Sainte Marie, '"L'interprétation créatrice"', 4; Simler, 'Art 1188 à 1192 – Fasc 10', [13] ff.; Terré et al., *Droit civil*, 612 ff.; Deshayes, 'Les directives d'interprétation'; Chantepie and Latina, *Le nouveau droit des obligations*, 500; P. Catala 'Interprétation et qualification dans l'avant-projet de réforme des obligations', in *Etudes offertes à G Viney* (Paris: LGDJ, 2008), p. 243; G. Viney, P. Jourdain and S. Carval, *Traité de droit civil, Les conditions de la responsabilité* (Paris: LGDJ, 2013), pp. 458 ff.

[97] L. Josserand, obs. under CA Lyon 7 December 1928: *DP* 1929.II.17; Etienney-de Sainte Marie, '"L'interprétation créatrice"'.

[98] Old Art. 1160 of the 1804 Civil Code.

[99] Old Art. 1135 of the Code.

the Principles of European Contract Law (PECL) and the Draft Common Frame of Reference (DCFR), which deal with the implication of terms separately from interpretation.[100] This development achieves greater certainty and coherency through the formal distinction of the two processes in their objectives and how they operate.

## 6.4 Standard-Form Contracts and the *Contra proferentem* Rule

Prior to the 2016 reforms there was thought to be a pressing need for regulation of how standard-form contracts are interpreted, with two issues giving rise to particular consternation. First, whether it is realistically possible to ascertain any common subjective intention of the parties from standard terms. Many argued that this simply could not be done,[101] since, by definition, standard terms are not negotiated and indeed characteristically are simply imposed by the stronger party in the relationship. An approach to interpretation that is appropriate in the context of negotiated contracts is unlikely to be suitable for standard terms, so the argument went. Second, on some occasions, the courts have interpreted the same clause in a standard-form contract in different ways, causing considerable uncertainty.[102]

These issues were addressed in the 2016 reforms by the *contra proferentem* rule being applied to standard-form contracts. New Article 1190 states that 'in case of ambiguity, a bespoke contract is interpreted against the creditor and in favour of the debtor, and a standard form contract is interpreted against the person who put it forward'. It is an objective approach to interpretation that does not look to the actual

[100] International contract law instruments have taken different approaches to this question: Art. 6:102 PECL and II.–9:101 DCFR is in the section on the contents and effects of contract; note, however, that Art. 4.8 of the Unidroit Principles addresses the implication of terms but in the section on interpretation.

[101] E.g. T. Revêt, 'L'uniformation de l'interprétation: contrats types et contrats d'adhésion', *RDC* 2015.199.

[102] Terré et al., *Droit civil*, 616, citing Civ 28 January 1907, two decisions DP 1908.5, S 1912.1.22. See also for the absence of intervention of the Cour de cassation in this area: Com 24 March 1965 Bull civ III No. 230; Civ 1, 21 May 1969 Bull civ I No. 169; Civ 1, 28 October 1970 Bull civ I No. 285; Chantepie and Latina, *Le nouveau droit des obligations*, 508; B. Nicholas, *The French Law of Contract*, 2nd ed. (Oxford: Oxford University Press, 1992), pp. 48–9; Revet, 'L'uniformation de l'interprétation', has shown that, through *dénaturation*, the Cour de cassation has on occasions imposed its own interpretation of clauses in standard form contracts but without ever acknowledging that it was doing so.

intention of the parties or the true meaning of their words but instead is concerned with rebalancing their obligations.[103]

The *contra proferentem rule* was already familiar in French law prior to the 2016 reforms, having been provided for in the 1804 Civil Code[104] and also applying to sale contracts pursuant to Article 1602 of the Civil Code and consumer contracts under Article L211–1 of the Consumer Code.[105] It is commonly justified on grounds of fairness, equity and the protection of the weaker party, and also as incentivising the party drafting the contract to do so with precision and clarity.[106]

With the inclusion of this provision, the section of the Code on interpretation now gives specific mention to standard-form contracts (in line with one of the stated aims of the 2016 reforms of designating specific provisions 'which only apply to standard form contracts'[107]). It also specifically requires the contract to be interpreted against the party that introduced the standard terms, rather than against the creditor.[108] In common with several other innovations in the reforms, this reflects the approach taken in a number of international contract instruments. For instance, Article 5:103 of PECL states that 'where there is doubt about the meaning of a contract term not individually negotiated, an interpretation of the term against the party who supplied it is to be preferred'. There is a similar rule in Article 4.6 of the Unidroit Principles and Article II-8:103(1) of the DCFR, albeit that its scope extends to all unclear terms rather than being confined only to those that are contained in a party's standard terms.

The introduction of the *contra proferentem* rule in the context of standard-form contracts has had a mixed reception in France; some commentators have responded more favourably than others.[109] What is clearly a positive development is the recognition that standard-form

[103] It is therefore objective in a different sense from Art. 1188 of the Civil Code.

[104] Old Art. 1162 of the 1804 Civil Code.

[105] Though, the impact of the rule differs in the consumer context as the *most* favourable interpretation for the consumer is to be adopted.

[106] Fauvarque-cosson, 'Les Nouvelles règles du Code civil' and 'L'interprétation du contrat'; Martial-Braz, 'L'objectivation des méthodes d'interprétation'; Terré et al., *Droit civil*, 610 ff.

[107] *Loi d'habilitation de l'ordonnance n°2016-131.*

[108] It has long been recognised by the Cour de cassation that in some circumstances, the creditor is not the person who drafts the contract and that protection should be against the latter, whose responsibility it is to draft a contract in clear and precise terms: Civ 1 22 October 1974 Bull civ I No. 271 and Simler, 'Art 1188 à 1192 – Fasc 10', [62]–[67].

[109] Revêt, 'L'uniformation de l'interprétation'; Etienney-de Sainte Marie, '"L'interprétation créatrice"', 14–15, 26 and 29.

contracts have unique characteristics which mean that any attempt to ascertain the subjective intention of the parties is likely to be unproductive. To the extent that the reforms achieve greater consistency in how standard terms are interpreted, this will also be helpful. There is equally much to be said for an approach that puts the risk of ambiguity onto the party who drafted the standard terms and was therefore able to prevent it.[110]

An alternative that would have mitigated the need for reform was for the Cour de cassation, rather than confining its appellate interventions to *dénaturation*,[111] to show greater readiness to rule definitively on recurrently contentious terms in standard-form contracts.[112] This has been the approach of the appellate courts in England, which have sought to establish uniform interpretations of standard terms in commercial contracts and generally avoided disturbing established constructions.[113] In the words of Lord Diplock in *Pioneer Shipping Ltd* v. *TP Tioxide Ltd*,[114] 'it is only if parties to commercial contracts can rely on a uniform construction being given to standard terms that they can prudently incorporate them in their contracts without the need for detailed negotiation or discussion'.[115] There are no separate rules for standard-form contracts, which are subject to the same principles as terms that have been negotiated, and the *contra proferentem* rule itself has fallen out of favour, being perceived to be unreliable and capable of leading to potentially arbitrary outcomes.[116]

This approach has much to commend it. Clear rulings that establish definite meanings for clauses that are widely used and susceptible to dispute can only be helpful in bringing certainty to contractual relationships[117] and,

[110] Jansen and Zimmermann, *Commentaries*, 773.

[111] Tricot, 'Le juge: le contrôle de dénaturation', 150–1.

[112] Simler, 'Art 1188 à 1192 – Fasc 10', [82] ff.; Tricot, 'Le juge: le contrôle de dénaturation'; Revet, 'L'uniformation de l'interprétation'.

[113] K. Lewinson, *The Interpretation of Contracts*, 5th ed. (London: Sweet & Maxwell, 2014), p. 4.08.

[114] *The Nema (No. 2)* [1982] AC 724.

[115] Ibid., 737 (Lord Diplock).

[116] *K/S Victoria Street* v. *House of Fraser (Stores Management)* [2011] EWCA Civ 904; [2012] Ch 497 at [68] (Lord Neuberger). On *the contra proferentem rule* and its relevance and role, see, recently, J. McCunn, 'Contra Proferentem Rule: Contract Law's Great Survivor' (2019) 39 *Oxford Journal of Legal Studies* 1, who argues that the rule still has a role to play. Note that English courts also take the view that terms (and even exemption clauses) should be given effect as representing the allocation of risk by the contracting parties, even if they are in a standard form.

[117] I am grateful to Professor Simon Whittaker for pointing out that it may be difficult to find evidence of the 'clear rulings' approach in the sort of commercial context in which it

where it is thought to be appropriate, prompting amendments to contract terms. It is doubtful that the *contra proferentem* rule will cure all of the difficulties that arise with the interpretation of standard-form contracts in France. The rule could potentially be applied inconsistently and the risk of the same terms being interpreted differently remains. There is also still no mechanism for bringing about a definitive ruling on specific clauses.[118]

## 6.5 Conclusion

The avowed aims of the 2016 reforms were to make French contract law more certain, predictable and fair while at the same time attractive to business and credible as an alternative to the major common law systems. There can be no doubt that the codification of principles that have been developed over time in the case law has brought the Civil Code much more up to date with the law as applied by the courts. In the context of contractual interpretation, a number of long-running controversies and debates have been addressed, in particular the dichotomy between the subjective and objective approaches to interpretation and the relationship between *interprétation créatrice* and *interprétation explicative*. The *dénaturation* power of the Cour de cassation has also been formally recognised and the *contra proferentem* rule is now used in the specific context of the interpretation of standard-form contracts. The reforms also bring a more modern and international approach to French contract law, which in part can be attributed to the extent to which the drafters were inspired by and drew upon a number of the international contract instruments. On any view, the increased clarity and certainty that have resulted are welcome.

It is, however, difficult to say whether the reforms will make French law more predictable and attractive to business. Despite the drafters having openly recognised that the courts can interpret a contract as would a reasonable person placed in the same situation as the parties, the French approach remains ideologically wedded to subjective interpretation. This has important consequences, particularly from a procedural perspective. Notably, interpretation remains a question of fact to be

is found in English law (for example, standard-form insurance contracts). As he pointed out, there may be less need in the French context to have recourse to standard terms as so many contracts are highly regulated by legislation, as is the case in the insurance context.

118 Tricot, 'Le juge: le contrôle de dénaturation'.

decided by lower courts, which exercise broad powers but say little as to their reasons in their short judgments, making it difficult to know how the principles of interpretation are actually applied in practice. As long as there is ostensibly a search for the subjective intention of the parties, the Cour de cassation is unlikely to disturb the first-instance finding and the practical reality is that relatively few decisions on interpretation are overturned.

Whether the changes made by the reforms to the law of interpretation will help French law be a more credible alternative to common law systems in this area of contract law is also hard to tell. This chapter has sought to show that, as with many other areas of contract law which have also been reformed,[119] the 2016 reforms have brought some sensible changes while leaving some issues unresolved. In England, the search for the declared intention of the parties and the exclusion of evidence of pre-contractual conduct as aspects of a strictly objective approach are thought to promote certainty, help contract planning and limit legal costs. However, while the process might be more transparent, the many high-profile cases on interpretation, divergences between appellate courts and powerful dissents in the judgments of those courts[120] show that England has also struggled to achieve stable and workable principles of interpretation. Ultimately, neither approach seems unarguably more attractive than the other.

[119] Rowan, 'The New French Law'.

[120] The most significant modern decisions on contract interpretation are *Investors Compensation Scheme* v. *West Bromwich* [1997] UKHL 8, [1998] 1 WLR 896; *Chartbrook Ltd* v. *Persimmon Homes* [2009] UKHL 38, [2009] 1 AC 1101; *Rainy Sky SA* v. *Kookmin Bank* [2011] UKSC 50, [2011] 1 WLR 2900; *Arnold* v. *Britton* [2015] UKSC 36, [2015] AC 1619; *Wood* v. *Capita* [2017] UKSC 24, [2017] AC 1173.

# 7

# Assessing (Divergent) Legal Development

COLM PETER MCGRATH

> A degree of doctrinal divergence is inevitable, but our study has suggested that this divergence is not uniform. Liability for medical injuries . . . is relatively homogeneous in different systems.[1]
>
> (Bell and Ibbetson)

Let us start, as lawyers often do, with texts, and, as comparatists often do, with texts from different jurisdictions, each taken from a mid-twentieth-century civil court. Each text addresses a familiar problem in medical liability that we will use to apply and explore Bell and Ibbetson's work: what if, when assessing fault in the context of diagnosis and treatment, the impugned conduct is generally accepted by some or all medical practitioners? The first text, from 1952, comes from an apex court, the German Bundesgerichtshof (BGH), where a dentist was sued for allowing his patient to swallow an unsecured 4 cm needle during a procedure:[2]

> From the fact that expert practitioners of dentistry ordinarily work with unsecured needles, the conclusion may be drawn that the defendant demonstrated the degree of care customary within his occupation. Yet, as noted, this is not determinative. Rather, more decisive is whether the objective required care has been observed. Presently, the protection of patients from incidents during treatment that threaten avoidable injury is the highest imperative.

The second, which arrived shortly thereafter in 1957, from the humble confines of the Queen's Bench Division in *Bolam* v. *Friern Hospital Management Committee*, saw a senior registrar choose not to inform their patient about, or adopt the use of, muscle relaxants during electro-convulsive therapy, with terrible injury resulting:[3]

1 J. Bell and D. Ibbetson, *European Legal Development: The Case of Tort* (Cambridge: Cambridge University Press, 2012), p. 179.
2 BGH 27.11.1952, BGHZ 8, 138, 141 (translation author's own).
3 [1957] 1 WLR 582, 587.

> I myself would prefer to put it this way, that he is not guilty of negligence if he has acted in accordance with a practice accepted as proper by a responsible body of medical men skilled in that particular art . . . Putting it the other way round, a man is not negligent, if he is acting in accordance with such a practice, merely because there is a body of opinion who would take a contrary view.

There are, of course, formal and stylistic differences between each utterance. The German collective, anonymous, final judicial exposition contrasts with a text individual to its author, McNair J, and interstitial, directed as it was to a jury. There are also, clearly, important substantive differences. Each case confronts the tension between directly policing patient safety and respecting plausible and possibly plural medical responses. The German court favoured the former, rejecting the idea that negligence might be avoided simply because a particular practice was accepted by practitioners. The English court, by contrast, emphasised that this was sufficient to avoid such a finding. These cases speak to a fundamentally different choice about the degree of control each body of knowledge, medical and legal, had over identifying actionable medical error. Our aim, in Bell and Ibbetson's mould, is to identify what drove the developmental narrative in each system and to reflect on what this reveals about their methodology.

## 7.1 Legal Development and the Comparative Stance

Bell and Ibbetson suggest that, broadly, legal development reflects a plural set of factors affecting a rule's meaning: the rule's formulation, interpretation, context and relevance, and the way in which it is used or enforced.[4] Their methodological framework for understanding how and why changes occur may require analysis of any or all of the law in the books, the legal outcomes and the relevant legal institutions.[5] These are presumed to exist symbiotically, with the latter providing the framework within which a presumed feedback loop of influence between the former two elements of a given system operates. For them, legal institutions are not tangibly institutional but instead an attempt to capture the intangible but nevertheless decisive elements of a legal system beyond a rule itself. This encompasses the dominant or accepted forms of reasoning and legal style as well as legal culture, which provides an equivalently central

[4] Bell and Ibbetson, *European Legal Development*, 4, 9.

[5] Ibid., 45–50.

framing device as 'a set of beliefs and attitudes (implicit and explicit) which give meaning to and condition activity'.[6] Their framework is completed by acknowledging the importance of siting analysis in the context of related areas of the law and the broader, extra-legal environment, rejecting a closed-system view of law. This is grounded in their hypothesis that path dependency is a key explanatory factor in legal development.[7] They hypothesise that internal pressure is likely to create systems that are remarkably sticky over time, with external influence required for change. However, substantial pressure or dissonance may be needed before reaching any tipping point, and non-change may be expected as much as change.[8] As such, they suggest uncovering the extent to which legal change is driven by internal or external factors is 'perhaps the most important question' for analysis.[9]

In our context, Bell and Ibbetson make a number of substantive claims about the development of medical liability between 1850 and 2000, focusing on an Anglo-French comparison, which, in part, we contrast here. Their central characterisation was that medical liability was an area where development has been 'substantially homogeneous'.[10] Speaking of medical practitioners, they suggest:[11]

> In general, in the nineteenth century, a relatively low standard of care was demanded of them, with the result that fault was difficult to prove. Courts were reluctant to challenge professional medical opinion about appropriate treatment. A change in approach is perhaps visible in the early twentieth century, but it was difficult for plaintiffs, and for the courts, to identify what a doctor had done wrong in using the new, complex technical apparatus that was becoming available. Through the second half of the century the law was increasingly plaintiff-friendly, with far higher standards being demanded of doctors and compensation becoming more easily available.

For our purposes, the relevant developmental narratives they identify are these: in the nineteenth century, whilst French courts deferred to

[6] Ibid., 45–6, 49.

[7] Ibid., 48–9.

[8] Ibid., 48. See also D. Ibbetson, 'Comparative Legal History: A Methodology', in A. Musson and C. Stebbings (eds.), *Making Legal History Approaches and Methodologies* (Cambridge: Cambridge University Press, 2012), p. 131.

[9] Bell and Ibbetson, *European Legal Development*, 50.

[10] Ibid., 74.

[11] Ibid., 84.

expertise,[12] English courts (really, juries) remained dominant.[13] The twentieth century saw a judicially driven, mid-century shift towards medical practitioners in England, encapsulated, they claim,[14] in the decision in *Bolam*, with a pro-patient reaction emerging only towards the century's end. France, by contrast, gradually abandoned deference with an increasingly low bar for fault.[15] The drivers they identify are, in the nineteenth century, the absence of dissatisfaction with the prevailing approach alongside robust insurance-driven defence of medical cases in England, with France experiencing a single high-profile prosecution pushing medical practitioners and courts to defend the role of expertise. The twentieth century emphasises the role of particular English judges in supporting the pro-practitioner shift, as well as differences in the procedural structures with the single, court-appointed expert in France preventing the naturally adversarial approach to medical evidence characteristic in England.[16] In what follows, we suggest that quite a different English narrative is plausible. Far from any fulcrum, *Bolam* reflects a long-settled approach to medical error. The German experience offers a stark contrast, given, as our texts suggest, the two systems appear to have been diverging as early as the 1950s.

## 7.2 Unpacking an Anglo-Germanic Comparison

As Bell and Ibbetson do,[17] we assume that the law in each system played out against a similar background of increasingly institutionally centred healthcare provision despite distinct national expression. From here, we first examine, how, if at all, medical practitioners internally approached medical error and, secondly, the formal legal position leading up to our highlighted texts. The relationship between these fields is a key factor in unpacking our comparison: to what extent did each legal narrative reflect

[12] Ibid., 87–8 referencing *Besançon*, 18 December 1844, S. 1845.2.602.

[13] Ibid., 87. See also W. Swain, 'The Development of Medical Liability in England and Wales', in E. Hondius (ed.), *The Development of Medical Liability* (Cambridge: Cambridge University Press, 2010), p. 37.

[14] Ibid., 98–9, drawing on *Hunter* and *Hatcher*, as discussed later.

[15] Ibid., 101–2.

[16] Ibid., 87–8, 103–4.

[17] Bell and Ibbetson, *European Legal Development*, 85.

a medical view or, instead, develop an alternative method of defining actionable medical error?[18]

### 7.2.1 *Internal Conceptions of Medical Error*

Within medical practice, there were two distinct forums where a medically driven discourse around error could arise: emerging occupational ethical frameworks and, often related, emerging disciplinary practices.

In Germany, both settled disciplinary structures and a clear, internal concept of medical error emerged during the nineteenth century. Medical advisory bodies had predated this process,[19] but, as in Baden in 1864, fresh structures emerged to provide official advice and self-regulation, often characterised by a local medical chamber's power to enforce ethical standards.[20] Increasing desire for more rigorous controls, reflected in the 1890 platform of the *Deutscher Ärztevereinsbund*,[21] saw the introduction of formalised disciplinary structures in the shape of the medical Honour Courts (*Ehrengerichte*) and in some cases a mandated code of conduct.[22] Although not first to emerge, the Prussian experience represents the most formalised, influential model.[23] The relevant Prussian legislation, the *Ehrengerichtsgesetz* 1899, required each medical chamber to establish an Honour Court (*Ehrengericht*). Their general jurisdiction over conduct required conscientious practice and that a practitioner 'showed himself worthy of the respect that his profession demanded, in his conduct both during and outside medical practice'.[24] Punishment ranged from

[18] The value of understanding both medical regulatory and legal viewpoints is emphasised in Quick's insightful work on patient safety, see O. Quick, *Regulating Patient Safety* (Cambridge: Cambridge University Press, 2017).

[19] C. P. McGrath, *The Development of Medical Liability in Germany 1800–1945* (Frankfurt: Vittorio Klostermann, 2019), pp. 19–21.

[20] C. Huerkamp, 'The Making of the Modern Medical Profession, 1800–1914: Prussian Doctors in the Nineteenth Century', in G. Cocks and K. Jarausch (eds.), *German Professions 1800–1950* (Oxford: Oxford University Press, 1990), p. 66.

[21] Founded in 1873, the *Ärztevereinsbund* represented medical interests at a national level, drawing on the developing network of local medical chambers throughout Germany.

[22] C. Huerkamp, *Der Aufstieg der Ärzte im 19. Jahrhundert* (Göttingen: Vandenhoeck & Ruprecht, 1985), p. 270.

[23] The picture was not homogenous, with Bavaria, for example, lagging behind until 1927: T. Riotte, 'Medical Negligence in Nineteenth-Century Germany', in S. Shuttleworth, M. Dickson and E. Taylor-Brown (eds.), *Progress and Pathology: Medicine and Culture in the Nineteenth Century* (Manchester: Manchester University Press, 2020), pp. 56, 68.

[24] A.-H. Maehle, 'Professional Ethics and Discipline: The Prussian Medical Courts of Honour, 1899–1920' (1999) 34 *Medizinhistorisches Journal* 309, 320.

warnings to substantial fines and withdrawal of voting rights or even membership of the chamber, with consequences for professional advancement. The lived experience of these structures is revealing. Maehle's work on the records of these Prussian courts reveals that many actions were initiated by fellow practitioners and largely concerned matters of reputation.[25] Yet he notes that there were also cases of straightforward mistreatment or malpractice and similar archival research on other regions concurs: Riotte is correct to view these disciplinary structures as forums for regulating the *quality* of medical conduct, not simply professional standing.[26]

Echoing the court practice of seeking advice from local university law faculties,[27] matters involving medical expertise were often handled directly by local medical bodies. This created a relationship between medico-legal scholarship and legal analysis that was at least symbiotic if not actively engendering in the former a tendency towards conceptual exposition.[28] In the context of medical error, this proved particularly impactful in the wake of a cause célèbre scandal in 1811 that saw Ernst Horn dismissed from the *Charité* after a senior colleague alleged that Horn had mistreated a psychiatric patient. Although the criminal prosecution failed in this case (also known as the 'Fall Horn'), it sparked in orthodox medical practitioners a much-contested debate over the appropriate conceptual definition of medical error.[29] The old terminology of the *Kunstfehler* (loosely translatable as 'professional error' but taken as a synonym for a culpable medical error)[30] was resurrected as the focus on this debate. With legal-historical and etymological roots in the first imperial criminal code – the 1532 *Carolina*[31] – redefining what

[25] A.-H. Maehle, *Doctors, Honour and the Law: Medical Ethics in Imperial Germany* (London: Palgrave, 2009) pp. 36–8; J. Taupitz, *Die Standesordnungen der Freien Berufe: Geschichtliche Entwicklung, Funktionen, Stellung im Rechtssystem* (Berlin: De Gruyter, 1991).

[26] McGrath, *Development of Medical Liability*, 25–8.

[27] F. Wieacker, *A History of Private Law in Europe*, trans. T. Weir (Oxford: Clarendon Press, 1995), p. 137, discussing *Aktenversendungen*.

[28] C. Crawford, 'Legalizing Medicine: Early Modern Legal Systems and the Growth of Medico-Legal Knowledge', in M. Clark and C. Crawford (eds.), *Legal Medicine in History* (Cambridge: Cambridge University Press, 1994), pp. 104–6.

[29] See generally J. Krähe, *Die Diskussion um den ärztlichen Kunstfehler in der Medizin des neunzehnten Jahrhunderts* (Frankfurt: Peter Lang Verlag, 1984).

[30] Riotte, 'Medical Negligence', 59.

[31] §134 of the so-called *Carolina* provided for fines and even imprisonment for those medical practitioners whose practice was '*unfleiss*' or '*unkunst*'. The leading study remains H. Kehr, *Ärztliche Kunstfehler und missbräuchliche Heilbehandlung, Eine*

constituted a *Kunstfehler* occupied considerable debate throughout the century, 'indicative of a renegotiation of doctors' accountability'.[32] This discussion naturally found oxygen in the burgeoning German medico-legal community.[33] Whilst initially practitioners wrestled with whether, in light of medicine's and medical practice's fluidity, concrete definition was possible at all, an 1870 opinion written by the great Prussian statesman, public health expert and pathologist Rudolph Virchow ultimately proved persuasive. In Virchow's definition, a *Kunstfehler* was an infringement of the 'generally recognised rules of the medical arts'.[34] This became the settled internal view of medical error and, with the intimate procedural connections between German courts and medical expertise, this process of refinement and redefinition provided a ready organising concept of error centred on medical praxis.[35]

By contrast the formal English structures had emerged earlier, in the form of the Medical Act 1858, and, with it, the creation of what would become the General Medical Council. The Council's disciplinary power lay in controlling the Act's Register of practitioners. Hansard reveals little by way of a rationale behind this power other than, 'if they were to have a register of duly qualified practitioners, they must have some authority to supervise and control'.[36] The fount of the relevant jurisdiction was section 29, which created two open-ended offences: criminal behaviour and 'infamous conduct in any professional respect', both leading to removal from the medical register.[37] Similarly, linking criminal conviction and potential removal provided further strong incentive to avoid getting prosecuted.[38] When the Court of Appeal was called to consider the term 'infamous conduct in any professional respect' in *Allinson* v. *GCMER*,[39] Lord Esher MR emphasised not only the seriousness of

*strafrechtsdogmatische Untersuchung zu Artikel 134 der Carolina* (Marburg: Görich & Weiershäuser, 1972).

32 Riotte, 'Medical Negligence', 57.

33 Krähe, *Die Diskussion*, pp. 64 ff.

34 R. Virchow, 'Kunstfehler der Aerzte', in R. Virchow (ed.), *Gesammelte Abhandlungen aus dem Gebiete der öffentlichen Medicin und der Seuchenlehre*, vol. 2 (Berlin: August Hirschwald Verlag, 1879), p. 519.

35 McGrath, *Development of Medical Liability*, 36–9.

36 Hansard, HC, vol. 150, col. 1414 2 June 1858.

37 R. Smith, *Medical Discipline* (Oxford: Clarendon Press, 1994), p. 38.

38 Ibid., 32.

39 *Allinson* v. *GCMER* [1894] 1 QB 750.

the conduct required, but the role of intra-professional views when deciding this.[40]

As in Germany, a range of behaviours were prosecuted. The early minutes of the Disciplinary Committee of the Council suggest that 'infamous conduct' was, in practice, a catch-all. Whilst cases of so-called 'covering' were myriad – a registered practitioner permitting practice by an unregistered colleague[41] – cases of neglect are few, with only seventeen investigated between 1859 and 1930, the facts being proven in nine.[42] These records demonstrate that malpractice, as envisaged by the Council, although seldom explicit, did appear, with a typical complaint being 'gross misconduct and culpable neglect of patients'.[43] Yet Smith has identified a number of convincing difficulties in this era for the profession when looking to these structures for regulatory guidance.[44] Until 1883 the Council supplied no public written guidance on the substance of disciplinary decisions. Newspaper reports might provide a window into proceedings, but decisions were generally unreasoned and, at any rate, the press was excluded until 1864. Even when official resolutions were taken, active dissemination could be slow: Adopted in 1883, the Council's first official warning was not actually publicised until 1887.[45]

Certainly, no less than in Germany, this was also a key period for emerging ethical frameworks, with Thomas Pervical's foundational *Medical Ethics* published in 1803, followed by Jukes Styrap's effort of 1878.[46] Yet no formal, codified model resulted, with the British Medical Association declining to adopt Styrap's efforts in 1882, reducing it to informal influence only. Again, the focus was often etiquette rather than patient-centred ethical standards, but there were outliers. A century after Percival, Robert Saundby, the first chair of the British Medical Association's Central Ethical Committee, produced his popular text on

40 Ibid., 760–1.

41 The period 1859–1930 sees around seventy-five cases being investigated, with thirty-two resulting in sanction.

42 Smith, *Medical Discipline*, 102.

43 GMC, *Minutes*, 25 November 1891, 151.

44 R. Smith, 'The Development of Ethical Guidance for Medical Practitioners by the General Medical Council' (1993) 37 *Medical History* 56.

45 Ibid., 58–60.

46 P. Bartrip, 'An Introduction to Jukes Styrap's *A Code of Medical Ethics* (1878)', in R. Baker (ed.), *The Codification of Medical Morality, vol. 2: Anglo-American Medical Ethics and Medical Jurisprudence in the Nineteenth Century* (Dordrecht: Kluwer Academic Publishers, 1995), p. 145.

medical ethics. Whilst duties to the profession, its authorities and the importance of respecting the opinions of one's brethren were tackled before the duties owed to patients, he was admirably, perhaps surprisingly, patient-focused: 'the interest and advantage of *their health* should alone influence his conduct towards them'.[47] Where he directly addressed the subject of malpractice, 'happily very uncommon in this country',[48] he looked outward to the law, rather than towards any internal rubric, briefly quoting from one and then summarising another well-known contemporary decision.[49] Tellingly, he noted the contemporary American approach – never formally adopted in England – that locality was a determinant of a practitioner's standard of care, tying this standard to the practice of one's peers as well as the fact that malpractice was difficult to establish, 'except in the face of gross carelessness, drunkenness or wilful neglect'.[50] There are also reasons to think these urtexts were less self-serving than is often assumed. Maehle's recent, detailed work on the Council's regulatory jurisdiction suggests both that a clear 'ethical compass' would have been visible through its praxis and that these efforts were more cognisant of patients' interests than has previously been thought.[51] Nevertheless, it is indicative for our purposes that when faced, in 1881, with allegations concerning a negligently performed autopsy, the Council relied on their solicitor's assessment rather than any internally generated frameworks in coming to a decision.[52]

Despite the broad similarities between regulatory structures in both systems, there was, then, a key difference between the internal medical discourses. Only in Germany, in response to the *Fall Horn*, did an identifiable conceptual approach to medical error emerge. The statutory power as enacted and understood in England failed to bear equivalent fruit. Although impossible to predict at the time, this would prove decisive for explaining our initial texts.

47 R. Saundby, *Medical Ethics: A Guide to Professional Conduct*, 2nd ed. (London: Griffin, 1907), p. 2. (emphasis added).

48 Ibid., 67.

49 Ibid., 67–8, discussing *Lanphier* v. *Phipos* (1838), 8 C& P 475 and, likely, *Perionowsky* v. *Freeman* 176 Eng Rep 873 (1866).

50 Saundby, *Medical Ethics*, 68.

51 A.-H. Maehle, 'Beyond Professional Self-interest: Medical Ethics and the Disciplinary Function of the General Medical Council of the United Kingdom, 1858–1914' (2020) 33 *Social History of Medicine* 41, 42–4.

52 Ibid., 48–9, eventually acquitting the accused.

### 7.2.2 *Legal Conceptions of Medical Error*

Turning to the formal legal rules, we look for the key tipping points that mark out each system's development. Here, the narratives we identify suggest a porous, reactive rule in Germany, shifting between interpretations, and, by contrast, the early and settled success of a rule in England. The German experience has received detailed consideration elsewhere,[53] so we map the basic pattern here before turning in greater detail to the English experience, where more groundwork is required.

#### Germany: Fault through a Medical Lens

Studying private law in Germany before the *Bürgerliches Gesetzbuch* (BGB) is challenging. A patchwork of codes augmented by the *gemeines Recht* generally resulted in different approaches to fault and the basis of any action.[54] For medical liability, this challenge is pronounced, with voluminous debate over the categorisation of civil actions dominated by the much-prized-in-the-era, if admirably unclear, Roman legal inheritance. Yet, whatever approach was taken before the BGB, the abstract standard of fault was generally regarded as simple negligence even if scholarly rhetoric supporting a gross negligence standard, whether as a matter of formal law or interpretive application, persisted throughout the century.[55] The leading criminal law statutes had, by the mid-nineteenth century, settled similarly but gross negligence had often been the standard beforehand.[56] Court practice in this era reveals a clear trend in practitioners' favour on account of two interlinked factors.

First, beginning with the practice of the criminal courts, the language and conceptual logic of the *Kunstfehler* as developed by practitioners themselves filled out the abstract, codified definitions of fault. In part this was an intellectual phenomenon, as leading legal authors reacted to Horn's prosecution. In part it was a practical matter, given that the criminal law – certainly after the arrival of the *Reichsstrafgesetzbuch* in 1871 – generally provided sounder footing for prosecuting injurious

[53] See McGrath, *Development of Medical Liability*.

[54] See M. J. Schermaier, 'Zivilrechtliche Verantwortlichkeit', in M. Schmöckerl, J. Rückert and R. Zimmermann (eds.), *Historisch-kritischer Kommentar zum BGB, Band II: Schuldrecht, Allgemeiner Teil* (Tübingen: Mohr Siebeck, 2007), p. 1028. On the shifting bases see McGrath, *Development of Medical Liability*, chapters 3 and 4.

[55] F. Zimmermann, 'Ueber das Rechtsverhältnis zwischen dem Arzte und dem Patienten' (1873) 56 *Archiv für Civilistische Praxis* 222; McGrath, *Development of Medical Liability*, 125–34.

[56] McGrath, *Development of Medical Liability*, 57–67.

practice. The *Reichsstrafgesetzbuch*'s relevant provisions provided fertile ground given the relevant offences (§§ 222 and 230) tied liability to the standard expected of the defendant's 'office, profession or trade'. Equally, as the *Reichsgericht* made clear throughout the 1880s, using the *Kunstfehler* as the practical content of the legal test for medical error set orthodox practice as arbiters over their unorthodox brethren,[57] albeit, conversely mere orthodox, licensed practice granted no immunity from action per se. Virchow's language of 'recognised' rules focused the court on what was actually accepted, as demonstrated by an unsuccessful appeal to the *Reichsgericht* in 1884 that saw an orthodox practitioner sanctioned for eschewing antiseptic safeguards.[58] Whilst civil actions were generally less common in this era, the leading academic literature acknowledged the role of medical practice in defining fault, often building from the Roman foundation of *imperitia culpae adnumeratur*.[59] The same melding of medical practice and legal standards through court adoption of the *Kunstfehler* was clearly visible in civil cases towards the end of the century.[60]

Secondly, medical expert opinion was embedded within legal processes, with courts heavily reliant on expert evidence from local medical chambers or designated state bodies. This echoed the long reach of the *Carolina* model, which had relied on medical judgement to unpack the key offences in §134. The terminological and conceptual creep of the *Kunstfehler* – based on an occupationally driven, sociological standard of care – was reflected in the published official expert opinions of relevant medico-legal administrative bodies.[61] As such, even if, by the end of the century, it was settled that the formal law imposed a standard of simple negligence, in practice this would likely have indulged any practitioner viewed as having followed recognised practice.

The arrival of the BGB finally provided a settled basis – whether contractual, delictual, or both[62] – for civil actions against practitioners and appeared to drive an immediate surge of such actions in the subsequent

[57] RG. 12.04.1882, Rechtsprechung des Reichsgerichts in Strafsachen 4, 313. See also RG. 14.01.1887, Entscheidungen des Reichsgerichts in Strafsachen 15, 182.

[58] RG. 03.07.1884, *Rechtsprechung des Reichsgerichts in Strafsachen* 6, 507.

[59] B. Windscheid, *Lehrbuch des Pandektenrechts* (Düsseldorf: Buddeus, 1866), vol. 2, pt II, §401, p. 120.

[60] McGrath, *Development of Medical Liability*, 125–34.

[61] Ibid., 39–46.

[62] D. Giesen, *International Medical Malpractice Law* (Tübingen: Mohr Siebeck, 1988), pp. 16 ff.

decades. Civil fault was decisively formalised in section 276 (2) BGB as a failure to demonstrate the care required in the given circumstances: *erforderliche Sorgfalt*.[63] As its drafters had intended,[64] this somewhat elliptical phrase came to be understood as an objective test of reasonable care.[65] Yet, in applying this to medical error, both academic literature and court practice retained the nineteenth-century practice.[66] Initially at least, the *Kunstfehler* remained covalent with legal analysis. Nevertheless, the increased academic and practical attention medical liability received in the early decades of the twentieth century drove a decisive legal shift. By the 1910s, the *Reichsgericht* was emphasising that demonstrating the absence of a *Kunstfehler* did not always mean *erforderliche Sorgfalt* had been provided. The courts also began to articulate normative standards of what could be expected from medical practitioners; a much-cited 1912 decision noting that 'the most careful practitioner does not operate with the safety of a machine' – failure to abide by recognised rules was not, itself, decisive of fault.[67] Academic literature also came to reflect and amplify the growing separation, emphasising the foreign-to-law roots of the *Kunstfehler* as it had been resurrected and applied in the nineteenth century.[68] This proved to be the tipping point. Despite outliers,[69] by the 1930s one leading legal text called openly to abandon the concept of the *Kunstfehler* altogether.[70] Whilst courts eschewed doing so, a series of decisions confirmed beyond doubt that the legal concept of fault, as set out in section 276 (2) BGB, provided the ultimate measure of medical conduct; putting it simply, 'not every *Kunstfehler* is a fault, and not every fault is a *Kunstfehler*'.[71] It may, of

[63] Schermaier, 'Zivilrechtliche Verantwortlichkeit', 1063 ff.

[64] N. Jansen, 'The Doctrinal Development of Fault in Germany 1850–2000', in N. Jansen (ed.), *The Development and Making of Legal Doctrine* (Cambridge: Cambridge University Press, 2010), p. 117.

[65] E. Rabel, *Die Haftpflicht des Arztes* (Leipzig: Veit, 1904), p. 11; and M. Rümelin, *Haftung in Klinischen Betrieb* (Tübingen: Mohr Siebeck, 1913), p. 2. This objectivisation has continued into recent decades, see C. Katzenmeier, *Arzthaftung* (Tübingen: Mohr Siebeck, 2002), p. 274.

[66] Rabel, *Haftpflicht*, 36–9; RG 14.03.1911 *Seufferts Archiv* 67, p. 102; RG 04.07.1916, noted in L. Ebermayer, *Der Arzt im Recht* (Leipzig: Georg Thieme, 1930), p. 136.

[67] RG. 01.03.1912 *Entscheidungen des Reichgerichts in Zivilsachen* 78, p. 435.

[68] McGrath, *Development of Medical Liability*, 171.

[69] K. Haberland, 'Ärztliche Kunstfehler', *Juristische Wochenschrift* (5–12 November 1932), 3304.

[70] F. König and H. Köstlin, *Haftpflicht des Arztes* (Leipzig: J. A. Barth, 1937).

[71] RG 12.05.1931, (1931) 7 *Höchstrichterliche Rechtsprechung* 1748; RG 23.02.1934; RG 08.02.1934, (1934) 10 *Höchstrichterliche Rechtsprechung* 786.

course, have been the case that, in practice, evidence of a *Kunstfehler* would often settle the matter,[72] but the converse had ceased to reliably hold.

Two important dynamics appear to have driven this decoupling process. The first was the willingness of the courts to de-emphasise the universal relevance of medical expertise. Not every clinical activity in relation to a patient was such that only medical opinion could assess it.[73] The second was that where there was significant divergence in the literature or, indeed, no settled practice at all,[74] courts exercised their own authority to set normative standards.[75] That the context for many key early twentieth-century decisions was the use of novel technologies or surgical advances suggests that increasingly scientific, technical medical practice in fact undermined the authority that practitioners had enjoyed in the nineteenth century.[76] By the time the new post-war state was established, then, and our 1952 decision arrived, German courts had ably defined and defended their own conceptual and – albeit slowly – normative view of acceptable medical conduct, distinct from medical views of the same.

## England: Medical Pluralism and Legal Dominance

More space must be given to the English narrative since we differ from Bell and Ibbetson's account of the developmental pattern in this respect. We begin with a reassessment of how the nineteenth-century law treated medical authority in negligence actions, before suggesting key reasons to think this approach ultimately remained undisturbed well into the twentieth century.

Although lacking the bookend of codification, the nineteenth century was an equally important formative period as negligence settled into a recognisably modern form during an era replete with malpractice claims. Four early decisions clarified two key doctrinal matters.[77] First, patients had a freestanding action in tort. Second, whether tortious or contractual, the default obligation was the same: reasonable care. As for the substance

72 As emphasised in RG. 08.02.1934, (1934) 10 *Höchstrichterliche Rechtsprechung* 786.

73 McGrath, *Development of Medical Liability*, 180–3.

74 RG 09.07.1913, *Entscheidungen des Reichgerichts in Zivilsachen* 83, 75.

75 RG 12.10.1934, (1935) 64 *Juristische Wochenschrift* 115; RG 04.02.1938, (1938) 67 *Juristische Wochenschrift* 1246.

76 McGrath, *Development of Medical Liability*, 197 ff., examining the role of X-rays, diathermy and techniques to avoid the retention of foreign objects after surgery.

77 *Seare* v. *Prentice* (1807) 8 East 348; *Pippin* v. *Sheppard* (1822) 11 Price 400 *Lanphier* v. *Phipos* (1838) 8 C&P 475; *Gladwell* v. *Steggall* (1839) 5 Bingham NC 736.

of fault, whilst the language of 'grossness' occasionally snuck in,[78] the keystone direction from Tindal CJ in *Lanphier* v. *Phipos* confirmed the expected standard of care was simple negligence.[79] A practitioner could not be damned simply because another, or they themselves, could have performed better; the question was, as Erle CJ put it, whether there was 'a competent degree of skill and knowledge'.[80] Certainly the language of 'ordinary' or 'common' care or skill was also often deployed,[81] but whether this spoke to juries setting the standard for themselves, or a standard that reflected settled medical practice is the decisive question.

As in Germany, it could certainly feel like the latter to *irregular* practitioners. In *Ruddock* v. *Lowe*,[82] the defendant represented himself as a member of the Royal College of Physicians and a 'master in the art of healing sexual disorders', treating the plaintiff's ills with mercury pills on an ongoing, lucrative basis. Sickening further, the plaintiff approached an orthodox practitioner who realised the problem and, appearing in the plaintiff's favour, deemed the treatment entirely improper. Unable to lead experts in defence, liability resulted. In *Jones* v. *Fay*,[83] a chemist without licence from the then Society of Apothecaries was alleged to have prescribed and peddled patent pills to the patient. Predictably, these were a healthy dose of mercury, not, as claimed, rhubarb. As Pigott B. directed the jury, medical evidence revealed such continuous dosing to be improper, leaving only the only question whether Fay had so acted; liability ensued. The same dynamic appeared in the criminal law.[84] Occupational status was irrelevant to the abstract standard required,[85] but, in practice, that standard looked to expert evidence of orthodox practice; indeed, 'meddling with things above his reach' might be enough itself to suggest negligence.[86]

78 See the contrast of 'gross ignorance and want of skill' with negligence in *Seare*.

79 *Lanphier* v. *Phipos*, 475; Bell and Ibbetson, *European Legal Development*, 86–7. See generally D. Ibbetson, 'The Tort of Negligence in the Common Law', in E. Schrage (ed.), *Negligence: The Comparative Legal History of the Law of Torts* (Berlin: Duncker & Humboldt, 1992), pp. 230–2.

80 *Rich* v. *Pierpont* (1862) 3 F&F 40.

81 Alongside *Seare* and *Rich* see also *Hall* v. *Semple* 1862 3 F&F 337; *Perionowsky* v. *Freeman* (1866) 4 F&F 977.

82 *Ruddock* v. *Lowe* 4 F&F 519; 176 ER 672, p. 673.

83 *Jones* v. *Fay* 4 F&F 525; 176 ER 675.

84 *Tessymond's Case* (1828) 1 Lewin 169; 168 ER 1000.

85 *R* v. *St John Long* (1830) 4 C&P 404; ER 759.

86 *R* v. *Markuss* (1864) 358 ER 599.

Turning to orthodox practitioners, where civil actions were the norm, Bell and Ibbetson – as does Swain[87] – suggest that the nineteenth century saw civil juries policing medical error in what amounted to ongoing lay scrutiny.[88] This sets the scene for their characterisation of McNair J's. jury direction in *Bolam* with which we started as an interpretive shift *in its own moment.*[89] Viewed as such, *Bolam* represents a bold mid-century judicial assertion of medical control over the legal assessment of medical error in contrast to such lay scrutiny: essentially one could not be found negligent where one's practice accorded with that accepted by others. By contrast, we suggest that whilst the civil jury's persistence into the first half of the twentieth century should not be overlooked – the formal finding lay with them where present – it goes altogether too far to suggest juries routinely engaged in such policing.[90] A recent and admirably comprehensive survey of relevant nineteenth-century decisions by Stein et al. reveals that not only did an unopposed expert always carry the day, but where, as became common, both sides led expert evidence, the practitioner won three in four cases in that period, with effectively no losses after 1866.[91] Although the jury was institutionally unavoidable, any role as a counterbalance or check on accepted practice appears doubtful when actual jury practice is accounted for.

We expand on this survey with a brief case study from a leading medico-legal text of the era. Drawing on overlooked periodical reports, it provides a compelling insight into the reception by medical practitioners of contemporary court practice concerning competing claims of medical expertise in negligence cases. In the first edition of his seminal treatise, *A Manual of Medical Jurisprudence*, in 1844, Taylor suggested that the disputes inherent in medical pluralism were frequently kept from court only by coroners, and was disdainful that it might appear 'as if the whole duty of a medical jurist consisted in his making the best of a case, on the side for which he happens to be engaged'.[92] He suggested courts instead required an authoritative board,

[87] Swain, 'Development of Medical Liability in England and Wales', 37 and 42.

[88] Bell and Ibbetson, *European Legal Development*, 87.

[89] Ibid., 98–9.

[90] Jury directions less focused on 'customary' care also appeared in the period: as in Tindal CJ's choice of 'reasonable and proper degree of care' in *Lanphier* v. *Phipos* (1838) 8 C&P 475, 479.

[91] M. A. Stein, C. P. Guzelian and K. M. Guzelian, 'Expert Testimony in Nineteenth Century Malapraxis Actions' (2015) 55 *American Journal of Legal History* 194, 195–6, 206.

[92] A. S. Taylor, *A Manual of Medical Jurisprudence* (London: Churchill, 1844), p. 361.

modelled on the Trinity Assessors, to adjudicate such disputes.[93] By 1846, reflecting his understanding of the law, a more nuanced view emerged: 'All that appears to be expected is a reasonable accordance in treatment with received professional doctrines'.[94] Two decisions in the interim underpinned his view. In the first, *Gibbs* v. *Tunaley*,[95] Parke B's direction, undisturbed by Tindal CJ on appeal, suggested that a defendant 'country practitioner' would not be held to the standard of an urban practitioner but 'the usual and ordinary amount of skill and care and attention which it was only reasonable to suppose he would possess'. The second, *Baker* v. *Lowe*, overlooked by later legal scholars, squarely engaged the issue.[96] Extensively reported in the medical and wider press, the case saw the surgeon-plaintiff countersued for malpractice. Captain Lowe alleged that Baker's negligent treatment of a gangrenous (or, gouty, as the *Times* opined)[97] toe required later amputation of the entire foot. The case directly raised the relevance of competing medical views of appropriate practice and their relation to fault. Eminent witnesses were led by both sides, including, for Baker, Robert Liston, who had conducted the amputation.[98] Depending on one's view, Baker's stimulating practice was either 'proper in such a case' or 'totally improper'.[99] Following Lord Denman's suggestion that it was hardly possible to do otherwise, Baker was acquitted. Wondering, not unjustly, 'Who shall decide when doctors (or surgeons) disagree?', the *Times* concluded: 'Not our humble selves certainly', doubting the jury would be any wiser.[100] Later public correspondence from Liston reported nineteen in twenty practitioners would have adopted Baker's course, given its endorsement in leading surgical works.[101] The public spectacle of expert against expert attracted criticism,[102] along with the mores of those willing to

93 Ibid., 361 and 404.

94 A. S. Taylor, *A Manual of Medical Jurisprudence*, 2nd ed. (London: Churchill, 1846), p. 361; consistent with his later works: A. S. Taylor, *The Principles and Practice of Medical Jurisprudence* (London: Churchill, 1865), pp. 502–3.

95 *Gibbs* v. *Tunaley* 1 CB 640; 135 ER 692, noted in Taylor, *A Manual*, 360.

96 Taylor, *A Manual* (1846), 360–1.

97 'Medical Testimony', *Times*, 18 February 1845, p. 8.

98 'Court of Queen's Bench', *John Bull*, 15 February 1845, p. 108; 'Medical Testimony' (1845) *London Medical Gazette*, NS vol. 1, p. 683.

99 'Medical Testimony', *Times*, 17 February 1845, p. 8.

100 'Medical Testimony', *Times*, 18 February 1845, p. 8.

101 'Court of Queen's Bench', *The Lancet*, 22 February 1845 (1121), 217; A rather more blunt view was taken in the *Gazette*: 'both these sets of witnesses could not have been in the right', (1845) *London Medical Gazette*, vol. 36, pt. 1, p. 127.

102 'Medical Testimony', (1845) *London Medical Gazette*, NS vol. 1, p. 683.

appear against a fellow practitioner.[103] Yet the principle Taylor drew from *Baker* remained in his work throughout the nineteenth century without question or contradiction. As Stein et al note, Taylor may have been drawing on his own view that medicine, as an art, lacked universal standards – thus the accepted custom of a given practice was the relevant measure of it – but whilst a more rigorous scientific counterpoint to this epistemic position would emerge over the nineteenth century,[104] Taylor's own casuistry drew from *Baker* an equivalent principle which not only pre-dates *Bolam* by over a century but, as the survey results suggest, fits convincingly with the reality of how civil claims for malpractice were handled throughout the nineteenth century.

What of other factors in the era? On the view presented here, any assumption that the Medical Act 1858 marked an important break in developments here must be suspect given *Baker* preceded it by thirteen years;[105] and that, in the Medical Act 1858, expert medical authority was reinforced to the favour of the registered, rather than suddenly, starkly immunised from scrutiny. Equally, whilst Bell and Ibbetson are surely correct that the arrival of the Medical Defence Union (MDU) in 1885 provided crucial practical support for maligned practitioners, it came too late to supress the type of litigation that would force courts to confront the relevance of accepted medical practice(s). As *Baker* suggests, organisations like the MDU arrived into, and could rely on, a climate in which the law already favoured practitioners compliant with accepted practice rather than acting as a tipping point in preventing a slide towards a more patient-friendly standard.[106]

If, then, the nineteenth century was an era in which, in reality, the standard of care closely tracked accepted medical practice, is there anything to suggest that juries in the early twentieth century had become more dominant such that *Bolam*, later, would represent a shift in the law? A comprehensive survey of the cases to 1957 lies beyond what can be explored here, but we nevertheless identify four plausible grounds to suggest the nineteenth-century model we have established here continued undisturbed up to *Bolam*.

[103] 'Baker versus Lowe', (1845) *London Medical Gazette*, NS vol. 1, p. 733; 'The Case of Baker v Lowe', *The Lancet*, 22 February 1845 (1121), p. 223.
[104] Stein et al., 'Expert Testimony', 201–2.
[105] Ibid., 206, drawing on Bell and Ibbetson, *European Legal Development*, 89.
[106] Bell and Ibbetson, *European Legal Development*, 88.

First, although much of the systematising legal literature around this period lacks specific discussion of medical negligence, the difficulties posed by competing medical narratives are reflected in one influential work. The first edition of Beven, in 1889,[107] acknowledged this challenge and emphasised the need to rely on expert evidence in response, remaining consistent into the early twentieth century.[108] If a defendant diverged from the majority view, the question became whether they were a 'scientific inquirer, possessed of the principles of a system and practicing them . . . or a mere ignorant pretender' – a question left, naturally, to medical evidence.[109] From the third edition, in 1908, he emphasised that novel treatments should not be regarded as negligent per se, suggesting recognition of the need to protect a space for reasoned medical practice and again relying on whether this was a *systematic* practice.[110]

Secondly, as Bell and Ibbetson note, there is strong doctrinal coherence between *Bolam* and surrounding case law.[111] Certainly, the idea that *Bolam* set out any novel proposition appears odd. Both *Hatcher* v. *Black* and *Hunter* v. *Hanley* had earlier emphasised a standard of care linked to accepted practice. In *Hatcher*, setting aside Denning LJ's rhetorical flourishes,[112] the decisive nature of professional opinion in relation to both claims was clear. Of the advice, 'the law did not condemn the doctor when he only did what a wise doctor would do'.[113] Of the treatment, 'the doctors for the plaintiff, and all the doctors had said it was a well-known hazard in such an operation, notwithstanding all care'.[114] *Hanley* – deployed in *Bolam* to emphasise the importance of respecting medical pluralism[115] – likewise adopted a sociological approach to the standard of care, at least in cases, as Lord President

107 T. Beven, *Principles of the Law of Negligence* (London: Stevens, 1889), p. 827.

108 T. Beven, *Negligence in Law*, 3rd ed., vol. 2 (London: Stevens, 1908), p. 1157; T. Beven, *Negligence in Law*, 4th ed., vol. 2 (London: Stevens, 1928), p. 1354.

109 Beven, *Principles* (1889), 828; see later, Beven, *Negligence* (1928), 1355.

110 Indeed, Beven viewed the real issue here as being whether the patient had been informed of any novel risks, Beven, *Negligence* (1908), 1162.

111 Bell and Ibbetson, *European Legal Development*, 89–99; Swain 'Development of Medical Liability in England and Wales', 42.

112 Swain, 'Development of Medical Liability in England and Wales', 27.

113 *Hatcher* v. *Black*, *The Times*, 2 July 1954. As Dr Black later put it: 'It was the sort of thing which, in the circumstances, nine out of ten doctors would have said', *Hatcher* v. *Black*, *The Times*, 30 June 1954.

114 *Hatcher* v. *Black*, *The Times*, 2 July 1954.

115 *Bolam* v. *Friern Hospital Management Committee* [1957] 1 WLR 582, 587. Following Salmond, *Hanley* assumed English and Scots law were aligned, see R. F. V. Heuston, *Salmond on the Law of Torts*, 11th ed. (London: Sweet & Maxwell, 1953), p. 511.

Clyde put it, concerning 'deviation from ordinary professional practice'.[116] In laying the boundaries of fault, accepted practice, and departures from it, were to be assessed by asking what it was medical professionals actually did.

Thirdly, this was not merely a directly contemporary phenomenon around *Bolam*; equivalent propositions are visible earlier in the century. In the *Vancouver General Hospital* decision, the Board agreed that, 'A defendant charged with negligence can clear his feet if he shows that he has acted in accord with a general and approved practice'.[117] This was adopted in the Court of Appeal the following year by Maugham LJ in *Marshall* v. *Lindsey County Council*:[118]

> An act cannot, in my opinion, be held to be due to a want of reasonable care if it is in accordance with the general practice of mankind. What is reasonable in a world not wholly composed of wise men and women must depend on what people presumed to be reasonable constantly do.

*Marshall* – the final authority at play in *Bolam* – was a potentially controversial decision, in part because of the spectre of broadened liability for hospitals.[119] Despite efforts in the House of Lords to re-cast the claim as not concerning medical expertise,[120] *Marshall*'s focus on a direct duty owed by the defendant itself makes it difficult to simply dismiss its relevance to core medical behaviour as contingent or mistaken.[121] Indeed, although dissenting on the point, Maugham LJ's view found support from Lord Russell on appeal,[122] and would later be cited approvingly by the House of Lords in *Whiteford* v. *Hunter*, which again directly raised the issue of medical pluralism and approved practice (the defendant surgeon winning).[123]

116 *Hunter* v. *Hanley* [1955] SC 200, 206.

117 *The Vancouver General Hospital* v. *McDaniel* [1934] UKPC 60, 5; *The Times*, 28 July 1934, per Lord Alness.

118 *Marshall* v. *Lindsey County Council* [1935] 1 KB 516, 540.

119 P. Mitchell, 'The Impact of Institutions and Professions on Fault Liability in England', in P. Mitchell (ed.), *The Impact of Institutions and Professions on Legal Development* (Cambridge: Cambridge University Press, 2012), p. 24.

120 *County Council of the Parts of Lindsey, Lincolnshire* v. *Marshall* [1937] AC 97. Most clear per Lord Macmillan at 119 but see also Viscount Sankey at 117; see also Roche LJ in the Court of Appeal at 556.

121 See H. Teff, *Reasonable Care* (Oxford: Clarendon Press, 1994), p. 179, n. 25, suggesting such dicta were alternatively justified in general terms beyond professional custom. Yet a close reading of Maugham LJ's judgment reveals he is entirely consistent in treating a question he did not view as a medical matter as one judged by 'good sense' rather than medical expertise, where, instead, he relied on *Vancouver*, at 541–2.

122 *Lindsey County Council* v. *Marshall* [1937] AC 97, 117.

123 *Whiteford* v. *Hunter* (1950) 94 SJ 758.

Juries, no doubt, prevented adherence to approved practice inevitably defeating a claim,[124] but, certainly given the nineteenth-century experience they were building on, these cases cannot be dismissed as mere outliers in the era and suggest an unbroken chain from the nineteenth century.

Finally, immediately preceding *Bolam* itself, Nathan's 1957 volume – the first serious attempt to systematise the law on medical negligence – adopted a practitioner-focused approach to fault when discussing the standard of care. Not only did this reference occupational rather than lay views in parsing the required degree of skill and care ('what is reasonably to be expected from the ordinarily competent practitioner of his class'),[125] but, citing *Vancouver* and *Whiteford* in support, he bluntly stated both: 'A practitioner cannot therefore be held negligent if he follows what is the general and approved practice in the situation', and, where there were different recognised approaches, one 'cannot be held negligent because he chooses one rather than the other'.[126] Nathan conceded that the ultimate decision lay with the courts (no mention of the jury) not the profession – customary practice could not obviate obvious risks – but could show no English authority for that proposition in practice.[127] Nathan's view was consistent with Salmond's – cited by Lord President Clyde in *Hunter* – who expressly endorsed the standard as that which could reasonably be expected from a 'normally skilful member of the profession',[128] and the approach adopted in *Vancouver* and *Whiteford*.[129] Perhaps unsurprisingly then, for all its later controversy, McNair J's direction in *Bolam* was met with an almost complete lack of surprise in both the medical and legal literature.[130] Had it truly marked a tipping point, one might have expected otherwise.

124 Teff, *Reasonable Care*, 179. See Bell and Ibbetson, *European Legal Development*, 99–100.

125 R. Nathan, *Medical Negligence Being the Law of Negligence in Relation to the Medical Profession and Hospitals* (London: Butterworth, 1957), p. 22.

126 Ibid., 25–6, 29.

127 Ibid., 26, instead citing *Anderson* v. *Chasney* [1949] 4 DLR 71 and *Van Wyk* v. *Lewis* [1924] App D 438. McNair J equally lacked English authority on the same point in *Bolam*. See also A. McCoid, 'The Care Required of Medical Practitioners' (1959) 12 *Vanderbilt Law Review* 549, 598: 'it appears that the standard throughout is largely one established by the profession itself'.

128 Salmond, *Torts*, 511.

129 Ibid., 509 n. (i); 510 n. (m).

130 Bell and Ibbetson, *European Legal Development*, 99; Swain, 'Development of Medical Liability in England and Wales', 43–6.

## 7.3 Assessing the Methodology of Legal Development

We conclude our analysis by asking three questions: What narrative emerges for each system? What does comparison reveal about the drivers of development behind our initial texts? Finally, what insights does Bell and Ibbetson's developmental focus provide for the methodology of comparative law?

Beginning with Germany, we suggest a three-stage process produced the Bundesgerichtshof's robustly pro-patient orientation. First, a settled definition of medical error was developed in medical circles. Second, this preceded key legal sources and was adopted as an interpretive lens for these sources. Third, as the law gained confidence, that reception came, like an unwelcome grain of sand, to be (r)ejected. By contrast, the English model is less a matter of influence shifting between actors, but, rather, the stately progression of an early settled model whereby the law captured the ground for defining and regulating medical error. *Baker* v. *Lowe*'s treatment in medical literature and the reality of court practice suggests that the rule later clearly framed in *Bolam* had, in fact, long been in place. The jury recedes from its suggested role as a robust check on medical practice and Denning LJ's pronouncements reflect continuing rather than novel or distinctive judicial attitudes.

In comparing these narratives, not only is the pattern of development different in each system, but the influence of particular elements clearly differs between the systems, ultimately resulting in our initial texts. In Germany, there was a shift away from a pro-practitioner interpretation towards a pro-patient one. In England, the development was that there was no change, at least to 1957. The crucial explanatory feature behind each of our initial texts, we suggest, is the external context in each system. Orthodox German medical practice, by providing courts with a concept to eventually orient themselves *against*, created space for an alternative, judicially driven conception of fault to flourish, downplaying the role of accepted practice. The absence of any such external pressure in England allowed legal conceptions of fault to dominate, with the practical result that the challenge of assessing medical pluralism had been internalised as early as the mid-nineteenth century as a matter of deference to accepted practice. As such, the law-in-practice continued to provide little solace to injured patients, with Denning LJ's ruminations and the historical record of jury practice suggesting little countervailing internal pressure in any case.[131] Bell

[131] A renowned comparative medical lawyer still felt, in 1988, that 'English courts appear to be coloured by a markedly deferential attitude towards the medical profession', D. Giesen, *International Medical Malpractice Law* (Tübingen: Mohr Siebeck, 1988), xi.

and Ibbetson's own Anglo-French comparison ultimately locates little change in the formulation or operation of the law, but far greater plasticity in how the simple rule – liability requires fault – was interpreted in each system.[132] Although individual explanatory features reflect a unique developmental path within each system, they conclude the patterns of development were 'substantially homogenous'.[133] By contrast, at least in the timeframe we have focused on here and allowing for the alternative narrative of the English sources we have constructed, the developmental paths, their drivers and their consequences lack such homogeneity.

Finally, we reflect on Bell and Ibbetson's methodology of studying comparative legal development as it generates insights for future comparatists. From our study here, we suggest three points emerge as essential.

The first is the importance of selecting the level of abstraction at which development is viewed. As noted, our conclusion differs from theirs. We suggest neither homogeneity of developmental patterns, nor homogeneity of influence by particular elements. For Bell and Ibbetson, studying legal development may uncover processes of both convergence and divergence. Indeed, it may be that the one is balanced by the other.[134] Here, they might respond that the locus of change in both our systems – the interpretation of the fault rule – is similar and that the fact each system deployed simple fault liability suggests a measure of convergence. This is, of course, correct, but highlights that the same set of narratives may plausibly be viewed at different levels of abstraction, what Bell and Ibbetson describe as the 'big picture' of comparison between systems may differ, as we suggest here, from detailed examination of the relevant rules in operation.[135] Clarifying the goal of comparing developmental patterns is thus important in that this allows the researcher to identify and justify the most relevant level of abstraction, a task equivalent to the challenge of how comparatists identify similarity at all.[136] Equally, concluding that systems share similar or contrasting developmental patterns at whatever level of abstraction tells us nothing per se about what drove those patterns. That provides the crucial insight into the inertial forces within any legal system in relation to its comparators but is not itself a necessary

[132] Bell and Ibbetson, *European Legal Development*, 36, 170.

[133] Ibid., 70, 156.

[134] Ibid., 172.

[135] Ibid., 153.

[136] G. Dannemann, 'Comparative Law: Study of Similarities or Differences?', in M. Reimann and R. Zimmermann (eds.), *The Oxford Handbook of Comparative Law*, 2nd ed. (Oxford: Oxford University Press, 2019), p. 390.

question to draw a fruitful conclusion, even if analysis will undoubtedly be enriched by making those connections.

The second is the importance of external, non-legal factors in driving legal change. In part this reflects Bell and Ibbetson's position on law as an open system, but in their conception, this distinction also carries normative weight, at least in the context of tort. A key insight of their work is that change driven by 'purely internal mechanisms' tended, without common influence, towards divergence between systems, while changes as a 'response to the external environment' tended towards functional convergence of legal outcomes, albeit leavened with a degree of divergence in how each system expresses this.[137] The idea of functional similarity and the '(in)famous' presumption of substantive similarity in outcomes has long dogged comparative legal analysis.[138] Although Michaels counsels that similarity between two solutions should be understood as pertaining only to their *function* as responses to common problems, Bell and Ibbetson's conclusion certainly suggests something more radical in that their definition of converging developmental patterns requires that they broadly reach the same substantive position, even with 'divergence at the level of the law in the books',[139] and not necessarily in the same timeframe. Certainly, there is no methodological presumption of developmental similarity at play,[140] but their suggestion that European systems have largely responded in similar ways to common external pressures is nevertheless striking given the scepticism occasioned by Zweigert and Kötz's original claim.[141] Applied to our own study, certainly the importance of external factors vindicates the need to account for the influence (or not) of the extra-legal environment in seeking to explain legal development. Rather than a common external influence, our comparison reveals there was a unique feature of the German experience that underpins our initial, divergent texts, suggesting that a granular understanding of the relevant external social context may sometimes be (exhaustingly!) necessary. What mattered was not,

[137] Ibid., 172–3.

[138] R. Michaels, 'The Functional Method of Comparative Law', in Reimann and Zimmermann, *Oxford Handbook*, 375.

[139] Bell and Ibbetson, *European Legal Development*, 179; generally 173–8.

[140] Indeed both clarify there is no deterministic theory on offer, only a methodology for studying legal development and the insights that draws in any given situation, Bell and Ibbetson, *European Legal Development*, 183; Ibbetson, 'Comparative Legal History', 134.

[141] K. Zweigert and H. Kötz, *An Introduction to Comparative Law*, 3rd ed., trans. Tony Weir (Oxford: Clarendon Press, 1998), p. 40.

adopting a broader view, the fact that modern medical practice emerged within each system in a similar period, it was the manner in which it did so and the decisive interest shown in Germany to matters of medical error that provided this vital external influence.

The third is the importance of legal culture and path dependency as explanations for legal change. Bell and Ibbetson concede that external factors cannot bring about legal change automatically.[142] A legally relevant individual or institution must be receptive or responsive to external stimulus. Indeed, the absence of such may lead to a lag in the law's response despite a common external driver. Once attention shifts to the law's response, as it must for lawyers seeking to explain legal development, they suggest that this will be governed primarily by established frameworks and habitual modes of analysis and categorisation: path dependency.[143] In adapting path dependency as an analytical framework for assessing legal development, they emphasise both the manifold focal points of legal decision-making and, as a result, the potentially under-appreciated extent to which change – rather than inertia – is possible, as well as the importance of conscious decision-making within institutional frameworks. From this, they draw two insights. One, a scepticism that legal development will naturally be smooth or incremental. The other, the challenge of identifying how and why any legal system *in a given moment* was open to influence from the extra-legal environment, viewing these tipping points as a set of interlocking responses rather than a purely unidirectional influence. Here, they hypothesise that court-driven systems such as the English common law may struggle to reach a tipping point, given the 'relative paucity' of legal formants, in contrast to systems that admit a broader range of formants.[144] Applied to our study, the overall picture is, by contrast, one of relatively smooth development in each system. In Germany, the pendulum may have swung from one interpretation to another but that process was a gradual steady eclipsing rather than an instantaneous jolt. Far from a paradigm shift, something more Darwinian, incremental (almost common-lawyerly) is revealed. The English narrative, is, on our account, defined by its stately

[142] Bell and Ibbetson, *European Legal Development*, 164, 176.

[143] Ibid., 24–32, 179. They suggest a path-dependent response for law might involve continuing with a welcome outcome, rather than the persistence of an inefficient or inapt outcome.

[144] Ibid., 165 and 3, drawing on R. Sacco, 'Legal Formants: A Dynamic Approach to Comparative Law' (1991) 39 *American Journal of Comparative Law* 1.

continuity. The fact that the law in both systems was so heavily case-driven and focused on interpreting a formally static rule plausibly explains the shared smoothness of these patterns. We have proposed that our initial texts can ultimately be explained by key differences in the extra-legal environment, but this is not enough to explain why in the moment this driver proved decisive. We suggest that it was the coincidence of the extra-legal discourse that developed in the aftermath of Dr Horn's prosecution with an era where German legal rules, institutions and legal culture were unsettled and open to influence that proved key. This set the stage for the later rejection of that discourse by a proudly legal conception of error.[145] Here path dependency pushed the legal view of error to assert itself in opposition to the previously internalised medical one. By contrast, both the absence of a competing, adoptable external discourse in England, and the presence of a settled legal framework that empowered accepted medical practice closed English law to any such influence, allowing the nineteenth century approach to progress, unhindered and path dependently, into the twentieth.

## 7.4 Conclusion

It is hoped that by turning attention to a system that was not considered by Bell and Ibbetson themselves we have achieved three things. The first is that we have provided a novel perspective on the ever-relevant topic of medical liability. The second is to have provided a plausible reframing of the relevant English sources and, in doing so, to have offered a persuasive counterweight to the notion that developmental homogeneity should be expected in the medical context, albeit as yet unexplored comparisons between further systems may enrich this broader debate. Finally, by reflecting on the model of studying legal development that Bell and Ibbetson adopted themselves, we have been able to develop and draw insights from their work in the hope that it will see fruitful use by other, future scholars of comparative law.

***

Having begun with a pair of texts, then, we end similarly, and personally. Time spent with John always emphasised to me that the law could only

[145] Bell and Ibbetson, *European Legal Development*, 88, noting the influence of the cause célèbre of the decision in *Hélie*.

be understood in the context of the world around it. This enterprise was not simply an intellectual pursuit, but often the practical reality of any given day. A stand-out memory in this regard, long cherished, is of a train trip to a conference with the man who would go on to become both my supervisor and mentor. Noting that the journey would be long, and that a change of reading material might be required, John produced the following from his briefcase: a doctoral thesis on French public law and that year's volume of Wisden, settling himself at ease with both as if that combination was the most natural thing in the world, which of course, for John, it was.

# 8

## Roundabout Law

MATTHEW DYSON

One of the most enduring intellectual threads I have picked up by learning from and working with John is the importance of how law is framed in the minds of legal actors. His approach to law itself spans many disciplines and discourses, but even if we just select one, and a largely doctrinal and technical one, the issue of framing is particularly revealing. A framework might develop from many places, such as a statutory or case law regime, or from how legal actors deal with a specific fact pattern in one area of law rather than another. A framework for approaching conflict and, over time, for managing legal change, is particularly important. This also links to John's leading work on path dependency: how legal actors can focus only on known forms of reasoning and solutions, closing down the routes into and out of legal rule-perceiving and rule-making.[1] What makes understanding reality even more difficult is the interaction between more than one legal framework, and that particularly comes down to the junctions between ideas and, indeed, legal systems.

This chapter will explore one particular junction, and starts from a mundane example drawn from the law relating to road traffic, an area I have had the pleasure of working on with John. And as John himself well knows,[2] the journey between Oxford and Cambridge might make one queasy for one simple reason: there are up to eighteen roundabouts, especially concentrated around Milton Keynes. I learnt this the hard way on my first research visit to Oxford in 2006. That was also around the time an introduction by John and David Ibbetson led me to spend some months at the Max Planck Institute for Foreign and Comparative Private

With particular thanks to David Ibbetson, Liz Fisher and, of course, for the inspiration, John Bell.

[1] See e.g. J. Bell, 'Path Dependence and Legal Development' (2012–13) 87 *Tulane Law Review* 787.

[2] Whether via the University of Leeds or otherwise.

Law in Hamburg. Of the many things I learnt in Hamburg, the most mundane was that there are few roundabouts in Germany.[3] That observation inspires this study on legal reasoning in general, and domestic law, comparative law and legal development in particular.

This chapter identifies and explores what I am calling 'roundabout reasoning', a process to resolve potential conflict between two or more objects by (a) a simple method of sequencing their consideration; (b) where actors apply it autonomously; and (c) consideration takes place through a neutral third space without reference to earlier states. Thinking through how such quotidian matters might unlock insights into legal reasoning highlights the value in studying legal frameworks. We can draw out insights about how mechanisms to resolve legal contradiction work, particularly how underlying unity of purpose can be found in otherwise conflicting objectives.

The chapter will:

1. briefly set out the road junction example that inspired this chapter;
2. set out roundabout reasoning as a development from more basic junctions;
3. apply roundabout reasoning within a comparative law setting;
4. apply roundabout reasoning domestically; and
5. apply roundabout reasoning in the context of legal development.

## 8.1 A Comparison with *Rechts vor Links*

First, we will start with a methodological assumption: that roads and road junctions are generally used in broadly similar ways, by similar vehicles, for similar purposes in Germany as compared to England. Matters such as which side of the road is driven on, and restrictions on vehicles, speeds, insurance and licensed users might be significant differences for some issues, but not for the basic premise of transportation by road. Within that usage, the function of a junction is to allow two paths to join and, where there is a potential conflict of use, to resolve it safely and efficiently. The right to proceed on the road and across the junction is a limited resource which more than one vehicle might wish to access at the same time. The different forms of junctions vary in their mechanisms and as to the relevance of decision-making and skill by the user. But the

[3] www.ruhr-uni-bochum.de/verkehrswesen/download/literatur/Brilon_roundabouts_2011_05_29_cit.pdf

user should always be able to know what the rule is, and any mechanism involved in the application of the rule should, if it fails, fail in a way that is safe. We start by considering unmarked junctions.

Germany employs a simple rule at small junctions where there are no other markings: *rechts vor links*. The vehicle on the right has priority over the vehicle to the left. This can be found in Regulation 8(1) of the General Road Traffic Regulations, Straßenverkehrs-Ordnung (StVO).[4] There are many such junctions, and the rule is very well known. Importantly, it applies whether the junction is a roundabout or not. For larger junctions presenting multiple individual junction decisions to be made, there are roundabouts, traffic lights and other systems. The *rechts vor links* rule on its surface does something similar to a roundabout wherever the need for a roundabout would arise, that is, to resolve a conflict of priority. It does this without requiring the physical existence of a roundabout. The road layout does not need to change to accommodate a turning circle in the centre of the junction and no road markings are necessary.

By contrast, in England the rules for unmarked junctions are less well known, phrased differently and not the same as for roundabouts. The Highway Code, published by the Department for Transport and the Driver and Vehicle Standards Agency, has rules which are enforced by criminal sanction, denoted by 'MUST' or 'MUST NOT'.[5] But the unmarked junction rules are not such rules, and breach of them is only admissible as evidence of breach of other rules. For example, the breach of such rules might constitute driving dangerously or carelessly, under sections 2 and 3 respectively of the Road Traffic Act 1988. In England, there is also no rule of priority at unmarked junctions.[6] Indeed, in the online format of the Highway Code, a question and answer section from 28 October 2013, which comes up first on the search function,[7] adds more detail:

> At an unmarked crossroads no one has priority. If there are no road signs or markings do not assume that you have priority. Remember that other drivers may assume they have the right to go. No type of vehicle has priority but it is courteous to give way to large vehicles. Also look out in particular for cyclists and motorcyclists.

[4] 'At intersections and junctions, vehicles coming from the right have the right of way.' Except where signed otherwise, or where the road to the right is a dirt road: https://germanlawarchive.iuscomp.org/?p=1290

[5] E.g. Rule 83.

[6] Rule 146 of the Highway Code (bullet point 4 of 6) and Rule 176.

[7] www.highwaycodeuk.co.uk/answers/who-has-priority-at-an-unmarked-crossroads

In short, in England there is no rule of priority at unmarked junctions. Instead, each engagement at the junction involves negotiation between the objects/actors there. Two further levels of guidance are provided. There is a very weak norm on decision-making, informing that it is 'courteous' to give way to large vehicles. There appear to be no possible legal consequences to ignoring this norm in English law. It is made even weaker by using antiquated language: 'courtesy' is not a word in common usage by anyone perhaps under fifty years old in England, and 'courteous' as an adjective is even rarer. Second, there is a norm of caution, giving greater awareness to the potential *presence* of other road users, including cyclists or motorcyclists, and the *assumptions* those road users might make. Also, note that the rule is given greater detail only in what appears to be an official question-and-answer section on a website.

English road traffic rules have instead developed around more formal markings, including using both roundabouts and mini-roundabouts (for smaller junctions and using a painted central space rather than a raised or inaccessible one). The roundabout grew out of the earlier 'traffic circles', some of the earliest examples of which are also in England, such as the Circus in Bath (built to mirror Stonehenge),[8] completed in 1768. The earliest specific set of rules associated with roundabouts were developed by the UK Transport Research Laboratory in the 1960s,[9] spreading out around the world from there. The precise development is a story beyond the scope of this work, but the roundabout's 'give way to the right' priority rule is the key rule for roundabouts in general. These rules are regardless of left- or right-hand driving. Newer roundabouts were copied in Germany after their success in England in the 1980s, and mini-roundabouts from the 1990s.[10]

Many countries have the same *rechts vor links* rule as in Germany, though they might perhaps have more roundabouts, and the rule can also be found in the Vienna Convention on Road Traffic 1968.[11] Indeed, a similar rule applies for shipping at sea, where there are no structured

[8] H. Conway and R. Roenisch, *Understanding Architecture: An Introduction to Architecture and Architectural History*, 2nd ed. (London: Routledge, 2005), pp. 35–6.

[9] https://web.archive.org/web/20160825085249/http://www.trl.co.uk/about-us/our-history

[10] W. Brilon, 'Studies on Roundabouts in Germany: Lessons Learned', paper presented at the 3rd International TRB-roundabout Conference, Carmel, Indiana, May 2011: www.ruhr-uni-bochum.de/verkehrswesen/download/literatur/Brilon_roundabouts_2011_05_29_cit.pdf.

[11] Art. 18.4: 4.

junctions.[12] By contrast, there is the *Boulevard* rule in some states of the USA, that drivers entering a larger road from a smaller one must give way to traffic on the larger road.[13] We might also note some Belgian objections that the rule is in fact outdated, and because not all parties understand the rule in the same way in practice, it leads to accidents and traffic lights are better.[14] Some countries require drivers to drive on the left, but give priority to the right, such as Australia.[15]

In summary, in England there is, for unmarked junctions, a comprehensive but imprecise rule requiring negotiation which could, theoretically, lead to stalemate, and a roundabout rule which is very similar to the German standard rule. In Germany, the answer given is comprehensive, but potentially inefficient and counterintuitive when applied to all types of junctions. Of course, given the importance of timing, both systems could in theory lead to a stalemate where a vehicle arrives at the same time at each road of a junction. Both are rules which do not themselves call strongly, or perhaps at all, to some wider deontological value: there is no normatively right answer. What, then, can junctions show us about how we might reason about law?

## 8.2 Roundabout Reasoning

The genius of junctions is how they resolve the potential contradiction in the direction of the two or more paths involved. This is true whether each path allows two-way travel or not, so long as there is a junction with more than one direction and more than one user of the system. The fact of junctions raises the possibility of a network of connected pathways and, ultimately, a system, a coherent body of paths and junctions. The more efficient the system, the more effectively junctions permit travel in the directions desired and the more effective are the junctions it uses.

[12] International Regulations for Preventing Collisions at Sea 1972, Regulations 15–17 mandate that two powered vessels give way by the one giving way to the other on the starboard, or right, side; see recently, *Evergreen Marine (UK) Limited* v. *Nautical Challenge Ltd* [2021] UKSC 6, with thanks to Michael Dyson for the suggestion.

[13] See e.g. *Palenchar* v. *Jarrett* 507 F Supp 2d 502, 509 (D Md 2007).

[14] B. De Brabander and L. Vereeck, 'Safety Effects of Roundabouts in Flanders: Signal Type, Speed Limits and Vulnerable Road Users' (2007) 39(3) *Accident Analysis and Prevention* 591–9.

[15] Transport and Infrastructure Council, Australian Road Rules (Parliamentary Counsel's Committee, 2019), Rules 72 and 73: www.pcc.gov.au/uniform/2019/Australian-Road-Rules-22November2019.pdf; they are model rules, to be implemented by states and territories.

Conceptually, this network is a map of the law, and the objects travelling might be thought of as fact patterns being processed by legal actors. In particular, what the roundabout does for road users is similar to what some junctions between legal frameworks can do.

There is indeed something intriguing about roundabouts as specific instances of junctions. For example, one issue is their efficiency: there is some evidence that roundabouts can improve traffic flow in certain situations and hence why their use has grown in Germany more recently. This efficiency seems to be linked to how they work. Roundabouts not only assign a priority, like a gate or a traffic light. They create a unified and mandatory direction for travel through the junction. Every incoming object's direction of travel is turned to fit a curve around a central point. In its most common form, this involves changing each largely straight line into the same tight curve for the duration of the junction. There is a single intermediate direction of travel for anything travelling through the junction, a common direction across the many shapes the network takes.

In addition, roundabouts, while circular, are in another sense decentralised: objects navigate the junction without relying on other forms of authority. The junction relies on decision-making by users of the system, with information available to them, and without further rule-making or application by a central authority. It does not have to rely on other infrastructure.

Roads in Germany (and many other countries) do not *physically* use roundabouts as extensively as England: this is the observable effect of a legal difference. The 'give way to the right' rule has the practical effect of resolving conflict in a similar way to a junction, but it is only a priority rule, not a directional rule. The layout of the particular junction might allow passage without similar directions of travel at all, and normally does. What the roundabout requires is that the incoming objects be rendered equal and uniform, in an intermediate form, as they pass through the junction. That intermediate or third state is completely independent from the entry and exit. Of course, passage through the junction is not only a question of priority of entry, it will include questions of other objects inside the junction already, or waiting to progress through the entry and exit points from the junction. But consideration inside the junction process can be summarised for practical use as based on a system of priority of consideration, whatever the reasons for progression.

It is these three distinctive features of roundabouts that constitute 'roundabout reasoning': it resolves potential conflict between two or more objects by (a) a simple method of sequencing their consideration;

(b) where actors apply the method autonomously; and (c) consideration takes place through a neutral third space without reference to earlier states. Roundabout reasoning provides an effective way for legal actors to handle the interfaces between pathways. This applies to pathways of thought as much as pathways of traffic. The process operates to isolate the relevant issues, strip them of some of their background, and enable effective decisions about how to route them within the system. It is a process to help legal actors make the best decisions, and give objects the best chance of navigating the junction successfully. From here, we will explore roundabout reasoning by applying it in three contexts in the next three sections: comparative methodology, domestic legal rules, and as a gateway to legal development.

## 8.3 Roundabout Comparisons

Roundabout reasoning adds to how comparative law can understand legal transplants. Comparative law is not short of terminology to assist its work but there is a gap a roundabout would fit right into. This is the particularly famous discourse around legal transplants. Alan Watson's leading work popularised the language of transplants,[16] for a process that he argued was central to the development of law. He argued that legal systems develop most significantly by implementing objects, particularly rules, from other legal systems into the domestic system. However, no single method or set of terminology is perfect.[17] Each seeks to capture more elements of the movement or the result, like 'borrowing',[18] 'legal pluralism'[19] and so on. A slightly different focus then developed: onto the nature of the object's integration into the receiving legal system. Three important examples are Sacco's 'legal formants',[20] Teubner's 'legal

16 Starting with A. Watson, *Legal Transplants: An Approach to Comparative Law* (Edinburgh: Scottish Academic Press, 1974); see e.g. W. Ewald, 'Comparative Jurisprudence (II): The Logic of Legal Transplants' (1995) 43 *American Journal of Comparative Law* 489.

17 See generally, D. Nelken, 'Legal Transplants and Beyond: Of Disciplines and Metaphors', in A. Harding and E. Örücü (eds.), *Comparative Law in the 21st Century* (London: Kluwer, 2002).

18 R. Sacco, 'Legal Formants: A Dynamic Approach to Comparative Law (Installment II of II)' (1991) 39 *American Journal of Comparative Law* 293, at 397–401.

19 U. Baxi, 'The Colonial Heritage', in P. Legrand and R. Munday (eds.), *Comparative Legal Studies: Traditions and Transitions* (Cambridge: Cambridge University Press, 2003).

20 R. Sacco, 'Legal Formants: A Dynamic Approach to Comparative Law' (Installment I of II) (1991) 39 *American Journal of Comparative Law* 1; and Sacco, 'Legal Formants' (Installment II of II).

irritants'[21] and Örücü's musical metaphors of 'transposition' and 'tuning'.[22] Each captures a slightly different perspective of the process of reception, and they came in a short period from 1995 to 2002, a nuanced and insightful part of the cresting wave of comparative methodology scholarship as the last century turned.

Sacco argued that any particular manifestation of law is the result of a core idea, a formant, built upon with other layers of cultural and other constructs. The formant could be stripped back, and transplanted, to be re-clothed in the new system. Sacco suggested that lawyers themselves realised that:

> living law contains many different elements such as statutory rules, the formulations of scholars, and the decisions of judges – elements that he keeps separate in his own thinking . . . The jurist concerned with the law within a single country examines all of these elements and then eliminates the complications that arise from their multiplicity to arrive at one rule. He does so by a process of interpretation.[23]

He went on to contend that 'Borrowing and imitation is . . . of central importance to understanding the course of legal change'[24] and that 'the birth of a rule or institution is a rarer phenomenon than its imitation'[25] as part of his argument about how formants moved. Sacco focused slightly less on the processes applied to the relevant objects, but his insight is very useful in seeing how the object that leaves one place might be different to the one that arrives in another.

Teubner used loaded and highly evocative language to describe the new, often transplanted idea as an 'irritant', a thing which needs both adjustment and adjusting to. Like the grit that starts a pearl, something new and very different can be created by a legal system adjusting to something it has taken in. The work was significant in highlighting the degree of mutual adjustment that happens, and the 'foreignness' that an object might continue to have, but in terms of the recipient system's responses and the possibilities for new forms and development that ensue.

[21] G. Teubner, 'Legal Irritants: Good Faith in British Law or How Unifying Law Ends up in New Divergences' (1998) 61 *Modern Law Review* 11.

[22] E. Örücü, 'Law as Transposition' (2002) 51 *International & Comparative Law Quarterly* 205.

[23] Sacco, 'Legal Formants' (Installment I), 22.

[24] Sacco, 'Legal Formants' (Installment II), 394.

[25] Ibid., 397.

Örücü's work uses a musical scheme as a preference over 'transplant', but it appears she intends it for only larger-scale works:

> The term 'transposition' is more apt in instances of massive change based on competing models, in that here the pitch is changed … legal institution or rule … [with] transposition occurring to suit the particular socio-legal culture and needs of the recipient … Developments of our day can be seen as instances of transposition, and the 'tuning' that takes place after transposition by the appropriate actors of the recipient is the key to success.[26]

Transposition and tuning might then be done by different legal actors, in different processes, and tuning is an ongoing process for the whole system. It seems Örücü was thinking of tuning to a problem, not tuning to an objective norm of what a note played by an instrument should be:

> It is internal tuning that is required and the tuners should ordinarily be the domestic judges. However, for successful transposition, tuning is necessary at all levels, including legal education. In all cases, even old instruments have to be tuned to new problems, such as in the case of electronic commerce or Internet fraud. One could go further and say that every time a court distinguishes from a prior case, it is undertaking tuning and sometimes transposing a rule or principle from some other area of law to solve the problem at hand.[27]

It is here that the roundabout reasoning can turn the discourse in a useful direction. The roundabout posits a neutral third state between the orientation of the entry and exit of the object in relation to the legal system. That neutral state is the curve around the central point of the roundabout, mandatory for all objects, and all objects look the same once in that state, and their source and destination are unknown and largely unknowable.

There is something of each of the three methodological approaches to post-transplant integration in how roundabout reasoning works. Roundabout reasoning strips out some of the lawyers from the 'formant', the object without origins, free for the system to then redirect it. It also reduces the risk of irritation in the negative sense, by transitioning from 'other' to 'self' and aligning to the routes in the system on the other side of the junction. Like the concept of an 'irritant', roundabout reasoning involves give and take: the circular motion is the middle ground between any two directions. Finally, in a sense, the process of tuning itself is about

[26] Örücü, 'Law as Transposition', 207.
[27] Ibid., 208.

finding a neutral state – in this case a reference pitch that the instrument should be pitched at, before it is then used to play music in that pitch. None of those three methods speaks to the merits of the objects at a junction, and nor does roundabout reasoning.

At the same time, roundabout reasoning offers detail beyond that in those three methodologies. It provides a means to adapt all objects, and what the intellectual parameters for success are. The neutral space does not presume the validity of the recipient space – the very thing found wanting for there to need to be some kind of transplant – nor does it presume the perfection of the incoming object. The key to success is how much a neutral conception can be found. It is another form of a pure point within comparative law, finding the right *tertium comparationis* for producing valuable insights into legal phenomenon. There is no clear rule in advance; it depends on the object, the issues, the host and the origin location, as well as the purposes of the legal system there and the legal actor doing the comparison. Of course, there are also occasionally wider-scale transplants, the transpositions that Örücü was thinking of, like the German codes being adapted in Japan. In those contexts, the junctions might be most relevant not in formal legal rules, but in how legal cultures understand and implement those rules.

An example in English law is the passing of the Human Rights Act 1998, implementing on a domestic level the European Convention of Human Rights (ECHR). The coming into force of the Act was delayed by two years in order to retrain legal actors, particularly judges, to be ready to apply the ECHR domestically. It has a number of elements, but one important aspect is the duty to interpret legislation in line with the ECHR to the extent it is possible to do so, under section 3. The mechanism to comply with the HRA involves: (a) priority, with the starting point the national law; (b) individual judges empowered to navigate the junction without a centralised authority; and (c) the integration of the two sets of frameworks being carried out through a neutral space, an interpretative duty rather than through a merits assessment or direct comparison of rules.

Compared to the *rechts vor links* rule, the neutral third space is possible for large junctions and small. Indeed, roundabout reasoning is context-sensitive: it frames the neutral space as varying with the size of the junction. Larger conduits require larger junctions, and roundabout reasoning scales effectively, and allows ideas to mix within their own order inside the junction's circular space. Applied to legal transplants, in the process of crossing the roundabout the object might be affected by other neutral objects within the junction. The condition for their relevance is that they too are using the junction, that legal actors within the system have given them a path that reaches the same place as the originally foreign object, and legal actors thought to have them in the junction at the same time. This analogy brings out even more of the dynamic and multifactorial issues underlying the formant, irritant and tuning approaches. There are micro- and macro-levels to the physical expression of roundabouts which help their reasoning play out.

On the micro-level, the roundabout might benefit from further physical expression, such as multiple lanes spiralling out from the centre, traffic lights or other infrastructure, shaping the movement into and interactions within the neutral space. Objects within the space might be guided through a specific default route based on lanes on entry, and it requires specific decisions and negotiation within the neutral space to change that default exit. The larger junctions require a more distinctive and larger central point to exert its presence as a means of ensuring smooth movement through the junction.

On the macro-level, the pattern of routes and junctions creates a network across the relevant space. In terms of legal change, existing routes tend to branch off, rather than break new ground or be closed off. Branching is the lower-cost upfront option, even if it will not always be the most efficient way to traverse the space, especially not as time brings changes to the landscapes' features. At any given moment, it will be easier to build on existing directions than redesign sections of the network.

Both levels involve 'routing', and that leads us to the concept of path dependence. This concept, first known to economics and other social sciences, uses the same language of transport infrastructure, particularly language associated with paths, and is effectively complemented by discussion of junctions. In simple terms, path dependence means that 'once a path is chosen, this choice itself affects possible future action to the point of locking in earlier paths even when this becomes comparatively inefficient'.[28] Hathaway has gone further, in a description all too reminiscent for drivers negotiating an unfamiliar roundabout:

> The theory further suggests that the opportunities for significant legal change in a common law system are brief and intermittent, occurring

[28] F. G. Sourgens, 'The Virtue of Path Dependence in the Law' (2016) 56 *Santa Clara Law Review* 303, 305.

> during critical junctures when new legal issues arise or higher courts or legislatures intercede. Moreover, it leads to the unsettling conclusion that the order in which cases arrive in the courts can significantly affect the specific legal doctrine that ultimately results.[29]

Hathaway's work might have focused on precedent, but it neatly highlights how legal change is not very predictable *ex ante* and that early outcomes may become locked in. The law evolves gradually over time, drawing on an existing stock of legal solutions, punctuated by periods of rapid adaptation.

Bell's work on path dependence highlights how legal systems could be more open to breaking out on new paths than the traditional view might suggest, particularly if legal change is understood in a comparative light.[30] In addition, the network might work well in multiple ways:

> Path dependence is connected with notions of embeddedness. The economics literature suggests that there are a number of equilibrium points at which a system of social practices can settle down in a stable way. Path dependence takes as its assumption that there are a number of arrangements of affairs in society that are equally efficient and beneficial.[31]

Bell picks out the different levels of embeddedness possible in the system:

> A feature of a legal system will be deeply embedded not simply because there is a habit of dealing with an issue in a particular way. To talk of something as a 'habit' or 'practice' tends to focus on discrete aspects of a legal system which may be easily separated from the rest of the system. Real embeddedness involves not just a special rule but also the way in which it connects significantly to other parts of the law, especially when it is underpinned by structural or organisational aspects of the system. Path dependence follows very often from such features of a legal system because it is very difficult to change institutional arrangements.[32]
>
> If a rule is embedded in a conceptual structure that has connection to other ideas, then it will be necessary to take account of this. Sometimes a concept needs to be removed . . . or sometimes a new concept needs to be introduced . . . New concepts may well work best as a bypass around the established conceptual framework.[33]

29 O. Hathaway, 'Path Dependence in the Law: The Course and Pattern of Legal Change in a Common Law System' (2001) 86 *Iowa Law Review* 101, 105.

30 J. Bell, 'Path Dependence and Legal Development' (2013) 87 *Tulane Law Review* 787, 788.

31 Ibid., 797.

32 Ibid., 805.

33 Ibid., 809–10.

Roads can sometimes be decommissioned, but bypasses are somewhat more common: a route around an area of difficulty or difference is instituted, leaving the old route for rarer or specialised use. To take just one topical example from an infrastructure rather than legal setting, there is a junction in Dresden where a traffic signal has been red without interruption for thirty-four years. Next to the red signal there is a sign indicating that a driver can proceed with caution. If you wish to turn right from Ziegelstraße into Güntzustraße, you can do so once you have stopped, and if the way is clear. Since the junction is controlled by traffic lights, all exits from it have to have a light, but a green light would imply permission to proceed even if the way was not clear, which would be a contradiction. And, for a while at least, it's cheaper to pay €5,500 a year in maintaining the light than to change the road layout.[34]

The roundabout reasoning adds to path dependency by articulating a mechanism for successful change. It links identity to route, direction and even speed. It acknowledges the necessity of change in objects at junctions, and does so dynamically, respecting the pressures on the junction at that point in time. It will be selected as a means to form certain types of junctions, where the directions and objects require greater regulation in their interaction, and an interaction free from further central authority. Rather than simply deciding which object at a junction has priority, the roundabout unifies the objects and decides on that priority, albeit that priority is determined by a very simple system building on information on time and physical location. Roundabout reasoning could be deployed whenever a junction is desired; indeed, a cheaper version could be deployed through the *rechts vor links* rule, without the infrastructure. But the argument in this chapter is that the neutral intermediate space is a key part of roundabout reasoning's success.

We turn now from comparative theory and path dependence to look at how roundabout reasoning might be seen in some specific examples within national legal systems.

## 8.4 Roundabout Domestic Laws

Thinking in terms of roundabout reasoning also helps us see that some issues in domestic law are under-analysed. One promising approach for roundabout reasoning is in unpacking the relationship of different

[34] www.thelocal.de/20150615/there-is-a-light-that-never-goes-out

objects within the legal system. Whether the intermediate state was in fact the original form, or can really be generalised as a neutral concept giving rise to specific expressions which are not derivative, is a difficult question not often addressed or answered.

Sometimes legal objects have a similar form to each other despite being placed in different parts of the legal system. The most common reason is that the objects share historical origins. The original object is only later placed as a junction between frameworks, but started as a freestanding concept. The borderline between tort and crime has such instances. In England, examples would be assault and battery, public nuisance and harassment. The English law against harassment is just such an example: the Protection from Harassment Act 1997 specifies a rule, not to harass, in section 1, and that rule is given the form of a criminal offence in section 2, and means are provided of claiming damages in a civil court in section 3. The neutral space contains a duty relating to the conduct, not to the procedures, norms or remedies associated with that rule. The fact that there are not many such examples is itself revealing, including that there are no specific torts for sexual battery, murder, theft and many other well-known offences which cause harm.

Sometimes the objects might arise from the same place, but the history is more clouded and the links less obvious. One example in English private law is an 'assumption of responsibility' generating some kind of obligation to act, often an obligation to take care.[35] This could arise in tort law, bailment and other areas, but it could not necessarily be said to be originally grounded in any one of them. There are historically significant instances of it, such as perhaps the first treatise engaging with the tort of negligence being one formally on bailment.[36]

Another way roundabout reasoning might help is to directly recognise duties that are expressed not as freestanding duties, but as in some sense linked to the area of law in which they first appear but having also a junction with another area of law. In England, breach of statutory duty is a means of creating a civil claim for harm caused by the breach of a duty in a statute where the statute does not itself expressly create civil liability for harm caused by breaching the statutory duty. The statute will normally have an enforcement mechanism of some kind, just not a civil one.

[35] For recent argument in this direction, see e.g. D. Nolan, 'Assumption of Responsibility: Four Questions' (2019) 72 *Current Legal Problems* 123.

[36] D. Ibbetson (ed.), *Sir William Jones, An Essay on the Law of Bailments* (Cardiff: Welsh Legal History Society, 2007).

The claimant has to show that, despite the absence of an express reference to creating civil liability in the statute, that is what Parliament intended. It is a factor against civil liability that the statute does impose a criminal penalty since, it can be argued, the criminal penalty appearing alone shows that is all Parliament wished to supply as an enforcement mechanism.[37] A famous example of a more general integrative technique is §823(2) BGB; §823(1) requires anyone who intentionally or negligently injures the protected interests of German law, life, body, health, freedom, property or another right, to pay compensation to that person. German law further adds, in §823(2), that the same duty to compensate is owed by someone who breaches a norm intended to protect another, so long as it is done with fault. A protective norm, or *Schutzgesetz*, will be found in many criminal offences which might not otherwise be fitted easily within §823(1), and in any case, civil liability is much easier to establish once the criminal liability has been found. But in both the English and the German forms, the language is of an underlying duty. That duty might be expressed in a statute that concerns primarily criminal law, but the constituent duty is given expression in tort law.

One way to apply roundabout reasoning, used by some legal systems, is to apply a neutral term such as 'unlawful act' in order to integrate norms from two networks. This intermediate concept is, in a sense, the legal formant that allows objects transfer across relevant borders; pushing an object into that state and out again according to some priority and through the behaviour of ordinary users of the system is, in effect, roundabout reasoning. For example, Dutch law's key definition of an unlawful act is as, amongst other things, 'an act or omission in violation of a duty imposed by written law' and all criminal laws must be in written form (in addition, breaching social standards of due care also generate liability).[38] This naturally means that every criminal act is also the base unit for then layering on the components for tort liability. French legislation does not do so expressly, but apparently began to do so as a free translation of the Roman *damnum injuria datum*.[39] It will be

[37] *Carroll* v. *Barclay (Andrew) and Sons, Ltd* [1948] AC 477, 489–90, 493; *Biddle* v. *Truvox Engineering Co.* [1952] 1 KB 101, 103; *Cutler* v. *Wandsworth Stadium* [1949] AC 398; and see also Goodhart's note on this case in (1946) 62 *Law Quarterly Review* 316, 317.

[38] Art. 6:162, *Burgerlijk Wetboek* (Dutch civil code).

[39] J.-L. Halpérin, 'French Doctrinal Writing', in N. Jansen (ed.), *The Development and Making of Legal Doctrine* (Cambridge: Cambridge University Press, 2010), pp. 80–1.

immediately apparent that what makes the act unlawful might be tightly bound up with other aspects of liability, especially notions of fault and notions of individual rights.[40]

These cases are perhaps slightly different to a concept being given effect in another area of law, without actually being a neutral or translated form. For instance, in Brazil, a conviction crystallises the obligation to pay compensation for the damage done by the crime: Article 91(I) of the Código Penal.[41] This is certainly conceptually interesting, and in line with some legal systems which analyse tort liability as stemming from an 'unlawful act', including crimes. However, in practice it might be more symbolic than meaningful and has often not led to greater compensation. In fact, the procedurally most significant provision across tort and crime was in the protection of the integrity of the legal system by binding any later civil court to the facts a criminal court must have been grounded on.[42] This has the effect of making a second action[43] in respect of loss easier, since the conviction will supply much of the evidence for the civil claim. It uses a substantive model: the conviction binds later civil courts over the legal questions that are the same. In a sense, either the criminal law has effect in a later civil case, or there is some kind of rule superior to criminal law and civil law which is being picked up and carried over. This second possibility looks a lot more like roundabout reasoning. Conversely, in England, a criminal conviction can be evidence of the facts upon which it must have been founded, for the purposes of any later civil claim on the same facts.[44]

## 8.5 Roundabout Legal Development: The Effects of Giving Way

Finally, roundabout reasoning can help us understand legal development. We turn now to look at two different paths of development, in two different countries, both actually starting from *rechts vor links* fact patterns. Both relate to the growing complexity in societies, including technological risks, the extent of social solidarity or the willingness for a loss to go uncompensated and, fundamentally, how the mode of argumentation affects how the

[40] The integrative techniques in contract law, whether through public policy, illegality or otherwise, are sadly beyond the scope of this chapter.

[41] 'tornar certa a obrigação de indenizar o dano causado pelo crime', so more directly 'makes real' or 'makes true' the obligation.

[42] Brazilian Civil Code, Art. 935.

[43] Code of Criminal Procedure (*Código de processo penal*), Arts. 63 and 64.

[44] Civil Evidence Act 1968, s. 11; see also s. 13.

law develops. From roundabout reasoning, we see two routes. First, conceptualisation without a neutral intermediate legal space, and no legal development; second, a neutral space and a period of significant change.

An example in Germany is a classic example of the risk of failure in a junction: commonly known as the *No red light* case.[45] This was an attempt to generate strict liability, liability regardless of fault, in the absence of a specific provision of German law which permitted it. It was a push against a strong normative and even cultural view that tort law required fault unless the legislature had found otherwise.

A driver approaching a junction found a traffic light not working ahead of him, and the only other relevant vehicle was approaching a road to his left; thinking he therefore had default right of way at a non-functioning traffic light junction, he proceeded into the junction. The driver on his left was approaching the junction, and the traffic light in front of him in fact showed a green light in his favour; thinking he had right of way because of the light, he proceeding onto the junction. A crash occurred. It transpired that the traffic light system as a whole had not failed, but the light facing the first driver had failed. The junction rule system had a flaw: the traffic lights could fail for one entry point without failing for all. Neither driver was at fault. The claim was brought against the state as the local authority was responsible for the traffic lights. The Bundesgerichtshof rejected the claim. It held that 'The legislature has only expressly stipulated strict liability for individual exceptions, which it has outlined in more detail . . . because it considered an exception to the principle of fault to be necessary here'. Despite the evident unfairness of the rule, the formal structure of norm-creating was adhered to, and statutory interpretation did not permit any other rule to be analogised or otherwise bent to fit these facts. It is an example of a failed attempt to change German tort law, and its facts were based on a failed system of junction rule priority rules.

Roundabout reasoning was, in a sense, not deployed in *No red light*. On the facts themselves, there was no physical marking to require the objects passing through the junction to adopt a neutral and circular way around the junction. The first driver relied only on the *rechts vor links* rule itself. As a matter of legal reasoning, there was a decision on priority, based on deference to legislative decision-making, or, put another way, reluctance by courts to take those decisions, or take them in favour of

[45] BGH, 15 October 1970.

strict liability. That was, in effect, also a claim to require external authority, not rely on the decision-makers involved at that junction. In effect, it was a claim to need a green light from the legislature. But most importantly for present purposes, there was no attempt to frame liability as being based on strict liability, as seen in the context solely of the normative and institutional claims about tort law in Germany.[46] No new neutral space was created to mediate a new rule coming into German law. Priority was assigned to the integrity of a system predicated on fault and legislative decisions to create strict liability. Like the German law of delict in general, courts were not willing to mediate the minefield of risk-regulation in place of fault, or socialise risks, but left that to the legislature for formal rules, for private behaviour such as insurance, and for the extensive state social security system.

For our second example, still using the same right-before-left rule but with vibrant legal development, we turn to Spanish law. In the twentieth century, Spanish tort law has seen very significant development in fault in order to make it easier for those who suffer harm to claim compensation.[47] Tort liability is still based on a general clause of liability for damage caused by fault laid down in the Spanish Civil Code (CC) of 1889, in Article 1902: 'He who, by action or omission, by his *culpa* or *negligencia*, causes harm to another, is obliged to compensate for the harm caused.'

This general clause is then supplemented by several instances of strict liability, both in the Code (Articles 1905–10) and in 'special statutes' such as those governing motor vehicle accidents[48] and environmental liability,[49] and the state's liability for harm caused by its agents is strict.[50] Spain does not have a general rule of liability for damage caused by things.

The Civil Code is slightly unusual in that it actually defines fault or *culpa* (Article 1104 CC): a lack of care according to the circumstances of time, space and the persons involved. This is the key form of fault in civil

46 See generally J. Bell and A. Janssen (eds.), *Markesinis' German Law of Torts* (Oxford: Hart, 2019), chapter 7.

47 See generally, e.g., L. Fernando Reglero Campos (ed.), *Tratado de Responsabilidad Civil* (Navarra: Aranzadi, 2008), chapter 2.

48 Royal Legislative Decree 8/2004 of 29 October, por el que se aprueba el texto refundido de la Ley sobre responsabilidad civil y seguro en la circulación de vehículos a motor (BOE No. 267 of 5 November 2004) (hereinafter LRCSCVM).

49 Act 26/2007 of 23 October, *de Responsabilidad Medioambiental* (BOE No. 255 of 24 October 2007) (hereinafter LRM).

50 Act 40/2015 of 1 October, *de régimen jurídico del sector público* (BOE No. 236 of 2 October 2015), Arts. 32–7.

liability in practice, just as in England and France. It is expressly and necessarily an open-textured standard, so 'that it is not possible to reduce or synthesise it into narrow rules to be applied' but instead it should be applied with all the complexities of the facts in view, subject to overarching review by cassation.[51] It is a purely objective standard, unlike the subjectivised version of negligence used in Spanish criminal law.[52]

At the start of the twentieth century, aware of what was happening with the growth of strict liability in France, the Spanish too began to consider 'objectification' of fault in response to social and economic development; this involved the Tribunal Supremo, itself a body drawn from practitioners and academics and aware of the wider intellectual trends.[53] From 1942, the Tribunal Supremo said culpa was a question of law, rather than a question of fact, and thereby allowed itself wider space to quash the trial court's verdict, the better to change the law on a wider scale.[54] One of the earliest of these efforts in fact failed: there were some unsuccessful efforts to analogise sources of strict liability or reverse burdens of proof, such as from animals to cars.[55]

However, the civil courts found leeway elsewhere. These methods achieved greater coverage for tort liability, but formally did so through adapting the standard or the burden of proving fault, rather than creating strict liability. They have been the subject of significant academic work.[56]

First, courts have applied a highly demanding standard of care: *in lege Aquilia et levissima culpa venit*.[57] In particular, the mere fact that the tortfeasor behaved in accordance with regulatory or technical standards ('regulatory compliance' defence), or what was provided in any necessary

[51] STS 20 December 1930 [1930–1] RJ 1365.

[52] J. Santos Briz, 'Unidad de concepto de la culpa', in J. A. Moreno Martínez (ed.), *Perfiles de la responsabilidad civil en el nuevo milenio* (Madrid: Dykinson, 2000), pp. 593–5; see also V. Silva Melero, *Tecnicismo jurídico civilista en el Derecho penal* (Oviedo: Universidad de Oviedo, 1950), pp. 116–18.

[53] I. González Pacanowska and M. García-Ripoll Montijano, 'The Impact of Institutions and Professions in Spain', in P. Mitchell (ed.), *The Impact of Institutions and Professions on Legal Development* (Cambridge: Cambridge University Press, 2014), pp. 171–2. See also Campos (ed.), *Tratado*, 260–75.

[54] S. Cavanillas Múgica, *La transformacion de la responsabilidad civil en la jurisprudencia* (Pamplona: Aranzadi, 1987), pp. 46–8.

[55] I. González Pacanowska, 'The Development of Traffic Liability in Spain', in W. Ernst (ed.), *The Development of Traffic Liability* (Cambridge: Cambridge University Press, 2010), pp. 174–6.

[56] See generally the detailed work of Cavanillas Múgica, *La transformacion*.

[57] See E. Font Serra, *La acción civil en el proceso penal: Su tratamiento procesal* (Madrid: La Ley, 1991), p. 14.

licence issued by the public administration, was not in itself enough to prove sufficient care was taken.[58] One of the foundational cases was the Supreme Court's judgment of 29 June 1932: a train company had to show a higher standard of care in its operations 'for the simple reason that the person who creates a risk of harm must answer for its consequences'. Additionally, the care required of professionals is much higher than that applicable to ordinary people (pursuant to Article 1104 CC).[59]

Second, and perhaps most famously, Spanish courts reversed the standard of proof of fault. The first such cases were in 1943, and were then repeated and expanded for much of the next half-century. The first significant case was decided on 10 July 1943. The defendant driver was in breach of the Traffic Code and his conduct was the only plausible cause of the injury to a cyclist; it was later explained that the driver had increased the risk of harm, and that was enough to invert the burden of proof.[60] The foundation for the decision was the standard 'give way to the right at an unmarked junction' rule. The trial court had found the driver not liable on the basis he had sounded his horn and that the curvature of the road inhibited visibility, but the Tribunal Supremo overturned the decision, dismissing those grounds as being insufficient to find that there was no liability. However, it went further, and held that the fact of the damage shifted to the person who caused it the burden of proving the question of fault – here, that there was no fault. It is particularly significant as a case where in fact the law probably did not need to change in order to find liability, but the Tribunal Supremo used it as a vehicle to do so. Previous road traffic cases had typically been heard by the criminal chamber, perhaps giving the civil chamber here more space to break with the earlier tradition.[61]

The roundabout reasoning comes clearly into play in marking out a neutral space between strict liability and fault: one of the grounds for reversing the burden of proof was a neutral space: the theory of risk (*teoría del riesgo*).[62] The Supreme Court did not require some external

58 E.g., Cavanillas Múgica, *La tranformacion*, 446–509.

59 See F. Reglero Campos, 'Los sistemas de responsabilidad civil', in F. Reglero Campos and J. M. Busto (eds.), *Tratado de responsabilidad civil*, 5th ed. (Cizur Menor: Thomson Aranzadi, 2014), pp. 265 and 298.

60 See also STS 31 October 1943 [1943] RJ 856; see, then, e.g. STS 9 April 1963 Collección Legislativa. Jurisprudencia Civil, 1963, No. 354.

61 González Pacanowska, 'Traffic Liability', 174–6, esp. fn. 71; J. M. Rodrîguez Devesa and A. Serrano Gomez, *Derecho Penal Español. Parte General* (Madrid: Dykinson, 1995).

62 See generally, A. Ruda-Gonzalez, 'Regulating Risk through Private Law: The Spanish Approach', in M. Dyson (ed.), *Regulating Risk through Private Law* (Cambridge:

authority, and it prioritised compensating those who suffer loss in a modern society over the doctrines which previously required the claimant to prove fault. This happened through the neutral intermediate space of risk. Risk was the basis for creating liability without the claimant proving fault, but still within the trappings of code provisions requiring fault. Indeed, legal scholarship usually speaks of risk grounding a presumption of fault so strong that it is almost impossible to rebut. It is sometimes called 'as-if strict liability' or 'quasi-strict liability' (*responsabilidad cuasiobjetiva*).[63] This reasoning was said to be strengthened by a link to another code provision, the liability for the acts of others (pursuant to Article 1903 CC). Risk reasoning in general has grown in prominence in Spanish tort law in the twentieth century, hand in hand with compulsory insurance. Moreover, associating liability with risk creation is often aligned with maxims from Roman law, such as *ubi commoda, ibi incommoda*; *ubi lucrum, ibi onus*; or *cuius commoda, eius et incommoda*, linking benefits to burdens.

Finally, in some cases the courts have concluded that the mere occurrence of damage suggests that the defendant was negligent. This expression is similar to the reasoning behind the reversal of the burden of proof, but here it could operate without reference to that burden. An early example of this was a case in 1931 setting out a principle that interpretation should favour the victim, the so-called *pro damnato* principle,[64] and be according to the time and understanding in which they are interpreted (Article 3.1 CC).

All in all, this brought liability in fault under the Civil Code very close to strict liability while expressly not analogising with strict liability provisions in the Code (not an unusual route), or creating strict liability by judicial fiat (the least plausible route).

From the 1990s there has been a counter-movement, case law seeming to demand more as to the proof of fault and definitely not reversing it automatically.[65] In general, risk-reasoning has been reigned in somewhat,

Intersentia, 2018). See also F. Gómez Pomar, 'Carga de la prueba y responsabilidad objetiva' (2001) 1 *InDret* 1, www.raco.cat/index.php/InDret/article/view/81064/105539

63 E.g. STS 186/2000, STS 2 March 2000 'the jurisprudence of the Tribunal Supremo ... tends towards the emblematic establishment of *responsabilidad objetiva*, but it has never brought about this liability in an absolute and radical way'.

64 STS 31 October 1931 [1931] RJ 2218.

65 See Ruda-Gonzalez, 'Regulating Risk', 152–3. STS 22 January 1996, with multiple decisions on the same day from reporting judges, A. Barala y Trillo-Figueroa and J. Almagro Nosete, including 1950/1992, 2265/92 and 2265/1992; STS 18 March 1999, 3065/1994.

and restricted to dangerous activities. It seems to have flowed from decisions about tort liability having become too extensive, and has been linked to a change, perhaps a weakening, in the strength of risk-reasoning.

## 8.6 Conclusion

Attempting to prioritise sources as a means to resolve legal disputes is not new. In Roman law, when it was no longer possible to adequately decide the authority of conflicting texts, in the sense of both which texts are historically accurate and which have authority over each other, Emperor Valentinian III introduced in 426 CE the *Lex Citandi*.[66] In short, it prioritised the texts of five of the classical jurists, and gave somewhat simple numerical rules to decide between them. It did not require any further calls to a centralised decision-maker, but it did not engage in the frameworks each author was building, merely allowing any two or more provisions to be resolved out of conflict. However, as Joshua Getzler has pointed out, in deciding on priority, what starts as a simple priority becomes both a redefinition of authority and a complex set of interactions.[67] In the twentieth century, English lawyers generalised the roundabout to solve a slightly different problem, but it too engaged with questions of priority, centralisation and proxies for substantive content.

This chapter was inspired by John's engagement with legal frameworks and how they join each other. It has played out an idea from comparative law, to domestic law, to legal development. It has also proposed that 'roundabout reasoning' resolves potential conflict between two or more objects by (a) a simple method of sequencing their consideration; (b) where actors apply it autonomously; and (c) consideration takes place through a neutral third space without reference to their earlier states. This reasoning was explored as a matter of comparative legal theory, drawing out how it adds to existing work on what a legal system does with objects, or rules, as they enter the system. In particular, it articulates one way to align the object with the new framework it is entering by formulating all traffic through that junction in terms of a neutral space.

[66] CTh. 1, 4, 3; see generally, A. J. B. Sirks, *The Theodosian Code: A Study* (Friedrichsdorf: Tortuga, 2007).

[67] J. Getzler, 'Citation and the Authority of Opinions in Roman and Jewish Law: The Snake Oven Revisited', in J. Hallebeek, M. Schermaier, R. Fiori, E. Metzger and J.-P. Coriat (eds.), *Inter cives necnon peregrinos: Essays in honour of Boudewijn Sirks* (Göttingen: Vandenhoeck and Ruprecht Unipress, 2014), p. 291.

The success of reasoning like this turns in part on how effective that neutral space is, and how much users accept the value of it. Two cases on the very *rechts vor links* rule gave us examples of this difficulty at play. We saw one example of an attempt to reframe German law out of the limits of strict liability creation. The court's judgment seems to have been too clearly in the furrows of established reasoning about parliamentary decision-making over strict liability. By contrast, in Spain, reconceptualising the work of at least some of tort liability being about the wrongful imposition of risk was enough to shape three aspects of fault reasoning without having to push all the way to quasi-strict liability. That might highlight the difference between the *rechts vor links* rule and roundabouts. The roundabout builds a physical infrastructure to make permanent the shifting through a neutral space, rather than just prioritising the entry points to the junction, and requiring decisions by those on the ground.

Exactly how embedded reasoning is, and how it carries through normative claims, is vital to understanding legal frameworks and their junctions. Some particularly interesting questions merit further study, including what kinds of 'accidents' or errors happen in roundabout reasoning, and whether there are even better forms of legal reasoning for comparativists, domestic lawyers, and for those generally seeking legal change.

# 9

# A Comparative Reflection on Chilean Economic Torts

CRISTIÁN A. BANFI

Unfair competition law belongs to the realm of private law. Its concern is to protect individual business adversaries from abusive and wrongful acts through preventive remedies and secondarily via tort compensation.

This study is written in gratitude for Professor John Bell, who wisely, generously and kindly taught me, as a postgraduate student in Cambridge, how to do comparative law seriously.

The chapter analyses Chilean tortious (extracontractual) liability for pure economic loss (PEL) caused by unfair commercial practices from an Anglo perspective. It shows that the general rules on tort, enshrined in the Civil Code of 1855 (CHCC), proved insufficient for prospective competitors to bring tort law suits: they had to wait until the Unfair Competition Act 2007 (UCA) was passed. Although the parties can choose between a claim in tort or under UCA, the case law on tortious liability for unfair competition is conspicuously missing; instead, case law under the UCA rapidly developed after its enactment. Chilean courts have not displayed the level of creativity characteristic of English judges when deciding on unfair competition, yet they have interpreted the UCA in a way that attracts the comparatist's attention.

I will argue that, rather than denying compensation for negligently inflicted PEL for lack of causation and uncertainty of damage, consistency with the existing law and legal policy requires that Chilean courts weigh against the wrongdoer's right/freedom of competition the victim's right to redress for harm caused by business rivalry. This can be done in different ways. First, trade opponents do not owe one another a duty of care, hence carelessly caused PEL is a side effect of legitimate commercial strife. Second, although competitors often injure one another intentionally,

This chapter is part of Fondecyt Regular Projects no. 1200176 and no. 1180680. I thank Professor Paula Gilliker and Dr Sophie Turenne for their comments on an earlier draft. The usual disclaimer applies.

courts should limit the overall principle of fault congruently with economic freedom, by subjecting liability to the tortfeasor's intention to harm the claimant or to procure the breach of contract, as the case may be, or at least to gross negligence (*culpa lata*), which the CHCC equates to intention (*dolo*). Thirdly, although unlawful means is conceptually a separate ingredient of the generic unfair practice – the latter being defined as 'conduct contrary to good faith or good customs that, through *illegitimate means*, aims at diverting customers from an agent of the market',[1] in practice Chilean courts subsume unlawful means under fault. Thus, unlawful means is identified with the breach of the duty to act in good faith/good commercial customs or with the specific conduct expressly prohibited by statute.[2]

This chapter is divided into four sections. Section 9.1 describes the basic tenets, functions and conditions of extracontractual liability and in particular how Chilean courts avail themselves of gross negligence as a liability-control device, similar to the role played by intention in other legal systems. Section 9.2 argues that tortious liability between commercial rivals should be limited through the requirement of intention (*dolo*) or gross negligence (*culpa lata*). In respect of unfair competition, the mental element of intention, more stringent than mere carelessness, is crucial for counteracting the risk of limitless liability and litigation arising from negligence-based liability for PEL. Section 9.3 reviews the recent case law on tortious interference with contract under the UCA, and compares it with English law. It suggests that if Chilean courts are to enforce tortious liability for interference with contracts as a specific instance of unfair competition, they should follow the more conservative English pattern when weighing the third party's freedom to compete against the claimant's contractual rights. Chilean law should recognise liability for inducing breach of contract (subject to the defendant's intention to cause the breach)[3] and liability for interfering with contractual performance without causing any breach (subject to the defendant's intention to harm the claimant, as in the tort of intentionally causing loss by unlawful means).[4] Section 9.4 summarises the main conclusions drawn from the foregoing reasoning.

[1] Art. 3 UCA.

[2] Art. 4 UCA (such as passing off, malicious falsehood and inducing breach of contract).

[3] *Lumley* v. *Gye* (1853) 118 ER 749.

[4] *OBG* v. *Allan* [2008] 1 AC 1.

## 9.1 Explaining Chilean Extracontractual Liability

Tortious liability comprises the wrongdoer's obligation to repair the harm done to the victim by an intentional (delict) or negligent (quasi-delict) act or omission – namely, an illicit (wrongful) conduct – regardless of any previous agreement.[5] The claimant must generally prove the defendant's *dolo* ('a positive intention to inflict injury upon another's person or property')[6] or *culpa* (which includes negligence and intention to harm, yet strictly speaking means carelessness), and that the claimant was personally injured as a direct consequence of that wrongful behaviour.[7] The existence, quantification and certainty of damage are factual issues within the trial court's jurisdiction,[8] whereas causation and fault are normative issues under the Supreme Court's control, via cassation, whereby the lower courts' final decisions applying the law incorrectly are annulled.[9]

Compensation for damages is tort law's central function. The balance between the wrongdoer and the victim – a relationship based on corrective justice – is altered by the injury but then rectified through tort compensation, usually as a sum of money equivalent to (no more, no less than) the harm inflicted on the victim, thereby preventing them from being unjustly enriched.[10] As in English law,[11] Chilean law compensates tort victims for their losses as if they had not been injured. However, the type of injury sustained is critical in England, and carelessly caused PEL (unlike personal or proprietary damage) is only occasionally awarded in order to avoid hindering economic activity.[12] By comparison, Chilean courts grant full compensation irrespective of the kind of harm suffered. Moreover, while the English intentional torts entail wider liability,[13] in Chile whether the defendant acted intentionally or negligently is in

[5] Art. 2314 CHCC.

[6] Art. 44 CHCC.

[7] Art. 1698 CHCC.

[8] SC.4/9/2002.RDJ.99.1ª.186.

[9] SC.28/1/1999.RDJ.96.4ª.71. Art. 764 CPC.

[10] SC.8/7/1935.RDJ.32.1ª.422.

[11] *Livingstone* v. *Rawyards* (1880) 5 App. Cas 25 at 39 per Lord Blackburn.

[12] The major exceptions for PEL concern negligent misstatements by banks or auditors in offering advice in financial matters, thereby injuring claimants who entered into unprofitable business: *Hedley Byrne & Co.* v. *Heller & Partners* [1964] AC 465; *Caparo Industries Plc* v. *Dickman* [1990] 2 AC 605 (although no liability was found in these cases).

[13] *Smith New Court Securities Ltd* v. *Scrimgeour (Asset Management) Ltd* [1997] AC 254 at 279–82 per Lord Steyn; J. Goudkamp and D. Nolan (eds.), *Winfield and Jolowicz on Tort*, 20th ed. (London: Thomson Reuters, 2020), p. 194, n. 321.

principle immaterial: the award of damages primarily hinges on the magnitude of harm inflicted on the victim whatever the tortfeasor's blameworthiness.[14] Tort liability only indirectly serves to punish wrongdoers, to prevent or discontinue harm through precautionary (injunctive) measures, to provide for reparation in kind (specific performance) and to divest defendants of their illicit gains.[15]

Tort liability follows from the breach of the generic or specific duty not to harm others negligently or intentionally.[16] Fault is the overall tort rule whereby courts balance the litigants' conflicting interests. So, victims must bear their losses unless deliberately or carelessly caused by someone else. *Culpa* justifies and limits the duty to compensate for harm which is attributed to the wrongdoer through the causation test.[17]

Here I should emphasise that, although case law is officially an indirect authority in Chile, and *stare decisis* is excluded even in respect of the Supreme Court's findings,[18] case law has been crucial in filling the legislative lacunas and elaborating the law of delict from the general principle of *culpa*, which demands continuous interpretation and specification through court decisions. However, Chilean judges have interpreted tort rules cautiously and have lacked the ability to innovate and refine principles. Further, the absence of *stare decisis* and clear judicial reasoning – as it is hidden behind vague categories like *causation* and *culpa*, which are seldom examined thoroughly – renders case law unpredictable in key aspects, such as the determination of fault.

Courts define negligence through various criteria: the intensity and probability of harm, the social value of the defendant's activity, the costs of avoiding damage, etc.[19] They compare the defendant's act with the applicable standard of care, thus squaring with the notion of doing or not doing what a reasonable person would or would not do.[20] Although the CHCC does not define fault, under Pothier's influence it adopted in Article 44 (a general liability provision) the Roman tripartite division of fault: gross negligence (*culpa lata*) – which is aligned with intention to

[14] SC.27/10/1983.RDJ.80.4ª.121.

[15] A. Alessandri, *De la responsabilidad extracontractual en el derecho civil chileno* (Santiago: Imprenta Universitaria, 1943), pp. 123, 533.

[16] Arts. 2314–29 CHCC.

[17] SC.13/11/2002.GJ.269.39.

[18] Art. 3 CHCC.

[19] E. Barros, *Tratado de responsabilidad extracontractual*, 2nd ed. (Santiago: Jurídica de Chile, 2020), I, pp. 112–29.

[20] *Blyth* v. *Birmingham Waterworks* (1856) 156 ER 1047 at 1050 per Alderson J.

harm (*dolo*) in civil law generally, slight negligence (*culpa leve*, equivalent to the reasonable person standard) and slightest negligence (*culpa levísima*). Fault implies the absence of diligence in the performance of a contract or in the execution of an act. Foresight is intrinsic to negligence ('the possibility of foreseeing what has not been foreseen')[21] and to causation (the harm imputable to the wrongdoer). The defendant is liable for the harm that a reasonable person would have foreseen. Further, direct harm is generally also foreseeable. Thus, through foreseeability, courts resolve the issue of causation with relative ease, using the but-for test.[22] Whether damage was a direct effect of the delict and whether harm was foreseeable when the tort was committed are factual problems within the trial courts' discretion.[23] By contrast, since unforeseen or unforeseeable harm is regarded as too remote, it is generally unrecoverable.

The tripartite division of fault is traditionally restricted to contract law, while the slightest negligence would bring about tort liability.[24] Therefore, tortfeasors must answer for all harms arising from delict or quasi-delict.[25] However, since *culpa leve* is the residual and appropriate category to measure the behaviour that can legitimately be expected from strangers in extracontractual relations, tort liability (except for intentional or grossly careless illicit acts) should be limited to direct and foreseen and/or foreseeable losses.[26]

*Dolo* is satisfied by *dolus directus*: the intention to harm the claimant as an end.[27] An obvious illustration is the unfair competitive act aimed at ruining rivals. Indeed, the exercise of a right becomes wrongful if it is solely targeted at injuring others. But since *dolo* is defined by statute (and statutory definitions are binding), the claimant must show the defendant's intention to injure, although proof can be indirect and inferred

21 SC.17/10/1972.RDJ.69.4ª.168.

22 R. Domínguez, 'Aspectos de la relación de causalidad en la responsabilidad civil con especial referencia al derecho chileno' (2001) 209 *RDUC* 7 at 14.

23 SC.12/8/1953.RDJ.50.1ª.288.

24 SC.7/4/1958.RDJ.55.1ª.35.

25 Conversely, contractual liability (except for deliberate or grossly negligent breach) is confined to the risks that the parties could contemplate and distribute when concluding their agreement, Art. 1558 CHCC. The restriction of compensation emerged from old French law, generalised by Pothier, reiterated in Art. 1150 *Code Civil* and adopted in *Hadley* v. *Baxendale* (1854) 156 ER at 151 per Alderson J.

26 C. Banfi, 'Por una reparación integral del daño extracontractual limitada a los hechos dolosos o gravemente negligentes' (2012) 22 *Ius et Praxis* 3–32. This idea finds recent support: SC.13/7/2015.26201-14; SC.29/12/2016.45946-16; Barros, *Tratado*, I, 86–8, 95–8.

27 Art. 44 CHCC.

from facts:[28] courts can establish serious, precise and concurring presumptions of the defendant's intention based on that evidence.[29] The classic examples do not concern commercial rivals, but they show that courts further confine *dolo* to malice ('the deliberate purpose of causing harm')[30] such as the obstruction by the owner of a servient tenement of a drainage canal merely for disturbing the dominant tenement owner's easement.[31]

However, *dolo* is not realistically satisfied by the defendant's disinterested malice but typically includes the infliction of loss as a means to another end, namely: to seek a benefit.[32] Thus, there is room for extending *dolo* to recklessness (*dolus eventualis*): to foresee and accept the victim's harm as a likely consequence of the defendant's act. This finds support in certain cases which define *dolo* as deliberate wrongful conduct, including recklessness.[33]

Yet recklessness should be irrelevant in private law where gross negligence is equated with intention in contract and tort.[34] This is because gross negligence resembles the intentional acceptance of a harmful effect. Gross negligence is therefore assessed more stringently than mere fault, though it is easier to prove than intention. Thus, since Chilean courts often restrict *dolo* to malice, while *culpa lata* involves the same effects as *dolo* but can be established with less effort, there is room for gross negligence being used more extensively by case law.

Courts further hold that tort compensation includes all direct losses flowing from delict and quasi-delict alike.[35] However, for the benefit of legal consistency, foresight should regulate negligence not only in contract but also in tort. Compensation should be confined to the direct and foreseeable harm arising from a quasi-delict, whilst intentional or grossly negligent torts ought to entail liability for all direct losses (including unforeseeable and unforeseen ones) arising therefrom, comparable to

[28] SC.31/7/2006.RDJ.103.1ª.596.

[29] SC.29/3/2012.7226-09.

[30] SC.6/1/1920.RDJ.18.1ª.405 at [1]. CASantiago.2/9/2010.3377-08 at [12].

[31] SC.19/10/1943.RDJ.41.1ª.266.

[32] Alessandri, *Responsabilidad*, 163.

[33] CAIquique.18/6/1953.RDJ.50.4ª.81.

[34] Art. 44 CHCC. SC.9/8/1944.RDJ.42.1ª.244. Compensation includes all direct losses flowing from intentional or grossly negligent breach of contract: Art. 1558 CHCC; SC.10/11/1920.RDJ.19.1ª.415.

[35] See above, n. 25.

the English intentional economic torts.[36] The retributive or extra-compensatory rationale for increasing contractual liability in the presence of intention or gross negligence, based on Article 1558 CHCC, should equally govern tortious liability ensuing from such obnoxious conduct.[37]

Thus, negligence is the failure to foresee what a reasonable person would have foreseen; hence compensation cannot include harm beyond that expectation. But where the victim is intentionally or grossly negligently injured, the wrongdoer should assume responsibility for all losses consequential upon their conduct. As Gordley posits, where the damage is intentionally inflicted it is immaterial whether the agent could foresee the risk that happened: the agent is liable 'simply because he wanted the harm that he caused to occur'.[38] Similarly, gross negligence 'creates risks so great and so easy to avert as to manifest a wilful indifference to the consequences to others. And so, once again, we have reached an ancient conclusion: *culpa lata dolo aequiparatur*, gross negligence amounts to an intentional wrong'.[39] Consequently, notwithstanding that the defendant's gross negligence is contrasted with an objective standard of (minimum) care,[40] it unveils reckless unconcern for the claimant's interests. Hence *culpa lata* brings about the same legal effects as *dolo*.[41]

Specifically, where trade adversaries are involved, tortious liability should be restricted in harmony with freedom of competition, through the requirement of intention or gross negligence. Thus, while English courts only exceptionally have awarded compensation for carelessly caused PEL,[42] Chilean courts avail themselves of gross negligence as a control device similar to intention.[43]

[36] See above, n. 13; H. McGregor, *McGregor on Damages*, 19th ed. (London: Thomson Reuters, 2014), pp. 1754–72, 1804–31.

[37] C. Banfi, *Responsabilidad civil por competencia desleal* (Santiago: Thomson Reuters, 2013), pp. 158–64.

[38] J. Gordley, 'Responsibility in Crime, Tort, and Contract for the Unforeseeable Consequences of an Intentional Wrong: A Once and Future Rule?', in P. Cane and J. Stapleton (eds.), *The Law of Obligations: Essays in Celebration of John Fleming* (Oxford: Clarendon Press, 1998), p. 194.

[39] Ibid., 198.

[40] *Culpa lata* is 'the failure to handle another's affairs with the care that even negligent and imprudent persons often employ in their own businesses', Art. 44 CHCC.

[41] 'This *culpa* amounts to *dolo* in civil matters', Art. 44 CHCC.

[42] See above, n. 12.

[43] Banfi, *Responsabilidad*, 184–92.

## 9.2 Limiting Tortious Liability Consistently with Freedom of Competition

### *9.2.1 A Loss of Profits*

In Chile, damage is widely understood as the infringement of a subjective right or legitimate interest in the claimant's person or goods.[44]

In particular, courts are not familiar with the expression 'pure economic loss', yet loss of profits (*lucrum cessans*) is a well-known legal category[45] that can be functionally equivalent to PEL.[46] Thus, in a 2008 case the claimant (an agricultural producer) commissioned a company to send from Chile several tonnes of special rose-hip therapeutic oil to an importer domiciled in Japan. The defendant communicated to the importer and the Chilean health authorities that the product was polluted with pesticide. The importer sent the load back to Chile, refusing to purchase it. Subsequently it was shown that the product was uncontaminated. The claimant brought a tort action to recover loss of profits arising from the defendant's false accusation. The defendant was found liable for carelessly damaging the claimant's commercial reputation. His false, serious and negligent accusation prevented the transaction from succeeding. The claimant was awarded the price of the frustrated export up to the amount proved at trial.[47]

*Lucrum cessans* occupies the middle ground between *damnum emergens* (highly certain damage) and loss of chance (which is recoverable as a value assigned to the possibility of making profits).[48] To prove *lucrum cessans*, the claimant must compare their actual situation with the gain they might have got had they not been injured; for example, weighing the transactions made before against those made after suffering harm (by analogy), or determining the income that they would have earned had the tort not been committed (by projection). Claimants must also establish the likelihood of that loss happening in the future, and that it flowed directly from the defendant's conduct.[49] It has been proposed that courts should merely require evidence of the reasonable probability (not mere

[44] SC.6/11/1972.RDJ.69.4ª.181.

[45] 'Compensation for damages includes *damnum emergens and lucrum cessans*', Art. 1556 CHCC.

[46] CASantiago.7/12/1984.RDJ.81.4ª.266.

[47] CAConcepción.30/12/2008.360-05; SC.15/11/2011.3516-09.

[48] SC.24/4/2019.7108-17.

[49] R. Domínguez, 'Consideraciones en torno a la noción de daño en la responsabilidad civil: Una visión comparatista' (1990) 188 *RDUC* 125, 148.

possibility) of suffering *lucrum cessans*, given that this kind of harm lacks absolute certainty. Nor should courts demand proof of the exact amount of loss if it has been shown that the claimant has effectively sustained it. It ought to suffice that the loss of profits was presumed from the fact that the claimant had been deprived of work for a long period due to the defendant's act. Courts are not bound by codal rules which limit compensation in contract but have ample discretion to award damages for lost profits in tort, including lump sums.[50]

Courts, however, frequently reject compensation for lost profits, holding it speculative, thereby demanding proof of the reasonably expected income, at least for a certain period, under normal circumstances.[51] Trial courts award non-pecuniary damage instead, which is often inferred from the direct victim's death or injury.[52]

Thus, although all kinds of damage intentionally or negligently caused must be compensated, the prospect of PEL being awarded is not auspicious: courts are likely to reject it on the grounds of uncertainty of harm and lack of causation. This procedure is consistent with the widely accepted (in Chile) duty not to harm others carelessly, and with the fact that corporeal goods and incorporeal interests, such as contractual rights and purely financial interests, are equally protected by the right of property enshrined in the Constitution and the CHCC. Nevertheless, even if this method practically limits liability and attains results analogous to the English economic torts, in a business context it mistakenly assumes that competitors owe each other a duty of care while the reverse is true: carelessly caused harm is a side effect of legitimate business struggle.[53] Therefore, discarding liability for lack of causation or uncertainty of damage can solve the tension between the litigants' conflicting interests, but at the expense of misunderstanding the gist of competition and sacrificing the liberty to compete. Also, this technique makes liability dependent on causation and damage, whereas it is the defendant's conduct that should really matter.[54]

[50] J. Díez, *El daño extracontractual* (Santiago: Jurídica de Chile, 1997), pp. 57 and 182.

[51] SC.28/5/2002.GJ.263.170.

[52] SC.24/10/2000.GJ.244.98.

[53] Banfi, *Responsabilidad*, 12, 208, 236–7; Barros, *Tratado*, I, 168–9, II, 963–5. Cf. M. Tapia, 'Competencia desleal por culpa' (2017) 29 *RCHDP* 165, arguing that unfair competition requires mere negligence, not intention as he initially claimed in 'Responsabilidad civil por actos de competencia desleal en el derecho chileno' (2007) 14 *CEJUA* 85–94.

[54] It is noteworthy that French courts restrict tort liability in commercial competition similarly to English courts, albeit they reach this outcome following a different path.

Accordingly, a better approach should acknowledge that negligently caused PEL is a collateral consequence of a commercial battle which is justifiable, however fierce it is. The wide principle of *culpa* should be tempered by requiring proof of the defendant's intention to injure the claimant or at least gross negligence, which is statutorily equivalent to the former and similar to recklessness: it discloses a notorious disregard for the claimant's interests. A mental element stricter than mere carelessness is crucial for tortious liability to perform preventive and retributive functions, alongside its primary compensatory role, in respect of unfair competition. The intentional or grossly negligent infliction of PEL often exposes the abuse of the right/liberty to compete, an abuse which is manifest in unfair practices. So, the requirement of intention to harm (which can only be proved indirectly, as an inference from unfair behaviour) is coherent with freedom of competition, which is part of the economic liberty that has constitutional value.[55] It is true that this suggestion might seem inconsistent with the principle of *culpa*, and it might also expose the lower courts which adhered to that proposal to their decisions being quashed via cassation for infringing that canon. Case law, however, has reinterpreted this principle in line with the UCA under which unfair practices are intentional torts.[56]

### *9.2.2 Gaining Insights on Limitations from Other Legal Systems*

We suggest that the role of tort liability in the regulation of business battles must remain a limited one. In line with freedom of competition, compensation for PEL should be restricted since commercial contenders naturally and intentionally harm one another. Liability should be refused except for specific torts (as in England) or extreme behaviour against good commercial customs embodying the agent's intention or reckless indifference to harm the claimant (as in §826 BGB). Here, Chilean law has much to learn from the English conservative regime.

Rather than discriminating between diverse categories of damage, the French courts reinterpret fault as comprising not only negligence (or even intention to harm) but also the breach of the duty to behave honestly in business strife, that is, courts demand *concurrence déloyale*, G. Wagner, 'Comparative Tort Law', in M. Reimann and R. Zimmermann (eds.), *The Oxford Handbook of Comparative Law*, 2nd ed. (Oxford: Oxford University Press, 2019), pp. 1006–10.

55 Art. 19 No. 21 Chilean Constitution.

56 Banfi, *Responsabilidad*, 213–38.

English law generally denies liability for carelessly inflicted PEL,[57] compensation for which must be sought through the intentional economic torts. By comparison, if liability is to be enforced consistently with freedom to compete, Chilean courts ought to require the defendant's intention or gross negligence, and this should in turn stretch the duty to compensate to all direct losses. First, intention is more reprehensible than simple carelessness as wrongdoers know their acts will produce a result disapproved by the law. Second, total disregard for legal prohibitions – or for another's interests – surely exceeds negligent conduct. Third, extra compensation is consistent with the greater difficulty in assessing harm and in establishing the causal link between the wrongful conduct and the injury.[58]

Indeed, Chilean courts already award more damages to victims of deliberate acts. Although tortious liability mainly serves to compensate for the victim's harm, Chilean trial courts perform a camouflaged punitive function: formally, they recognise a purely reparatory policy to restore the victim's status quo;[59] implicitly, they use retributive criteria to order higher awards of non-pecuniary injury within their discretion.[60] Yet the nature of the defendant's conduct[61] and the gravity of the defendant's fault[62] stand out as punitive strands. Through this concealed method, courts elude the risk of their decisions being quashed, since punitive damages – which are clearly associated with criminal liability – are not enshrined in the law. It is suggested that the retributive criteria used by courts to award higher sums for non-pecuniary harm could be extended to intentionally or grossly negligently caused PEL. Courts would not need to wait until Congress allows punitive damages: they can simply rely on Article 1558 CHCC.[63]

The alternative control device, based on mere negligence, is conceptually unsound. Although courts can restrain a negligence-based liability by holding PEL to be uncertain, remote or unproven, this method takes for granted that trade competitors owe each other a duty of care when they do not. As Fleming asserted, the crucial issue in the tort of negligence is to limit liability, amongst others, through the concepts of duty and

[57] S. Deakin and Z. Adams, *Markesinis and Deakin's Tort Law*, 8th ed. (Oxford: Oxford University Press, 2019), pp. 124 ff.

[58] Barros, *Tratado*, I, 171–3, 427–8.

[59] SC.16/10/1970.RDJ.67.4ª.424.

[60] SC.14/9/1987.RDJ.84.4ª.137.

[61] SC.13/11/2003.GJ.281.104.

[62] SC.2/12/1998.FM.481.2737.

[63] See above, nn. 25 and 34.

causation. Likewise, a general principle of liability for negligence may produce order, albeit not necessarily sound case law: 'An undifferentiated approach may satisfy the quest for uniformity but is unlikely to produce desirable decisions'.[64] Extending this analysis to business rivalry, Chilean courts could opt for curbing liability through an intentional element which is consistent with the essence of competing. For the sake of legal consistency, they should qualify the principle of *culpa* in line with freedom of competition.

Here they can find a valuable guide in the floodgates argument that led Anglo-American tort law into foreclosing the recovery of carelessly caused PEL.[65] The fact that English case law severely restricts liability between commercial competitors through a mental element more severe than mere negligence and unlawful means, shows the vitality of the floodgate argument. Through the economic torts, courts can counteract the risk of limitless liability and litigation attributed to negligence-based liability for financial harm.

In turn, Chilean courts could restrict liability through the requirement of the defendant's intention to harm the claimant or gross negligence. This control mechanism may not only prevent floods of litigation;[66] it may also confine liability to abusive misconduct, thus signalling that the role of tort liability in the regulation of business battles must remain limited. If tortious liability is to be imposed consistently with freedom of competition, compensation for PEL should be restricted since commercial contenders naturally and intentionally harm one another. Liability should then be refused except for specific torts (as in England) or extreme behaviour against good commercial customs embodying the agent's intention or reckless indifference to harm the claimant (as in §826 BGB).

### 9.2.3 *Abuse of Rights*

Currently, Chilean law accepts the principle of liability for intentionally inflicted harm even if it is brought about when exercising a subjective right, including personal (contractual) rights and real rights (such as

[64] J. Fleming, 'Remoteness and Duty: The Control Devices in Liability for Negligence' (1953) *Canadian Bar Review* 471, 481.

[65] *Ultramares Corp* v. *Touche* 255 NY 170 (1931) at 179, Cardozo CJ; *Caparo Industries Plc* v. *Dickman* [1990] 2 AC 605 at 621–2 per Lord Bridge.

[66] Thus, the Chilean Supreme Court knew about 12,000 cases during the second half of 2017 only. See www.decs.pjud.cl

property). Subjective rights are relative and limited externally by statute or by contract to permit a peaceful coexistence between individuals enjoying equal freedom. They are also constrained internally: they must not be exercised abusively. This means that right-holders abuse their rights if they act within the external margins defined by the law but exceed the internal bounds of the right at risk.[67] So, the modern abuse-of-rights doctrine attempts to moralise the law, and it provides a strong justification for imposing tort liability for damage arising from the abnormal exercise of rights.[68] More importantly, the abuse of rights limits and justifies tort liability for intentionally caused economic harm along with yielding content to unfair practices. In fact, the most notorious case of abuse of rights involves deliberately caused harm, which helps to regulate liability between trade opponents.

The intentional infliction of harm without justification is the paradigmatic case of abuse of rights, or under the American prima facie tort theory.[69] Chilean courts usually associate the abuse of rights with the defendant's malice. The abuse of rights in its most intense sense provides the best examples of this. The classic case concerned a buyer of a car who, having found defects in it, made exaggerated requests to the claimant (car-seller), who resisted them. Through a newspaper advertisement, whereby the defendant offered his car for sale, he denigrated the automobile brand and the seller. The court found that the defendant had abused his right of property which only allowed him to offer his car for sale without injuring the claimant. The defendant was declared tortiously liable.[70] Today this case would arguably be dealt with as malicious falsehood under the UCA.

[67] Barros, *Tratado*, I, 655.

[68] L. Josserand, *De l'esprit des droits et de leur relativité*, 2nd ed. (Paris: Dalloz, 1939). Cf. M. Planiol, *Traité élémentaire de droit civil*, 10th ed. (Paris: LGDJ, 1926); G. Ripert, *La règle morale dans les obligations civiles* (Paris: LGDJ, 1949).

[69] '[P]rima facie, the intentional infliction of temporal damage is a cause of action, which as a matter of substantive law, whatever may be the form of pleading, requires a justification if the defendant is to escape.' *Aikens* v. *Wisconsin* 195 US 194 (1904) at 204 per Holmes J. See also *Porter* v. *Crawford & Co.*, 611 S.W.2d 265 (Mo. Ct. App. 1980). In *Aikens*, Holmes cited Bowen LJ's dictum ('intentionally to do that which is calculated in the ordinary course of events to damage, and which does, in fact, damage another in that other person's property or trade, is actionable if done without just cause or excuse', *Mogul Steamship* v. *McGregor* (1889) LR 23 QBD 598 at 613), yet this does not represent English law: *Allen* v. *Flood* [1898] AC 1; *OBG Ltd* v. *Allan* [2008] 1 AC 1.

[70] SC.15/11/1927.RDJ.25.1ª.501.

Nonetheless, abuse of *process* is perhaps the form of abuse that most typically creates tort liability in Chile. This also uncovers a certain judicial inclination to confine the abuse of rights to very extreme misconduct, such as the intentional, reckless or grossly negligent causation of damage.[71] Moreover, although the Chilean courts have distinguished several variants of the abuse of rights (including carelessness, abnormality, absence of legitimate interest and conduct contrary to good customs or good faith), they tend to confine the abuse of rights to malicious behaviour.[72] Accordingly, the abuse of rights is rather like an alternative manner of describing intentionally inflicted harm.

This said, the malicious exercise of a right is a strange hypothesis of abusive conduct, proof of which is hard and can easily be negated through justification. The claimant must bring evidence that the defendant intended to injure them as a means to another end or acted grossly negligently. Indeed, the intention to harm can be surmised from the absence of utility for the defendant. For instance, it can be inferred from the irrational act of digging a water well seeking no benefit whatsoever.[73] Thus, we see that the abuse of rights serves to justify liability for unfair practices and to understand the need for compensating intentionally inflicted PEL. However, although the abuse of rights can also consist of negligent behaviour, tort liability for PEL arising from competition should be limited to *dolo* or *culpa lata* in order to preserve economic freedom.

The abuse of rights thus reveals wrongful conduct and makes tort actions more persuasive. By extension, the abuse of the right to compete renders unfair commercial practices unlawful. The connection between unfair competition and the abuse of rights is evident in systems lacking specific legislation, such as French law, but also even when unfair competition is statutorily forbidden, as happens under the UCA. The only difference is that claimants can choose between using the tort principles or the special statute.[74]

[71] SC.23/7/2013.8243-12.

[72] CASantiago.9/11/1992.GJ.149.58.

[73] Art. 56 Chilean Waters Code.

[74] Until 2007, there were no reported economic tort cases based on the CHCC's general provisions although legal scholars had long before recognised the possibility of suing in tort the accomplice in the breach of another's contract. The situation changed dramatically since the UCA was enacted. See below Section 9.3.

### 9.2.4 *Wrongfulness*

Wrongfulness helps to control liability for harm caused between business opponents when it is subsumed under intention or gross negligence, that is, abusive and unjustified conduct. Wrongfulness is not generally regarded as an independent ingredient of tortious liability, it is rather subsumed under *culpa*: the breach of a duty of care imposed by the law.[75] It can alternatively comprise the breach of the general duty not to harm others, the violation of a specific statutory duty intended to protect the class of persons from the type of harm corresponding to the claimant's rights (*culpa infraccional*) or the infringement of another's rights. In the latter two cases, the act is presumed to be culpable.[76]

Here, the treatment of a breach of a statutory provision is comparable to that in England (where the victim injured by the violation of a statute the purpose of which is to protect them against such harm can bring a tort action for breach of statutory duty). Similarly, Chilean courts consider the breach of statute by the defendant as the cause of the claimant's harm if the claimant falls within the statutory protection. There must be a sufficient connection between the defendant's breach of the rule of conduct and the claimant's (statutorily protected) interest and damage.[77] So, while fault is generally included in wrongfulness, the breach of statutory duty constitutes wrongfulness from which fault is deduced.

However, wrongfulness can also be embodied in harm and causation: the defendant's conduct is treated as wrongful because it culpably and directly injured the victim. Accordingly, there is no need for distinguishing wrongfulness from fault, damage and causation: wrongfulness is invariably understood as the breach of duty.[78] Thus, even if wrongfulness seems more suitable for providing legal certainty about the prohibited conduct in a casuistic system such as the English legal system, the fact is that a broad fault principle, like that of Chilean law, absorbs wrongfulness. Eventually, whether wrongfulness is autonomous or incorporated into fault is a formal choice only. Courts must always evaluate the litigants' conflicting interests and clearly establish which types of injurious conduct are unacceptable. It is worth emphasising that, in a business context, the harm derived from business competition is at first sight

[75] SC.12/8/1981.RDJ.78.4ª.120.

[76] SC.20/7/1992.RDJ.89.1ª.90.

[77] SC.22/4/1998.GJ.214.115.

[78] E. Descheemaeker, *The Division of Wrongs: A Historical Comparative Study* (Oxford: Oxford University Press, 2009), p. 17.

justified, unless the defendant abused their right to compete through the perpetration of conduct prohibited by the UCA.[79]

## 9.3 Chilean Case Law under the Unfair Competition Act

Both unfair practices and torts in Chilean law involve similar kinds of intention and harm as both fall in the private law sphere. However, unfair practices are mainly remedied through preventive actions, whereas tort law fulfils a circumscribed role in this arena. In Chile, tort law plays a limited function in deterring and punishing unfair practices as compared with alternative legal and extra-legal mechanisms. As described in the previous section, tort actions provide compensation for individual harm flowing from unfair practices, and the UCA – the first Chilean systematic legislation on the topic – has invigorated tort law. However, in fact, other remedies than compensation are better at preventing unfair practices from happening, and I now consider both the UCA case law and these remedies.

Unfair practices are prima facie intentional and illicit acts. Wrongfulness is a necessary requirement since competition is normally legitimate, however fierce it might be. So, although a sweeping clause such as Article 3 UCA only formally differs from the delict rules enshrined in a civil code[80] such as the CHCC,[81] it can promote the enforcement of tortious liability against reprehensible business conduct.

As the case law illustrates, litigants and courts have increasingly used the general delict principles to deal with unfair practices since the UCA allows them to sue for damages in tort relying on the general rules set forth in the CHCC.[82]

It is worth mentioning that, while the UCA refers to protecting competitors, consumers and any person injured in their legitimate interest by unfair practices, it primarily applies to commercial competitors. This is evident in the general clause[83] and the specific unfair acts sanctioned by

[79] M. Inostroza argues in 'El ilícito concurrencial general en la Ley N° 20.169 sobre competencia desleal' (2017) 23 *Iuset Praxis* 21 that unfair competition would demand independently unlawful means alongside the defendant's mental element. Time does not permit consideration of this point; suffice it to say, however, that this requirement would in practice seem undistinguishable from the generic and specific acts prohibited by the UCA.

[80] A. Kamperman, *Unfair Competition Law* (Oxford: Clarendon Press, 1997), p. 69.

[81] Arts. 2314 ff. CHCC.

[82] Art. 5 (d) UCA.

[83] Art. 3 UCA.

the UCA.[84] In addition, the UCA offers a wide range of private law remedies to prevent unfair practices (and, as said, to compensate for individual harm). Thus, any person directly threatened or affected in their legitimate interests can claim the cessation and/or prohibition of the unfair practice;[85] request the declaration of such conduct;[86] and/or ask for the removal of the effects arising from the unfair practice through the publication of the judgment at the defendant's expense.[87]

Since the enactment of the UCA, the Chilean Supreme Court has decided more than 150 cases, yet only exceptionally has it delved into the ingredients of the economic torts. Only a few examples of the main kinds of unfair commercial practices decided by courts can be offered here.

### Passing Off

The claimant (Acepta.com) and the first defendant (SouthConsulting) compete in the provision of electronic billing services. SouthConsulting contracted with the second defendant (Google) to the effect that web users were redirected to SouthConsulting's webpage upon writing down the claimant's trademarks. Accepta.com sought a declaration from the court that SouthConsulting passed off its services as if they were Accepta.com's, to enjoin it from continuing to do so and to hold it liable for loss of profits and non-pecuniary harm. The court allowed the remedies in kind as SouthConsulting had intended to divert customers from Acepta.com into its own firm, thereby causing confusion amongst Google's users. Rather than making a mistake, SouthConsulting deliberately and fully consciously violated Acepta.com's rights by including in its advertising the direct rival's trademarks which SouthConsulting (unlike Google) could not ignore. The tort action was rejected since *lucrum cessans* (including what Acepta.com had named as 'non-pecuniary') was not shown at trial.[88]

### Misleading and Comparative Advertising

FASA and CV are drugstore companies and aggressive competitors in Chile. CV carried out an advertising campaign comparing hundreds of drugs sold by it against FASA's equivalent products. CV deliberately

[84] Art. 4 UCA.
[85] Art. 5 (a) UCA.
[86] Art. 5 (b) UCA.
[87] Art. 5 (c) UCA.
[88] 3CivilCourtSantiago.28/11/2012.55530-09; CASantiago.24/3/2014.484-13.

chose three of its drugs, declaring them to be the most consumed ones in the relevant market, and stated that its prices were lower than FASA's. CV excluded from its campaign the generic medicines, notwithstanding that they represented a high percentage of the drugstores' sales. CV hid the fact that the drugs included in its promotion favoured its club members only. FASA filed the four actions under the UCA.

The court ordered CV immediately to cease its advertising campaign. Comparative advertising, the court reasoned, must be demonstrably truthful and use lawful means, thereby highlighting the qualities of one's products without attacking those of a rival. The fact that the advertising campaign at issue was directly and exclusively targeted at FASA showed the defendant's intention to lure the claimant's customers. FASA also sought compensation for the costs incurred in investing in advertising and relocating its trademarks, loss of profits from the drop in sales from the beginning of CV's campaign until the legal proceedings commenced, and reputational damage.

Although CV had intended to harm FASA, the court dismissed the tort lawsuit as neither harm nor the causal link were shown. The fall in FASA's sales, the court expressed, could be explained by reasons unrelated to CV's behaviour. And although there was no evidence of the detriment of FASA's prestige other than the value of the claimant's assets, this supposed harm, the court thought, could be ameliorated as a result of the advertising campaign being forbidden.[89] The Court of Appeal confirmed this judgment but also allowed the tort claim. It held that the unlawful means are implicit in any conduct contrary to good faith or good commercial customs.[90] The Supreme Court approved the lower court's decision. CV, it held, had simply disagreed with the trial court's appraisal of the facts, which is beyond cassation.[91]

### Malicious Falsehood

Danone and Soprole compete in the Chilean market for the sale of yogurt. Soprole undertook an advertising campaign through a TV spot where a famous model recommended to women Soprole's yogurt to counteract intestinal problems. She said: 'forget about the bad stuff and stay with the good one'. Danone filed an action for malicious falsehood

[89] 17CivilCourtSantiago.30/6/2010.23423-07.
[90] CASantiago.23/7/2012.4155-10.
[91] SC.29.11.2012.8196-12.

arguing Soprole's advertising campaign discredited Danone's yogurt, which had previously been promoted by the model's (also celebrity) sister on TV. Soprole proved its advertising campaign relied on scientific research about the consumers' perceptions. The court dismissed the claim for absence of a mental element. It held that competition is a legitimate activity the effect of which (to grab a rival's clientele) is lawful. Without the wrongdoer's intention to harm a rival or reckless indifference conduct cannot be deemed contrary to good faith or good customs.[92] The judgment was upheld on appeal, yet unfair practice was objectively construed (as the violation of the duty of loyalty which market agents must observe) without requiring a mental element.[93]

### Inducing Breach of Contract

Case 1. The defendants were journalists working for the claimant's advertising agency under employment contracts which included a non-compete clause, an obligation not to attract the claimant's clients and a prohibition from hiring the claimant's employees within two years after the contracts finished. The defendants resigned their jobs and soon afterwards were employed in top positions by the claimant's competitor. Subsequently the latter hired and enticed several of the claimant's employees and clients. The claimant sued the defendants for unfair competition. The action was rejected. Although the defendants intentionally and successfully diverted the claimant's clients, thereby breaking their obligations with the claimant, the court concluded that they had not acted in bad faith, that is, with 'a fraudulent attitude and the intention to harm the other contracting party'. In the court's view, the fact that the claimant's clients followed the claimant's employees with whom they had established personal links of trust, as is customary in the advertising business, excluded the use of unlawful means.[94]

Case 2. Tais was the sole distributor and seller of the claimant's (Christian Dior) luxurious cosmetics and perfumes in specialised shops located in the wealthy areas of Santiago. During their relationship, Tais sold those goods only very occasionally at promoted prices in its inelegant store located in a down-market area of the city. When the contract

[92] 12CivilCourtSantiago.26/5/2015.5096-12.

[93] CASantiago.25/5/2016.11068-15.

[94] 8CivilCourtSantiago.12/7/2012.15139-11; SC.31/7/2014.11531-14.

was about to expire Tais refused to resell the products in stock to the claimant, as it had committed itself under the covenant, and instead transferred them to the first defendant (Garmont), a company owned by the second defendant (García, formerly Tais' general manager). Garmont sold the remaining goods at very low prices in Tais' store and in an additional shop under its name, which was decorated with Christian Dior's furniture. Christian Dior sued the defendants for inducing Tais to break the distribution contract, seeking from the court to declare the defendants liable for unfair competition.

The lower courts dismissed the claim. Although Tais had arguably broken its obligation with Christian Dior – and although the very conduct prohibited by the UCA demonstrates bad faith – the defendants had not acted in bad faith or used unlawful means.[95] The Supreme Court annulled the Court of Appeal's decision, holding the defendants liable on several grounds.

Firstly, unlawful means is not a separate but a redundant ingredient of the unfair conduct. It can be embodied in the violation of the good faith or good commercial customs. It can also (or alternatively) be incorporated into the specifically prohibited conduct. In the instant case, the unlawful means used by the defendants consisted of the generic unfair practice[96] and the inducement of breach of contract.[97] Here García aimed at extending the distribution contract in terms not authorised by Christian Dior, with the aid of a third party (Garmont) closely related to García, thus injuring the claimant's legitimate interests.

Secondly, unfair competition involves the breach of objective rules of conduct – or the standard of a decent entrepreneur[98] – without need for any intention, yet this is typically involved.[99] Indeed, the consumers would not be properly protected if liability required proof of the defendant's intention or even negligence. Therefore, courts should follow an objective approach in order to determine if those rules, deduced from good faith, were actually contravened.

Thirdly, the applicable standard of conduct imposes a duty not to act in such a manner that depreciates the exclusivity of the claimant's product. The defendants did not take care of the places where and the

[95] CASantiago.10/7/2014.3053-13 at [4].

[96] Art. 3 UCA.

[97] Art. 4 (f) UCA.

[98] Barros, *Tratado*, II, 963–4.

[99] O. Contreras, *La competencia desleal* (Santiago: Ediciones UC, 2012), pp. 97–100, 162.

prices at which they sold Christian Dior's goods, nor did they preserve the claimant's select consumers of luxurious, exclusive and renowned products. Instead, they commercialised them at very low prices in a popular shop. Hence they undermined the consumers' perception of Christian Dior's world-famous brand, thereby likely causing the claimant's clientele to be diverted to the defendants.

Fourthly, inducing breach of contract demands proof of the defendant's intention, mere negligence being insufficient. The agreement interfered with by the inducer need not be in force but this tort covers situations where the defendant causes a contracting party to break their post-contractual obligations owed to the claimant. The fact that the defendants were well informed about the operation of the business (as evident in the long-term contract between Christian Dior and Tais) suggests that they also intended to attract Christian Dior's customers for their own benefit. So the defendants intentionally interfered with the performance of Tais' duty under the contract with the purpose of drawing in Christian Dior's clientele. This is quite irrational conduct in any event. Indeed, the defendants and Tais could have charged much higher resale prices for the products in stock than they actually obtained.[100]

Case 3. The claimant entered into an agency agreement with an Austrian manufacturer (Forsttechnik) to sell Forsttechnik's forestry machinery in Chile. The claimant honestly believed he was Forsttechnik's exclusive agent. Shortly afterwards the defendant started to sell those machines in Chile. The claimant sued the defendant for inducing breach of contract. The action was dismissed as the defendant (not the claimant) was Forsttechnik's exclusive representative.[101] Interestingly, unfair competition was defined as 'an intentional act, aimed at diverting clientele, committed in bad faith or with intention to harm'.[102] The claimant sought the annulment of the decision, arguing it had proved the unfair conduct which, in their view, did not include a mental element. The motion was ruled out as an attempt to alter the facts established at trial.[103]

Therefore, courts have not agreed on whether the generic act is just the breach of an objective standard of care or – as in inducing breach of contract – it comprises a mental element.

[100] SC.25/11/2015.23680-14.

[101] 1CivilCourtTalcahuano.21.3.2014.3344-13.

[102] CAConcepción.16/4/2015.547-14 at [6].

[103] SC.22/6/2016.6722-15.

## 9.4 Comparative Observations on Tortious Interference with Contract

The economic torts are fertile for drawing comparisons and learning from foreign experiences. The fact that domestic laws are heavily influenced by national traditions and idiosyncrasies attracts the comparatist's interest. In fact, national jurisdictions deploy procedural and substantive mechanisms to control unfair practices without adhering to a given legal family.[104]

Chilean case law on the matter shows that the generic conduct and the specific torts enshrined in the UCA cannot be committed accidentally: wrongdoers foresee and intend to – or recklessly or grossly negligently – harm rivals. Beyond the UCA, however, case law on tortious liability for unfair competition is conspicuously missing. Although legal commentary endorses a principle of liability for knowingly and culpably assisting with the breach of another's contract,[105] and asserts that the accomplice and the defaulting promisor must answer for all the harm caused to the claimant (despite the fact technically they are not joint tortfeasors but commit separate wrongs),[106] there are almost no reported cases. In fact, in a solitary and recent case, the tort action brought against the accomplice in the breach of another's contract was dismissed for lack of causation and for the reason that the defendant's intention to harm the claimant was not proved.[107]

A possible explanation for the paucity of tort actions against accomplices for the breach of someone else's contract is that litigants heavily rely on contractual remedies to protect personal rights, as case law shows. For example, one defendant promised to sell his real estate to the claimant – who paid the price beforehand – but finally sold it to third parties, who knew this transaction implied the breach of the claimant's option. The claimant filed *acción pauliana* (which serves to rescind a contract made between a debtor and a third party to the creditor's detriment, subject to proof of the contracting parties' knowledge of the debtor's insolvency)[108] to annul the sale and cancel the registration of the

[104] F. Henning-Bodewig, *Unfair Competition Law* (The Hague: Kluwer, 2006), p. 3.

[105] Alessandri, *Responsabilidad*, 62–3; J. López and F. Elorriaga, *Los contratos*, 6th ed. (Santiago: Thomson Reuters, 2017), p. 392.

[106] Barros, *Tratado*, I, 446–9.

[107] 23CivilCourtSantiago.8/2/2017.28.967-11; CASantiago.18/4/2018.5552-17; SC.22/10/2018.13188-18; C. Banfi, 'El contrato y los terceros', in A. Vidal (ed.), *Estudios sobre derecho de los contratos* (Santiago: Thomson Reuters, 2018), pp. 933–51.

[108] Art. 2468 CHCC.

property under the purchasers' name, alleging damages in both contract and tort. Interestingly, the tort (not the contractual) action succeeded: the defaulting promisor had acted unlawfully and negligently in knowingly depriving the claimant of the property for which the latter paid in advance, even though the claimant failed to prove the defendant's *dolo* he had pleaded.[109] The claimant could have sued the purchasers as accomplices in the breach of contract, yet for unexplained reasons he did not.[110]

Similarly, where the defendant had unilaterally terminated a construction contract, thereby preventing the builder from continuing the works by entrusting them to a third party (the latter knowing of that contract), the builder unsuccessfully claimed damages for deliberate breach of contract: he could not prove the defendant's intention to harm.[111] A tort claim against the accomplice might have been more auspicious, and particularly helpful if the contract-breaker was insolvent.[112] Moreover, prospective claimants could take advantage of the fact that courts award tort compensation for all direct losses even if the defendant acted with mere negligence.

Tort law can safeguard the proprietary dimension of contractual rights, reinforce contractual remedies and supplement the gaps left by privity of contract. It can also deter outsiders from inducing or participating in the breach of another's contract, increase the security in transactions and diminish the risk of debtors' insolvency. A moderate tort can be useful if promisees are averse to the risk of revealing confidential information or deteriorating their contractual relationships.[113] To the contrary, commercial certainty would be undermined if outsiders were liable for carelessly failing to find out whether the defaulting promisor had already contracted with the claimant so the subsequent agreement with the contract-breaker infringed the first covenant.[114]

[109] SC.26/1/2000.RDJ.97.1ª.36.

[110] R. Domínguez, 'Comentario de Jurisprudencia' (2000) 209 *RDUC* 177.

[111] CASerena.29/5/2003.27568-02; SC.6/5/2004.2656-03.

[112] C. Pizarro, 'Comentario de Jurisprudencia' (2005) 4 *RCHDP* 193–8.

[113] V. Palmer, 'A Comparative Study (from a Common Law Perspective) of the French Action for Wrongful Interference with Contract' (1992) 40 *American Journal of Comparative Law* 297, 323, 334–5.

[114] Inducing breach of contract would reach disproportionate breadth if it embraced careless interference with unenforceable or terminable at-will agreements, as held in *J'Aire Corp.* v. *Gregory* 24 Cal.3d 799 (1979).

Thus, I argue that if Chilean courts are to enforce tortious liability for interference with contracts as a specific instance of unfair competition, they should follow the more conservative English pattern when weighing the third party's freedom to compete against the claimant's contractual rights. Chilean law should recognise liability for inducing breach of contract (subject to the defendant's intention to cause the breach)[115] and liability for interfering with contractual performance without causing any breach (subject to the defendant's intention to harm the claimant, as in the tort of intentionally causing loss by unlawful means).[116]

The intention in inducing a breach of contract flows from the causal link between the defendant's conduct and its effect: the inducer wishes and provokes the breach of contract; one who prevents performance seeks and causes the claimant's harm. The intention requirement also implies that contractual rights enjoy stronger protection than economic interests in business at large. The mental element isolates abusive conduct from legitimate competition, and it excludes tortious liability founded on simple fault or bad faith which might lead to excesses. Moreover, the intention ingredient finds support in the UCA, which defines inducing breach of contract in terms of seeking to persuade a contracting party to break their obligations to the defendant's competitor.[117] But not every contract interfered with justifies the imposition of liability: the contract must not be illegal, anticompetitive, unenforceable or terminable at will.

Whether the defendant intended to cause the breach of contract or to harm the claimant can be surmised from the fact that they knew or should have known of the contract interfered with. Here Chilean courts could learn from the English case law: there is no need for the defendant to be fully aware of the contract involved,[118] yet they must have been able to realise that they could contribute to the breach of contract and consequently damage the claimant's interests.[119] The defendant's knowledge in the relevant activity are indications from which courts can infer the intention to harm.[120]

[115] *Lumley* v. *Gye* (1853) 118 ER 749.

[116] *OBG* v. *Allan* [2008] 1 AC 1.

[117] Art. 4(f) UCA.

[118] *Dimbleby & Sons Ltd* v. *NUJ* [1984] 1 WLR 427, 433–4 per Lord Diplock.

[119] *Stratford* v. *Lindley* [1965] AC 269, 323–4 per Lord Reid.

[120] *Merkur Island Shipping Corp.* v. *Laughton* [1983] 2 AC 570, 608–9 per Lord Diplock.

Indeed, the defendant acts knowingly and intentionally not only if aware of the contract interfered with, but also if disregarding the means whereby they could know of it:

> Even if they did not know of the actual terms of the contract, but had the means of knowledge – which they deliberately disregarded – that would be enough. Like the man who turns a blind eye . . . For it is unlawful for a third person to procure a breach of contract knowingly, or recklessly, indifferent whether it is a breach or not.[121]

Thus, the mental element is proved if the defendant recklessly neglected the possibility of causing or facilitating the breach of the contracting party's obligations to the detriment of the claimant, because 'a conscious decision not to inquire into the existence of a fact is in many cases treated as equivalent to knowledge of that fact'.[122] Similarly, it is held that 'even if true "knowledge" could only be obtained by reading the contract itself, there was sufficient Nelsonian blindness to justify an alternative finding that [the inducer] were reckless as to the existence of the exclusivity provision'.[123]

However, while English law does not extend this effect to gross negligence, in Chile, the defendant equally acts knowingly if grossly negligently ignoring the chance of influencing or provoking the breach of the claimant's contract. Then, actual or constructive knowledge is a strong indication on which the court can conclude that the accomplice in the breach of a third party's contract either intended to cause this outcome, or was recklessly indifferent (or grossly negligent) to it and did nothing to prevent the claimant from being injured.

Foreign solutions should not be unthinkingly transplanted into Chile but adapted to the country's needs. Comparative law also helps to discard unworkable solutions. The English approach to economic torts is not just compatible with Chilean law; it is worth emulating.

## 9.5 Concluding Remarks

Chilean courts traditionally deny liability for carelessly caused PEL, treating the latter as uncertain or too remote a consequence of the defendant's act. However, in the specific area of unfair competition, they

[121] *Emerald Construction Co.* v. *Lothian* [1966] 1 WLR 691, 700–1 per Lord Denning MR.

[122] *OBG Ltd* v. *Allan* [2008] 1 AC 1 at [41] per Lord Hoffmann.

[123] *One Money Mail Ltd* v. *Ria Financial Services* [2015] EWCA Civ 1084 at [26] per Longmore LJ.

accept tortious liability for carelessly caused PEL but often condition tort actions and remedies in kind on proof of the defendant's knowledge, or intention to harm the claimant, or intention to procure the breach of contract. The outcome is analogous to that achieved in England. More importantly, it is a sound approach: a mental element stricter than bare negligence is what makes unfair competition abusive and wrongful. As business adversaries owe one another no duty of care at all, liability should hinge on that intention, reckless or grossly negligent disregard of the competitor's interest.

Only a few claims under the UCA have been successful. This is partly due to the intricate proof of intention and causation. It has been hard for claimants to show unfair conduct worth a punishment targeted at deviating a rival's clientele. First, the courts have imposed an unusually high standard of proof in civil proceedings, as if misbehaviour were to be shown beyond any reasonable doubt, whereas the evidence should be weighed on the balance of probabilities. Second, the courts seem to expect that the mental element which defines unfair competition must be proved directly, whereas, in truth, intention can only be inferred from the evidence gathered at trial.

Occasionally, Chilean courts have understood unfair practice objectively, namely without requiring intention – as an act inconsistent with good faith or good commercial customs. With respect to these cases, it has been argued that this interpretation is flawed. Indeed, intention to harm, reckless indifference or at any rate gross negligence is the gist of commercial misconduct. Unfair practices cannot be perpetrated 'accidentally', hence the victim's right to be compensated must be balanced against the tortfeasor's liberty to compete. In sum, a mental element more stringent than simple carelessness is a reasonable qualification of the overarching principle of *culpa* in commercial competition. Merely suffering harm – even if it is negligently inflicted – is just a side effect of legitimate business struggle. Intentionally, recklessly or grossly negligently caused harm reveals abusive, wrongful, unfair behaviour.

# 10

# Judicial Identity Crises

## The French and European High Courts

MITCHEL DE S. O.-L'E. LASSER

This chapter, written as a contribution to John Bell's *festschrift*, focuses on subject matter dear to John's heart: the development of the role of the judiciary in France and Europe. I use it as a means to pivot from my new book on the recent reforms to the judicial appointments process to the two great European courts[1] – the European Court of Justice (the ECJ) and the European Court of Human Rights (the ECtHR) – to a new project that brings me back to my own academic origins and my academic origins with John: the French high courts (and especially the Cour de cassation).

Let me start by stating the basic thesis in very broad terms, which will then be refined over the course of the chapter. In brief, I believe that the high European judiciaries from Strasbourg, to Luxembourg, to Paris (and probably through London, Madrid and more) are in the midst of an existential crisis. On the one hand, they have been ebullient for some time.[2] Not only have they become stunningly powerful institutional actors whose authority has moved past the interpretive, to the normative, to the political, to the constitutional levels, but they are also fully cognisant of this new state of affairs.[3] As a result, they have become

[1] M. Lasser, *Judicial Dis-Appointments: Judicial Appointments Reform and the Rise of European Independence* (Oxford: Oxford University Press, 2020).

[2] Indeed, they have done so for significantly longer than the comparative legal literature has tended to realise. John Bell offers excellent examples from France, for example, dating back well into the 1970s. See e.g. J. Bell, *Judiciaries within Europe: A Comparative Review* (Cambridge: Cambridge University Press, 2006), p. 70.

[3] In 2017, for example, John Murray, the retired Chief Justice of Ireland and former judge of the ECJ, then serving as the president of the Advisory Panel of Experts on Candidates for Election as Judge to the ECtHR, published the following in his 'Exchange of Views' with the Council of Europe:

> It is important that [ECtHR judges] have experience of such high level because, as I have said before, judges are called upon to interpret the Convention in a way that can impact on major social and political issues

increasingly adamant – and at times downright strident – in defending and even expanding their prerogatives on a broad range of fronts, ranging from judicial independence, to judicial councils, to judicial appointments, to judicial authority, to the judicial role in the separation of powers. On the other hand, the very recognition and assertion of this new status goes a long way towards depriving them of the traditional bases of their legitimacy: their secondary or derivative position relative to the political branches of government, their merely positivist and interpretive relation to law, the institutional bases of their professional legitimacy, and so on.

This has put European judges on the horns of a dilemma that they are now trying desperately to work through. The difficulty is that the judiciary is not alone in being aware of this new state of affairs. So is everyone else, ranging from the political branches of government to the general public (via the popular press), never mind enlightened academics. At the very moment, therefore, that the judiciary blossoms into a full-fledged institution of government (in the United States, we use the seemingly tautological term 'coequal branch'), at the very moment that the judiciary not only privately but publicly avows this status to the world at large, it must find some new way to construct its legitimacy. And this, it turns out, is not so easy. It takes substantial and protracted effort. And it is often not terribly clear what exactly is at stake or what might be the eventual outcome.

This chapter quickly sketches out two case studies that offer different, yet related, attempts to reconstruct judicial legitimacy in contemporary Europe. The first focuses on the judicial appointments reforms concerning the ECJ and the ECtHR, reforms that connect to a broader series of interlocking reforms. The second turns to ongoing debates concerning

> at national level. First there is the law and then there is its interpretation by judges, and then the interpretation is the law. That is the modern reality. The time of Montesquieu, the era when the judge was the so-called mouthpiece of the law, is long gone. So the calibre of judges refers to people who can make judgments on sensitive issues like the status of the embryo or whether you can trade in embryos for research purposes or the right to suicide and so on. A Court must be capable of dealing with these sensitive issues and where the boundary of Convention obligations and national sovereignty needs to be drawn.

Steering Committee for Human Rights, Committee of Experts on the System of the European Convention on Human Rights (DH-SYSC), Exchange of Views between Mr John Murray, President of the Advisory Panel of Experts on Candidates for Election as Judge to the European Court of Human Rights and the Ministers' Deputies (1 March 2017), DH-SYSC-I(2017)016, 4 May 2017.

the use of judicial analytics, the reform of the traditional French mode of composing judicial decisions, and other measures designed to increase access to French judicial reasoning.

## 10.1 The European Judicial Appointments Reforms

This section addresses the first of two case studies that demonstrate the tremendous effort being put into reconstructing judicial legitimacy via judicial reform: the European judicial appointments measures culminating in the establishment in 2009 and 2010 of blue-ribbon panels of experts to vet candidates to sit on the ECJ and the ECtHR. Contrary to appearances, the *status quo ante* regarding appointments to both courts effectively empowered the national governments to appoint judges of their own choosing. True, appointments to the ECJ were to be made by 'common accord of the governments of the Member States'.[4] But this actually meant that each government would be able to select its own judge without serious threat of being challenged: the unanimity requirement empowered each individual government not so much because it could exercise veto powers over the judges proposed by others, but because it could freely appoint its own judge, lest it play tit-for-tat with any potential challenging government. The reality at the ECtHR was similar, despite a seemingly very different appointments procedure. Formally, the Parliamentary Assembly of the Council of Europe (PACE) would elect one of the three candidates put forward by each of the contracting parties. In practice, however, the national governments had a broad array of informal mechanisms for signalling their preferred candidate; and the PACE almost always duly obliged by 'electing' this candidate to sit in Strasbourg, thereby maintaining a system of intergovernmental comity. Furthermore, the relatively short and renewable six-year judicial term at both European courts traditionally allowed any government to replace a judge who had earned its displeasure.[5]

The 2009–10 European measures altered this state of affairs. They created the two blue-ribbon vetting panels: the Article 255 Panel (255 Panel) for appointment to Luxembourg and the Advisory Panel of

[4] See Article 253 of the Treaty on the Functioning of the European Union.

[5] The ECtHR only changed its appointments to nine-year non-renewable judicial terms with the passage of Protocol 14 to the Convention for the Protection of Human Rights and Fundamental Freedoms, amending the control system of the Convention, Strasbourg, 13 May 2004, in force 1 June 2010, CETS 194.

Experts on Candidates for Election as Judge to the ECtHR (APE) for appointment to Strasbourg. As we shall soon see, however, it would be a mistake to treat the establishment of these vetting panels as one-off events: their creation was but the most visible product of a decades-long effort at judicial reform that yielded a broad package of interlocking measures on issues ranging from judicial appointments, to judicial independence, to judicial quality, to judicial gender balance, to judicial councils and more. The 2009–10 timeframe is thus misleading: the reforms actually date back over twenty-five years to the post-1989 accession era.

### *10.1.1 The Council of Europe Reforms*

The history of the ECtHR is too well known to warrant detailed recounting here. We need merely remember a few key points that demonstrate just how wary the original contracting parties were of an international human rights court that might interfere with national authorities. First, the European Convention on Human Rights (ECHR)[6] as originally constructed did not even establish the ECtHR. Article 46 of the ECHR stated that '[a]ny of the High Contracting Parties may at any time declare that it recognises as compulsory … the jurisdiction of the Court', which effectively meant that signatory states could refuse the Court's jurisdiction altogether. Worse, Article 56 specified that until eight states accepted such jurisdiction, the ECtHR would not come into existence at all. The result was all too predictable: although the Council of Europe drafted the ECHR in 1950, it took almost another ten years for the ECtHR to be established. Second, the ECHR allowed contracting states to refuse to allow individuals to petition for redress against violations of the ECHR. Finally, the ECHR established an institutional structure that worked actively to limit recourse to the ECtHR. It created a powerful filtering institution, the Commission, which would dismiss the great majority of cases as 'inadmissible' and resolve the rest by diplomatic compromise; and it established an intergovernmental Committee of Ministers that would handle all interstate cases. The net result was that only a tiny number of cases ever made it before the ECtHR, which operated on a part-time basis for the first thirty-five years of its existence.

[6] Convention for the Protection of Human Rights and Fundamental Freedoms, Rome, 4 November 1950, in force 3 September 1953, 213 UNTS 221; ETS 5 (ECHR).

All of this changed suddenly in the early-to-mid 1990s, as the former Eastern Bloc states applied for accession to the Council of Europe. Needless to say, the most important reform was to become Protocol 11: in 1993, the Committee of Ministers finally decided to back the merger of the Commission and the Court, which would result in a full-time European Court with compulsory and original jurisdiction. Gone were the days of the Commission's handling of complaints through diplomatic compromise ('friendly settlements'); individuals would now directly petition the Court as of right and the Court would hand down formal judicial decisions in response.[7]

But this was hardly the end of the matter. To the contrary, the judicial reforms have continued ever since. Those reforms have progressed on multiple fronts at once. The first involved 'judicial independence'. In 1994, the same year that the Committee of Ministers signed on to Protocol 11, it also passed its Recommendation 'On the Independence, Efficiency and Role of Judges'.[8] Explicitly linking judicial independence, democracy, the separation of powers and the rule of law, the Ministers' Explanatory Report stated:

> 1. Within the framework of the activities undertaken to promote and guarantee the efficiency and fairness of civil and criminal justice, it was decided to prepare a recommendation on the independence, efficiency and role of judges
> 2. Indeed, the Council of Europe includes among its aims the institution and protection of a democratic and political system characterised by the rule of law and the establishment of a constitutionally governed state, as well as the promotion and protection of human rights and fundamental freedoms.
> 3. The recommendation on the independence, efficiency and role of judges recognises and emphasises the pre-eminent and significant role played by judges in the implementation of these aims. The independence of judges is one of the central pillars of the rule of law. The need to promote the independence of judges is not confined to individual judges only but may have consequences for the judicial system as a whole.[9]

[7] The European Heads of State endorsed this decision in the Vienna Declaration. See Explanatory Report to Protocol 11 to the Convention for the Protection of Human Rights and Fundamental Freedoms, restructuring the control machinery established thereby, p. 5.

[8] Committee of Ministers, Recommendation R (94) 12 (13 October 1994).

[9] Ibid., 6.

Therefore, from the moment that the ECtHR became a full-time court with compulsory jurisdiction over individual human rights complaints, Council of Europe institutions forged a strong conceptual link between the importance and independence of the judiciary.

Almost immediately, the Council of Europe passed (and eventually passed over and over again) a mountain of measures under the banners of judicial independence, judicial quality and the like. The 1994 Recommendation made strong assertions about selection, promotion and discipline of domestic judges:

> All decisions concerning the professional career of judges should be based on objective criteria, and the selection and career of judges should be based on merit, having regard to qualifications, integrity, ability and efficiency. The authority taking the decision on the selection and career of judges should be independent of the government and the administration. In order to safeguard its independence, rules should ensure that, for instance, its members are selected by the judiciary and that the authority decides itself on its procedural rules.[10]

Ensuing measures then imposed increasingly precise demands to induce national governments to adopt this perspective when making judicial appointment decisions, to both the domestic and the European benches.

These measures included a specific institutional mandate: all member states should create some kind of independent authority that would be responsible for governing matters relating to judicial selection, promotion and discipline. This authority – in essence, a judicial council – should be composed predominantly of 'judges elected by their peers following methods guaranteeing the widest representation of the judiciary'.[11] As the Consultative Council of European Judges, established by the Committee of Ministers in 2000, insisted in its very first policy paper, such a formally established 'independent authority' should govern all aspects of the judicial profession and do so on the basis of formal and public procedures.[12]

This institutional structure would not only protect judicial independence, but also promote and ensure the competence and quality

[10] Ibid., 2.

[11] European Charter on the Statute for Judges, DAJ/DOC (98) 23 (1998), [1.3].

[12] Consultative Council of European Judges, 'Opinion No. 1 on Standards Concerning the Independence of the Judiciary and the Irremovability of Judges', CCJE (2001) OP No. 1 (CCJE Opinion 1).

of candidates for judicial office. The preamble to the 1998 European Charter on the Statute for Judges fuses these elements together into a unified package:

> Being concerned to see the promotion of judicial independence, necessary for the strengthening of the pre-eminence of law and for the protection of individual liberties within democratic states, made more effective;
> Conscious of the necessity that provisions calculated to ensure the best guarantees of the competence, independence and impartiality of judges should be specified in a formal document intended for all European States;
> Desiring to see the judges' statutes of the different European States take into account these provisions in order to ensure in concrete terms the best level of guarantees;
> Have adopted the present European Charter on the statute for judges.[13]

Having constructed this package of requirements, the European institutions then extended its applicability to the European as well as the domestic judiciary. As the Consultative Council of European Judges (CCJE) explained, it is 'vital that the appointment and reappointment of judges to the courts interpreting [the European] treaties should command the same confidence and respect the same principles as national legal systems'.[14] The European judicial appointments, independence and quality debates had expanded seamlessly from the domestic to the supranational realm.

This expansion led to a veritable explosion of European measures in Strasbourg. For their part, national authorities would have to institute and abide by formal and transparent procedures for the selection and nomination of candidates to fill vacancies on the ECtHR, to issue a formal call for candidates in the appropriate specialised press, to include at least one woman in their slate of three nominated candidates, and so on.[15] But measures were directed to the European authorities as well. Preparing for the entry into force of Protocol 11, the PACE's Committee on Legal Affairs and Human Rights thus acted in 1995 'to improve [the PACE's] own procedure for examining the candidatures and for the selection of candidates, for more efficiency and professionalism'.[16] ECtHR judicial

13 European Charter on the Statute for Judges, DAJ/DOC (98) 23 (1998).

14 CCJE Opinion 1 at [56].

15 See ibid.

16 PACE Committee on Legal Affairs and Human Rights (Rapporteur: Lord Kirkhill), 'Report on the procedure for examining candidatures for the election of judges to the European Court of Human Rights 1', Doc 7439, 1403-15/12/95-1-E (1995).

candidates would now be made 'to fill in a model curriculum vitae, so that the Assembly will have comparable information at its disposal' when selecting among candidates. The member state governments would now be required to transmit its candidates' CVs in alphabetical order, so that these governments would be unable to declare their own preference.[17] Finally, the three candidates would be interviewed by a newly created PACE sub-committee, which would assess their qualities in order to make a recommendation to the Plenary Assembly.[18]

As all of these reforms make quite clear, the Council of Europe's judicial reforms had been continually on the Strasbourg agenda for a solid fifteen years by the time the sitting President of the ECtHR, Jean-Paul Costa, issued his dramatic call for the establishment of the APE in 2010.[19] And as we shall see in the next section (10.1.2), the establishment of the APE later that year hardly put an end to the judicial debates or reforms.

### *10.1.2 The European Union's Judicial Reforms*

The European Union's reforms on the judicial appointments front do not appear to be as substantial or persistent as those generated by the Council of Europe institutions. Some of the reasons for this disparity is historical/geographic; some is institutional. As suggested above, the European judicial reforms did not suddenly appear in 2009–10. They began in earnest in the early-to-mid 1990s, which is to say, in the immediate aftermath of the fall of the Berlin Wall, precisely during the period when a large cohort of former Eastern Bloc countries from Central and Eastern Europe rushed to accede to the Council of Europe and the European Union.

This mass accession impacted the Council of Europe more quickly and more radically than it did the EU. After all, accession to the Council of

17 See PACE Recommendation 1429 (1999), 2004 PACE Recommendation 1649 (2004) and PACE Resolution 1432 (2005).

18 PACE Committee on Legal Affairs and Human Rights (Rapporteur: Lord Kirkhill), 'Report'.

19 Costa wrote: 'In terms of the future of the Court and therefore the Convention system, one of the decisive factors will be the quality of its Judges. Whatever reforms are undertaken, the system will fail if judges do not have the necessary experience and authority.' Letter from Jean-Paul Costa, President of the European Court of Human Rights, addressed to member states' Permanent Representatives (Ambassadors) on 9 June 2010, in Committee on Legal Affairs and Human Rights (Rapporteur: Wohlwend), 'Report on National procedures for the selection of candidates for the European Court of Human Rights', PACE document 12391 (6 October 2010) Appendix, http://assembly.coe.int/nw/xml/XRef/X2H-Xref-ViewPDF.asp?FileID=12764&lang=en

Europe requires little more than signing up to a Human Rights Treaty; accession to the EU, however, is a notoriously complex and painstaking process. As a result, after the fall of the Berlin Wall, some twenty-one countries from east of Berlin acceded to the Council of Europe before the first acceded to the EU (in the 2004 enlargement).[20] At least as important was the challenge raised by the particular countries involved, which included not only those that would eventually accede to the EU, but also many that would never have qualified for EU admission in the first place, not to mention the distinctive challenges posed by Russia itself.

Second, the institutional and procedural structure surrounding judicial appointments profoundly affected ensuing developments. Judging from outward appearances, one might assume that the EU was shielded from some of the challenges faced by the Council of Europe: appointment to the EU judiciary is effectuated 'by common accord of the Governments of the Member states'.[21] This looks like a veto system: were any government to refuse to consent to another's proposed judicial candidate, the appointment could not go through. In truth, however, this arrangement functioned in an almost diametrically opposed manner: each government could select its judge with relative impunity, lest it play tit-for-tat with any potential challenging government's own judicial candidate.

The net result of these differences was that the EU was not really forced to face the judicial appointments challenges prompted by mass eastern accession until the mid-2000s – that is, at least ten years later than the Council of Europe.[22] And even when it did, it was greatly aided by the very same 'common accord' mechanism that had heretofore empowered the member states to appoint their chosen judges with impunity. When, in the wake of the Discussion Circle debates of the EU's Constitutional Convention, the EU decided to create the 255 Panel to vet proposed judicial candidates to the EU judiciary, the Panel was greatly empowered by the 'common accord' appointments mechanism. If the 255 Panel decided to oppose a given judicial candidate, appointment

[20] All of the following countries acceded to the Council of Europe prior to the EU's 2004 enlargement: Hungary (1990); Poland (1991); Bulgaria (1992); Estonia, Lithuania, Slovenia, the Czech Republic, Slovakia and Romania (1993); Latvia, Moldova, Albania, Ukraine and North Macedonia (1995); Russia and Croatia (1996), Georgia (1999); Armenia and Azerbaijan (2001); Bosnia and Herzegovina (2002); and Serbia (2003).

[21] Article 253 of the Treaty of Lisbon amending the Treaty on European Union and the Treaty establishing the European Community, Lisbon, 13 December 2007, in force 1 December 2009, OJEU, C 306.

[22] Lasser, *Judicial Dis-Appointments*, Parts I–II.

would now require that the member state governments positively and unanimously agree to override the Panel's negative judgment. But this was far too embarrassing to occur. As a result, the 'common accord' mechanism had changed completely in meaning and effect: instead of each *government* having a unilateral power to *make* any appointment, the *255 Panel* had the unilateral power to *block* any appointment.

The 255 Panel then used this dominant tactical advantage to lay out its own ground rules for appointment to the EU judiciary (ground rules that, as we have just seen, the Panel was effectively empowered to enforce unilaterally). The 255 Panel published a series of 'Activity Reports' that not only summarised its decisions regarding the suitability of candidates to EU judicial office, but also laid out in detail the criteria it had applied (and would continue to apply) to assess such candidacies.[23] The first notable feature of the 255 Panel's assessment is that it places a burden of justification on the governments proposing each candidate:

> [T]he panel . . . asks the government proposing the application to pass on the essential reasons why it chose the proposed candidate and a letter explaining the reasons for the application and a bibliographic list of the candidate's publications. The panel also asks for information on the national procedure that led to the candidate being selected, inviting the government to say inter alia whether there was a public call for applications, whether a national selection committee was set up and if so how the national selection committee was made up and what it recommended.[24]

This passage effectively announces that the Panel has taken on the task of assessing not only each proposed candidate, but also (if only implicitly) the national procedures by which the member state has selected and proposed that candidate.

The 255 Panel then set out in painstaking detail the assessment criteria it would henceforth apply to the candidates themselves. Those criteria fell into six broad categories: 'the candidate's legal expertise, professional experience, ability to perform the duties of a Judge, assurance of independence and impartiality, language skills and aptitude for working as part of a team in an international environment in which several legal systems are represented'.[25] Spending multiple pages elaborating on each of these criteria, the 255 Panel effectively imposed its requirements on the member state governments, who

[23] See e.g. 'First Activity report of the panel provided for by Article 255 of the Treaty on the Functioning of the European Union', Brussels, 17 February 2011, 6509/11 Cour 3 Jur 57.

[24] Ibid., 6.

[25] Ibid., 8–9.

understood not only that the 255 Panel had the effective power to reject unilaterally any candidate it deemed unsuitable, but also that it was perfectly willing to do so: as soon as it was established, the 255 Panel started rejecting a substantial percentage – almost a quarter – of all new candidates proposed by the member state governments to sit on the ECJ and the General Court in Luxembourg.[26]

### *10.1.3 Transitional Conclusion*

The rise of the European judicial appointments debates and reforms led to the signal establishment of the two European judicial vetting panels in 2009 and 2010. But the establishment of the APE and the 255 Panel represented neither the beginning nor the end of the debates regarding judicial appointments, judicial independence, judicial quality, judicial councils, etc. It was but one of the many outcomes (albeit a particularly important one) that grew out of the judicial debates that had raged since the early-to-mid 1990s, the period of large-scale accession of former Eastern Bloc countries to the Council of Europe and the EU. And as we shall see, their establishment did not magically solve the tensions that had prompted their creation in the first place.[27]

For our purposes, the European judicial appointments reforms demonstrate several important features. First, it is noteworthy that they occurred in the first place. After all, the EU and the Council of Europe did not bother with any such reforms from their creation in the 1950s until the Accession period beginning in the 1990s. Second, these measures were intimately intertwined with a series of thematically and procedurally adjacent reforms, such as those concerning judicial independence, judicial quality and the like. Third, the thrust of these reforms greatly empowered the judiciary at both the European and national levels to control a broad range of institutionally important issues, ranging from judicial appointments, to training, to discipline, to organisation and self-management. But even more, they reworked the judiciary's relation to the political branches of government, and to the executive in particular. Fourth, as we shall argue in Section 10.3, this reworking has effectively been constitutional in nature, as both a

[26] See Article 255 Panel, Third Activity report of the panel provided for by Article 255 of the Treaty on the Functioning of the European Union 9 (No. SN 1118/2014) (13 December 2013).

[27] See below, Section 10.3.

theoretical and practical matter. Finally, the judicial empowerment created by this transformation has also triggered significant anxiety: the judiciary would have to find new ways to ground the legitimacy of its rising constitutional status, which then tended to trigger further judicial anxiety and empowerment.

## 10.2 The French Reforms

At first blush, the French reforms may appear less important or coherent than the European ones. But they too form a cluster of projects that demonstrate a brooding anxiety over the bases of judicial authority and legitimacy. This section will tie the sensational example of the recent French policy decision to criminalise the use of judicial analytics to broader – if seemingly unrelated – reforms regarding French judicial procedure and the publication of French judicial reasoning. The French judiciary, no less than the European one, has been seesawing between demonstrations of empowerment and vulnerability.

### *10.2.1 The Criminalisation of Targeted Judicial Analytics*

In the spring of 2019, the French modified their administrative and judicial organisation codes in a perplexing manner: they decided to forbid the 'reutilisation' of the names of the judges who have decided published judicial decisions 'in order to evaluate, analyse, compare or predict these judges' real or supposed professional practices'.[28] Not content to state the prohibition, they backed it up with penalties of five years of imprisonment and fines of up to €300,000![29] What could possibly have provoked such a draconian (and seemingly paranoid) legal development?

[28] 'Les données d'identité des magistrats . . . ne peuvent faire l'objet d'une réutilisation ayant pour objet ou pour effet d'évaluer, d'analyser, de comparer ou de prédire leurs pratiques professionnelles réelles ou supposées': see Article 33 of Loi no. 2019-222 du 23 mars 2019 de programmation 2018–2022 et de réforme pour la justice.

[29] See ibid. Such punishment is unusually severe by French standards. By means of comparison, Article 431-6 of the French Penal Code states: 'Directly inciting an armed and unlawful assembly, whether by yelling or giving public speeches, or by posting or distributing writings, or by transmitting writing, speeches or images by any other means, is to be punished by imprisonment of one year and a fine of €15,000. Where the incitement is acted upon, the penalty is increased to imprisonment of seven years and to a fine of €100,000.'

International condemnation was swift and more or less universal.[30] Comparative legal commentators seized on this reform and drew a direct line between the traditional opacity of French judicial decisions and this latest attempt to deny the agency and importance of French judicial decision making.[31] The critique made surface sense. After all, ever since the French Revolution, the rules and practices surrounding French judicial decision making have worked rather effectively to downplay the independent and normative role played by the French judiciary. Revolutionary-era rules forbade the judiciary to interfere with the legislative and executive branches of government. The Napoleonic Code denied judges the power to make binding legal rules. The traditional – and notoriously opaque – form of the French judicial decision insisted on unsigned, collegial judgments without concurrences or dissents, composed as single-sentence syllogisms less than a single page long.[32] How in keeping with this tradition, therefore, that the French system would now ban the use of judicial analytics to examine the decisional tendencies of particular judges.

Leaving aside the fact that comparatists' classic critique of French judicial traditions has never been entirely justified on its own terms,[33] the current chorus of criticism rarely makes enough of the fact that the recent French reforms actually stem from a concerted push to make judicial decision making much *more* accessible, not to shield it from public view. This reform drive, known as the 'Open Data' initiative, was triggered by the 2016 passage of the Law for a Digital Republic, which was an extremely broad legislative measure that sought to overhaul and improve French digital life. In addition to promoting internet access, the protection of personal data, and so on, this law made an important

[30] See e.g. Artificial Lawyer, 'France Bans Judge Analytics, 5 Years in Prison for Rule Breakers', www.artificiallawyer.com/2019/06/04/france-bans-judge-analytics-5-years-in-prison-for-rule-breakers/; M. Langford and M. R. Madsen, 'France Criminalizes Research on Judges', https://verfassungsblog.de/france-criminalises-research-on-judges/; M. Livermore and D. Rockmore, 'France Kicks Data Scientists Out of Its Courts', https://slate.com/technology/2019/06/france-has-banned-judicial-analytics-to-analyze-the-courts.html; N. Kuhlmann, 'The Forbidden Tree of Knowledge', https://legalempirics.com/10.25527/re.2019.09/the-forbidden-tree-of-knowledge/

[31] See e.g. Langford and Madsen, 'France Criminalizes Research on Judges'.

[32] See M. Lasser, *Judicial Deliberations: A Comparative Analysis of Transparency and Legitimacy* (Oxford: Oxford University Press, 2004), chapter 2.

[33] See ibid., chapters 6, 10 and 11.

change with regard to the French state: it established a sweeping default rule that the state must make digitally available all information and public data in its possession.[34]

This Open Data mandate applied to the judiciary as much as to executive branch agencies. As a result, the French courts were now to operate under a default rule that all of their judgments were to be made freely available on the internet. It is hard to convey the magnitude of the shift that this represents. As I have explained elsewhere, the French judicial system has long functioned on the basis of a distinctive publication regime.[35] Although the French could freely request copies of judgments directly from the courts' registries, only a tiny percentage of judgments were ever published, and these usually in extremely summary form.[36] This magnified the role of French publishers and academics: they effectively curated the judiciary's jurisprudence by selecting, identifying and publicising the judiciary's output – they amplified their own impact on French legal developments. The publishers decided which judgments to publish and whether to do so in merely summary form. And because even a judgment quoted in full consisted of short and relatively opaque single-sentence judicial syllogism, publishers would typically supplement any they deemed sufficiently important by publishing it in tandem with a longer academic 'note' that deciphered its meaning, import and qualities (or faults). As a result, academic commentary played a crucial mediating and framing function whose normative weight complemented and rivalled that of the judgments it was commenting on.[37] For the French courts to make all of their judgments freely available on the internet without any of the selection, framing and critical filters traditionally imposed by the judiciary, the publishers and academia (*la doctrine*) therefore represented a dramatic increase in the accessibility and transparency of the courts (and of their jurisprudence) to the French public.

But the reform was not self-executing, and it posed significant challenges, ranging from the technical, to the institutional, to the juridical, to the philosophical. The main problem lay with privacy concerns: with the

[34] Needless to say, this sweeping default rule is subject to exceptions and limitations. One of these, concerning personal information, will be discussed below. See also Lasser, *Judicial Deliberations*, 329.

[35] See ibid., chapters 6 and 8.

[36] For a brilliant analysis of the traditional French relation between the practice of legal publication and the creation of judicial norms, see E. Serverin, *De la jurisprudence en droit privé: Théorie d'une pratique* (Lyon: Presses universitaires de Lyon, 1985).

[37] See Lasser, *Judicial Deliberations*, 329.

ever-increasing capacity to mine massive data sets, the online revelation of the identity of those involved in court proceedings could quickly devolve into significant privacy violations. The solution was theoretically simple: to anonymise the judgments. This represented an enormous endeavour, but it posed no major policy problems with regard to the litigants. But then came the thorny problem of court personnel, including especially the judges themselves.

The ensuing debates on the occultation of the judges' names from their own judgments were heated. Loïc Cadiet, a seasoned professor at the Law Faculty of Paris-1, was put in charge of a commission to examine how the Open Data initiative should be put into effect in the French judiciary; and the Commission's report reveals large-scale disagreement over judicial anonymisation.[38] Many, such as the Chief Justice of the Cour de cassation, the Conference of appellate court presidents, the presidents of the courts of first instance and the national bar argued forcefully in favour of the online publication of judicial names: in addition to satisfying the Open Data mandate, such openness advanced the analysis of legal divergences and trends, increased predictability, promoted the democratic need for transparency, and thus militated against secrecy. Others, however, such as the head of the Conseil d'Etat and the majority of public prosecutors, argued forcefully against such online publication. Not only should judicial consistency and predictability be accomplished by institutional means within the judiciary, but online publication also invited the deployment of judicial analytics targeted at specific judges. Such 'judicial profiling' would promote strategic argumentation and forum shopping, which would inevitably favour well-funded parties and damage the unity, authority and independence of the courts.

The Open Data reform and its application to the judiciary demonstrate that the criminalisation of targeted judicial analytics was not a freestanding policy judgement intended to reinforce the misleadingly opaque and mechanistic appearance of French judicial decisions. It was actually a compromise solution to a dilemma posed by a ground-breaking and transparency-*enhancing* reform. The French judiciary was fundamentally, if not unanimously, in favour of the democratic virtues of judicial transparency. But it also feared for the personal privacy of its judges and for the integrity of French judicial authority and procedure: massive

[38] See L. Cadiet, *L'Open Data des décisions de justice: Mission d'étude et de préfiguration sur l'ouverture au public des décisions de justice* (Paris: Ministère de la justice, 2018), www.justice.gouv.fr/publication/open_data_rapport.pdf

amounts of information would suddenly become electronically available for data-driven analysis by well-funded and self-interested parties who could put supercomputing to tactical use in ways that might pressure individual judges, thereby compromising their decisional independence. The compromise was simple: rather than conceal the personal identity and information of judges (as would be done for litigants), such judicial information would remain fully visible, now freely available online. However, the 'reutilisation' of the published 'identifying data of the judges or of the members of the courts' registries for the purposes or effect to evaluate, analyse, compare or predict their real or supposed professional practices' would be criminally sanctioned.[39] The idea was to promote the democratic transparency of the judiciary while minimising the risk of privacy breaches and of data mining by powerful, well-funded and tactically savvy actors who might otherwise leverage them against particular judges and the French judicial system as a whole.

### *10.2.2 The Reform of French Judicial Decision Writing*

The form of the French judicial decision has long been the source of horrified fascination for outsiders.[40] From the time I first met John Bell at a grand conference held at the Cour de cassation, I have worked hard to debunk the myths surrounding the iconic unsigned, collegial, single-sentence judicial syllogism of the traditional Cour de cassation or Conseil d'Etat judgment. It has been a hard sell. Common lawyers (and US common lawyers in particular) are loath to accept that a legal system could be intelligently and honourably run on the basis of such cryptic and mechanical judicial pronouncements. To read the comparative literature, the French must be either retrograde formalists or misleading hypocrites: either they must believe that short, codified commands really can mechanically resolve just about any controversy, no matter how novel or complex, or they must be cynically masking the reality of French judicial creativity behind the cover conveniently offered by the Revolutionary-era fear of a *gouvernement des juges*.

The reality is that the French have been consistently experimenting with judicial reform over the last few decades. As I have written elsewhere, these reform efforts are the product of complex interactions at the intersection

[39] Ibid., n. 27.

[40] See e.g. J. Dawson, *The Oracles of the Law* (Ann Arbor: University of Michigan Press, 1968), chapter 5; R. Pound, *Jurisprudence* (St. Paul: West Publishing, 1959), vols. 1 and 3.

of the French and European judicial orders. Some of these interactions represent internal jockeying between the troika of French 'high courts': the Cour de cassation, the Conseil d'Etat and the Constitutional Council.[41] But external interactions between these high French courts and the high European courts in Strasbourg and Luxembourg have prompted significant changes to French judicial authority and decision making practice. Not only have the European courts effectively demanded that the French courts exercise judicial review over the French political branches of government (if only in the name of European law), but their 'fair trial' jurisprudence has also triggered important changes to French internal decision-making procedures.[42]

Such French judicial reform efforts continue to this day. This section briefly introduces two closely related examples: both the Cour de cassation and the Conseil d'Etat have recently engaged in sustained projects to reform the traditional style of their published judicial reasoning in order to produce more thoroughly, straightforwardly and transparently reasoned judgments. Indeed, even the Constitutional Council modified its own style of decision writing in a similar manner.[43] Our two examples demonstrate that the courts' reforms are significantly overlapping, but that the Cour de cassation had particularly ambitious and comprehensive plans.

## The Conseil d'Etat Reform

In October 2010, Jean-Marc Sauvé, the formidable leader of the Conseil d'Etat, tasked a working group (chaired by Philippe Martin, the Associate President of the Conseil's Litigation Section) to re-examine the Conseil's traditional style of composing its judgments. Now that law had become more complex and the Conseil's audience had become broader and less specialised, it was time to reconsider whether the Conseil should not

41 I place the term 'high courts' in quotations in order to acknowledge the definitional complication that neither the Conseil d'Etat nor the Constitutional Council are part of the French judiciary and that arguably neither (and especially not the Constitutional Council) is a court at all.

42 See M. Lasser, *Judicial Transformations: The Rights Revolution in the Courts of Europe* (Oxford: Oxford University Press, 2009), chapter 4.

43 See Constitutional Council, Decisions No. 216-539 QPC and 2016-540 QPC of 10 May 2016. I do not include a presentation of this reform both for space reasons and because the Constitutional Council effectively presented it as a fait accompli without offering a detailed public explanation of its motivations.

explicate[44] its judgments in a more sustained manner. As a further benefit, such a development might improve the translatability of the Conseil's judgments, which would help their diffusion at the European and international levels.[45]

The resulting Martin Report, delivered in 2012, offers a detailed set of proposals for modifying the structure and content of Conseil d'Etat judgments. The time had come to abandon the Conseil's traditional single-sentence syllogisms structured by a parade of 'whereas' clauses: 'this mode of composition ... perhaps no longer permits the administrative judge to give to a broader audience as full and clear an account as possible of how an ever more complex law is being applied'.[46] It continued:

> It soon became apparent [to the Working Group] that the objective of improving the intelligibility of judgments, which responds to an expectation of both private and public litigants, relies as much on the form and style of those judgments as it does on their content, and that their mode of composition had above all to permit as clear, precise and complete an expression as possible of the reasons for which the judge has adopted a given solution.[47]

The single-sentence judgment with its parade of 'whereas' clauses should be replaced by short sentences that end in a period. The judgment should be structured in short paragraphs that cover only one subject 'in order to guarantee the rigour of the reasoning and the legibility of the decision'. The paragraphs might even be numbered. Subject headings and subheading should increasingly be used. This should all help to render 'more analytically and completely the [judgment's] legal reasoning'. Furthermore, the judgment should 'indicate the interpretive method (such as reference to legislative history, use of legal analogy, purposive or teleological reasoning, etc.) by which the court elucidates the significance of a legal rule'.[48] In short, the Martin Report proposed a major reworking of the traditional form of Conseil d'Etat judgments.

[44] The French verb is 'motiver', which is difficult to translate. It means to provide legal reasons.

[45] J.-M. Sauvé, Lettre de Mission du 20 octobre 2010 à Philippe Martin, in 'Rapport du groupe de travail sur la rédaction des décisions de la juridiction administrative' (April 2012), p. 218 (Martin Report).

[46] Ibid., 6.

[47] Ibid., 7.

[48] Ibid., 46.

The Conseil put its new compositional guidelines into effect on 1 January 2019.[49] These guidelines were instituted and explained in its official 'Manual on the composition of the judgments of the administrative tribunals' (Manual).[50] The Manual explained:

> The composition of a judgment manifests for the public law judge the search for an *equilibrium* between the sometimes contradictory demands and constraints upon him: the writer must concern himself with the intelligibility of the judgment he is preparing, of its authority and of its acceptability to the parties; but he cannot forget that the litigation he is handling is not the only one on his docket and lose sight of the overall capacity of the public law tribunals to respond to an ever increasing demand for justice.[51]

The Manual clearly represents an attempt to balance competing demands, several of which are rather telling newcomers in the French legal psyche. In particular, the French judiciary has come to believe that it must expend added effort on the composition of its judgments. Far from being mechanical applications of self-applying rules, the judgments must be made more intelligible, not merely for intelligibility's sake, but because their authority and acceptability depends on it. The Manual is therefore deeply cognisant of the judiciary's varied audiences, ranging from 'citizens or journalists interested in a case', to other judges and jurists 'who are interested in the contribution that the decision makes to [the court's] jurisprudence and to its doctrinal position', and so on.[52] The courts, in short, must take responsibility for their interventions and take account of their publics.

This is not to say that this growing consciousness of, and public accountability for, French judicial action represents a total renunciation of the traditional French approach to high-level judicial decision making. Not at all: the Manual counterbalances this push towards transparent judicial explanation with overt appeals to the traditionally institutional bases of French judicial legitimacy. Writing in particularly pedantic terms, it warns:

[49] Conseil d'État, 'Vade-mecum sur la rédaction des décisions de la juridiction administrative', www.conseil-etat.fr/content/download/152050/file/Vade-mecum-Redaction-decisions-de-la-juridiction-administrative.pdf

[50] Ibid.

[51] Ibid., 4.

[52] Ibid.

> The [judicial] writer must therefore work hard to ensure the coherence and clarity of the judgment, the rigour of its legal reasoning, the precision of its factual findings, the quality of its expression and the concision of its style, always adopting the measured, sober and objective tone that characterises [the French] public law tribunals.[53]

Indeed, for all that the reform pushes towards a direct style of composition and more explicit reasoning, it refuses to relinquish the characteristically syllogistic form of traditional French judicial pronouncements, never mind their univocal and collegial construction. In a section tellingly entitled 'Methodology (1) – The Deductive Construction of the Administrative Judge's Rationales', the Manual announces:

> The rationales are constructed by following the order of a major proposition that exposes the legal rule, a minor [proposition] that assesses the facts pertinent to the case, and a conclusion that applies the legal rule to the case facts. The legal motivation must therefore precede the factual finding and the conclusion of the syllogism.
>
> This deductive construction . . . directly serves the explanatory function of the judgment, thereby conferring to it a general coherence that permits it to be better understood, and thus, better accepted by the litigants. It does not, however, imply the written transposition of all of the stages or all the reasons that convinced the judge, in his innermost conviction, to adopt his reasoning. Said otherwise, although the decision must indicate to the parties the rationales of the judgment, it is not required to expose to them all of the rationales for these rationales: although, for example, the judge must reveal the interpretation he gives to a legal rule, he is not held to explain whether he was convinced to adopt this reading by virtue of textual, contextual or analogical reasons.[54]

As should be apparent, the Conseil is trying to walk a fine line between two modes of generating legitimacy: offering a relatively transparent and forthcoming explanation to its audiences and maintaining the classic indicia of the irrefutable logic and authority of its institution.

### The Cour de Cassation Reform

Not to be outdone by the Conseil d'Etat and the Constitutional Council, the Cour de cassation undertook its own rather bold reforms. The reforms were vigorously pursued by its president, Bertrand Louvel, who immediately made clear his intention to transform the Cour's constitutional status and working methods. At the speech marking his formal

[53] Ibid., 5.
[54] Ibid., 9.

investiture as 'Premier président' of the Cour in 2014, Louvel explicitly drew inspiration from the model offered by the ECJ and ECtHR:

> The rise in power of the European courts ... leads our Court to envisage in some circumstances altering its traditional role of strictly controlling the application of law. The often interdisciplinary reasoning of these courts' judgments invites us to evaluate better the impact of our decisions in social and economic terms, both national and international, beyond only the legal analyses that [traditionally] represent the culture of the Cour de cassation.[55]

Working from these foreign models, Louvel directly challenged French legal orthodoxy. Speaking in highly charged terms, he all but declared the traditional French approach a stunted historical anachronism:

> In truth, our national tradition is having trouble breaking free of the very ancient model under which we continue to live, which was conceived in the 18th century by Chancellor Maupeau and put into effect by Bonaparte.
>
> The philosophy of this system was summarised in 1766 by Louis XV in the following terms: 'It is from me alone that the courts hold their existence and authority.' This formulation was barely updated in 1964 by General De Gaulle, who believed that no judicial authority could exist that was not conferred and maintained by the President of the Republic.
>
> Beyond the extremism of this position, we find once again the archaic idea of the submission of the Judiciary to the Executive that continues even today to stand in the way of the achievement of an authentic separation of powers in our system of rule of law.[56]

Louvel was not fiddling around the edges of French traditions. He therefore spearheaded reforms that began with the traditional form of Cour de cassation judgments, but that went well beyond merely formal modifications. In his opening remarks to the Commission he had convened to examine the form of the Cour's judgments, he explained:

> Far more than in the past, the citizen refuses to accept legal solutions that are imposed on him without his understanding them. It is important, therefore, that the judiciary explain its decisions.
>
> Long gone are the days when social structures, limited communications and technical knowledge offered so much stability that the judiciary, like the

[55] B. Louvel, Discours d'installation en qualité de Premier président de la Cour de cassation (16 July 2014), www.courdecassation.fr/files/files/Evenements%20Cour/andience/Discours_PP_140716v2.pdf

[56] Ibid. Maupeou attempted to help salvage the monarchy by abolishing the ancien regime's powerful *parlements*. They were restored upon the death of Louis XV.

> legislature, could dispense with the perpetual need to re-examine the utility of a given solution in terms of evolving social and economic demands.
>
> Many ask that the judiciary in particular make explicit the legal reasoning that entered into a given judgment as well as the technical, economic and social data that determined its decision . . .
>
> Some fear that should the Cour break free of the legalist principles bequeathed by our national tradition, its creative role might grow. Our Cour is accordingly confronted by a major challenge: if it does not update the traditional bases of its authority and prestige, younger and more enterprising courts may well supplant them with their own.[57]

In these remarks, one can see quite clearly the scope and ambition of the proposed reforms.

The Commission's final Report (Jean Report) did not disappoint. Stressing the need for democratic transparency, it reiterated Louvel's assertion that contemporary governing elites must publicly explain and justify their decisions in a generally accessible manner.[58] In order to do so in an environment in which the Cour hands down almost 20,000 cases a year and in which the mass of its jurisprudence can be subjected to undifferentiated big data analysis, the Cour must now 'prioritise and spell out [its jurisprudence], lest its normative information be diluted in an undifferentiated and ever expanding mass'.[59]

These related impulses to prioritise, explicate and publicise the Cour's judgments undergird the Report's primary proposals. The Report proposes, for example, that the Cour systematically expand (the more suggestive French term is 'enrichir') its legal explanations in all important cases.[60] The judgments' form should also be simplified: paragraphs should be numbered and the traditional parade of 'whereas' clauses should be abolished in favour of direct sentences. In short, the Cour's judgments should be made more comprehensible and be more widely distributed, especially by electronic means.[61]

[57] B. Louvel, Motivation des arrêts de la Cour de cassation (14 September 2015), www.huyette.net/2015/09/la-motivation-des-arrets-de-la-cour-de-cassation.html

[58] 'Rapport de la Commission de réflexion sur la réforme de la Cour de cassation', p. 138 (April 2017) [Jean Report], www.courdecassation.fr/files/files/R%C3%A9forme/Archives/Rapport%20sur%20la%20r%C3%A9forme%20de%20la%20Cour%20de%20cassation.pdf

[59] Ibid., 137–8.

[60] Ibid., 152. The categories of such important cases include judicial overrulings, fundamental rights cases, foundational legal questions, proportionality cases, unification or development of jurisprudence, and so on, see ibid.

[61] The French Open Data legislation now requires this, see Section 10.2.1.

But more fundamental yet is the way the Jean Report discusses the taboo embedded in the question of form: the judicial citation to prior judgments. The traditional French approach to this issue is that the courts should not make such citations, lest they suggest that court decisions possess important normative authority; after all, the French judiciary is explicitly forbidden to make law.[62] The danger is that such citations might lead other courts to treat them as if they did, thereby making it so.

What is so interesting is how the issue is now being discussed in the French legal literature, including in the reports and policy documents generated by the French high courts themselves: not only do the debates increasingly call this orthodoxy into question, but they also do so in startling new terms. In particular, the debates increasingly abandon the traditional French term for prior judicial holdings – *jurisprudence* – in favour of a term that would traditionally have been anathema: *les précédents*! It is hard to convey what a major conceptual shift this really represents, complete with its latent procedural, institutional and even constitutional presuppositions. Indeed, merely using and thus normalising the term probably constitutes as significant a leap as actually permitting *les précédents* to be cited by the courts in their judgments.

The Conseil d'Etat had addressed the citation issue five years earlier in its Martin Report, but in relatively measured terms (in both form and substance). It had explained:

> In conclusion, although certain members of the Working Group [on the composition of the Conseil's judgments] continue to have strong reservations about the idea of introducing any references whatever to prior judgments by the administrative tribunals because precedents lack obligatory force, the majority of the Group's members believe that reference to leading cases, identified as such, that resolved a legal question offers a useful piece of information to litigants.[63]

This passage openly reveals the debates and disagreements within the Conseil on this classic issue. While it recognises the standard objection to judicial citations (craftily using the term 'precedent' to underscore the traditional disapproval of the term and idea), it is sufficiently politic to use less charged terms when explaining that the majority now approve of

[62] This refusal dates back to the Revolution. See Articles 10 and 13 of the Code de l'organisation judiciaire tit. II, 16–24 August 1790; Articles 4, 5 and 1355 of the French Civil Code.

[63] Martin Report, 32.

judicial references to 'leading cases' that offer litigants 'a useful piece of information'.[64]

The Cour de cassation's Jean Report makes no such tactful concessions. In a truly ground-breaking move, it formally proposes that in all important cases, the Cour should 'cite *les précédents* whenever this appears necessary, especially in cases in which the Cour is overruling its prior jurisprudence or in which the Appellate Court has failed to follow the settled jurisprudence of the Cour de cassation'.[65] Indeed, as if to stress the magnitude of its own proposal, it underlines that the Conseil's Martin Report had also endorsed referring to leading cases, but that the Conseil's own leader, Jean-Marc Sauvé, had stymied the idea. Writing in striking – if spectacularly opaque – terms, Sauvé had proclaimed:

> If the French administrative judge wishes to develop and expand the motivation of his judgments without sacrificing the rigour of his legal reasoning, it is unlikely that he would soon refer formally to the judgments of other courts or, for that matter, to his own jurisprudence. In accordance with Article 5 of the Civil Code, he does not intend to be seen to recognise their normative function. Such is the tribute that the French administrative judge continues diligently to pay to the heritage of the French Revolution.[66]

By directly quoting Sauvé's contrary position (and his own reference to Revolutionary traditions), the authors of the Cour de cassation's Jean Report effectively underlined their own intention to break from hallowed French legal traditions and to reorient the practices and bases of French judicial authority and legitimacy.

But the Jean Report was not content to limit itself to endorsing (and normalising) citations to 'precedent', however major such a shift might be in its own right.[67] Instead, it linked this terminological and

[64] The Report uses the term 'décisions de principe', which I have translated as 'leading cases', but that includes the notion that these judgments have intentionally taken a firm position on a previously contested legal issue, see ibid. Cleverly, the Martin Report did indeed use the term *précédents* at various points in its analysis but refrained from doing so when making formal proposals, see Martin Report at 30, 31, 32, 39, 50, 94.

[65] Jean Report, 154, Proposition 34.

[66] J. M. Sauvé, 'Comprendre et réguler le droit globalisé ou comment dompter la Chimère?' (20 May 2015), www.conseil-etat.fr/actualites/discours-et-interventions/comprendre-et-reguler-le-droit-globalise-ou-comment-dompter-la-chimere#_ednref1

[67] That said, the Jean Report certainly did not skimp on its use of the term *les précédents*, which appeared fully twenty-seven times, see Jean Report.

conceptual intervention to an ambitious procedural proposal that was designed to maximise the Cour's ability to focus its energies on – and amplify the influence of – its most important judgments. The Jean Report argued that the Cour should institute a systematic triage process for identifying and handling the truly important cases buried among the thousands that come before it annually.[68] It proposed establishing 'clearly identified pathways for the differential treatment of appeals': a first path for simple cases, a second for typical ones, and a third for those appeals that demand 'in-depth treatment'.[69] The Jean Report wrote overtly of the need to detect the most 'important cases' within its docket, to which the Cour could then devote special attention. It proposed tasking the Cour's Advocate General in particular with producing impact statements that would 'evaluate the economic, social, philosophical and human consequences of proposed decisions'.[70]

In summary, the Jean Report offered a deliberate and cohesive plan to take charge of the Cour's docket, to organise it procedurally so as to direct its analytic focus and maximise its doctrinal impact, and to compose and publish the resulting judgments in a manner designed to justify and publicise their holdings. It therefore represented an organised strategy to reset the foundations of French judicial authority and legitimacy. Indeed, the Jean Report had no intention to mask this integrated project or to downplay its implications regarding the extent and bases of French judicial power. To the contrary, it brazenly discussed how its proposals reflected, effectuated and supported the Cour's *politique jurisdictionnel* (jurisdictional/institutional policy) and *politique jurisprudentielle* (jurisprudential/doctrinal policy) – terms and notions that could hardly be more jarring to French legal traditionalists. As the Jean Report, its proposals, its vocabulary and its worldview demonstrate so clearly, the days are long gone when French high court judgments anchored their legitimacy in the image of an impassive and disinterested institution piously applying the mechanical dictates of codified law. The high courts are now increasingly comfortable presenting themselves openly as active and volitional players that consciously seek to formulate, impose and publicise their institutional and jurisprudential policy.

68 See www.courdecassation.fr/files/files/Publications/Rapport%20annuel/rapport-annuel_2021.pdf (offering the Cour's docket statistics).

69 See Jean Rapport, 84–128.

70 Ibid., 108.

## 10.3 Conclusions

The European and French judicial reforms examined in this chapter are significantly historically overlapping and have been so for significantly longer than might at first appear. Although the European judicial vetting panels were established in 2009–10, they are embedded in a series of interlocking reforms that date back to the immediate aftermath of the breakup of the former Eastern Bloc in the 1990s. Similarly, although the French reforms that resulted in the Martin and Jean Reports and in the revamping of French high court decision-writing style date from the last eight years or so, they too go back at least to the 1990s, when the ECtHR began using the ECHR's 'fair trial' guarantee as a means to pressure legal systems designed on the French model to revamp the decision-making procedures of their high courts.[71]

The judicial reforms have continued doggedly ever since. On the one hand, the reforms make perfect sense. The judiciary has, after all, exploded in prominence and power throughout Europe since the Second World War, at both the national and supranational levels. There was a time when this rise in power was relatively little appreciated outside of those legal (and especially legal academic) circles attuned to European and domestic constitutional and judicial developments.[72] As the Brexit debates demonstrated all too well, however, no one fails any longer to understand the centrality of the high national and European courts: remarkably enough, not only Theresa May, but even the British tabloids treated escaping the jurisdiction of the ECJ as if it were as important as stopping unwanted immigration.[73] The domestic high courts have not failed to attract

[71] See e.g. *Borgers* v. *Belgium*, App. no. 12005/86 (ECHR, 30 October 1991); *Vermeulen v. Belgium*, App. no. 19075/91 (ECHR, 20 February 1996); *Lobo Machado* v. *Portugal*, App. no. 15764/89 (ECHR, 20 February 1996); *Reinhardt and Slimane-Kaïd* v. *France*, Apps. Nos. 23043/93 and 22921/93 (ECHR, 31 March 1998).

[72] One need only think of the classic literature on the ECJ, which worked hard to raise consciousness regarding the ECJ's pivotal role in the construction of Europe. See e.g. K. Alter, *Establishing the Supremacy of European Law: Making of an International Rule of Law in Europe* (Oxford: Oxford University Press, 2003); H. Rasmussen, *On Law and Policy in the European Court of Justice: A Comparative Study in Judicial Policymaking* (Nijhoff: Dordrecht, 1986); A. Stone, *Governing with Judges: Constitutional Politics in Europe* (Oxford: Oxford University Press, 2000); J. Weiler, 'The Transformation of Europe' (1991) 100 *Yale Law Journal* 2403.

[73] In the words of Theresa May:

> But let's state one thing loud and clear: we are not leaving the European Union only to give up control of immigration all over again. And we are

attention either, whether as vectors of European law or as increasingly prominent constitutional actors. It only makes sense, therefore, that the judiciary would feel pressured to justify its expanding authority and to reconstruct the bases of its legitimacy accordingly.

On the other hand, it is hard not to marvel at the full extent to which the French and European high courts have leveraged to their advantage the apparent need to justify and legitimate their newfound powers. In a long series of interlocking reforms, both the French and European high courts have managed to further increase their already burgeoning clout. The European courts have come out of this process with their judges significantly empowered relative to their respective national executive branches. For the most part, appointments to the ECJ and the ECtHR – and for that matter, to the national courts – have effectively come to require domestic selection processes controlled largely by independent judicial councils, themselves populated primarily by national judicial figures. To these national processes has been added an increasingly independent and rigorous European component, itself controlled overwhelmingly by high-ranking national and European judicial figures.[74] As a result of the developments, European (and domestic) judges have been significantly – though certainly not completely – liberated from their traditional vulnerability to heavy-handed executive branch control, at both the appointment and reappointment phase.

This is certainly not to suggest that such developments have always gone smoothly. They have not. Precisely because they limit the traditional capacity of executives to call the shots on judicial appointments, and thus to demand a certain level of fealty by 'their' judges serving in Strasbourg and Luxembourg, the reforms have been resisted at almost every turn. Even after the passage of most of the European judicial appointments reforms (including the establishment of the vetting panels), governments have done their level best to game the appointments systems by strong-arming their national judicial councils and by using assorted stratagems to telegraph their wishes to the European

> not leaving only to return to the jurisdiction of the European Court of Justice. That's not going to happen.
>
> We are leaving to become, once more, a fully sovereign and independent country – and the deal is going to have to work for Britain.

T. May, 'Britain after Brexit: A Vision of a Global Britain', www.independent.co.uk/news/uk/politics/theresa-may-speech-tory-conference-2016-in-full-transcript-a7346171.html

74 Both the 255 Panel and the APE are composed overwhelmingly of judicial notables.

institutions involved in the appointments process, worked to subvert and/or circumvent the European judicial vetting panels, threatened and retaliated against their own and even other countries' judges, and so on.[75] But such episodes only underline the full extent to which those governments have come to fear their loss of control over ever more powerful judicial actors. The felt need to justify and legitimate the exercise of ever-increasing European judicial power has effectively led to a further increase of that power.

The same can be said for the French judicial reforms, which seek to shift French judicial legitimacy from its longstanding institutional basis towards a more discursive model. The Cour de cassation, the Conseil d'Etat and the Constitutional Council have all recently modified their traditional writing styles to generate more thoroughly and transparently argued judgments. All now try actively to take into consideration the need to explain and justify their decisions to a general public that is understood to demand more than syllogistic, single-sentence, judicial fiats framed as mechanical applications of codified law.

Here, too, the developments have not always gone perfectly smoothly, as the criminalisation of targeted judicial analytics demonstrates all too clearly. But this threatened sanction only underlines the full dimension of the changes that have brought the judiciary into public consciousness. Yes, the increased spotlight on judicial decision making has triggered a newfound sense of French judicial vulnerability. But this vulnerability is not only a *result* of the increasingly transparent exercise of rising French judicial power, but also the *cause* of further French judicial reforms of the kind proposed under the Louvel presidency of the Cour de cassation. Finally, these reforms are explicitly designed to empower the French high courts even further to engage self-consciously, overtly and effectively in policy-making initiatives: they are designed precisely to maximise the Cour's ability to focus its energies on – and amplify the influence of – its most important judgments, now identified unabashedly as *les précédents*. How far things have come since I first met John Bell, the finest of all scholars of French and European judicial cultures.[76]

[75] See Lasser, *Judicial Dis-Appointments*, chapters 3, 5 and 10.

[76] See e.g. L. N. Brown and J. S. Bell, *French Administrative Law*, 5th ed. (Oxford: Oxford University Press, 2001); J. Bell, *French Legal Cultures* (Cambridge: Cambridge University Press, 2001); J. Bell, *Judiciaries within Europe: A Comparative Review* (Cambridge: Cambridge University Press, 2006); J. Bell, S. Boyron and S. Whittaker, *Principles of French Law*, 2nd ed. (Oxford: Oxford University Press, 2008).

# 11

# Researching Judicial Cultures in the European Union

## Lessons from John Bell

ELAINE MAK

John Bell has conducted ground-breaking research on courts. Central qualities of his work are an original angle of research questions, a broad comparative scope combined with a strong analytical view, attention paid to legal cultures and societal contexts, and the use of team collaborations with scholars in other countries. These publications as well as conversations with John have inspired much of my own research. Moreover, I am indebted to him for his guidance with regard to the design and realisation of my research projects. For a volume in honour of John, it seems appropriate to put a spotlight on the lessons which can be learnt from his work by scholars who, like me, are interested in understanding the role and functioning of judiciaries in evolving legal and societal contexts.

With this aim in mind, my contribution outlines main insights from John's comparative analysis in his book *Judiciaries within Europe*,[1] regarding the factors which shape the character of a judiciary. I discuss how further research on courts can benefit from these insights, drawing examples from a current research project on judicial cooperation in the European Union.[2] At the same time, this chapter aims to provide some thoughts on legal scholarship in contemporary societal and academic contexts. In particular, I will address the phenomenon of legal

[1] J. Bell, *Judiciaries within Europe: A Comparative Review* (Cambridge: Cambridge University Press, 2006).

[2] This chapter integrates parts of a published analysis, presented in E. Mak, N. Graaf and E. Jackson, 'The Framework for Judicial Cooperation in the European Union: Unpacking the Ethical, Legal and Institutional Dimensions of "Judicial Culture"' (2018) 34(1) *Utrecht Journal of International and European Law* 24. The research was conducted with the help of a Vidi grant (2016) from the Netherlands Organisation for Scientific Research (NWO).

globalisation and how to study this, expanding on John's analysis of this topic.[3] Besides paying tribute to the lessons that John has taught me, I hope that this chapter also provides some useful 'food for thought' for current law students and early career legal scholars.

The analysis in this chapter focuses on the concept of 'judicial culture'. John described this concept in *Judiciaries within Europe* and applied it in a comparative analysis regarding the judicial systems of France, Germany, Spain, Sweden and England. In his words, this notion concerns the 'features that shape the way in which the work of a judge is performed and valued within particular legal systems'.[4] It is a central notion for understanding the role and practices of judiciaries. Whereas John's analysis concerned national legal systems, increased judicial interactions beyond national borders give rise to new questions for legal research. A distinction can be made between different types of legal development which affect national judiciaries: 'international' for the binding obligations of states under treaties developed in the framework of international organisations, 'supranational' for the *sui generis* legal order of the EU, and 'transnational' for interaction between (actors in) different legal orders on a voluntary basis, e.g. concerning the exchange of ideas and best practices. In this respect, the EU is particularly interesting as an object of study, because of its combination of supranational and transnational legal development and the important role of judiciaries in both respects. The analysis in this chapter will highlight conceptual and methodological challenges which need to be addressed when conducting research on national judiciaries in this evolving European context.

This chapter is structured around some central methodological considerations of legal research on judicial cultures. The analysis in each section starts with a summary of insights from the research of John Bell, which is then commented and expanded on. Section 11.1 addresses the definition of judicial culture and Section 11.2 continues with the operationalisation of this concept in legal research. Section 11.3 concerns the design of research on judicial cultures in Europe in relation to current developments. Section 11.4 contains brief concluding remarks.

[3] J. Bell, 'Researching Globalisation: Lessons from Judicial Citations' (2014) 3(3) *Cambridge Journal of International and Comparative Law* 961.

[4] Bell, *Judiciaries within Europe*, 2.

## 11.1 Defining 'Judicial Culture'

John Bell's conceptualisation of judicial culture brings to the fore the interplay of values and practices when it comes to the development of judiciaries as institutions (Section 11.1.1). We can gain a better understanding of this conceptualisation if we analyse it in relation to the concept of legal culture (Section 11.1.2). Taking into account the trend of legal globalisation (Section 11.1.3), the conceptualisation of judicial culture can be refined in order to make it suitable for an analysis of judiciaries in a transnational legal context, such as the EU (Section 11.1.4).

### *11.1.1 Judicial Culture as Values and Praxis*

In John Bell's definition, judicial culture encompasses both a set of ideas and a praxis, particular to the legal community, the institutions of government and the wider community.[5] This conceptualisation addresses judicial functioning as a whole, i.e. both the primary process of judging and the judicial organisation. Ideas regarding judicial culture are expressed in the moral and social values of a specific community and in the legal rules concerning judicial organisation and the judgment of cases. The praxis that is a part of judicial culture concerns the approaches to judging that have developed over time in a specific legal system. This includes approaches to legal interpretation, i.e. the content of the judicial activity, and the handling of court procedures, i.e. the context in which judicial decisions are made.[6]

This notion of judicial culture encompasses a contextual element. After all, the values and praxis relating to the judicial functioning cannot be considered separately from the community or communities in which they developed. As such, the notion can be used as a starting point for legal research, which will need to take into account relevant legal sources and institutions as well as contextual aspects (e.g. legal, sociological, political and economic) regarding their meaning and functioning.[7]

[5] Ibid., 2.

[6] Ibid.

[7] From a methodological point of view, this approach fits with the analysis of S. Taekema, 'Relative Autonomy: A Characterisation of the Discipline of Law', in B. van Klink and S. Taekema (eds.), *Law and Method: Interdisciplinary Research into Law* (Tübingen: Mohr Siebeck, 2011), pp. 33–52.

In his book *Judiciaries within Europe*, John Bell analysed the institutional features of judiciaries, which 'provide the framework not only for stability, but also for continuity and change'.[8] The professional role of individuals is shaped in part by this institutional setting, e.g. through initial training and the opportunity to accumulate professional experiences. Judiciaries as institutions can be understood in different ways: as decision-making bodies in a hierarchical structure, as constitutional institutions in a balance of powers, as social institutions which help solve societal issues, and as a group of legal professionals within legal and professional communities. Only through an analysis which addresses both formal and informal aspects of judicial functioning, e.g. organisational arrangements as well as networks, can we obtain insights that connect these different dimensions.[9]

### *11.1.2 Understanding the Concept of Judicial Culture*

The presented conceptualisation of judicial culture connects with a concept that is probably more familiar to many legal scholars: that of legal culture. The concept of legal culture is the classic tool used within legal scholarship to describe patterns of legally oriented social behaviour and attitudes. It enables demonstrating the significant effects of social pressures on legal change.[10] However, the concept is not without criticism. It has been argued that the term is too vague and impressionistic as a concept to be useful in finding explanations of the patterns and processes of change in specific legal contexts.[11] In particular, the concept of legal culture can be divided into many different elements – such as attitudes, knowledge, expectations and values – which are not so easy to reassemble.[12] Furthermore, no straightforward answer exists to the question on how to operationalise legal culture in an analysis of specific elements, their interrelations and the connection with other types of cultures (for example, religious, political or economic culture).[13]

[8] Bell, *Judiciaries within Europe*, 350.
[9] Ibid., 350–1.
[10] D. Nelken, 'Thinking about Legal Culture' (2014) 1 *Asian Journal of Law and Society* 255.
[11] R. Cotterrell, 'The Concept of Legal Culture', in D. Nelken (ed.), *Comparing Legal Cultures* (Abingdon: Routledge, 1997), p. 13. See also S. Engle Merry, 'What Is Legal Culture? An Anthropological Perspective', in D. Nelken (ed.), *Using Legal Culture* (London: Wildy, Simmonds and Hill, 2012), pp. 52–76.
[12] Nelken, 'Thinking about Legal Culture', citing Von Benda Beckmann.
[13] Ibid.

Despite this criticism, specific conceptualisations of legal culture can be helpful for 'finding a common language to understanding and evaluating differences in patterns of legally oriented behaviour'.[14] Based on such a common language, elements of coherence and change can be analysed.[15] In this regard, conceptualisations that focus on attitudes and values can be criticised for being static and for presupposing the existence of unchangeable cultures.[16] By contrast, a conceptualisation of legal culture as something that is learnt – a view elaborated by Dutch sociologist Geert Hofstede – seems particularly useful for the analysis of developments in legal cultures.[17]

The concept of judicial culture has not yet been used with the same frequency in the academic literature as legal culture and, most likely as a consequence, has not yet been conceptualised in an in-depth manner.[18] Further attention to this concept is essential, however, for enabling sound and thorough studies on judiciaries as institutions in evolving legal and societal contexts. Moreover, this conceptualisation could contribute to the theoretical understanding of the broader concept of legal culture. Let us have a closer look at both of these aspects.

### *11.1.3 Integrating the Trend of Judicial Globalisation*

Cross-border legal-cultural elements have become prominent in recent years. Gunther Teubner has argued that national laws have been downgraded to 'mere regional parts of [a global] network which are in close communication with each other'.[19] Anne-Marie Slaughter has attached a more positive connotation to the changing role of courts, which according to her have become involved in a 'global community of

[14] Ibid.

[15] Ibid.

[16] J. Smits, 'Legal Culture as Mental Software', in T. Wilhelmsson, E. Paunio and A. Pohjolainen (eds.), *Private Law and the Many Cultures of Europe* (Alphen aan den Rijn: Kluwer Law International, 2007).

[17] Ibid.

[18] John Bell is one of the few authors who have conducted such a conceptual analysis. See further K. Å. Modéer, 'From "Rechtsstaat" to "Welfare-State": Swedish Judicial Culture in Transition 1870–1970', in W. Pue and D. Sugarman (eds.), *Lawyers and Vampires: Cultural Histories of Legal Professions* (Oxford: Hart, 2003), p. 153.

[19] G. Teubner, 'Legal Irritants: Good Faith in British Law or How Unifying Law Ends Up in New Divergences' (1998) 61 *Modern Law Review* 16.

courts'.[20] Their analyses classify a perceived increase of interconnections between legal systems and actors in these systems as indicative of a trend of legal globalisation.

From a normative-theoretical perspective, this idea of 'globalisation' of laws and legal systems corresponds with an assumption of universality, meaning the equal and indiscriminate application of supranational or international law in national legal systems. This view on globalisation also corresponds with a cosmopolitan outlook, i.e. a conception of 'the world as a single entity, with resonances between people irrespective of their location, nationality and culture' and a conception which involves concern for the way in which 'legal actors can access legal regimes beyond their state's domestic framework'.[21]

John Bell has nuanced the views expressed by some scholars regarding the pervasiveness of legal globalisation. Based on an analysis of available research on transnational judicial citations, notably studies by Michal Bobek and by me,[22] he argues that signs of converged practices of national courts in solving common problems for now mostly concern areas of mandatory cooperation, i.e. cooperation based on international or supranational laws, and that 'global' mindsets of judges are harder to find.[23] Yet, regardless of one's view about legal globalisation, it is clear that legal actors, including judges, can no longer delimit their focus to one legal culture only. This certainly is the case in the sphere of mandatory judicial cooperation created by the EU.

Regarding judiciaries in Europe, this trend of legal globalisation prompts research on the effects of the EU legal integration on the judicial function in member states. The development of EU law and judicial mechanisms for its application has added additional tasks to the function of national judges, in particular the role of national courts as EU judges. Furthermore, the judicial function in the EU context is valued not only on the basis of national constitutional values but also on the basis of fundamental European legal values, such as democracy and the rule of

[20] A.-M. Slaughter, 'A Global Community of Courts' (2003) 44 *Harvard International Law Journal* 191.

[21] Bell, 'Researching Globalisation', 961.

[22] M. Bobek, *Comparative Reasoning in European Supreme Courts* (Oxford: Oxford University Press, 2013); E. Mak, *Judicial Decision-Making in a Globalised World: A Comparative Analysis of the Changing Practices of Western Highest Courts* (Oxford: Hart, 2013).

[23] Bell, 'Researching Globalisation', 980.

law, and the social values of pluralism and solidarity.[24] From within the member states, moreover, many judges have knowledge of, and sometimes experience with, the laws of other national systems, which informs their decision making. In this way, 'top-down' supranational as well as 'bottom-up' transnational influences on judicial functioning in the EU invite a rethinking of the notion of judicial culture.

### *11.1.4 Refining the Concept of Judicial Culture*

As an epistemological tool, judicial culture connects with Patrick Glenn's definition of 'legal tradition', which he has described as the received information from the past that governs current laws and legal practices.[25] 'Culture', for the purpose of studying influences on judicial systems and professionals in these systems, can be connected with the 'mental software' possessed by those belonging to a specific community.[26] This term 'mental software' was coined by Geert Hofstede and defines culture as 'the collective programming of the mind which distinguishes the members of one group or category of people from another'.[27] This conceptualisation acknowledges the susceptibility of culture to change, related to the development of the meaning attached by the individual to facts and behaviour.[28]

With regard to judging, the development of the views and approaches to judging of judges in national highest courts provides a helpful example for understanding what a judicial culture is and how it can develop. To start with, highest court judges can be classified as belonging to different groups with each group having its own 'mental software'. Indeed, in the contemporary legal context, where international, supranational and comparative legal sources are increasingly relevant, some judges – who could be called 'globalist' judges – have opened up to the possibility of finding persuasive arguments for the judgment of cases in non-binding foreign legal sources. By contrast, others – who could be called 'localist' judges –

[24] Article 2 Treaty on European Union.

[25] H. P. Glenn, *Legal Traditions of the World: Sustainable Diversity in Law* (Oxford: Oxford University Press, 2014).

[26] Smits, 'Legal Culture as Mental Software'.

[27] G. Hofstede, *Cultures and Organisations: Software of the Mind* (New York: McGraw-Hill, 1997), p. 5.

[28] Smits, 'Legal Culture as Mental Software', referring to C. Geertz, *The Interpretation of Cultures* (New York: Basic Books, 1973).

have shown themselves reluctant to walk this path.[29] Factors which influence the adherence to one or the other of these groups include a judge's personal interest in comparative legal studies as well as personal encounters with foreign legal systems through legal education, working experiences abroad or the judge's personal life.[30] In this sense, the development of the views and practices of new members of a community, such as law students with an ambition to enter the judicial profession, is influenced by the existing 'mental software(s)' to which they are exposed. The appropriation of a specific culture could therefore be said to consist of a process of individual learning. At the same time, the culture that is learnt is a 'moving target' in the sense that it will keep evolving based on the meaning that all members of the group attach to facts and behaviour in the context in which they interact with each other.

In addition to this possibility of different judicial views and approaches in different groups of judges, the geographical aspect of culture also requires a further clarification. Culture in Hofstede's definition does not necessarily correspond with national territory. One country can encompass more than one legal culture and specific legal cultures might be a part of more than one national legal system.[31] With regard to judging, this is illustrated by the geographical distribution of the common law and civil law traditions. The common law model, in which the judge has a leading role in the development of the law through precedents, has spread throughout the English-speaking world. Meanwhile continental-European countries as well as countries in Latin America and Asia have adopted the civil law perspective in which the judge is conceptually constrained to the task of applying the laws enacted by the legislative authorities.[32] At the same time, these two traditions can co-exist within one legal system. One such example is Canada, where the common law tradition is dominant, but the civil law tradition underlies specific areas of law in the province of Québec.[33] Besides these possibilities of cross-

[29] Mak, *Judicial Decision-Making in a Globalised World.*

[30] Ibid. Regarding the importance of experience abroad for the development of individual views, see also M. Goodwin, 'The Importance of Elsewhere', inaugural lecture Tilburg University, 29 April 2016, www.youtube.com/watch?v=TsjO4NNSxuc

[31] Smits, in 'Legal Culture as Mental Software', criticises conceptualisations of legal culture, which connect primarily with nation states.

[32] Glenn, *Legal Traditions of the World*, also describes how the differences between these legal traditions have become less pronounced in the course of their development over time.

[33] See www.justice.gc.ca

national and coexisting legal cultures, differences can develop due to local interpretations, as demonstrated by the connection of a legal tradition with a specific national legal system. For example, the style of judicial reasoning in the French legal system is still apodictic in nature, whereas judges in the French-inspired Dutch legal system have developed a more elaborate way of reasoning.[34] The relevance of nationality in this context can be explained by the connection of the judicial style of reasoning with the role of the judiciary as a national institution with a developed homogenous approach to judging cases within its jurisdiction.

Based on this conceptual analysis, it appears that the views and approaches to the judicial function among judges are open to differentiation. In this regard, individuals do not belong to one culture only, but to a variety of cultures simultaneously.[35] Judges – as well as other legal professionals and policy makers – can sometimes connect with cultural elements related to their national legal system, such as the national conception of 'good faith' in contract law or of the 'rule of law' principle. They can at other times connect with cross-border cultural elements such as principles of *lex mercatoria* or the conception of a 'fair trial' under the European Convention on Human Rights.[36]

Fundamentally, the analysis in this section demonstrates that the development of a shared judicial culture across national borders could be a natural next step in the evolution of 'mental software' of judges in member states of the EU. An alignment of national judicial cultures would consist of the development of a critical mass among legal professionals in favour of an approach of consistent reference to shared cross-border legal-cultural elements rather than only national legal-cultural elements (in as far as divergence exists between these elements). How, then, can we study such a process of possible alignment?

## 11.2 Operationalising Judicial Culture

If we want to gain more insight into the characteristics and development of judiciaries in relation to a judicial culture, we will need to identify variables which can be described and compared. In other words, the concept of judicial culture needs to be operationalised. According to John

[34] Mak, *Judicial Decision-Making in a Globalised World.*

[35] Smits, 'Legal Culture as Mental Software', referring to A. Sen, *Identity and Violence: The Illusion of Destiny* (New York: Norton, 2006).

[36] Ibid.

Bell, four main factors come to the fore, which shape the character of a judiciary.[37] In this section, I will analyse how these factors can be fine-tuned for research of judicial cultures in the EU context. These factors are: relevant historical developments (Section 11.2.1), the task relating to the judicial role (Section 11.2.2), the organisational structure of the judiciary (Section 11.2.3) and values for the judiciary (Section 11.2.4).

### *11.2.1 History*

In his analysis of European judiciaries, John Bell starts out from the idea that judicial tasks and judicial organisation are shaped in the practices which develop over time in countries. The development of judiciaries as social groups concerns a process of historical experience rather than the implementation of a design based on constitutional theory.[38] This process can be related to the model of the reflective practitioner, in which 'reflection is a problem-solving exercise' and 'experience leads to reflection and change'.[39] In this regard, the development of judiciaries over time more often consists of a gradual adjustment of judges to conjunctural events rather than of changes based on institutional planning.[40]

According to John Bell, an historical influence on the development of the five judiciaries examined in his book is visible with regard to the shape of procedures relating to specific judicial tasks, such as the inclusion of lay judges or juries in procedures in some areas of the law.[41] He observes that a notable historical influence concerns judicial law making. This role has developed and gained authority to a larger extent in legal orders where judges were involved in pre-legislative processes than in systems where this was not the case. Previous experiences formed an important motor behind the development of this judicial involvement.[42]

Developed patterns regarding the judicial function tend to persist because of path dependence, meaning that 'established legal approaches to the solution of issues will determine the way in which new situations or new problems are handled in the present and in the future'.[43] Legal

[37] Bell, *Judiciaries within Europe*, 351.

[38] Ibid., 351.

[39] Ibid., 354.

[40] Ibid., 378.

[41] Ibid.

[42] Ibid., 352–3.

[43] M. Siems, *Comparative Law* (Cambridge: Cambridge University Press, 2014), p. 239, cited by Bell, 'Researching Globalisation', 962.

scholarship which pays attention to path dependence is able to explain specific developments of legal systems, including developments regarding judicial institutions.

My own approach corresponds with this view. As an illustrative example, I mention here my research focus on the specific feature of constitutional (in-)flexibility for explaining the development of legal systems and their institutions. This feature concerns 'the relative openness of the constitutional framework of a specific legal system as concerns the expression of normative change'.[44] The '(in-)flexibility' of a constitution is the parameter which explains to what extent this constitution allows for the integration of normative changes, based on evolving societal views, into the legal framework for government.[45] The degree of (in-)flexibility of a constitutional framework depends on the detail of constitutional rules and the possibility for modification of these rules as well as on the approach to judicial interpretation of the constitution and the influence of external legal sources (e.g. international law) on the legal system.[46] Taking into account these factors in an analysis of the development of legal systems, e.g. with regard to 'global' interactions of judges, can assist us in understanding similarities and differences between countries.

In research regarding judiciaries in the EU, it is relevant to pay attention to the origins and goals of the EU and to look for connections with national histories when analysing developments. With regard to judicial culture, current developments tie in with the European Commission's agenda for judicial cooperation. The ambition to strive for a shared judicial culture was first articulated in April 2010 by Viviane Reding, then Vice-President of the European Commission responsible for Justice, Fundamental Rights and Citizenship. Reding underlined the necessity for further alignment between judicial systems after the entry into force of the Lisbon Treaty (2009).[47] This treaty has increased the EU's competences regarding judicial cooperation in civil and criminal matters (Title V of the Treaty on the Functioning of the European Union) and has given legal force to the Charter of Fundamental Rights of the EU (2000). In this context, the objectives of providing effective legal remedies and human

[44] E. Mak, 'Understanding Legal Evolution through Constitutional Theory: The Concept of Constitutional (In-)Flexibility' (2011) 4(4) *Erasmus Law Review* 196.

[45] Ibid., 197.

[46] Ibid., 197–202.

[47] V. Reding, 'A European Law Institute: An Important Milestone for an Ever Closer Union of Law, Rights and Justice', speech at the European University Institute, 10 April 2010, https://ec.europa.eu/commission/presscorner/detail/en/SPEECH_10_154

rights protection in the EU create a strong impetus for alignment of national judicial values and procedures. Her successor, Commissioner Věra Jourová, adopted this agenda and focused on the enhancement of mutual trust between the judiciaries of member states through European judicial training and improved access to information.[48]

More unity between European judicial systems is also promoted from another direction. Beside the 'top-down' developments from the European Commission, we can identify a 'bottom-up' tendency of alignment between the judicial systems of EU member states. Aspects of these systems have converged under the effects of European legal integration and globalisation of laws and legal systems. On the one hand, EU harmonisation has occurred with regard to substantive laws and procedures and institutional aspects of judicial organisation.[49] On the other hand, judiciaries in Europe have aligned their interpretations of legal concepts and their working methods to a certain degree through the institutional dynamics of transnational judicial communication, entailing the finding of inspiration in foreign legislation, case law and scholarship and in informal exchanges, for example in networks.[50]

When designing research on the current development of judicial cooperation in the EU, it is worthwhile to refer to John Bell's analysis of the gradual adjustments which judiciaries have made in previous stages of the EU legal integration. In *Judiciaries within Europe*, he makes the following observations:

> Adjustments in the absence of planning are a feature of the European dimensions of the judiciaries discussed here. The doctrines of direct effect and the supremacy of European Community law were not clearly stated in the original treaties of the European Communities or in the British accession through the European Communities Act 1972. It was therefore for the judges to adjust to the values put in place by the European Court of Justice in 1963–4. Whereas the French Cour de cassation responded in 1975, the Conseil d'Etat and the Conseil constitutionnel both took until after the end of the Gaullist era and after the Single European Act of

48 V. Jourova, 'Answers to European Parliament Questionnaire' (2014), https://ec.europa.eu/commission/commissioners/sites/cwt/files/commissioner_ep_hearings/jourova-reply_en.pdf

49 Concerning judicial organisation, see for example the 'Copenhagen criteria' for accession to the EU by new member states (2003), https://ec.europa.eu/neighbourhood-enlargement/policy/glossary/terms/accession-criteria_en

50 E. Mak and D. S. Law, 'Transnational Judicial Communication: The European Union', in D. S. Law (ed.), *Constitutionalism in Context* (Cambridge: Cambridge University Press, 2022), pp. 236–60.

> 1986 before they adopted more similar positions in 1989 and 1988 respectively. The German courts had similar hesitations. Developing a sense of direction in such changed circumstances requires a political sense among the judges of what is going to last. Developing such a collective sense among the members of a supreme court, let alone among the lower judges, requires much internal discussion. The decision is often prepared by what Lord Devlin called 'rumblings from Olympus' – there were musings that indicated a potential change of direction. Without a formal debate, there was a gradual realisation of 'the spirit of the times', often coinciding with changes in key personnel.[51]

### *11.2.2 Task*

The character of the judicial role is influenced by the tasks that are assigned to the judiciary. John Bell has rightly observed that adjudication is a 'major defining task' of judiciaries in Western legal systems. Still, using adjudication is a social decision, as 'the involvement of judges in the resolution of social problems through their core task of adjudication is only one option among many for handling social problems'.[52] Reasons for assigning certain tasks to the judiciary include the mission of the legal system, e.g. to be leading in a certain area of law or to resolve problems of citizens, and the availability of other institutions to pick up certain tasks, taking into account inter alia expertise and reputation.[53] Also, serendipity plays a role, e.g. the availability of resources or generalisable models at a moment of reform.[54]

Bell observes that '[t]he particular tasks of judges will involve them in different relationships with other social actors. Constitutional adjudication will bring to the fore relations with politicians, whilst criminal law will bring close connections with the media'.[55] Whereas judicial tasks are not directly connected with the organisational structure of the judiciary, there is a relationship with procedural arrangements. In this regard, Bell points out differences between criminal procedures. For example, judges will prepare and act differently depending on whether they are functioning in an adversarial system or dealing with an inquisitorial trial.[56]

[51] Bell, *Judiciaries within Europe*, 379.
[52] Ibid., 356.
[53] Ibid., 356–7.
[54] Ibid., 357.
[55] Ibid.
[56] Ibid., 358.

A look at judiciaries in the EU confirms the variety in 'social decisions' which have been made regarding judicial tasks. Indeed, judicial cooperation remains complicated because of differences between views on the judicial function and the developed practices of judging in different EU member states. For instance, a judge in the Netherlands can be a member of a political party.[57] This judge should take a monist view on the relationship between EU law and domestic law,[58] and might be reluctant to execute a judgment from another EU member state where corruption within the judiciary is still a recognised problem.[59] By contrast, judges in some other EU member states are not allowed to be a member of a political party.[60] They should take a dualist approach to the relationship between EU law and domestic law,[61] and they may still be struggling to bring their judicial system up to standard in terms of realisation of the principle of the rule of law.[62]

It is helpful to keep in mind these aspects when conducting research on judiciaries. Rather than looking for a set of shared characteristics, it is more feasible to compare judicial systems in terms of 'family resemblances'.[63] Furthermore, a contextual analysis should pay attention to developing normative views on the judicial function. An example concerns the increased emphasis on procedural justice in some legal systems, e.g. concerning the rights of crime victims to speak during a trial. Another example is the call in some countries for T-shaped legal professionalism – i.e. a combination of 'deep' legal knowledge and skills and 'broad' interdisciplinary insights – to address contemporary legal issues.[64] In this respect, John Bell's reference to external expectations with regard to the judiciary is pertinent. Such expectations can come

[57] *NVvR-Rechterscode* (Judges' Code) (2011) para. 2.3.2, https://nvvr.org/uploads/documenten/nvvr-rechterscode.pdf

[58] M. Claes, *The National Courts' Mandate in the European Constitution* (Oxford: Hart, 2006), p. 205.

[59] See Transparency International, *Corruption Perceptions Index* (2019), www.transparency.org/en/cpi#

[60] See codes of conduct for judges in inter alia Estonia, Finland, Hungary, Latvia, Lithuania and Portugal as well as former member state the United Kingdom (England and Wales).

[61] E.g. Germany, Italy. See Claes, *National Courts' Mandate*, 198–9.

[62] See further Section 11.2.4.

[63] See also M. M. Shapiro, *Courts: A Comparative and Political Analysis* (Chicago, IL: University of Chicago Press, 1981).

[64] E. Mak, *The T-Shaped Lawyer and Beyond: Rethinking Legal Professionalism and Legal Education for Contemporary Societies* (The Hague: Eleven International Publishing, 2017), pp. 7–8.

from other legal professionals, e.g. advocates, or from the wider societal and political community, e.g. in media debates or proposals for legal reform. These expectations stand in connection with expectations raised by members of the judiciary, e.g. senior judges with a high profile in debates on the profession.[65] Attention paid to these expectations can help clarify which actors have been influential in the normative debate on judicial tasks in a legal system and provide insight into the dynamics between professional and societal expectations regarding the judiciary.[66]

### *11.2.3 Organisational Structure*

The way in which a judiciary is organised has an influence on individual judges. In the words of John Bell, '[i]ndividuals become judges by becoming part of an organisation that has its own ethos and range of activities and procedures'.[67] He identifies the nature of the judicial corps as the most important organisational factor that shapes the character of the judiciary. This 'corps' is 'the socially and institutionally defined group to which a judge belongs and in which she operates'.[68] An important feature concerns the number of divisions in the judicial corps and related aspects such as the function and formation of specific groups and their relations with other professional groups inside and outside of the judicial corps. In case of more radical separations, e.g. between administrative judges and other groups (France) or between judges and the bar (France, Sweden, Spain), there is less of a basis for mutual understanding between groups and less space for joint reflections on the development of the law.[69] The organisation of professional education and training is often linked to divisions in the judicial corps and thereby reinforces separations into distinct groups.[70]

John Bell discusses the particularities of hierarchy and leadership within a judicial organisation. Because of the particularities of the judicial function, '[t]here has to be a combination of the exercise of authority to

65 Bell, *Judiciaries within Europe*, 380–2.

66 See also E. Mak, 'Het gezag van de juristen: een normatieve reflectie', in A. Berlee, M. Bovens, J. Buiting, A. R. Mackor, E. Mak, J. Silvis and E. Tjong Tjin Tai, *De toekomst van de jurist, de jurist van de toekomst (Handelingen Nederlandse Juristen-Vereniging)* (Deventer: Wolters Kluwer, 2020), pp. 19–25.

67 Bell, *Judiciaries within Europe*, 359.

68 Ibid.

69 Ibid., 360–2.

70 Ibid., 364.

ensure tasks are performed properly with a significant element of collegiality which respects the independent professional status of those being managed'.[71] Bell points out types of leadership which can develop in relation to specific roles. He distinguishes between institutional leadership, e.g. of highest courts in shaping legal development, and individual leadership relating to professional status or personal authority.[72] Bell also discusses managerial roles regarding the organisation of courts and judicial careers. In this regard, the relationship with a ministry is an important element that shapes the character of a judiciary. Within the diverse landscape of national approaches, a common feature seems to be the ministerial influence on available resources.[73]

I share John Bell's observation that '[t]he extent to which management in relation to judicial activity is contentious depends on the aspect of the judicial role over which it is exercised'.[74] Insightful comparative research on experiences with judicial self-governance in Europe, in particular the role of judicial councils, has been conducted by David Kosař in a collaboration with legal scholars from a broad selection of countries.[75] He has emphasised 'the liquid nature of judicial self-governance and its responsiveness to political, social, and cultural changes'.[76]

John Bell further notices the features of social diversity in the judicial corps, the structure of contacts and influence, and collective action by judges through professional associations.[77] Among these features, the structure of contacts and influence has come to the fore as important in my own research. The role of judicial networks in Europe has been explored in more detail, and with the use of empirical legal methods (participant observation and interviews), by Erin Jackson.[78] In a similar vein, Niels Graaf conducted a 'longue durée' analysis of cross-references in German, French, and Italian public law scholarship in order to trace possible signs of alignment regarding national legal thinking on EU

[71] Ibid., 365.

[72] Ibid., 366.

[73] Ibid., 367.

[74] Ibid., 368.

[75] D. Kosař (ed.), 'Judicial Self-Governance in Europe' (2018) 19(7) *German Law Journal*, special issue.

[76] D. Kosař, 'Beyond Judicial Councils: Forms, Rationales and Impact of Judicial Self-Governance in Europe' (2018) 19(7) *German Law Journal* 1571.

[77] Bell, *Judiciaries within Europe*, 368–72.

[78] See Mak, Graaf and Jackson, 'The Framework for Judicial Cooperation in the European Union'. *Inside European Judicial Networks*, dissertation to be defended in 2023.

law.[79] John Bell has noticed the importance of research on these 'informal' aspects. An understanding of changes of 'period style', i.e. the defining characteristics of a judiciary at a certain moment in time, can only come about if we study both the role of formal institutions in legal development and the role of informal systems which contribute to the development of the collective view. This insight calls for an analysis of legal sources such as court decisions as well as research on 'the fora in which judges are able to discuss potential developments'.[80]

### *11.2.4 Values*

Based on his research, John Bell has concluded that '[t]he dominant values of the judicial role at any one period are actually a compromise between historically received ideas, external views of the political, social and legal communities, and internally generated ideas within the judiciary itself'.[81] In his book, he discusses the values of judicial creativity in law-making, judicial independence and conceptions of the judicial role as a public office or as a bureaucratic job.

With regard to law-making creativity, firstly, Bell's analysis of continental legal systems as well as the English legal system clarifies that 'there has been a "period style" about the degree of creativity in interpreting legislation that is thought appropriate'.[82] Currently, the judicial creation of norms is accepted to some degree, although we should keep in mind that most court cases concern 'routine legal questions and routine solutions'.[83] Secondly, the value of judicial independence gets shaped into institutional arrangements as a response to identified threats to that independence in a particular country. This contextual development explains why conceptions of judicial independence and developed practices can differ between countries.[84] Bell's contextualised analysis and comparison of a number of European legal systems is insightful as a means for understanding similarities and differences in this regard. The value which concerns the judicial role as such, finally, connects with the

[79] N. Graaf, *Judicial Influencers: Scholarly Use of Foreign Law and the Convergence of German, Italian and French Ideas on the Position of National Constitutional Courts in the EU Legal Context, 1989–2012* (PhD dissertation, Utrecht University: 10 October 2022).

[80] Bell, *Judiciaries within Europe*, 380.

[81] Ibid., 372.

[82] Ibid.

[83] Ibid., 373.

[84] Ibid., 374.

legitimacy of the judiciary. A role of judges as public office holders, e.g. in constitutional cases, provides legitimacy in the form of an independent role next to the other branches of government. A role of judges as bureaucratic functionaries, relating to professionalism in conformity with the rule of law principle, provides an instrumental legitimacy where judges uphold standards of justice.[85] An interesting observation concerns the development of codes of ethics for judges. While written codes existed in only a few countries when Bell conducted his research in the early 2000s,[86] a proliferation has occurred since then.[87] Although we can see a lot of similarities between standards, differences exist in specific areas and can be traced back to 'the tradition of the judicial community, reinforced by both training and discipline'.[88]

Bell's analysis confirms that the development of judicial cultures, in a national as well as in a multi-level legal system, takes place within a specific normative framework. Beside these values, the societal trends in a specific day and age shape laws and legal institutions. Lord Thomas of Cwmgiedd has described this interplay between fundamental values and contemporary trends with reference to Thomas Jefferson's adagium: 'On matters of style, swim with the current, on matters of principle, stand like a rock'.[89]

For the EU, the basic framework for the judicial function is set by the principle of the rule of law.[90] Relevant contemporary trends are the 'top-down' and 'bottom-up' developments and connected challenges for achieving unity between judicial systems in the EU. Against the background of these trends, questions arise as to how European and transnational tendencies in judicial cooperation can develop further in the 'post-Lisbon era'. From a political and societal perspective, conflicting postures of support and resistance regarding the process of European

[85] Ibid., 377.

[86] Ibid., 377–8.

[87] G. Di Federico, 'Judicial Accountability and Conduct: An Overview', in A. Seibert-Fohr (ed.), *Judicial Independence in Transition* (Berlin: Springer, 2012), pp. 87–118; E. Mak, 'Researching Judicial Ethical Codes, or: How to Eat a Mille-Feuille?' (2018) 9(3) *International Journal for Court Administration* 55–66.

[88] Bell, *Judiciaries within Europe*, 378.

[89] Lord Thomas of Cwmgiedd, 'The Centrality of Justice: Its Contribution to Society and Its Delivery', in J. Cooper (ed.), *Being a Judge in the Modern World* (Oxford: Oxford University Press, 2017), pp. 166–7.

[90] Article 2 Treaty on European Union.

legal integration are likely to influence the balance that is struck in EU legislation and governance between the unity and diversity of laws and judicial systems.[91] Indeed, events such as the euro crisis, the refugee crisis, the 'rule of law' crises in Hungary and Poland and the Brexit vote underline the vulnerability of the European project, which started out with the goal of achieving an 'ever closer union'.[92] However, transnational issues, including the sheltering of refugees and combating terrorism, have simultaneously prompted a call for increased cooperation between states in Europe.[93] Judges are likely to be influenced by these political and societal developments in their shaping of domestic laws[94] and possibly also in their alignment of practices towards a shared European standard for the sound and fair administration of justice.[95]

Against the background of these developments, conceptual clarity and comparative reflections on judicial culture have become more pertinent. They can help us explain and assess systemic threats to the rule of law in EU member states, in particular the political pressure on judiciaries in Poland and Hungary.[96] Indeed, the developments in these member states make clear that a common ground in Europe regarding the principles of the rule of law and judicial independence is shaky, to say the least. Moreover, these developments are illustrative of the persistent influence of historically developed views and practices regarding the judicial function in national legal systems, in this case the continued influence of communist political ideologies.

The process of legal integration in the EU has become even more complex and multi-faceted after the Brexit referendum in 2016. The United Kingdom's departure from the Union raises numerous legal questions. From the perspective of the development of legal systems,

[91] For a conceptual clarification on postures of support and resistance of transnational influences, see V. C. Jackson, *Constitutional Engagement in a Transnational Era* (Oxford: Oxford University Press, 2009).

[92] See J. Peet, 'The Future of the European Union: Creaking at 60', *The Economist* (25 March 2017), www.economist.com/news/special-report/21719188-it-marks-its-60th-birthday-european-union-poor-shape-it-needs-more

[93] Ibid.

[94] Jackson, *Constitutional Engagement in a Transnational Era*, outlining the influence of the views of judges on the development of domestic constitutional law.

[95] Mak, *Judicial Decision-Making in a Globalised World*, 237–9.

[96] See e.g. P. Gyöngyi, 'The Obligation of Judges to Uphold Rules of Positive Law and Possibly Conflicting Ethical Values in Context: The Case of Criminalization of Homelessness in Hungary' (2020) 49(2) *Netherlands Journal of Legal Philosophy* 196–217.

Brexit can be expected to have consequences for the development of substantive laws as well as legal institutions in the European Union and in the United Kingdom. In the new constellation, there is no longer any sphere of mandatory interaction between legal actors and therefore no automatic 'cross-pollination' in legal interpretation or in the development of organisational arrangements and procedures. Still, the issue of retained EU case law is one example of a continued formal connection between the United Kingdom and the EU leg system.[97] With regard to legal research, analyses based on a sound conceptual framework can provide useful insights for understanding and guiding the development of judiciaries in this new context.

## 11.3 Designing Further Research on Judicial Culture(s) in Europe

Besides starting-points for the conceptualisation and operationalisation of judicial culture, John Bell's research provides insights regarding methodological design of research on judicial cultures in Europe. For further research, we can learn useful lessons regarding the design of an analytical framework (Section 11.3.1), the choice of topics and research approaches (Section 11.3.2), and the engagement in team collaborations (Section 11.3.3).

### *11.3.1 Analytical Framework*

John Bell's comparative analysis of European judiciaries provides explanatory insights into the development of judiciaries as institutions in national legal systems. With regard to a possible alignment of national judicial cultures towards in the EU, an added component is that research will have to consider the normative foundation which could allow for the development of a shared 'European judicial culture'.

After all, a constitutional normative framework for the judicial function is still under construction at the EU level. Indeed, constitutional consensus currently does not exist regarding the main requirements for judicial functioning under the rule of law. At present, such consensus between EU member states holds challenges related to differences in main areas relating to the judicial role and functioning, these being: (1) the judiciary's

97 See the regulations on retained EU case law and the UK courts: European Union (Withdrawal) Act 2018 (Relevant Court) (Retained EU Case Law) Regulations 2020, www.legislation.gov.uk

position in the political balance of powers;[98] (2) the conception of the judicial role in law development and law enforcement;[99] and (3) societal values regarding justice and rights protection.[100] Moreover, the European Commission's ambitions reach further than the realisation of a basic consensus, as do specific 'bottom-up' processes of transnational borrowing developed by national courts in the EU member states. The achievement of a 'true' European judicial culture, as envisaged by these actors,[101] demands striving for alignment of values, rules and practices for judicial functioning beyond the minimum level of compliance with the rule of law, defined here as the prevention of the arbitrary use of power.[102]

In this regard, liberal-democratic constitutional norms provide a foundation for judicial cultures in the EU and set conditions for change.[103] At the core, the national judiciaries in member states have a dual role to play. On the one hand, they are the institutions in the rule-of-law framework that embody the principle of access to justice and the protection of fundamental rights in a national legal order. On the other hand, they are the 'linchpins' between their domestic legal order and international and supranational legal orders, in particular in their role as 'decentralised' EU courts.[104] Research on the development of judiciaries in the EU context should address both roles and connect with an external normative framework, e.g. derived from constitutional theory, in order to assess the possibility of alignment between different views and practices which have developed in the member states. An ambition in my current research project is to develop such a normative-theoretical assessment.

[98] See A. Seibert-Fohr (ed.), *Judicial Independence in Transition* (Heidelberg: Springer, 2012). See also Bell, *Judiciaries within Europe*, 375.

[99] M. van Hoecke and M. Warrington, 'Legal Cultures, Legal Paradigms, Legal Doctrine: Towards a New Model for Comparative Law' (1998) 47 *International and Comparative Law Quarterly* 495; R. A. Posner, *How Judges Think* (Cambridge, MA: Harvard University Press, 2008); M. de Visser, *Constitutional Review in Europe: A Comparative Analysis* (Oxford: Hart, 2013).

[100] D. Schraad-Tissler and C. Kroll, *Social Justice in the EU: A Cross-National Comparison* (Gütersloh: Bertelsmann Stiftung, 2014); A. Williams, *The Ethos of Europe: Values, Law and Justice in the EU* (Cambridge: Cambridge University Press, 2010).

[101] See Reding, 'A European Law Institute'.

[102] See E. Mak and S. Taekema, 'The European Union's Rule of Law Agenda: Identifying Its Core and Contextualizing Its Application' (2016) 8(1) *Hague Journal on the Rule of Law*, 25–50.

[103] Mak, *Judicial Decision-Making in a Globalised World*, 14–35.

[104] B. de Witte et al. (eds.), *National Courts and EU Law: New Issues, Theories and Methods* (Cheltenham: Edward Elgar, 2016), p. 5.

### *11.3.2 Topics and Research Approaches*

John Bell's research provides a reflection on the object of legal research in a globalised context. He has argued that 'the national (or sub-national) legal system remains an important feature of legal experience and needs to be factored into any project on globalisation'.[105] Bell indicates the 'enduring effects' of the legal systems developed in nation states.[106] Firstly, these effects encompass the professional formation of lawyers, which influences the way in which they will approach legal problems. Secondly, these effects include the phenomenon of path dependence.

With regard to legal research in a globalised context, Bell argues that 'a more sectorial approach to the place of international and comparative law is the way forward, rather than focusing on grand scale claims about globalisation'.[107] After all, the globalised legal context is characterised by variety in the loci of problem-solving, including roles for national actors, supranational and international actors, and private as well as public actors. Moreover, national legal systems contain specific frameworks which demarcate the scope of action of these actors.[108]

Keeping this advice in mind, research on judiciaries in the EU can benefit from comparative as well as interdisciplinary approaches to legal research. Research which demonstrates the benefits of these approaches has been developed by inter alia Mitchel Lasser and Ran Hirschl, who have combined legal, sociological and historical elements in their research on judiciaries in different countries.[109]

Furthermore, the scope of examined objects could be broadened. As Bell has pointed out, '[m]uch of the recent evidence adduced to demonstrate globalisation comes from the analysis of judicial decisions'.[110] Further insights on the development of legal and judicial cultures can be obtained by considering other issues, e.g. cross-references in legal scholarship, exchanges in transnational judicial networks or the influence of codes of ethics on judicial functioning.[111]

105 Bell, 'Researching Globalisation', 961.
106 Ibid., 962.
107 Ibid., 965.
108 Ibid.
109 M. de S. O. l'E. Lasser, *Judicial Transformations: The Rights Revolution in the Courts of Europe* (Oxford: Oxford University Press, 2009); R. Hirschl, *Comparative Matters* (Oxford: Oxford University Press, 2014).
110 Bell, 'Researching Globalisation', 967.
111 See further Section 11.3.3.

### 11.3.3 Team Collaborations

A final important topic which John Bell has addressed in his work concerns teamwork in legal research. In his words:

> A lone scholar can tackle a universal problem in broad terms without worrying about the specific circumstances in which it is instantiated. But if the problem involves the interaction of a multiplicity of levels of legal regulation and those multiple levels may have differential results between countries, then it becomes difficult for a single scholar to undertake the necessary research.[112]

This analysis certainly applies to the study of judiciaries in the evolving EU context. Citing John Bell again: 'A fuller picture of globalisation requires both coverage of a wide variety of countries and a variety of analyses, statistical, interview-based, and the reading of texts, and an understanding of the contexts out of which these materials are all arising.'[113] Interestingly, the Dutch academic context seems to offer good starting points for building such collaborative research. First of all, law schools have recently joined forces to collaborate on a number of selected themes, which include the development of conflict-solving institutions, such as courts, and empirical legal studies.[114] Moreover, training for students regarding doctrinal, comparative and empirical legal research methods is increasingly becoming mainstream in the law schools, preparing a next generation for collaborative comparative and interdisciplinary legal scholarship. Finally, a national debate on recognition and rewards for academic work has brought arguments to the fore in favour of a change of research funding schemes aimed at consortia rather than at single scholars with 'star status'.[115]

It should be noted that increased team collaboration in legal scholarship gives rise to new reflections on academic practices, e.g. regarding the authorship of publications. In this respect, lessons can be learnt from developed practices in other disciplines, for example the social sciences, where team work has been the standard for a longer time.[116]

112 Bell, 'Researching Globalisation', 981.

113 Ibid., 982.

114 Law Sector Plan 2018.

115 VSNU Recognition & Rewards, https://vsnu.nl/recognitionandrewards/recognition-and-rewards/index.html

116 E. Mak and K. van den Bos, 'Van super(wo)man naar teamprestaties? Over auteurschap in de rechtswetenschap' (2019) 68(10) *Ars Aequi* 804–8.

## 11.4 Concluding Remarks

In the final pages of *Judiciaries within Europe*, John Bell writes:

> The tools of analysis of organisational theory and in particular of institutional culture enable one to identify the features shaping particular judicial institutions. By immersing oneself in the way a judiciary works, one can identify the interplay of features, before then moving to compare. Of course, one's initial hypotheses are informed by initial comparative research, giving a pre-understanding of what might be useful from a comparative perspective and not merely to those from a particular jurisdiction. But that pre-understanding has to be revised in the light of further research. The reader will hopefully take this work as the starting point for her own pre-understanding and improve upon its analysis.[117]

My aim in this chapter has been to describe how John's work has indeed been a starting point and inspiration for much of my research. His analysis has helped me to gain a pre-understanding of the legal systems covered in his study. Also, his work has inspired me to explore the perspectives of organisational theory and institutional culture as helpful angles for contextualised legal research on judiciaries. With the modest aim of expanding on John's work, rather than improving on his very clear and complete analyses, I hope to be able to further contribute to our understanding of the development of judiciaries in Europe and to continue discussions on this topic with John for as long as he finds these interesting!

[117] Bell, *Judiciaries within Europe*, 382–3.

# John Bell's Principal Publications

[* = Books or edited collections]

## A.1 General Articles and Book Chapters on Comparative Law

### *A.1.1 Books*

J. Bell, *Judiciaries within Europe* (Cambridge: Cambridge University Press, 2006)

J. Bell (ed.), *Studies in UK Law* (London: BIICL, 2002)

J. Bell and M.-L. Paris (eds.), *Rights-Based Constitutional Review* (Cheltenham: Edward Elgar, 2016), pp. 409–29

### *A.1.2 Articles and Book Chapters*

J. Bell, 'The Value of Micro-Comparison', in H. Dedek (ed.), *Cosmopolitan Jurisprudence. Essays in Memory of H. Patrick Glenn* (Cambridge: Cambridge University Press, 2021), pp. 64–82

'Judicial Review in the Administrative State', in E. Ballin, S. Lavrijssen, J. de Poorter (eds.), *Judicial Review in the Administrative State* (The Hague: TCM Asser Press, 2019), pp. 3–26

'Administrative Law', in R. Zimmermann and M. Reiman (eds.), *Oxford Handbook of Comparative Law* (Oxford: Oxford University Pres, 2019), pp. 1251–74

'The Reform of Delict in the Civil Code and Liability in Administrative Law', in J. S. Borghetti and S. Whittaker (eds.), *French Civil Liability in Comparative Perspective* (Oxford: Hart, 2019), pp. 425–43 (French version also available in *Revue des Contrats*)

'Sources of Law' (2018) 77 *Cambridge Law Journal* 40–71

'Is Comparative Law Necessary for Legal Theory?', in M. Del Mar and M. Lobban (eds.), *Law in Theory and History: New Essays on a Neglected Dialogue* (Oxford: Hart, 2016), pp. 127–45.

'Comparative Law and Fundamental Rights', in J. Bell and M.-L. Paris (eds.), *Rights-Based Constitutional Review* (Cheltenham: Edward Elgar, 2016), pp. 409–29

'Researching Globalisation: Lessons from Judicial Citations' (2014) 3(3) *Cambridge Journal of Comparative and International Law* 961–82

'The Importance of Institutions', in M. Adams and D. Heirbaut (eds.), *The Method and Culture of Comparative Law: Essays in Honour of Mark Van Hoecke* (Oxford: Hart 2014), pp. 207–19

'Path Dependence and Legal Development' (2013) 87 *Tulane Law Review* 787

'Continental European Jurisprudence 1850–2000', in M. Lobban and J. Moses (eds.), *The Impact of Ideas on Legal Development* (Cambridge: Cambridge University Press, 2012), pp. 100–26

'The Argumentative Status of Foreign Legal Arguments' (2012) 8 *Utrecht Law Review* 8–19

'Legal Research and the Distinctiveness of Comparative Law', in M. Van Hoecke (ed.), *Methodologies of Legal Research* (Oxford: Hart, 2011), pp. 155–76

'The Relevance of Foreign Examples to Legal Development (2011) 21 *Duke Journal of Comparative and International Law* 431–60

'Legal Research and the Distinctiveness of Comparative Law', in M. Van Hoecke (ed.), *Methodologies of Legal Research* (Oxford: Hart, 2011), pp. 156–76

'La culture', in P. Legrand (ed.), *Comparer les droits résolument* (Paris: PUF, 2009), pp. 247–77

'Sweden's Contribution to Governance of the Judiciary', in M. Andenas and D. Fairgrieve (eds.), *Tom Bingham and the Transformation of the Law* (Oxford: Oxford University Press, 2009), pp. 221–39

'Codes and Codification in National Law', 'Code Napoleon' and 'French Law', in P. Cane and J. Conaghan (eds.), *Oxford New Companion to Law* (Oxford: Oxford University Press, 2008)

'Administrative Law in Comparative Perspective', in E. Örücü and D. Nelken (eds.), *Comparative Law: A Handbook* (Oxford: Hart, 2007), pp. 287–312

'Reflections on Continental European Supreme Courts' (2004) 24 *Legal Studies* 156–68

'Public Law in Europe: Caught between the National, the Sub-National and the European?', in M. Van Hoecke (ed.), *Epistemology and Methodology of Comparative Law* (Oxford: Hart, 2004), pp. 259–69

'Comparing Public Law', in A. Harding and E. Örücü (eds.), *Comparative Law in the 21st Century* (Amsterdam: Springer 2002), pp. 235–47

'Lay Judges' (2002) 5 *Cambridge Yearbook of European Legal Studies* 293–310

'Judicial Cultures and Judicial Independence' (2001) 4 *Cambridge Yearbook of European Legal Studies* 47–60

'La comparaison en droit public', in Société de Législation Comparée, *Mélanges Tallon* (1999), pp. 33–44

'Mechanisms for the Cross-Fertilisation of Administrative Law in Europe', in J. Beatson and T. Tridimas (eds.), *New Directions in European Public Law* (Oxford: Hart, 1998), pp. 147–67

'The Europeanisation of Constitutional Law', in T. Watkin (ed.), *The Europeanisation of Law* (London: BIICL, 1998), pp. 70–89

'Comparing Precedent' (1997) 82 *Cornell Law Review* 1243–78

J. Bell, 'De la nécessité d'un droit administratif', *Actualité Juridique – Droit Administratif*, 50th anniversary special issue 20 June 1995, pp. 99–108

'Comparative Law and Legal Theory, in W. Krawietz, N. MacCormick and G. H. von Wright (eds.), *Prescriptive Formality and Normative Rationality in Modern Legal Systems* (Berlin: Duncker & Humblot, 1994), pp. 19–32

'Convergences and Divergences in European Administrative Law' (1992) 1 *Rivistà Italiana di diritto pubblico communitario* 3–22

'Conceptions of Public Policy', in P. Cane and J. Stapleton (eds.), *Essays for Patrick Atiyah* (Oxford: Oxford University Press, 1991), pp. 88–112

J. Bell and I. de Lamberterie, 'Long-Term Contracts', in D. Harris and D. Tallon (eds.), *Contract Law Today* (Oxford: Oxford University Press, 1988), chapter 5

'Disputes, Rules and Method: The Tswana Way' (1983) 3 *Oxford Journal of Legal Studies* 405–16

## A.2 Comparative Tort Law

### *A.2.1 Books*

J. Bell and A. Janssen, *Markesinis on the German Law of Torts* (Oxford: Hart, 2019)

J. Bell and D. Ibbetson (series eds.), *Comparative Studies in the Development of the Law of Torts in Europe*, 9 vols. (Cambridge: Cambridge University Press, 2010–12)

J. Bell and D. Ibbetson, *European Legal Development: The Case of Tort*, vol. 9 in J. Bell and D. Ibbetson (series eds.), *Comparative Studies in the Development of the Law of Torts in Europe* (Cambridge: Cambridge University Press, 2012)

J. Bell and A. W. Bradley (eds.), *Governmental Liability: A Comparative Study* (London: BIICL, 1991)

J. Bell, D. Fairgrieve and M. Andenas (eds.), *Tort Liability of Public Authorities in Comparative Perspective* (London: BIICL, 2002)

### *A.2.2 Articles and Book Chapters*

J. Bell, 'Tort Law and the Moral Law: Anglo-French Divergences' (2021) 80 *Cambridge Law Journal* 833–60

'Continental European Jurisprudence', in M. Lobban and J. Moses (eds.), *The Impact of Ideas on Legal Development* (Cambridge: Cambridge University Press, 2012)

'Continental European Jurisprudence', in vol. 7 of J. Bell and D. Ibbetson (series eds.), *Comparative Studies in the Development of the Law of Torts in Europe* (Cambridge: Cambridge University Press, 2012), pp. 100–126

'The Development of Tort Law', in H. Koziol and B. C. Steininger (eds.), *European Tort Law 2007* (Berlin: De Gruyter, 2008), pp. 2–23

'Introduction', in J. Bell, D. Fairgrieve and M. Andenas (eds.), *Tort Liability of Public Authorities in Comparative Perspective* (London: BIICL, 2002), pp. xv–xxvi

'Governmental Liability in Tort' (1996) 6 *National Journal of Constitutional Law* 85–104

## A.3 Books and Articles on French Law

### *A.3.1 Books*

J. Bell and F. Lichère, *Contemporary French Administrative Law* (Cambridge: Cambridge University Press, 2022)

J. Bell, *French Legal Cultures* (London: Butterworths, 2001)

J. Bell, S. Whittaker and S. Boyron, *Principles of French Law* (Oxford: Oxford University Press, 1998)

J. Bell and L. N. Brown, *French Administrative Law* (Oxford: Oxford University Press, 1993)

*French Constitutional Law* (Oxford: Oxford University Press, 1992)

### *A.3.2 Articles and Book Chapters*

J. Bell, 'Les sources non-écrites de la Constitution', in T. d'Habiba Abbassi and J. Rosetto (eds.), *Mélanges Dominique Rousseau* (Paris: Lextenso, 2020), pp. 857–65

'External Dimensions of the French Constitution' (2018) 57 *Virginia International Law Review* 493–514

'The Role of Doctrinal Writing in Creating Administrative Law: France and England Compared' (2018) 15 *Glossae* 140–54

'Consequential Reasoning in France', in S. Glanert (ed.), *Comparative Legal Reasoning: Essays in Honour of Geoffrey Samuel* (London: Wildy, 2018), pp. 94–108

'Secularism French Style' (2017) 23 *European Public Law* 237–44

'Disciplining Prisoners' (2014) 20 *European Public Law* 15–21

'From "Government Commissioner" to "Public Reporter": A Transformation in French Administrative Court Procedure?' (2010) 16 *European Public Law* 533–8

'Interpretative Resistance Faced with the Case-Law of the Strasbourg Court' (2008) 14 *European Public Law* 137–42

'Property and Legal Culture in France', in P. Birks and A. Pretto (eds.), *Themes in Comparative Law* (Oxford: Oxford University Press, 2002), pp. 83–96

'The Criminal Liability of Politicians in France' (2001) 3 *Cambridge Yearbook of European Legal Studies* 65–78

'The Concept of Public Service under Threat from Europe? An Illustration from Energy Law' (1999) 5 *European Public Law* 189–98

'Independent Administrative Authorities in France' (1997) 3 *European Public Law* 474–84

'Administrative Liability in French law' (1996) 2 *European Public Law* 337–43

'English Law and French Law – Not So Different?' (1995) 48 *Current Legal Problems* 64–101

'France: Current Developments' (1995) 1 *European Public Law* 16–22

'The French Pre-Trial System', in C. Walker and K. Starmer (eds.), *Justice in Error* (London: Blackstone Press, 1993), pp. 226–45

'Discretion and Administrative Procedure in France and England', in L. Torchia (ed.), *Il procedimento amministrativo: profili comparati* (Padua: CEDAM, 1993), pp. 7–31

'Reflections on the Procedure of the Conseil d'Etat', in G. Hand and J. McBride (eds.), *Droit sans frontières: Essays in Honour of L. Neville Brown* (Birmingham: Holdsworth Club, 1991), pp. 211–34

'Equality in the Case-Law of the Conseil constitutionnel' (1987) 1987 *Public Law* 426–46

'A French Lesson in Judicial Review' (1982) 2 *Oxford Journal of Legal Studies* 142–5

## A.4 Jurisprudence

### *A.4.1 Books*

J. Bell and Sir G. Engle, *Cross on Statutory Interpretation* (London: Butterworths, 1987)

J. Bell and J. Eekelaar (eds.), *Oxford Essays in Jurisprudence* (Oxford: Oxford University Press 1987)

J. Bell, *Policy Arguments in Judicial Decisions* (Oxford: Oxford University Press, 1983)

### A.4.2 *Articles and Book Chapters*

J. Bell, 'Sources of Law', in *English Private Law*, 1st ed. by P. Birks 2001; 2nd ed. by A. Burrows 2007; 3rd ed. by A. Burrows 2013 (Oxford: Oxford University Press)

'Analogy and Parable in Legal Reasoning', in M. Delmar and C. Michelon (eds.), *The Anxiety of the Jurist* (London: Ashgate, 2013), pp. 241–56

'Legal Texts and Operational Enactments', in H. van Schooten (ed.), *Semiotics and Legislation: Jurisprudential, Institutional and Sociological Perspectives* (Liverpool: Deborah Charles, 1999), pp. 71–9

'Interpreting Statutes over Time', in F. Ost and M. Van Hoecke (eds.), *Time and Law: Is It the Nature of Law to Last?* (Brussels: Bruylant, 1998), pp. 31–53

'Policy Arguments and Legal Reasoning', in Z. Bankowski, I. White and U. Hahn (eds.), *Informatics and the Foundations of Legal Reasoning* (Dordrecht: Kluwer, 1993), pp. 73–98

'Public Interest: Policy or Principle?', in R. Brownsword (ed.), *Law and the Public Interest* (Beiheft: ARSP, 1993), pp. 27–36

'Discretionary Decision-Making: A Jurisprudential View', in K. Hawkins (ed.), *The Uses of Discretion* (Oxford: Oxford University Press, 1993), pp. 89–111

'Policy Arguments in Statutory Interpretation', in J. van Dunné (ed.), *Legal Reasoning and Statutory Interpretation: Rotterdam Lectures in Jurisprudence 1986, 1988* (Arnhem: Gouda Quint, 1989), pp. 55–79

'The Judge as Bureaucrat', in J. Bell and J. Eekelaar (eds.), *Oxford Essays in Jurisprudence* (Oxford: Oxford University Press, 1987), pp. 33–56

'The Acceptability of Legal Arguments', in D. N. MacCormick and P. Birks (eds.), *The Legal Mind* (Oxford: Oxford University Press, 1986), pp. 45–65

## A.5 Comparative Law Writings on English Law for a Foreign Audience

J. Bell, 'La responsabilité de l'administration en droit anglais: caractéristiques générales, torts et compensation' (2013) 147 *Revue française d'administration* 691–704

'La Ve République vue du Royaume-Uni' (2009) 1(77) *Revue française de droit constitutionnel* 41–53

'La Révolution constitutionnelle au Royaume-Uni' (2000) 2 *Revue de Droit Public* 414–36

'La Ve République vue de Grande-Bretagne (1998) 5–6 *Revue de Droit Public* 1877–83

'L'expérience britannique', *Le Service public, Actualité Juridique - Droit Administratif*, special issue 20 June 1997, pp. 130–5

'Le règne de droit et le règne du juge', in P. Delvolvé (ed.), *L'Etat de Droit, Mélanges en l'honneur de Guy Braibant* (Paris: Dalloz, 1996), pp. 15–28

'Justice et politique: le cas du Royaume-Uni' (1995) 3 *Justices* 25–39

'Que représente la souveraineté pour un britannique?' (1993) 67 *Pouvoirs* 107–16

'Le fondement du contrôle juridictionnel de l'Administration', in P. Legrand (ed.), *Common Law d'un Siècle à l'autre* (Montréal: Blais, 1992), pp. 57–86.

'Le débat au Royaume-Uni', in CERAP (ed.), *Le contrôle juridictionnel de l'administration: Bilan critique* (Paris: Economica, 1991), pp. 73–90.

'Le juge administratif anglais, est-il un juge politique?' (1986) 38 *Revue internationale de droit comparé* 791–810

'Droit Anglais', in R. Rodière (ed.), *Les vices du consentement dans le contrat* (Paris: Pedone, 1977)

# INDEX

www.ingramcontent.com/pod-product-compliance
Lightning Source LLC
LaVergne TN
LVHW011808200926
848484LV00005B/1103